HUNT

# Hunters, Predators and Prey

## Inuit Perceptions of Animals

Frédéric Laugrand and Jarich Oosten

berghahn
NEW YORK · OXFORD
www.berghahnbooks.com

Published in 2015 by

Berghahn Books

www.berghahnbooks.com

© 2015, 2016 Frédéric Laugrand and Jarich Oosten
First paperback edition published in 2016

**Library of Congress Cataloging-in-Publication Data**

Laugrand, Frédéric.
    Hunters, predators and prey : Inuit perceptions of animals / by Frédéric
Laugrand and Jarich Oosten.
        pages cm
    Includes bibliographical references and index.
    ISBN 978-1-78238-405-2 (hardback) — ISBN 978-1-78533-337-8
    (paperback) — ISBN 978-1-78238-406-9 (ebook)
    1. Inuit—Rites and ceremonies. 2. Inuit—Hunting. 3. Human-animal
relationships—Nunavut. 4. Animals—Folklore. I. Oosten, J. G., 1945–
II. Title.
    E99.E7L368 2014
    398.24′5—dc23

                                                        2014000897

**British Library Cataloguing in Publication Data**

A catalogue record for this book is available from the British Library

ISBN 978-1-78238-405-2 hardback
ISBN 978-1-78533-337-8 paperback
ISBN 978-1-78238-406-9 ebook

# Contents

✳

# Figures

# Acknowledgements

This book is the result of research we conducted for more than fifteen years. We received the support of many Inuit elders. Many of them have passed away now. We are grateful to them for sharing their recollections and knowledge with us.

Ollie and Lizzie Itinnuaq, Peter Suvaksiuq, Josie Angutinngurniq, and Job and Eva Muqyunniq organized and hosted the elders workshops in Kangiq&iniq (2000 and 2002), Arviat (2003 and 2005), Kugaarruk (2004), and Maguse River (2011). Ollie Itinnuaq, as well as Job and Eva Muqyunniq, are no longer with us. Susan Sammons of Nunavut Arctic College, who always supported our work, has also passed away. We remain very much indebted to them.

Many Inuit helped us in organizing the workshops, translating the recorded material or giving support to our project in other ways. We thank Henry Kablalik, Noa Tiktak, Atuat, Lisa Koperqualuk, Gloria Putumiraqtuq, Sarah Silou, Betsy Annahatak, Myna Ishulutaq, David Serkoak, Louise Flaherty and Alexina Kublu for their help. We also thank John MacDonald and Louis Tapardjuk for granting us access to the interviews of the Iglulik Oral Traditions Project as well as for their hospitality during our research in Iglulik. We are grateful to Bishop Reynald Rouleau, Father Robert Lechat, Father André Dubois and Lorraine Brandson for supporting and facilitating our research in the field and in the archives. We wish to express our gratitude to many colleagues, friends and graduate students whose stimulating ideas enriched classes, conferences and the writing of many papers.

We are particularly grateful for the comments and discussions of our work at different stages and occasions by our colleagues, particularly Peter Armitage, David Anderson, Cunera Buijs, Florence Brunois, Robert Crépeau, Denys Delâge, Philippe Descola, Louis-Jacques Dorais, Robert Fréchette, Jean-Guy Goulet, Roberte Hamayon, Pierre-Jo

Laurent, Marie Mauzé, Toby Morantz, Sylvie Poirier, Cornelius Remie, Bernard Saladin d'Anglure, Olivier Servais, Birgitte Sonne, Michèle Therrien, Vladimir Randa, Christopher Trott and Anne-Marie Vuillemenot. Robert Fréchette from Avataq Cultural Institute kindly provided us with excellent photographs from his collection.

We thank the journals *Anthropos, Arctic Anthropology, Polar Record, L'Homme*, and the Avataq Cultural Institute for their permission to reprint parts of our articles in this book.

Finally, our research activities in the field were financed by the Social Sciences and Humanities Research Council of Canada (SSHRC) and the Department of Culture, Language, Elders and Youth of Nunavut (Canada).

Frédéric Laugrand
Jarich Oosten
Quebec City, August 2014

PART I

# INTRODUCTION

# CHAPTER I

# Theoretical Perspectives

> While we still have our body functioning so that we are still breathing
> the breath of life that was given to us by God, while we still have to
> step on the earth before we part with her, we cannot live a life that is
> completely different from what we have got. This is known from time
> immemorial. Therefore you cannot neglect it as long as our body is
> still alive. These were the reasons why the elders wanted us to know
> about these things, that is being cruel to animals and in addition, that
> the game animals that we hunt for food, are the things that come from
> God. From the time earth came into being and subsequently after
> that, game animals were placed so that humans can use them for
> sustenance. That is the reason why they are, right up to this day.
> —George Kappianaq, IE 330

In recent years, the study of human-animal relations has developed
so much that it has become a field of research in its own right.[1] The
emphasis has shifted from symbolic approaches to ethno-zoological,
ecological and environmental perspectives.[2] In this book, we will adopt
an anthropological perspective that gives priority to the participants'
views (see Oosten 2005). In this approach we do not explore whether Inuit knowledge of animals and their environment is symbolic or experi-
ential, technical or spiritual, modern or traditional.[3] These distinctions
make little sense to the participants anyway, as the very connections
between these various levels are essential to the nature of their knowledge of animals and their world. Rather, we focus on the organization,
dynamics and developments of this knowledge itself. It is quite clear
that Inuit knowledge transformed considerably in the twentieth century, when Inuit gradually left the hunting camps to settle in small permanent communities, embracing Christianity and modernity. Today,
Inuit knowledge is usually referred to as Inuit *qaujimajatuqangit*,[4] in

the context of Nunavut as a new political entity. Ideas and values that are central to Inuit knowledge play an important role in contemporary conflicts and debates focusing on the hunt of animals such as caribou, belugas, polar bears, whales and so forth. Inuit strongly resent external attempts to manage animals as if they were a limited resource. Now that Inuit have become familiar with Western concepts relating to animals and their environment, and the Nunavut government has taken responsibility with respect to the management of wildlife, Inuit have tried to reconcile the different perspectives.

However, Nadasdy (2003) is quite right when he argues that the idea of co-management of wildlife and other resources and land claims processes are based on Euro-American concepts of 'knowledge' and 'property' more than on local aboriginal perspectives and that incompatibilities between aboriginal views and perspectives with Western ones are still significant (see Nadasdy 2003; Cruikshank 2004). In many respects the implementation of new bureaucracies does not help the hunters faced with new expectations and new rules. As Nadasdy observes, 'In many ways First Nations offices across Canada now resemble miniature versions of federal and provincial/territorial bureaucracies. They are staffed by fish and wildlife officers, lands coordinators, heritage officers, and a host of other First Nations employees who deal regularly with their bureaucratic counterparts' (2003: 2). These transformations had and still have numerous and far-reaching effects for all aboriginal groups, including Inuit. People have to learn new ways of speaking to be understood by wildlife, biology, and bureaucratic resource management officers. They have to put aside many of their beliefs and practices and trust these new relationships with old colonial institutions at a time when the financial and international markets tend to impose their own logics, as in the case of mining activities and the protection of the environment.

Inuit therefore look to *qaujimajatuqangit* for guidance, as this knowledge allowed them to survive for thousands of years. In this book we explore the richness of Inuit traditions, the perceptions, practices and stories relating to animals and the land. We focus on the ethnographic data and leave aside substantial discussions about the relation between traditional/indigenous knowledge and wildlife management. In discussing the academic debates on human-animal relationships, we will confine ourselves to a broad outline of the main currents in the debates and focus especially on topics that are relevant to our understanding of Inuit perceptions and practices.

In the anthropological field of human-animal relationships, four main streams of research can be discerned. They build on the pioneering work of anthropologists such as Irving Hallowell in North America and André-Georges Haudricourt in the Pacific. They were inspired by a variety of structuralists such as Claude Lévi-Strauss, Mary Douglas and Edmund Leach, and by historians of nature such as Keith Thomas in Great Britain and Robert Delort in France, and lately by philosophers such as Gilles Deleuze and Felix Guattari.

## Gift and Reciprocity

The first group of important anthropological studies of human-animal relations was inspired by the famous theories of exchange of Marcel Mauss, influencing Robert Brightman, Ann Fienup-Riordan and Marshall Sahlins[5] at the University of Chicago. The question of to what extent relations between hunters and prey can be considered reciprocal exchange became an issue of debate among scholars working with hunter-gatherers.

In *Bringing Home Animals* (1979), a detailed study on Mistassini Cree hunters of northern Quebec, Adrian Tanner refers to Mauss and Sahlins. He views Cree religion as an ideology combining shamanism and Christianity. Drawing on information collected during various fieldwork sessions in the late 1960s and 1970s as well as on classic ethnographic sources (especially Speck but also Rogers, Rousseau, etc.), Tanner questions the relation between Cree religious practices and their productive activities, showing that both spring from the same cognitive source. He examines the transformation of the religious ideology of the Mistassini Cree and their rites and beliefs relating to hunting and trapping with the onset of the fur trade. He opposes the 'religion of the bush' to the 'religion of the settlement', reflecting on a contrast between the hunting domain and the cash sectors of the economy. Such a dualism has been reported in many northern communities in the sub-Arctic and Arctic regions, but on closer scrutiny the boundary is not always clear.

Tanner also shows that Cree ritual and religious activities organize complex relationships in which hunters often have to force or trick their prey. Tanner explains how two modes of production gradually emerged, a capitalist one in the settlement and a domestic one based on subsistence hunting and trapping. Tanner (1979: 207) explains that Cree hunters could be divided into two groups, those having a reputation for skill in religious techniques and those skilled in non-religious techniques. He points out that these various techniques are not considered antagonistic. Tanner provides much of the ethnographic information on what he calls 'the ecology of hunting' and on the ritualization of space, on rites of hunting divination (such as the shaking tent, the steam tent or scapulimancy, usually performed with porcupine or caribou shoulder blades), ritual relations between hunters and game animals, and respect for the animals killed. Some of his observations are quite relevant with respect to Inuit hunters.

A first point raised by Tanner is an ethnographic problem. As Tanner (1979: 26) states, 'Many of these rites are barely noticeable, and by themselves seem trivial superstitions. However, they can be shown to be parts of a system that has the organized purpose of controlling, predicting and explaining the behaviour of game animals, and the behavior of imaginary beings which are believed to influence the animals, or are identified with particular natural phenomena.' This is also valid for Inuit hunting practices. Many small rites, divinatory signs and rules easily escape ethnographers, as these gestures are part of the hunting routine.

Hunting usually requires preparatory rites, and it would be interesting to compare the steam tent ritual, which was already declining during Tanner's fieldwork among the Mistassini Cree, with the Inuit *nunagiksaqtuq* practice. Both rituals are clearly performed and intended to prepare and secure a good hunting season. The cleansing activities involved indicate that hunters cannot enter the animal domain without adequate precautions and preparations. The settlement also appears as a dirty place in contrast to the bush or the tundra.

Another point to be noted is the importance of dreams for hunters to predict their hunting success (Tanner 1979: 124). According to Tanner, a dream about a female human being often forecasts success in hunting. This is also true for the Inuit. Tanner (1979: 132) rightly concludes that hunting divination involves various levels of communication and its explicit purpose is to communicate with the animals and the agencies that control them.

Regarding human and animal relations, Tanner (1979: 138) distinguishes three major models for interaction based on three types of social relationships: (1) male-female, the victim being represented as the female lover of the hunter (see also Preston [(1975) 2002: 21] regarding bear hunting); (2) dominance-subordination, when 'magic is used to compel an animal to approach the hunter or in some other way allow itself to be caught', or when the shaman makes game animals come to the hunter, or in cases of animals who have masters; and (3) equivalence. In the third case, Tanner uses the notion of 'friendship' to qualify the relation between a hunter, usually a well-experienced hunter, elder or shaman, and the animal. In this case, good hunters are said to have animals that act as pets, such as a goose. The hunter has to make offerings to his animal friend, and the relationship stops when the hunter dies. Much later, Peter Armitage (1992: 2) observed, 'Among the Innu people of eastern Quebec and Labrador, religious beliefs about animal masters and other spirits also continue to play an important role in shaping human behaviour.' He identified about ten animal masters, such as Papakashtshihk for the caribou, Nisk-napeu for the geese, Mashkuapeu for the bears, and so forth. Whereas the male-female metaphor certainly applies to Inuit hunting, a distinction between dominance-subordination and equivalence is not very helpful in understanding Inuit hunting.

Finally, Tanner provides many details about ritual aspects of killing animals, exploring the cases of the bear and the beaver. He describes the use of charms, clean clothing, decorations, offering of tobacco and so forth, and the various ways to show respect to the prey. He particularly distinguishes three separate occasions when ritual actions are required: (1) when the meat is brought into the dwelling of the hunter, (2) during the eating of the meat and (3) when the inedible remains are disposed of (Tanner 1979: 153). Hunters have to show gratitude and respect towards the animal by treating its body properly; this extends hunters' good fortune to future hunts. Numerous taboos are mentioned, such as food offerings, rules of serving food and so forth. Among these, the *asawaapin* is listed as a key operation, and it leads to Tanner's main thesis, which consists of a greeting ritual performed by children running out and greeting the hunter as he comes in with his prey. With respect to animals, Tanner (1979: 173) concludes that human-animal relations imply a series of prestations and counter-prestations: 'Men make gifts to the animal world, that is, to the bush, and in return are the recipients of gifts of game animals killed by the hunters.' Furthermore, Tanner observes:

> During the third phase of the hunting cycle great stress is laid on the boundary separating the human domain (the inside of the dwelling) from the animal domain (the outside, and the bush). The *asawaapin* taboo keeps the domestic group inside as the hunter brings in the animal.... The doorway ... permits the entry of the gift animal, while the chimney is used to send the offerings of food put in the fire back to the outside. This gives a model of exchange between man and animal. (1979: 173–74)

Regarding the respect hunters and their kin have to show towards the animal, Tanner (1979: 157) emphasizes that the kill has to be placed in a certain way so it can see the path, such that the animal should be 'laid on the floor of the dwelling in the middle of the family area, facing the door', and Tanner concludes, 'The reason given is that the animal may see out through the door, and see how the hunter went out when he left to go hunting.' Similar rules for positioning the prey can be found among Inuit hunters.

In *Grateful Prey: Rock Cree Human-Animal Relationships* (1993), Robert Brightman, a student of Sahlins, shows how the contrasting principles of reciprocity and domination play an essential part in human-animal relations in Cree cosmology. Using Rock Cree oral traditions extensively, Brightman argues that Cree human-animal relationships are complex and ambivalent. He explains that hunted animals are sometimes conceived of as giving themselves to the hunters in response to the hunter's respectful treatment of them as non-human persons, and sometimes as elusive adversaries.

According to Brightman, animals have their specific forms but reveal themselves as humans in certain contexts, such as death or rituals. Brightman (1993: 176) recalls that animals were initially human beings who lost their humanity: 'In the bush, they assume theriomorphic form and lose cultural attributes. When "killed" their disembodied spirits "come to be like human", and the perishable carcass is the medium through which human hunters seek to exchange with them. Thereafter, they are reborn or regenerate, lose their cultural attributes, and the cycle begins anew.' Brightman (1993: 119) thus connects respect for the animal to its regeneration. Rock Cree say that some animals become very old and can eventually die, and that their souls then move to a post-mortem place. But before that, animals like to renew themselves. A way to respect them is to dispose of their bones in trees in order to protect them from dogs. Brightman adds that Cree even use empty cans to hang the bones in the trees.[6]

Cree, like Inuit and most other aboriginal peoples, are neither ecologists nor conservationists[7] but hunters. According to Brightman, Cree have always regarded abundance of game as a gift to be fully used with gratitude. In the nineteenth and twentieth centuries, Cree hunters were deeply involved in the fur trade and participated actively in the depletion of game. Yet, Cree stories of animals always emphasize attitudes of respect for the animals and the need to communicate with them through dreams, visions and rituals. Brightman does not explore the issue of the moral discourse of the hunters that was later developed by Fienup-Riordan for the Yup'ik in Alaska.[8] She argued that the foundation of the relationship between human and animals was neither economic nor social but moral (Fienup-Riordan 2007: 239). After Arthur J. Ray, Brightman (1993: 103) was one of the first anthropologists to describe the exchange between animals and hunters:

[Religious observances] materially affect the efficiency of hunting and trapping in an environment where animals consciously regulate hunters' access to them. If these acts are performed correctly, it is said that slain animals will be reborn and voluntarily offer themselves to hunters by entering traps and allowing themselves to be killed with guns. Cree sometimes say that hunters can only kill animals when this voluntary self-sacrifice occurs. If the practices are omitted or performed incorrectly, it is said that animals will fail to be reborn or will withhold themselves from hunters by frustrating attempts to kill them.

Brightman (1993: 119) and Fienup-Riordan (1990: 167) argue that, respectively, Rock Cree and Yup'ik Eskimos see their kills as 'infinitely renewable'. Thus, animals are not a finite resource, as they are perceived by Western specialists of game management and biologists. For the natives, as Fienup-Riordan (1990: 167) puts it, 'The perishable flesh of both humans and animals belied the immortality of their souls. All living things participated in a cycle of birth and rebirth, contingent on right thought and action by others as well as self.' Biologists simply cannot accept such a conception and consider it a native belief that can be falsified by scientific evidence. According to Fienup-Riordan (1990: 168), humans as well as animals possess awareness (*ella*), which allow individuals a sense of control over their destiny. Such a conviction is not acceptable to modern science, which attaches little importance to the self-awareness of animals in debates on management and control.[9]

Fienup-Riordan (1994: 51) explains that because of this awareness in the animal, the hunter has to treat his prey properly; otherwise the animal will not give itself to the hunter anymore (see also Bodenhorn 1989, 1990). Thus, when seals are killed, they know the exact manner in which they are handled after they have been caught. If a hunter is not respectful, the seal will not go to him anymore. When human beings respect animals, their awareness will develop further and they will become elders credited with a strong and powerful mind. Sharp (2001: 66, 187), who worked with the Dene, went a step further, arguing that animals, not human beings, are knowledgeable: 'What differentiates animals from humans is the fact that humans do not know; they do not have the power/knowledge to survive unaided.' In that respect, pets are also said to be unable to care for themselves, in contrast to wild animals, which are 'self-sufficient.... No one, no person, no being, no power needs to teach the animals; they know.'

In Inuit society animals are aware of the transgressions of human beings and will retaliate if they are not respected. Human beings are aware of this, as the survival of society depends on it. The fate of animals and human beings is interconnected. We will explore to what extent reciprocity is a feature of Inuit hunting and how the notion of the gift is embedded in Inuit hunting.[10]

## Personhood and the Ontology of Engagement

British anthropologists, inspired by the debates on hunter-gatherer societies, proposed a phenomenological perspective to define the relations between hunter-gatherers and their environment. This is the second main stream of anthropological research on human-animal relations. After Irving Hallowell, Tim Ingold (1988, 1996, 2000) argued that many indigenous peoples do not create a division between nature and culture, but that instead in many societies the borders between the human and non-human realms are permeable. Humans and non-humans are subject to metamorphosis. Ingold (2004: 33) states, 'Metamorphosis is not a covering up, but an opening up, of the person to the world', since a person taking many forms can also take many perspectives. Such a perspective inspired Ingold to propose the notion of 'poetics of dwelling'. With Nurit Bird-David (1990, 1991, 2006), he developed 'an ontology of engagement', characterizing animism as a mode of knowledge founded on experience and being in the world. For Ingold and his followers, such an ontology is marked by relationality (and not essence) and has to be treated on equal terms with Western science. It is not simply a system of knowledge, but rather a way of being in the world.[11] The conflicting views that result from these ontologies are very different from those of Western societies. There is no escape from this 'mental model', which accommodates 'beings that are really non-human into schemes of representation that construct them as social and therefore human' (Ingold 2004: 34). In many societies, in tropical Asia as well as in Siberia, hunters engage in social relationships with non-human beings, spirits as well as animals, who in exchange for offerings are benevolent and generous with them. Relations between humans and animals are marked by intimacy and reciprocity. The consumption of game by hunters and the sharing of meat are fundamental acts marking the importance of exchange and the existence of a common identity.

Assessing the nature of the relations between hunters and animals is central to the debate. Ingold (2000: 52) argues, 'The animals participate as real-world creatures endowed with powers of feeling and autonomous action, whose characteristic behaviours, temperaments and sensibilities one gets to know in the very course of one's everyday practical dealings with them. In this regard, dealing with non-human ani-

mals is not fundamentally different from dealing with fellow humans.'
Adapting Schütz's definition of sociality to the relations between hunters and prey, Ingold states, 'Sociality is constituted by communicative
acts in which the I (the hunter) turns to the others (animals), appre-
hending them as persons who turn to him, and both know of this fact'
(2000: 52; quoted in Nadasdy 2007).[12]

The notion of ontology has become quite popular in anthropology
in the last decennia. It is central to some philosophical debates on the
nature of being, reality and existence. In our approach we focus on
the perspectives of the participants. Our goal is to gain a better understanding of these perspectives and to contribute to a dialogue between
Inuit and outsiders.

A dialogue implies an exchange between different value systems,
and little purpose is served by assessing the truth, reality or nature of
one value system in terms of another. Therefore, we do not use notions
such as truth, ontology or reality in the description and analysis of
Inuit worldviews. The questions raised by Ingold are very important,
and we will especially explore the notion of personhood in Inuit human-animal relationships.

With respect to the relations between humans and animals, Ann
Fienup-Riordan (1994) adopted a similar approach for the Alaskan
Eskimos, introducing the notions of 'relational morality', 'compassion
and restraint' and 'ethical views' (Fienup-Riordan 2007). She argues
that animals should be considered non-human persons and emphasizes the notions of respect between human beings and animals. She
rightly reminds us of the sensitivity of animals and their ability to see
and hear what occurs in the human world (Fienup-Riordan 2007: 249).
As her work is closer to our own field, we will explore this perspective
in this book and investigate to what extent it is shared by Canadian
Inuit.

## Animism: Beyond the Nature versus Culture Dichotomy

The third stream of anthropological research was developed in the
1980s when Philippe Descola gave new incentive to the study of human-
animal relations. Descola took his inspiration from Marx, Lévi-Strauss
and Haudricourt. In *La nature domestique* (1986) and especially in *Par-
delà nature culture* (2005) he examines the notions of nature and culture. He considers this contrast too evolutionist and ethnocentric to
do justice to the complexity of human-animal relationships in other
societies and instead proposes a new model on the basis of four great

ontologies or cosmologies: totemism, analogism, animism and naturalism. As Descola (2005: 176; our translation) puts it,

> Confronted with someone, human or non-human, I can assume that he
> has physical and interior features identical to mine, or that his interior-
> ity and physicality differ from mine, or that we have similar interiorities
> and different physicalities, or that our interiorities are different and our
> physicalities analogous. I will call the first combination totemism, the
> second one analogism, the third one animism and the last one naturalism.

By distinguishing physicality from interiority and developing a structural scheme based on these categories, Descola reduced the different
ontologies of the world into four basic models.[13]

In Descola's approach the notion of animism is especially relevant
with respect to the indigenous people of the Americas, including the
Arctic cultures. It implies that people attribute social features as well as
the status of a person to all animated and/or inanimate beings in their
environment. In such a universe the intrinsic qualities of beings remain the same, whereas differences manifest themselves especially in
bodily appearances. In this perspective, the animistic ontology inverts
the naturalistic perspective of Western societies that, since Descartes,
has considered the intrinsic qualities of human beings and animals
as different, and at the same time accepts a Darwinist evolutionary
view emphasizing continuity on a physical level. Descola's model is
stimulating, but one has to keep in mind that features of the four ontologies he discerns are in fact all present in most societies – but, at
some period and depending on the context, some may take precedence
over others.[14] Descola observes that among the Achuar of Ecuador, animals are treated like humans, even like kin, though they are sometimes
killed. Quoting an Achuar, he writes that animals are considered as beings that are not entirely human, as they lack some elements (Descola
2005: 21). Inuit do consider animals as sentient animated beings, yet
they are not completely human. We will explore how the notions of
*tarniq*, shade, the miniature image of a being, *inua*, the human person
or owner of a being, and *atiq*, the name, all organize the relations between human beings and animals.

## Perspectivism: When the Point of View Is Located in the Body

The importance of the body was emphasized by Claude Lévi-Strauss
in a famous anecdote. He contrasted the European conquistadores trying to figure out if Native Americans from Brazil had souls with the

same Native Americans who were trying to understand what kind of bodies they had by immersing their dead bodies in water. Viveiros de Castro (1998: 469) referred to this anecdote when he built his model of perspectivism, according to which 'the world is inhabited by different sorts of subjects or persons, humans or non-humans, which apprehend the world from distinct points of view'. In this respect, animals see themselves differently than how humans see them. He views the body as the primary locus of perception. Viveiros de Castro initially worked with the Araweté and developed his theoretical model after reading the work of Tania Lima (1999), who had conducted research among another group, the Juruna. His work had a great impact on Brazilian anthropologists such as Aparecida Vilaça (2000, 2005) and Carlos Fausto (2007) (see also Kohn 2007). Carlos Fausto (2007), for instance, developed the idea that Amazonian cosmologies are organized by two models: the model of predation, mainly dominant in Amazonia, and the model of reciprocal exchange, strongly represented in North America. These authors all contributed to the development of a theory of perspectivism that can be summarized in two phrases: 'the body makes the difference' and, paraphrasing Leibniz, 'the point of view is located in the body' (Viveiros de Castro 1998: 478). Viveiros de Castro argues that the Amerindians postulate a metaphysical continuity and a physical discontinuity in beings, the first emanating from animism and the second one from perspectivism. The spirit, not conceived as an immaterial substance but as a reflexive form, integrates, whereas the body (conceived not as material substance, but as active affection) differentiates (Viveiros de Castro 1998). In this view the shaman becomes the key operator in perspective logic. Capable of changing his body, and thus his perspective, he can interact better than anyone else with different beings.

Viveiros de Castro (1998: 482) also discussed the notion of metamorphosis, linking it to what he calls the 'doctrine of animal clothing', showing that masks are instruments:

> It is not so much that the body is a clothing but rather that clothing is a body. We are dealing with societies which inscribe efficacious meanings onto the skin, and which use animal masks endowed with power metaphysically to transform the identities of those who wear them, if used in the appropriate ritual context. To put on a mask-clothing is not so much to conceal a human essence beneath the animal appearance, but rather to activate the powers of a different body.

In a recent volume entitled *Métaphysiques cannibales*, Viveiros de Castro (2009) investigates the work of Deleuze and Guattari and further develops his theory, claiming the necessity to 'decolonize' the discipline by introducing a new form of relativism in which Latour (2009a: 2) saw 'a bomb with the potential to explode the whole implicit philosophy so dominant in most ethnographers' interpretations of their material'. Viveiros de Castro once again defended the idea of multi-naturalism against an idea of culture that only belongs to the naturalist perspective. He argued that perspectivism is by no means a local variant of animist ontology, as suggested by Descola, but rather a completely different system, 'an intellectual structure that contains its own theory' (Viveiros de Castro 2009: 44) and has its own philosophy: 'What these persons see ... – and therefore what they are as persons – constitutes precisely the philosophical problem posed by and for indigenous thought' (Viveiros de Castro 2009: 21; quoted in Brightman et al. 2012: 3). One may, however, wonder how Amazonian thought comes so close to French philosophy, as most ideas developed by Viveiros de Castro in fact come from Deleuze and Guattari. Moreover, for Viveiros de Castro, perspectivism is a system that, like Ingold's ontology of engagement model, is somehow 'incommensurable'. He concludes that 'we can't think like the Indians but, we can at the most, think with them' (Viveiros de Castro 2009: 169).

Viveiros de Castro's ideas raised considerable criticism by Santos-Granero (2009), Terence Turner (2009) and Laura Rival (2005) in South America and Charles Stépanoff (2009) in Siberia. But his perspective was a great influence on Amazonian specialists (see Césard et al. 2003), as well as on specialists working in Asia (see Pedersen 2001 regarding Mongolia).

More recently, Rane Willerslev used such an approach to study the mimetics of the Yukaghir hunters of Siberia, who are able to adopt not only the perspective of the hunter but also that of the prey, leading Willerslev to postulate a double perspective (2004: 641; 2007).[15] Willerslev (2007: 104) also introduced the notion of 'mimetic empathy' to explain that if the animal gives itself to the hunter, it does so only if the hunter appears to be sexually attractive to his prey, friendly and harmless. This empathy is what suspends the disbelief and hostility of the animal so that it can now give itself as prey to the hunter. With respect to Inuit hunting, such a view sounds rather romantic, especially when Willerslev compares it to what the spectator feels watching a beautiful Hollywood film. Inuit never express such a 'mimetic empathy', as hunting is a serious and dangerous business that may require not only seduction but also violence.

Willerslev (2007: 95) uses Viveiros de Castro's approach of perspectivism, but tries to bring it 'down to earth', to use an expression he borrows from Ingold. His point is that perspectivism should not be approached in terms of representation or as a cosmological abstraction, but rather in terms of action, engagement and practice.

The studies of Ingold, Descola, Viveiros de Castro and others deal with crucial issues such as corporality, the relation between body and clothing, and metamorphosis. These notions refer to a 'highly transformational world', to use an expression of Rivière's (quoted in Viveiros de Castro 1998: 471) to describe Amazonian ontologies. In this book, we explore to what extent these notions are relevant in the Arctic. We will see that in Inuit society an awareness exists that boundaries between human beings, spirits and animals may collapse and transformations between different categories often occur in the context of shamanism and storytelling. The boundaries have to be maintained by ritual rules; otherwise, society itself will collapse. This explains why Inuit are always trying to maintain and preserve the correct relationships between human beings and non-human beings.

The theoretical perspectives referred to above raise important questions, not only with respect to the relations of hunters and prey in other societies, but also with respect to our understanding of these relationships. Categories such as animism, person, rationality and reciprocity have a long and complex history in anthropological debates. Like the categories used by the aboriginal people themselves, they are by no means clear and are used in a variety of ways depending on the context. Therefore, they should be used with some caution. Moreover, although these concepts are important analytic tools in anthropological debates, they often have little meaning for the participants themselves. It is worthwhile to explore what the central issues are in the debates among the hunters themselves. Obviously we do not wish to subordinate the aboriginal perspectives to Western perspectives or shift the debates from a discussion of aboriginal categories to a more familiar discussion of the meaning of Western concepts such as nature, person or subject. In the case of the Inuit we might opt to discuss notions such as soul, spirit and person instead of Inuit categories such as *tarniq, inua* or *atiq,* but the participants themselves would resent such a shift of debate. In Inuit society the complex relationships between animals and human beings are not expressed in a philosophical discourse on the nature of animals but in the rules of respect relating to animals, as well as in the stories that deal with the interactions between animals and human beings. In this book we will focus on the perspective of the participants and explore the organizing principles of their perceptions and practices relating to animals. First we will present the ethnographic data in separate chapters. Then we will examine Inuit perspectives of the animal world in a more comparative and theoretical perspective.

This book primarily offers an ethnographic study, based on our understanding of Inuit views and perspectives after many years of close collaboration with Inuit elders in activities focusing on the transfer of knowledge between elders and youth. Non-Western patterns of thought are not easily accessible and challenge our own commonsense notions. As Julie Cruikshank puts it, 'One contribution anthropology can continue to make is through ethnography that shows how particular local formulations can continue to complicate – and to surprise – universalising common-sense, expectations about what we mean by knowledge' (2004: 32).[16] By providing the verbatim texts from the elders, we offer the reader an opportunity to distinguish the information given by the participants from the interpretation we provide. We are well aware that in the translation, selection and organization of these verbatim texts interpretation is already at work. There is no such thing as description without interpretation (see Brightman 1993: 28; Ingold 2004), but we still try to give an accurate and sensitive description of Inuit perspectives on animals. According to Brightman (1993: 34), 'humans, animals, and categories of interaction between them are organized by sets of propositions that are themselves complex signs' and 'the existence and meaning of each animal-as-sign is based on overlapping dimensions of resemblance and difference with the others'. We may add that human beings constitute the point of reference for these resemblances and differences. Therefore, we will examine each animal in detail and in different domains of thought and action. We will discuss the place of each animal in relation to human beings as well as to other animals living in Inuit territory.

## The Field of Anthropological Study Approach

In his famous 1904 work *Seasonal Variations of the Eskimo*, Mauss (1979: 19) notes, 'There exist, not one, but many Eskimo societies whose culture is sufficiently homogeneous that they may be usefully compared, and sufficiently diverse that these comparisons may be fruitful.' He argued, 'The Eskimo offer such a privileged field of study because their morphology is not the same throughout the year.' Inspired by Mauss, the Leiden structuralists developed the notion of the field of anthropological study (FAS) to handle cultural variation in a specific area.

In a field of anthropological study, local variations are examined as cultural variants linked by transformations in time and space. Only by charting the cultural diversity and richness of local traditions can we do justice to the complexity of a field of anthropological study. In the ethnographic literature on Inuit, many different groupings are distinguished. The names of these groupings are usually derived from the place where they lived. But in practice the borders between these groupings were quite flexible and dynamic as people moved from one area to another. In the nineteenth century, Boas (1888: 425) already recognized that Inuit could not be easily divided into tribes or other distinct groups: 'In my opinion a great difference between these tribes never existed. Undoubtedly they were groups of families confined to a certain district and connected by a common life.' In our comparison of local traditions, we thus do not assume that different groups can be clearly distinguished from each other.

Inuit traditions of knowledge are in important respects locally oriented. Knowledge of the land plays a central part in Inuit life. It is important to know how the animals move, where to hunt at which season, at which dangerous places one should not camp or hunt, or which specific rituals must be carried out before entering a particular area. One has to know where to go for trade or what trade goods are required at a particular place and time. Such knowledge largely determines where people will reside and how they will organize their travels. Obviously, it is historically embedded.

Inuit have always moved over large areas, taking their family traditions with them. Their knowledge depends not only on family traditions but also on local knowledge. Knowledge traditions cannot be identified with a particular local group, since groups as well as traditions are continuously changing. Thus, knowledge is often more strongly associated with a particular place than with a particular group. People have to know how the land and its animals should be respected to survive. They should avoid some places, bring offerings to other places and so on. Therefore, variation between groups as well as places should be taken into account if we wish to examine the variations and patterns, the diversity and richness, of the cultural variation in the whole area under study. Inuit emphasize the importance of the cultural differences between different areas. When Rasmussen (1930: 111) told Kibkarjut (a Padlirmiutaq) that he had heard another version of a story she had related, she explained:

> I had heard this story related somewhat differently among the Harvaq-
> tôrmiut where the woman who cuts off part of her face forms an item in
> the fantastic adventures of Kivioq, and when I asked whether the version
> here given might not be correctly remembered, the answer, given very
> energetically, was as follows: 'We tell you only that which we know our-

selves, and that which has been told throughout the ages in our tribe. You, who come from other peoples, and speak the tongue of other villages (dialect), and understand other Inuit besides ourselves, must know that human beings differ. The Harvaqtôrmiut know many things we do not know and we know many things they do not. Therefore you must not compare the Harvaqtôrmiut with us, for their knowledge is not our knowledge as our knowledge is not theirs. Therefore we tell you only what we know from our own villages.'

In 1997 Cornelius Nutaraaluk from Iqaluit commented, 'I think our stories vary from community to community even though they are the same *unikkaaqtuat*' (quoted in Oosten and Laugrand 1999a: 188). This terse proposition nicely states the problem of the FAS approach. Even though variation is the name of the game, that variation can only be adequately understood by assuming that underlying patterns are shared. In this book we will look for these patterns that shape regional diversity.

Our area of interest encompasses the Kivalliq (including the Nattilik area), the North Baffin area (including Iglulik) and the South Baffin area, from Kinngait (Cape Dorset) to Kangiqtugaapik (Clyde River) (see figure 1.1). The close cultural relationships between the Kivalliq and the North and South Baffin areas are well-known. In concentrating on these three areas, we give less attention to relevant connections

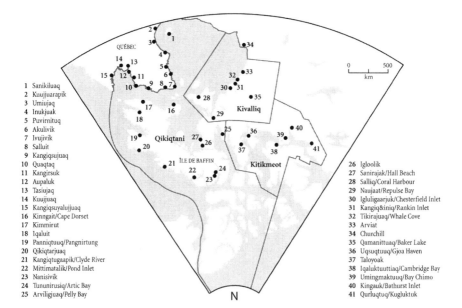

1　Sanikiluaq
2　Kuujjuarapik
3　Umiujaq
4　Inukjuak
5　Puvirnituq
6　Akulivik
7　Ivujivik
8　Salluit
9　Kangiqsujuaq
10　Quaqtaq
11　Kangirsuk
12　Aupaluk
13　Tasiujaq
14　Kuujjuaq
15　Kangiqsuyalujjuaq
16　Kinngait/Cape Dorset
17　Kimmirut
18　Iqaluit
19　Panniqtuuq/Pangnirtung
20　Qikiqtarjuaq
21　Kangiqtugaapik/Clyde River
22　Mittimatalik/Pond Inlet
23　Nanisivik
24　Tununirusiq/Artic Bay
25　Arviligjuaq/Pelly Bay

26　Igloolik
27　Sanirajak/Hall Beach
28　Salliq/Coral Harbour
29　Naujaat/Repulse Bay
30　Igluligaarjuk/Chesterfield Inlet
31　Kangiq&iniq/Rankin Inlet
32　Tikirajuaq/Whale Cove
33　Arviat
34　Churchill
35　Qamanittuaq/Baker Lake
36　Uqsuqtuuq/Gjoa Haven
37　Taloyoak
38　Iqaluktuuttiaq/Cambridge Bay
39　Umingmaktuuq/Bay Chimo
40　Kingauk/Bathurst Inlet
41　Qurluqtuq/Kugluktuk

**Figure 1.1.** Map of Nunavut, Canada.

to related areas (Inuinnait [Copper], Nunavik or West Greenland). However, we chose these three areas on the basis of the intensive interaction within the whole region and the availability of a rich corpus of ethnographic data and missionary archives. Moreover, most of the elders participating in our workshops came from these three areas.

Elders are highly respected, but the degree of knowledge they have of the old traditions varies for each of the three areas under scrutiny. In the nineteenth century whalers established whaling stations in South Baffin, and in 1894 an Anglican Mission post was founded. In the early 1900s most people converted to Christianity and most rituals and rules pertaining to animals were abandoned. As a result, elders from this area have hardly any firsthand recollections of the old traditions. For information on these old traditions, we mainly rely on the ethnographer Boas (1888, 1901, 1907) and the missionary Peck (Laugrand et al. 2006).

Christianity reached the North Baffin area in the early 1920s. Elders such as Rose Iqallijuq, Noah Piugaattuq and George Kappianaq from Iglulik, born in the beginning of the twentieth century, still had vivid recollections of the old traditions. Moreover, Knud Rasmussen interviewed many respected elders such as Aava and Ivaluardjuk in the early 1920s. Most of the North Baffin area became Anglican, but in Iglulik there was also a substantial Roman Catholic community.

The Kivalliq is probably the most complex area, where many different small groups used to live. A Roman Catholic mission was founded in Chesterfield Inlet in 1914, but it was not until 1935 that a mission was founded in Kugaaruk. Roman Catholicism was in many respects more tolerant of the old traditions than Anglicanism, and many elders in this area are quite knowledgeable about the old traditions. In the Kivalliq Roman Catholicism is most strongly represented, but there are also many Anglican communities.

Another problem is that each area has not been studied with equal attention, especially with respect to the traditions of the elders. In this respect Iglulik has a special position. In the 1970s Bernard Saladin d'Anglure interviewed many elders in this area, and in the 1980s Willem Rasing (1994) and John McDonald set up an interview project with Inuit elders in the community that eventually contained hundreds of interviews. In the 1990s and 2000s we interviewed several Iglulik elders in our workshops. As a result, we have access to many recorded views of Iglulik elders over a long period. That is not the case in most other communities. Obviously statements by Iglulik elders cannot be generalized for the whole area, but they certainly can have heuristic value for exploring ideas and values elsewhere.

In the past Inuit lived a nomadic life, choosing their campsites close to the places where they could catch game. If there were no game available, people would move to another campsite. People usually would not stay in one location for too long, as their residence depended on the seasons and the movements of the game. This intimate relationship between animals and people changed when people moved to permanent settlements in the 1950s and 1960s. The distinction between life in a settlement and life out on the land acquired new meanings. Life in the settlement was in many respects shaped by the Canadian administration, the Royal Canadian Mounted Police (RCMP) and the Anglican and Roman Catholic Churches. Out on the land, these institutions had little grip on the Inuit. Moreover, in the second half of the twentieth century life in the settlements became associated with all kinds of social problems, whereas life out on the land became associated with the much more healthy life of the *inummariit,* the true Inuit or ancestors, and Inuit *qaujimajatuqangit,* the knowledge associated with them. The *inummariit,* the 'real or genuine Inuit', were able to hunt and bring food to their families and camps.[17]

Today, people continue to hunt from their communities, but they usually have to cover much greater distances to reach the game than in the past. People try to retain their connection to the land and its animals by moving out on the land in spring and living the life of their ancestors in tents or cabins. Even though modern technology, with its snowmobiles, motorboats, radio and GPS, has obviously changed life on the land, maintenance of the correct relationships with the land and its animals remains a matter of great concern. People enjoy life out on the land and feel it connects them to the animals as well as to their ancestors.

When Inuit adopted Christianity, different camps and communities connected to the same great tradition, reducing cultural differences. Settlement in permanent communities and the foundation of Nunavut very much strengthened the impact of Canadian society on Inuit communities, subordinating cultural differences to Western ideology.

Because this book covers a period of two hundred years across such a huge area, generalizations cannot be avoided. But according to the FAS approach, we should not overestimate the importance of these generalizations, thus remaining aware of the value of the differences among the peoples studied.

## Sources

In this book we focus on the perspective of the participants. In the last decennia elders' views have been extensively recorded. The Oral

Traditions Project at Arctic College in Iqaluit, started by Susan Sammons in 1994, is a very rich source of information for the North Baffin and Melville Peninsula areas. We frequently refer to interviews with elders who participated in the Iglulik Oral Traditions Project, started by McDonald and Rasing in the mid 1980s. They are referred to by 'IE' (Iglulik elder) plus the number of the interview in the project. In many cases the English translation of these interviews is problematic, and wherever necessary we adapted punctuation and spelling.

The Iqaluit Oral Traditions Project covers South Baffin and parts of the Kivalliq. Courses in oral tradition in Iqaluit have been important sources of information. They consist of verbatim accounts of interviews of elders by Inuit students. They were published in Inuktitut as well as in English and cover a wide range of topics such as shamanism and cosmology, the transition to Christianity, and surviving and travelling out on the land.

Elders' workshops in the Kivalliq initiated and facilitated by the authors, also yielded much information. They had a different format. Elders discussed the old traditions pertaining to survival, shamanism, stories and other traditions. The aim of the workshops was to record the richness of the traditions of the past (see figures 1.2 and 1.3).

**Figure 1.2.** Ollie Itinnuaq from Rankin Inlet and George Kappianaq from Iglulik in a workshop organized in Rankin Inlet in 2002. Itinnuaq was raised by Anaqqaq, a famous shaman. Kappianaq contributed extensively to the Iglulik Oral Traditions Project. Photo: Frédéric Laugrand, 2002.

**Figure 1.3.** Job and Eva Murjungniq, two Ahiarmiut from Arviat, with Frédéric Laugrand on the left and Jarich Oosten on the right. Photo: Frédéric Laugrand, 2011.

Several workshops were published by Iqaluit Arctic College, such as *Inuit Qaujimajatuqangit: Shamanism and Reintegrating Wrongdoers* (Oosten and Laugrand 2002), *Surviving in Different Worlds* and *Hardships of the Past: Recollections of Arviat Elders* (Oosten and Laugrand 2007). The results of the workshops in Arviat (2006, 2007, 2010, 2011), Kugaaruk (2004), Baker Lake (2005) and Churchill (2008) have not yet been published. Therefore, we cannot indicate page numbers for these workshops, but instead refer to them by place name and year (e.g., Kugaaruk workshop, 2004).[18] Unpublished individual interviews are referred to by the year of the interview. In addition, we refer to rich sources on elders' views that have been published in the last fifteen years, such as *Inuit Nunamiut: Inland Inuit* by Mannik (1998) and *Uqalurait: An Oral History of Nunavut* by Bennett and Rowley (2004).

It is often more difficult to infer participant views from older sources. Fortunately, Knud Rasmussen made quite a point of recording the views of the participants themselves and is meticulous in providing the names of his main informants. Thus, he provided rich information on the Iglulik, Nattilik and Kivalliq areas. For the South Baffin area, ethnographic information provided by the Reverend E. J. Peck is extremely valuable (see figure 1.4). Much of his ethnographic informa-

**Figure 1.4.** At the beginning of the twentieth century the Reverend Peck provided Inuit in South Baffin with paper and pencil so they could make drawings of their life. In this drawing we see two scenes: The upper scene shows hunting at the seal breathing holes. The hunter on the left is ready to kill the seal; the other hunter appears to be watching. The second scene depicts a fully loaded sledge drawn by dogs. *Source:* Anglican Church of Canada/General Synod Archives/Peck Papers, M56-1, series XXXIII, 4–6, 8–13.

tion clearly consists of almost verbatim accounts of participants, but unfortunately he does not always provide the names of his informants in the presentation of these data. Such ethnographic data can be supplemented by those of other ethnographers such as Kumlien and Boas, but in their accounts the views of the ethnographer and those of the participants cannot always be clearly distinguished.

In this book we follow the rules of the standard Roman orthography as it is used in Nunavut today. The older sources, such as Boas, Peck and Rasmussen, use older orthographies, often based on Greenlandic traditions. We have retained those specific orthographies in the quotations. We also follow standard orthography in the spelling of the names of the elders, unless the elders have indicated a preference for another spelling (e.g., Kupak instead of Kupaq or Etanguat instead of Itanguat).

## The Organization of the Book

In this book on Inuit perceptions of animals, we focus on animals that take a central place in the Inuits' worldview. We provide a general introduction to the Inuit and the animals that populate their world in the chapters of part I, Introduction. In chapter 1 we discuss some of the main theoretical perspectives on human-animal relations developed by leading scholars in the field and develop our own approach to the study of human-animal relations. In chapter 2 we introduce the land, the sea and the sky as well as the animals that populate them. We show how the notions of *tarniq* (miniature image, shade), *inua* (person, owner), and *atiq* (name) shape the relations between human beings and animals in Inuit culture. In chapter 3 we focus on the relationship between the hunter and his prey and the importance of learning the correct ways of hunting.

Then, in part II, Life and Death, we begin to focus on specific animals. We first discuss the raven in chapter 4, an animal that holds a central place in many Arctic cultures as a creator and a trickster. In chapter 5 we focus on *qupirruit*, a category consisting of insects and other small life-forms. Like the raven, they have a trickster aspect and are associated with transformations of life to death and vice versa. They are considered inedible, as is the raven, and at the same time they eat what is inedible themselves.

In part III, Fellow Hunters, we examine two animals who are closely connected to Inuit hunters. In chapter 6 we discuss the dog, the animal companion of the hunter, and in chapter 7 the bear, considered to resemble a human being and a fellow hunter. The two animals are related to each other as *illuriik*—song partners, cross-cousins. They can be eaten, but as they are thought to be close to human beings and their meat is thought to taste like human flesh, there are restrictions on eating these animals.

In part IV, Prey, we examine the animals that are considered prey par excellence. In chapter 8 the caribou, the lice of the earth, who provide human beings not only with meat but also with furs that protect them against the cold. In chapter 9 the seals, the offspring of the fingers of the sea woman. And in chapter 10 the whale, the symbol of the whole; we then also discuss the renewal of whale hunting in recent years.

Finally, in the conclusions, we provide a comparative analysis of the ethnographic data presented in the book. We examine various theoretical and moral issues such as to what extent animals are human, the nature of the transformations of human beings into animals and animals into human beings, and the debate on the protection of animals.

## Notes

1. In the North American Arctic, research on human-animal relations first focused on the field of symbolic anthropology, mythology and ritual (see Juel 1945; Rainey 1947; Lantis 1947; Irving 1953, 1958; Soby 1970; Larsen

1970; Meletinsky 1973; Saladin d'Anglure 1990b; Blaisel 1993). Interest in the topic soon developed in the fields of ethno-linguistics (Rausch 1951), ethno-science (Paillet 1973) and geography, notably in ecology and economy (Roy 1971; Forbes 1986; Wenzel 1983, 1986, 1989; Usher 2000). In the field of arts the focus on animals increased in the 1980s (see Graburn 1980; Driscoll 1982, 1985). Today, all these trends are beginning to merge: see Dorais (1984), Randa (1989, 1994, 2002a, 2002b, 2003) and Feldman and Norton (1995) for ethno-linguistics and ethno-zoology; see Smith (1991), Donaldson (1994), Tyrrell (2005, 2006, 2007) and Dowsley (2007, 2010) for geography. At the end of the 1990s, studies on animals also appeared in a new field known as applied ecology/environmental studies (D. Armitage 2005; Berkes 2008).

2. Tanner (1979) and Willis (1990) offer good examples of symbolic approaches. The ecological or environmental perspectives developed in the 1980s continue to be very popular among geographers (see Wenzel 1986, 1991, 2004; Usher 2000; Berkes 2008; Tyrrell 2007, 2008). A good example of an ethno-zoological approach can be found in Clément (1995, 2012) for the Innu and in Randa (1994) for the Inuit.

3. For such discussions, see R. Nelson (1983: 15), Scott (1996), Nadasdy (2003) and Willerslev (2007).

4. On Inuit *qaujimajatuqangit* and the various debates surrounding it, see Arnakak (2002), Wenzel (1999, 2004) and Berkes (2008).

5. Sahlins's chapter *The Original Affluent Society,* in his book *Stone Age Economics* released in 1972, had a great impact on scholars in this field.

6. On these practices among the eastern Cree, see Preston ([1975] 2002: 97) and Tanner (1979: 169).

7. Animals are not supposed to suffer when they are killed, but this issue remains controversial; see Désveaux (1995) and Brightman (1993: 110–11). See also Krech (1999) and Nadasdy (2005) for further discussion of the myth of the 'ecological Indian'.

8. Fienup-Riordan (1999, 2000) discusses extensively hunting activities among the Yup'ik.

9. According to Sharp (2001: 68), the Chipewyan and many Dene groups believe that all animals except dogs reincarnate and 'become new again'.

10. According to R. Nelson (1983: 22), Koyukon people distinguish between animals that are possessed by spirits that can bring harm to anyone who offends them, causing illness, taking away luck or causing death (such as the bear, wolverine, lynx, wolf, and otter), animals that are possessed by spirits but are not vengeful (such as the beaver and marmot) and animals that have less powerful spirits and inflict minor punishments, mostly bad luck in hunting (such as birds, fish and other mammals).

11. See also Clammer et al. (2004) on the notion of 'figured worlds'.

12. Ingold's perspective has inspired many scholars (e.g., Clammer et al. 2004).

13. See Descola (2005: 163–80).

14. Latour (1993, 2009b) argued that Western societies are still ambiguous. Naturalism can be seen as the dominant scheme of interaction, but at the same time this view can be challenged, as illustrated by the title of one

of Latour's books, *We Have Never Been Modern* (1993). Eco-theology also gives more space to analogy.

15. On hunting and mimesis, see also Koester (2002) and Wisniewski (2007).

16. R. Nelson (1983: xiv) adopted a similar approach in *Make Prayers to the Raven,* acknowledging the role of a Western mind that often organizes and filters the data.

17. *Inummariit* are considered very knowledgeable hunters, and others often point to their generosity, patience and co-operative behaviour (see Brody 1979).

18. For the organization and methodology of these courses and workshops, see Laugrand and Oosten (2012a: 19–33).

# CHAPTER 2

# The Animals and Their Environment

## The Land, the Sea and the Sky

The animals inhabit *nuna*, the land; *tariuq*, the sea and *sila*, the sky. In Inuit culture, especially the land and the sea were a source of life. They provided the sustenance that allows human beings to survive in the harsh Arctic climate. The main prey were the caribou on the land and the sea mammals in the sea. Birds were hunted, but they were much less important prey than the caribou and the sea mammals (see figure 2.1).

In the past, land game and sea game were usually separated by ritual injunctions. Especially the transition from caribou hunting to seal hunting was strongly marked in this respect. The land and the sea apparently constituted different domains that had to be kept separate by ritual injunctions organizing the use and consumption of these animals.

## Nuna, *the Land*

The land represents the origin of human beings as well as of some animals such as caribou and especially *qupirruit*, insects and other vermin that were thought to come out of the earth spontaneously each year. Inuit myths of the origin of human beings tell us that in the past the first human beings were created from the earth, from *niaqutait*, hummocks of earth.[1] The first children were produced by the earth, and originally people ate earth (Rasmussen 1929: 110, 254). Earth was a source of life, and the first two people did not die, but returned to the soil (Oosten et al. 1999: 199). The reproductive and alimentary cycles were encompassed by the earth until human beings learned to reproduce themselves and to hunt for game. The earth must be respected, so it will not turn against human beings. Rasmussen (1929: 19) relates,

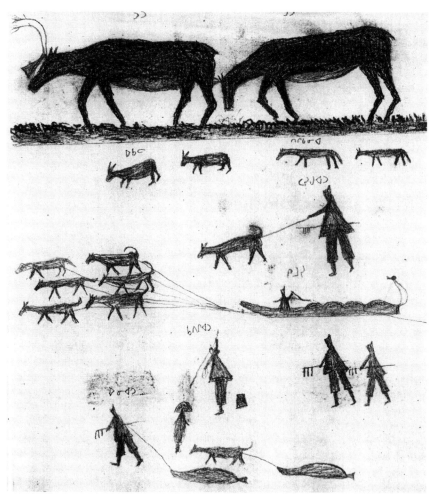

**Figure 2.1.** Caribou and seals are the most important prey. *Source:* Anglican Church of Canada/General Synod Archives/Peck Papers, M56-1, series XXXIII, 4–6, 8–13.

'The earth grew angry if men out hunting worked too much with stones and turf in the building of their meat stores and hunting depots.'

The Iglulingmiut believed that if people stayed in a place too long, the earth became hot, and this would affect their well-being. Eugene Amarualik (IE 287), from Iglulik, related how people would leave their old home after three years of occupation so that the land would not 'get hot' (*uunarsiqunagu*). For this reason, the camp had been moved from Avajja to Iglulik.

Living within a community is associated with hotness, and it is generally assumed that living on the land outside the community is healthy and refreshes and invigorates a person. Traditionally it was thought that places where no human traces could be found in the snow were especially appropriate for making contact with spirits and other non-human beings. People in the North Baffin area would go to such places and pray by shouting words (*qinngaq*) or the name of a person to seek help in a dangerous situation, to locate wildlife or to improve the weather (see Saladin d'Anglure 2001: 142–44).

The earth also holds the deceased. The dead were traditionally deposited out on the land, but today they are buried in cemeteries near the settlements, which preferably overlook the land or the sea. Thus, the land used to be covered with graves that were visited by relatives of the deceased and must be respected. The land is also covered with traces of previous inhabitants: tent rings, remains of sod houses, objects and *inuksuit,* stone markers in the shape of a human being.

The land and the sky cannot be owned by people. They are shared by those who live there. Inuit still consider themselves to be *nunaqqatigiit,* those who share the land, or *silaqqatigiit,* those who share the air, the wind and the weather.

When travelling on the land, people need to know where the good hunting areas can be found and which places are dangerous and should be avoided. Some places are only safe if certain rules are observed. Marble Island is well-known for the rules that apply to visitors; on first approaching the island, one has to crawl.

Kappianaq recalled various places near Iglulik that were considered dangerous: 'You would hear voices of people that were not part of the group you were with at that place.' He added that people should still respect these places, for 'even though we have become Christians, the land hasn't changed'. He emphasized that one should not challenge the wisdom of the elders: 'When people, through experience, have learned about these places, they caution others about them. If a person knowingly decides to challenge this knowledge and goes there, he will lose his strength. It is usually hills and high places that are dangerous.'

Lakes are also places that sometimes have to be approached with caution. At a workshop in Kugaaruk in 2004, Kupak from Naujaat related, 'Close to Aivilik, there is a lake. We were told never to camp near that lake for some reason. We can't camp there. We Inuit believe in these things. Some places can be scary and dangerous.' Reverend Armand Tagoona (1975) from Qamanittuaq gives the example of Dubawnt Lake: 'The Inuit are afraid of that lake, because, they say, it has big fishes, fishes that swallow human beings and even whole caribou.'

Graves demanded special respect. People would visit the graves of their relatives and namesakes. A visit to the grave of a dead person

was considered beneficial for the living person. Iqallijuq from Iglulik
related,

> Whenever we went to the land where my namesake was buried, my
> mother would always take me to the grave.... Now you can see me as an
> old lady: there were times when I almost died but I was able to recover
> because of visiting that grave. As a matter of fact, I was given the sacra-
> ment of last rites on two occasions when I was comatose. Both times I
> was able to recover, and so I know that it helps to visit the grave of your
> namesake. (quoted in Saladin d'Anglure 2001: 5)

Graves could be found all over the land, and people had to know the
places where the deceased were buried so they could observe the rules
pertaining to those places. In the 2003 workshop in Arviat, Peter Suvaksiuq from Arviat related that he was cured by honouring the wishes of the
deceased and visiting their graves:

> On an island there is a grave there. He used to tell people to stop there
> for tea. Three years ago while I was alone I went down there for tea. I
> wanted to find out what it was like. I took a thermos. The grave was ex-
> posed. You could see the bones. They weren't covered at all, at Qikiqtar-
> juat, just a little way from here. I had tea and I said I was tired of being
> sick. The next day I got rid of my sickness. When you test something
> sometimes it will really happen.

The land is also populated with many non-human beings that are
sometimes closely associated with particular animals. Thus, the *ijirait* are connected to the caribou, and some places are called *ijiralik*, a
place where *ijirait* live, and have to be treated with respect.

## Tariuq, the Sea

The sea is the home of the sea mammals (*puijiit*) that constituted
a major source of food. They originated from the fingers of the sea
woman, who was considered the owner of the sea mammals. Rasmussen (1929: 183) relates, 'The sea spirit Takánâluk demands taboo
for all sea animals because they were made from her fingers.' The
Iglulingmiut relate that Takaanaaluk Kapsaluk or Uinigumasuittuq,
'the woman who does not want to marry a husband', was invited by
a strange hunter to board his kayak. He turned out to be a stormy
petrel in human appearance and took her to a far country. They lived
together for some time. Later her father came to fetch her and per-
suaded his daughter to come back with him. When they travelled
home in their *umiaq*, boat, the petrel pursued them, creating a storm

with his wings. The father did not want to return his daughter to the bird and pushed her out of the boat. She clung to the boat with both hands. Her father cut off her fingers, joint after joint, and they turned into seals, bearded seals and walrus as they fell into the water. Then the woman sank to the bottom of the sea. She became the *inua* of the sea, the owner of the sea as well as the sea game (see Rasmussen 1929: 63–66). Different versions specify different sea mammals that came from her fingers. Boas (1888: 584) relates, 'The cruel father then took a knife and cut off the first joints of her fingers. Falling into the sea they were transformed into whales, the nails turning into whalebone. Sedna holding on to the boat more tightly, the second finger joints fell under the sharp knife and swam away as seals (*Pagomys faetidus*); when the father cut off the stumps of the fingers they became ground seals[2] (*Phoca barbata*).'

Peck (quoted in Laugrand et al. 2006: chap. 15) relates that from the fingers originated seals, bearded seals, walrus and whales. According to a Nattilik version (Rasmussen 1931: 381–82), fjord seals, bearded seals and walrus were created. In a more recent Iglulik version recorded by Alexina Kublu,[3] seals, square flippers (bearded seals) and beluga originated from the fingers.[4]

Thus, seals, bearded seals and whales were usually considered transformations of the fingers of the sea woman. Boas (1901: 528) reports, 'It is very remarkable that the walrus is not included in this series of regulations. It is explicitly stated that the walrus, the white whale and the narwhal are not subject to these laws, which affect only the sea animals that originated from Sedna's fingers.' Rasmussen (1931: 226) relates, 'Whenever people have been indifferent towards her by not observing taboo, she hides all the animals; the seals she shuts up in her in·aut: a drip-basin that she has under her lamp. As long as they are inside it, there are no animals to hunt in the sea, and mankind has to starve; the shamans then have to summon their helping spirits and conjure her to be kind again.' Then the *angakkuq*, the shaman, would have to descend to Sedna's house on the bottom of the sea, to calm her down and appease her. Once he had managed to do so and the Inuit had confessed all their transgressions and offences, she would be prepared to set the seals free again.

A different story or origin myth existed for the walrus (see page 284). The belugas also were usually not considered to be under the sway of the sea woman. The narwhal was thought to be a transformation of an old woman usually considered to be the mother or grandmother of the moon man. The story relates that he was hunting beluga with his (grand)mother. When she tied the harpoon line around her waist, he harpooned a big one, which drew her into the water. The old woman then changed into a narwhal.[5]

Like the land, the sea is also populated by non-human beings that may be associated with animal species. Thus, the *tuutaliit*, naked human-like beings living in the sea, are closely associated with the seals.

Even though the land and the sea constitute different domains, they are in many respects connected. Some land animals are thought to have a counterpart in the sea. Thus, we find many *qupirruit*, insects and other small life-forms, in the land as well as in the sea (e.g., the bumblebee and the bumblebee of the sea). The caribou is connected by its origin myth to the walrus, and the polar bear is at home in both domains.

## Sila, *the Sky*

Sila is a concept that embraces a wide range of related categories such as the sky, the weather and the 'outside' in general.[6] The direction of Sila is the direction in which the sun moves, and this is the direction that should normally be followed. Sila is associated with reason, and a person without Sila is a person without reason. Sila refers to the world and its order, as it is represented by the movements of the constellations in the sky.

In the Nattilik and Iglulik areas some mythical traditions are connected with Silaup inua or Narssuk, the spirit of the wind. Rasmussen (1929: 72; see also Rasmussen 1931: 210, 229–30) writes:

> Nartsuk, also pronounced Narshuk, was originally the child of a giant and his wife, both of whom were murdered, first the father, then the mother killed. This evil-doing turned the child into a spirit, which flew up into the sky and became the lord of the weather. It is always dressed in a full costume of caribou skin – a dress with tunic and breeches made in one piece, and very wide, as worn by children generally. When Nartsuk shakes his dress, air rushes out from all the loose space in his clothing, and the winds begin to blow.
>
> When the spirit of the winds keeps on blowing and there is no peace for men to go out hunting by land or sea, then a shaman has to go up into the sky and beat him, thrash him with a whip, until he calms down and the storms subside.

Nakasuk from Iglulik told Rasmussen that the 'wickedness of mankind turned him [the spirit of the wind] into a tonraq [helping spirit]' (1929: 230). Rasmussen (1929: 72) adds that if the weather was bad and the wind continued to blow, *angakkuit* had to calm him down. As Boas ([1888] 1964: 593) reports for South Baffin, 'Storm and bad weather, when lasting a long time and causing want of food, are conjured by making a large whip of seaweed, stepping to the beach, and striking out in the direction whence the wind blows, at the same time crying Taba (It is enough).'

Storms could also be caused by *silaat*, eggs that were found on the land. Rasmussen (1929: 203; see also Boas 1901: 493) writes, 'It is said that they are the children of the earth. Anyone killing such a *silaq* must observe the same taboo as a man who has lost his brother.' Today, *silaat* may still be found, and careful hunters will leave them alone. From these eggs grew white animals, but if they were prematurely broken, the weather became bad and fierce storms could arise. In similar traditions in the Nattilik area, *silaat* turned into musk oxen (Rasmussen 1931: 265). Pisuk from Kangiq&iniq recalled how he had found a *silaq* and had told his father about it:

> He said, 'Let's go and see what you saw.' I took him back there. The narrow part was pointed downwards. He told me it was an earth egg and that if I broke it, [it] would become very windy. He said if we were to cook it whole and eat it, then nothing would happen to the weather, but that the weather would really be aware of it if we broke it. When my father told me you were not supposed to break them, he seemed afraid. He said that if it was really an earth egg, then it would be fresh. It was as fresh as a newly laid egg. My mother cooked it and cut it into pieces, and my brothers and sisters and I all ate it. It was in the Saagluk area near Qamanittuaq. (quoted in Oosten and Laugrand 2002: 96–97)

*Silaat* will turn into large animals. Angutinngurniq from Kugaaruk commented, '*Silaat* is what they are called after they hatch. I have heard that the eggs are not all the same colour, but they all become *silaat*. They become different animals depending on the colour of the eggs' (quoted in Oosten and Laugrand 2002: 98).

The air is the domain of a variety of birds, most of them migratory visting the Arctic in the summer. The raven, the snowy owl and the ptarmigan are also present in winter. Birds may have a connection to the *tarniq*, the miniature image of a being that was later interpreted as the soul.

## Prey and Hunters

Animals and human beings are connected as prey and hunters. Animals are in many respects considered partners of human beings, and their relations are embedded in a cosmological framework that does not follow the rules of a modern zoological classification. According to Randa (2002b: 73), Inuit from Iglulik classify animals into five categories: (1) *nirijutit* (mammals, literally 'those who serve as food') – in that category animals are usually divided into the *pisuktiit* ('those who walk') or *nunamiutait* ('those of the land') and the *imarmiutait* ('those of the water') or *puijiit* ('those who emerge to breathe'); (2) *tingmiat* (birds); (3) *iqaluit* (fish); (4) *qupirruit* (insects and other small life-forms); and (5) *uviluit* (molluscs). Randa notes that all these categories encompass a number of animals, and that a few beings do not fit into these categories.[7] He examined many animals in detail and devoted a rich monograph to the polar bear.

In this book we do not cover the full range of Arctic animals; we limit ourselves to those that come to the fore in Inuit beliefs and practices. Some animals such as bears, caribou and seals are richly documented, whereas the ethnographic data on other animals such as wolves, musk oxen, rabbits and lemmings are less rich. As a consequence, they are only referred to obliquely in our book and covered very briefly.

Many scholars assume that animals can be considered sentient beings equivalent to human beings, but they seldom explain the specificity of each animal and the connections that exist between them. On closer scrutiny, each animal is quite specific in its features and connections to others. Therefore, we will not only explore species of animals, but also connect their use and symbolism. We will provide a careful investigation of Inuit categories of thought as they take shape in stories, rules of respect and personal experiences.

The most general term for animals is *uumajuit*, 'those who live'. Like the English word 'animal', derived from 'anima', breath, soul, it is not an exclusive category, as human beings also have life and breath. Inuit emphasize that their survival has always depended upon their capacity to hunt animals, and relations to animals are perceived as fundamental to their own existence. As survival has always depended upon the killing of animals, they are greatly valued in Inuit society.

People identify as Inuit because they hunt and eat animals. In 1975, Mosesie Idlout, from Resolute, stated, '[Although] I have learned more about the white man's ways … I am still Inuk because I grew up on Inuk food' (quoted in Freeman et al. 1998: 39). That same year, Peter Okpik from Gjoa Haven observed, 'This is the way I think. A person is born with animals. He has to eat animals. That is why the animals and a person are just like one.'[8] In these statements the ambivalence of the relation between human beings and animals is clearly expressed. Inuit can only remain Inuit by killing and eating animals, and in doing so the unity of human beings and animals takes shape. Inuit and animals may share a common identity, but their respective roles in their relationship are clearly defined as hunters and prey.

The notion of *niqituinnaq,* real or country food, is commonly used in Nunavik (see Dorais 1997) as well as in some Baffin Island communities (see Wenzel 1991: 136). It refers to the game and the fish provided by the hunters, in contrast to store-bought food associated with the *qallunaat,* white people. Food not only sustains people; it also produces social relationships through sharing and eating. Betsy Annahatak from Nunavik quoted Annie Grey and Tomassie Kudluk: 'Because food is what makes people be related to each other, we were told not to have it to ourselves while people are hungry.'[9] And Tomassie Kudluk added, 'Even among close siblings, food is what makes them have close relationships.'[10] Inuit culture therefore necessarily encompasses the animals that form the basis of Inuit identity and the foundation of their sociality (see Dorais 1997; Stairs and Wenzel 1992).[11]

In the past Inuit lived a nomadic lifestyle and followed the game (see figure 2.2). Although women could be hunters as well, men usually took care of hunting. Martha Nasook from Iglulik (IE 159) recalled how they used to wait for the hunters as children:

We were told that only if we heard the dog team returning, we had to smile when we entered; otherwise we should not smile. We found it diffi-

**Figure 2.2.** Inuit hunters and their women travelling inland for the caribou hunt. *Source:* Anglican Church of Canada/General Synod Archives/Peck Papers, M56-1, series XXXIII, 4–6, 8–13.

cult not to smile even if we did not hear the hunters returning. ... As there were no other noises except those of our own making, we could hear the dog team returning even when they were some distance away. Sometimes we would put our ears to the ground and hear the sleds gliding along the ground way before we could hear the dogs. Indeed, we could hear the sound of sled, we could tell if the sled had a heavy load.

In the summer time we used to spend the summer out in the mainland when we were hunting caribou. So, the hunters sometimes would spend days out from our main camp; so sometimes when we were running short on food we could see the hunters finally returning; so when we saw that the pack dogs were behind the hunter, we could tell that the dogs were packed, which told us that the hunter had caught caribou. In those days when a hunter was returning or had returned, there used to be excitement and jubilation, especially when a polar bear had been caught.

Not only daily life, but also the patterns of space and time were organized and structured by the animals.

The introduction of Western materials and implements changed hunting technology and the beliefs and practices relating to it. Today, Inuit hunters often acknowledge the extensive transformations of these techniques, which varied depending on the animals and the location of the hunt. Noah Piugaattuq (IE 248) described the transition in hunting caribou from bows and arrows to firearms:

It is said that when they started to use firearms, they found it so much easier to catch caribou; as a matter of fact, even when they hit part of the back bone, it did not even take another step when it fell down. ...

When one is hunting with arrows one must aim for the lungs or the heart. The hunter will only shoot when it is so close that it is surely a hit. When the caribou is too far and the hunter is doubtful whether he will hit the target, which is the lungs and the heart, they would use an arrowhead with offset lateral barbs with hitting the target anywhere in mind. Should he penetrate the caribou with this arrow around the legs, the arrow would penetrate deeper with each of the movements the caribou makes. ... That was the reason for the offset lateral barbs on the arrow, which were used to shoot a caribou that was too far to hit the proper target. When the caribou was close, the hunter would use an arrow that had a metal arrowhead that would kill the animal through the heart or the lung.

Today, the Inuit of northeast Canada have given up their nomadic lifestyle and live in permanent settlements, but many elders still rely on animals and their behaviour to predict the weather and the seasons. They connect animal behaviour to the wind, the sun and the moon. As Noah Piugaattuq (IE 246) explained,

You sometimes will notice the sea animals, especially the walrus [see figure 2.3], are all moving in one particular direction. That means that a prolonged prevailing wind is on its way and the walrus are moving against that wind. When this happens, it was deemed to be dangerous, so hunters were warned that they should stop hunting on the moving ice.... When the wind hits, it will last for three days and later it will start to slow down. It was known that the winds would be blowing for more than one day when the walrus are moving in the general directions....

When the caribou are moving to one general location, that means the path that they have taken will not see many caribou. These were the things that were used to forecast the availability of certain animals as well as the conditions. Different species of animals do not live together, but sometimes they appear as if they have the same thoughts, especially the land animals when they start to move in one general direction. As for the marine animals, they were mainly used to tell the weather forecast, because the sea usually reacts before the weather.

Although many Inuit no longer hunt, hunting still has a central place in their worldview and is considered essential to survival. In 1995, an Inuk from Sanikuluaq stated:

We, as Inuit, our tradition is fresh meat, and I know that it can keep the body in shape.... Only animals keep us strong as Inuit.... When we haven't taken seal blubber for a while, we weaken.... When we haven't

**Figure 2.3.** Like the caribou, the walrus is a gregarious animal, often appearing in multitudes. Photo: Robert Fréchette/Avataq Cultural Institute.

eaten fresh meat for a while, we get really tired. And then, when we do eat it, our body gets satisfied because we are Inuit.... Even if we eat white man's food, if we haven't eaten Inuit food for a while, we weaken. (quoted in Freeman et al. 1998: 45)

Only by hunting and eating country food can Inuit retain their strength. Thus, they depend completely on the animals they kill. The animals are thought to be aware of this and to give themselves up willingly to be killed by the hunter. In March 1995, Simionie Akpalialuk from Pangniqtuuq stated,

We have to go out and get [food].... I just can't go to the store and pick it up.... [Our] relationship to the land is very important because the land is alive, the animals and the sea itself; and you are interacting [with them]. ... Going to catch a whale, the feeling that you get is never what you get going down to the store. Going down to the store, you're on dead ground: all the buildings are dead. All items in there are dead, there's nothing alive ... but here in the North, it's a lot more.... You're not only just going there just for food, you're going there to interact with nature, to understand more of the animals. A whale gives of itself: it's an animal that you feel fully about, it's something that gives itself up to you and that's an important thing in our beliefs, that's still very strong. (quoted in Freeman et al. 1998: 42)

The killing of game is therefore not considered an act of violence by a human being towards an animal, but a meaningful act in which hunter and animal are connected as partners.

A key moment in any hunt is the killing of the prey and the enjoyment it brings to the hunter. George Kappianaq (IE 071) evokes that specific moment in the context of the walrus hunt, one of the most dangerous hunts:

I was taught how to use a harpoon in walrus hunts without using a rifle. This is when the walrus are not aware of your presence, when you approach them on the ice before they get a chance to dive away. This must be one of the joyous moments. All other thoughts are gone. Your only thought at this point is the walrus ahead of you. When you approach a walrus, one gets really excited with anticipation as you will get a chance to strike. When the walrus exhales, the noise seems to be quiet as you would strike when the walrus inhales. As the walrus starts to inhale, your concentration is centred on your target. As you aim, your thoughts are not wandering but on your target. This is the moment when you are filled with gladness [*alianait*].

The game provided meat for food, skins for clothing and blubber for fuel. Bones, sinews and bladders were all used to make implements.

If the game did not show itself to the hunters, people would starve and perhaps die. Whether animals allowed themselves to be killed depended to a large extent on the behaviour of the hunter, his wife and the community as a whole. Hunters would only be successful if people behaved respectfully towards the animals and observed the correct ritual injunctions. For example, a successful hunter should share his catch with his hunting partners, his family, his housemates and the community where he lived. Nobody should be left hungry after a catch. This obligation to give was, and still is, all-important. There is no obligation to give something back. But each hunter has to give, regardless of whether he has received something in the past.

Thus, animals and human beings were thought to share a common origin and in many respects a common nature. But they were also fundamentally different. Animals were prey and human beings were hunters; hunters should not become prey to the game.

## The *Tarniq* and the *Atiq*

Animals were endowed with consciousness. Like human beings, they had a *tarniq*, a concept often translated as 'soul'. The word *tarniq* is derived from the root *taaq-*, dark, and is best translated as 'shade' or 'miniature image'. The *tarniq* was usually located in a vital organ such as the kidneys or the liver. Animals as well as human beings had a *tarniq* that survived them after death. The *tarniq* was invisible to ordinary human beings, but it could be seen by *angakkuit*, shamans. The famous ethnographer Knud Rasmussen (1929: 58–59), who crossed the Arctic regions from Greenland to Alaska in the early 1920s, relates,

> The soul, tarniŋa or inuˑsia (inuusia), is that which gives to all living things their particular appearance. In the case of human beings it is really a tiny human being, in the case of the caribou a tiny caribou, and so on with all animals; an image, but very much smaller than the creature itself.
>
> The inuˑsia (meaning 'appearance as a human being') is situated in a bubble of air in the groin; from it proceed appearance, thoughts, strength and life, it is that which makes the man a man, the caribou a caribou, the walrus a walrus, the dog a dog, etc.[12]

Life depends on this miniature image, which is held inside a *pullaq* (bubble of air). When a person dies, the *tarniq* survives. According to Felix Pisuk from Kangiq&iniq, 'When I die my *tarniq* will no longer be a bubble. It will become the way you see me' (quoted in Kolb and Law 2001: 36).

The *tarniq* differentiated the appearance of a being. The *tarniq* of a human being was a miniature human being, and that of a caribou a miniature caribou. The health and vitality of a being depended on its *tarniq* as well. It might leave the body temporarily, but if it did not return, the separation between body and the *tarniq* would become final, and that being would die.

Ethnographers such as Franz Boas and Knud Rasmussen translated *tarniq* as 'soul', and after the transition to Christianity, *tarniq* became the Inuktitut translation of the Christian concept of soul. The *tarniit* of animals were supposed to incarnate again, whereas the *tarniq* of a human being would go to a land of the dead. It was expected that the shade of an animal that had been killed would reincarnate. If it had been treated well and had been respected by the hunter and his wife, it would allow itself to be caught again by the same hunter who had shown it respect. Peter Arnatsiaq from Iglulik told a story about an old bear who was full of facial scars because he 'would return to his being after his meat was all eaten up following his capture by the hunters. In those days any animal used to return after they had served their purpose to the human kind; this was known as *angiraaliniq*.' Arnatsiaq explained that the facial scars were the results of the attacks of the dogs as he was bitten by them each time that the bear was killed and butchered. 'After he had been used he would return home among the polar bears.'[13]

Whereas the continuity of animals was ensured by the reincarnation of nameless *tarniit*, the continuity of human beings was organized by a succession of *atiit*, names. Babies were named after deceased ancestors who would support their living namesakes. People might even have recollections of events in the lives of their deceased namesakes. To what extent there was a connection between the *tarniq* and the *atiq* is unclear. Sometimes it is suggested, but it is never strongly marked. Boas (1901: 234) relates the story of a hunter who recognized the soul of his deceased mother in a fox and therefore could not kill it. In the famous story of Arnaqtaaqtuq, told by Celestine Iqijjuk from Kivalliq, a rejected foetus reincarnated time and again in different beings, such as dogs, seals and caribou, until it was finally reborn as a human being.[14] The Arnaqtaaqtuq story starts with an *angiaq*, a miscarriage, suggesting that these things may happen when rules are transgressed, but no suggestion is made that this is a normal pattern. Human beings are connected to the ancestors through their names, whereas animals lack such a connection and live in a continuous circle of reincarnation. History is part of human society, not of the world of anonymous animals whose *tarniit* continually reincarnate.

The mortality of the *tarniq* was a topic of discussion in Inuit society. Oosutapik, one of Peck's informants in Cumberland Sound, told Peck that many *tuurngait* (helping spirits of the shamans) were able to kill the *tarniit* of animals so that the animals could be easily killed by hunters. However, another of Peck's main informants, Qoojessie, emphatically denied that this was possible, explaining that souls were immortal and could not be killed (quoted in Laugrand et al. 2006: 383–84).

The willingness of the game to be killed could also be explained in reference to its wish to change its body. Rasmussen (1929: 58) relates,

> Animals have in reality no objection to being killed by human beings, as long as the rules of life are observed by the latter. It may even happen, and not infrequently, that an animal will approach a human being, actually desiring to be killed by that particular person. An animal may perhaps be tired of being what it is; and since its soul cannot change its envelope until the body has been killed, it is natural that animals should sometimes wish to die.

Many Inuit believed that animals offered themselves to the hunter in order to be killed. If animals were hunted they would multiply; if they were not hunted, they would feel neglected and disappear. George Kappianaq (IE 454) recalled, 'Some animals can make themselves available. I suppose they want to be caught, so they make themselves available, or if they want to be turned to another species, so some animals make themselves available.' Animals were thus often described as giving themselves to the hunters, who would make good use of their meat.

The missionaries taught the Inuit that only human beings have souls, and this point of view was then adopted by Inuit, although there was always some debate. Thus, Piugaattuq (IE 453) stated that game animals do not have souls, and added, 'From what I have heard from Ittusarjjuat, I think that wolves might have souls, I am not certain.'

## Shared Origins

Human beings and animals are usually thought to have shared origins.[15] The Nattilik woman Nalungiaq told Rasmussen (1931: 208) that at first the world was dark:

> In the very first times there was no light on earth. Everything was in darkness, the lands could not be seen, the animals could not be seen. And still, both people and animals lived on the earth, but there was no difference between them. They lived promiscuously. A person could be-

come an animal, and an animal could become a human being. There
were wolves, bears, and foxes, but as soon as they turned into humans
they were all the same. They may have had different habits, but all spoke
the same tongue, lived in the same kind of house, and spoke and hunted
in the same way.

Thus, in the darkness there was no difference between human beings
and animals in terms of human appearance, language and habits. Their
relationship was marked by promiscuity. The animals that Nalungiaq
specified were all land animals and predators. When light was created
by the raven, wolves, bears and foxes no longer mingled with human
beings.

Before the introduction of Christianity it was believed that animals
had an *inua*, its person or owner. The suffix -*a* means 'its', 'his' or 'her'.
*Inua* therefore means 'its person', and depending on context it can also
be translated as 'its inhabitant' or 'its owner'.[16] The *inua* of a dog or a
kayak is the person who owns that dog or kayak. Places often also had
an *inua*. The *inua* of an animal or a place could take the appearance of
a human being, but such an *inua* was not really a human person. Stories relate how human beings visited places where the animals lived in
human appearance. Although ordinary people might be fooled, *angakkuit*, shamans, were able to perceive that such an *inua* was not a real
human person. An animal could also transform itself into a human being, and in a mythical past human beings were also able to transform
themselves into animals. Rasmussen (1929: 271) provides several stories about people who visited bears and wolves in human appearance.
The Kiviuq myths, relating the adventures of the great traveller Kiviuq
who travelled far and wide over land and sea, provide many stories
relating how Kiviuq married an animal in human appearance (e.g.,
a goose, a fox). The *tarniq* as well as the *inua* were visually marked:
the *tarniq* was a miniature image of a being and could only be seen
by shamans; the *inua* was the human appearance of a being, and only
shamans could perceive its true nature.

The word *inua* was also used for the owners of the moon, the sky
and the sea. The *inua* of the moon originally was a human being. After
an incestuous relationship with his sister, the two siblings were transformed into sun and moon. The *inua* of the sky, Sila or Narssuk, was
originally a giant baby who was mistreated and went up into the sky
and was associated with the weather, especially the wind. The *inua* of
the sea, the sea woman, was usually considered the owner of the sea
mammals. In South Baffin she was usually referred to as Sanna, 'the
one down there'. In the Iglulik area she was known as Takaanaaluk
Kapsaluk, 'the terrible one down there', and in the Nattilik area as Nu-

liajuk. When she withheld the game because of all the transgressions committed by human beings, an *angakkuq* had to descend to her house at the bottom of the sea to appease her and if necessary wrestle with her so that she would set the animals free again.

To what extent the *inua* of an animal, or the *inua* of the sea, 'owns' animals is an issue of debate among Inuit themselves. Ollie Ittinuaq, an elder from Rankin Inlet, observed in a workshop,

> I don't know if the animals have an owner. I have heard that animals belong to everyone. I have heard you can hunt them. I have never heard of anyone other than Nuliajuk that had any power over them. Mothers have power over their young because they [the young] cannot do things on their own. They follow their mother everywhere. My mother's grandfather was one of many people who saw Nuliajuk.... I cannot say who has power over animals. I have heard they were created by God. (quoted in Oosten and Laugrand 2002: 114)

Tivi Etok from Nunavik stated,

> There is a saying that goes like this: 'An animal roaming free on Earth does not have an owner. Therefore he who catches it becomes the owner.' That is an old saying. For instance, suppose I have a wife and I catch an animal. When I bring it to my wife's kitchen, then and only then does the animal belong to a person. Animals wandering the Earth do not belong to anybody. Only when someone catches the animal does that person get authority over it. It's up to him if he wants to host a feast. That was the law; the way it used to be. (quoted in Weetaluktuk and Bryant 2008: 163)

Whatever the interpretation, elders agree that animals have to be respected. If the rules of respect are not observed, either the *inua* of the animal, the sea, the sky or the moon will retaliate. The *inua* of a place might also retaliate in case of transgressions. George Kappianaq (IE 330) related, 'It is said that the river and the lake each have an *inua* (its person) who have control over the fish in that lake, and who tend to get upset very easily and will stop the fish from running. If people have verbally contended over the fish, because they are humans, the lake's *inua* can stop the fish for a period; then later on the fish can return.'

In the past, the unavailability of animals was associated with breaking rules. Qaggutaq (IE 169) from Iglulik recalled how in spring,

> A weir would be constructed at the mouth of the river so there would be plenty of fish. Because the tides are high the fish would get into the weirs so when the tide was receding the fish would be caught in these weirs. There were times when the fish did not get to the weirs. So that was interpreted that someone had breached a taboo.... If there was a shaman

in the camp, he would get to do consultation with the spirits by *qila* [head lifting] and the ritual of *saka* [invoking a helping spirit]. This was done, as there would be times when there would be absolutely no fish in the weirs. It was believed that after these consultations with the spirits had been performed, the fish would once again be able to enter the weirs.

Today the concepts of *inua* and owners of the game such as the sea woman and the caribou woman are no longer used. In the course of the twentieth century, the Inuit of northeast Canada adopted Christianity and integrated their traditional beliefs into the framework of the new religion. Animals to be hunted were no longer provided by non-human beings living out on the land and in the sea, but by God named *Nunaliurti or Anirnialuk* among the Catholics and *Guuti* among the Anglicans. The various prohibition rules (*pitailiniit, tirigusuusiit*) required by these non-human beings no longer had to be observed, because God had created the animals for the benefit of human beings. Rachel Uyarasuk, an elder from Iglulik, recalled that

> there was not going to be any more *pittailiniq* after we began to follow Christianity. Because animals were made by God to be food for humans, people were going to be able to eat whatever part of the animal they wanted to. When they started following religion, the *angakkuit* [shamans] let go of their powers, and people let go of their *pittailiniq*. (quoted in Oosten and Laugrand 1999b: 126)

Respect for animals, however, remained a central issue in Inuit hunting. Inuit are still convinced that if you do not respect animals or abuse them, animals are aware of this and will retaliate.

## Rules of Respect

If an animal was killed and treated with respect, the animal would feel welcome and would be prepared to let itself be killed again in a new incarnation. However, the killing of an animal also implied danger. The old Aivilingmiutaq Ivaluardjuk told Knud Rasmussen (1929: 56) in 1922:

> The greatest peril of life lies in the fact that human food consists entirely of souls. All the creatures that we have to kill and eat, all those that we have to strike down and destroy to make clothes for ourselves, have souls, like we have, souls that do not perish with the body, and which must therefore be propitiated lest they should revenge themselves on us for taking away their bodies.

In the past, the situation was even more precarious, as explained to Rasmussen by the *angakkuq* Anarqaq:

> 'In the old days, it was far worse than it is now', put in Anarqaq, 'Everything was more difficult, and our customs accordingly much more strict. In those days, men hunted only with bow and arrow and knew nothing of the white men's firearms. It was far more difficult to live then, and often men could not get food enough. The caribou were hunted in kayaks at the crossing of rivers and lakes, being driven out into the water where they could be easily overtaken in a kayak. But it was hard to make them run the way one wished, and therefore rules were very strict about those places. No woman was allowed to work there, no bone of any animal might be broken, no brain or marrow eaten. To do so would be an insult to the souls of the caribou and was punished by death or disaster. (Rasmussen 1929: 57–58)

According to Rasmussen (1931: 241),

> Animals turn into evil spirits in the same manner as humans when full respect is not shown them after their death. It is considered to be a matter of great importance that game animals, and especially caribou, should never have their flesh touched or their skin cured by unclean women. If this happens the soul of the animal will take revenge, not on the woman but on the man who first killed it and then allowed an unclean woman to come in contact with its body. In such cases the soul of the animal becomes a *tonraq kigloritoq*, literally a savage spirit, and the hunter who outlawed the soul is beyond redemption.

Inuit rules and customs were often referred to as taboos by anthropologists such as Boas and Rasmussen. They made long lists of taboos, treating them as if they were part of a generally acknowledged Inuit system of rules. But rules varied greatly in different areas. Inuit usually referred to these rules as *pitailiniq*, refraining from doing something, *tirigusuusiit*, specific injunctions imposed on a person, *tiringnaqtuq*, anything that is a cause of one needing to observe a *tirigusuusiq*, and *maligait*, accepted guidelines for doing things that need to be followed. Today the word *maligaq* is used as a translation for 'Canadian law' (see Kublu 2004). The Iglulingmiut had a reputation for being very strict in the application of rules, particularly with respect to the sea mammals. But there was great variation in the rules to be observed, not only in different areas, but also by families and even individuals.

Rules of respect governed a wide range of cultural behaviour. Some rules concerned the earth, others the relationships between human beings. Most rules had to do with animals and different parts of their bodies: the skins, bones, meat, sinews and so forth. They specified how different categories of people should or should not handle these parts in specific contexts. Respect towards wildlife took shape in a wide variety of principles, customs and rules. Not observing these rules would affect the availability of game, the health of people, the weather or other factors crucial to survival. Silas Kalluk from Qamanittuaq remembered, 'Some people were not allowed to eat hearts of animals or kidneys. They were rules that people followed and that is how it was. If they didn't follow rules, they would be neglected or a shaman may lose his helping spirit' (quoted in Mannik 1998: 188).

Women who were menstruating or had just delivered a child were particularly at risk for breaking rules. Rasmussen (1929: 98) reports, 'The worst offense against taboo which any woman can commit is concealment of menstruation or abortion. Women during the menstrual period are especially unclean in relation to all animals hunted, and may thus expose the entire community to the greatest danger and disaster if they endeavour to conceal their impurity.'

The statements by Ivaluardjuk and Anarqaq quoted above emphasize that the rules and customs were oriented towards the *tarniit* of the game, which should not be offended. The *tarniit* of the game should accept that it was killed and that its meat, skin and bones would be used by human beings. In observing these customs and rules, people showed their respect for the *tarniit,* which allowed the animals to die and human society to survive. We refer to these customs and rules as rules of respect to emphasize their relational nature. These customs and rules should not be viewed as systems of unwritten laws and rules that applied equally to all hunters, as each area, each family and even each individual had his or her own rules of respect to observe. They varied with gender and age, and special rules of respect might apply to different places.

Some rules of respect served a specific purpose, such as making a boy into a good hunter or a girl into a good seamstress. Most people observed these rules, as they valorized their results. As Aqatsiaq (IE 149) recalled,

> The little boys were discouraged to play the [string] game more than the little girls. It is said that when the boys were so used to playing the string game that it was dangerous for them when they waited for the seal in the breathing hole using a harpoon; the danger lay with the harpoon line. It is said that the ones that spent a good part of their time playing with the string game used to get tangled with it when they harpooned a seal. At one time a hunter lost his thumb when he harpooned a bearded seal. So for these reasons, the little boys were discouraged from playing too much string games.

Similarly, a number of basic principles in the rules of respect were found almost everywhere. Direct contact between sea animals and land animals should be avoided. Contact between menstruating women or women who have just delivered children and game should also be avoided. So should contact between relatives and campmates of a recently deceased person and the game.

However, it is hard to generalize, and the observance of these rules of respect was flexible and varied. In this book we will pay close attention to these rules of respect, and in discussing the various animals we will explore the rules of respect pertaining to them. They help us to clarify the relations between different animals as well as the relations between animals and human beings.

In the course of time, the observance of these rules of respect has changed. The *angakkuq* Arnaqaq pointed out to Rasmussen that before the introduction of guns rules were stricter. The adoption of Christianity also implied a break with the rules of the past. In the North Baffin area, the ritual of *siqqitiq* evolved to mark the transition from traditional beliefs to Christianity.[17] A meeting would be held, and the heart of an animal, usually a fresh seal, would be divided into pieces and eaten by all participants. As the eating of a heart was prohibited by traditional customs, especially for women, the ritual marked the transition to a new way of life, free of the restrictions of the old ways.[18] Rachel Uyarasuk from Iglulik participated in the ritual and recalled how it was intended to end the rules for the observance of rituals, for 'after they heard of religion, when they wanted to turn towards Christianity':

> When they decided they were going to *siqqitiq*, they went to the windbreak. It was nice outside. The sun was shining since it was spring. They brought a seal to the windbreak. They cut the seal open and took out the intestines, the liver, heart, the eyes, the tongue and they were all cut to small pieces. They did not have plates in those days, so they placed them on the seal. They were cut into tiny pieces and put together. In the end, the people were in a line, and each was given a piece of meat to put into the mouth. People were asked why they wanted to go through this ceremony. Every one of them replied, 'We are going through this because we want to take Christianity.' My mother told me, if I were asked, to say, 'I want to go to Jesus.' When the person giving the meat came to me, that person gave me an eye and a piece of intestine. It was cut small enough to chew. I was asked why I wanted to take religion. Here I was, just a child. I was old enough to speak. I replied as my mother instructed me: 'Because I want to go to Jesus when I die.' Every one of us was given a piece of meat. The meaning of this was that all these parts of a seal, the meat, the heart, the intestine were all parts of the *pittailiniq*, the taboos. And they were no longer going to be used or observed. There would be

no part of the seal that people would have to refrain from eating. This was not just the case for seal, but for all other animals as well. There were not going to be any more refrainings from eating any parts of any animal. This is why we were given bits and pieces of everything. (quoted in Oosten and Laugrand 1999b: 3)

The foods especially favoured in the *siqqitiq* were the heart and the other parts of the animal that had often been forbidden.

The transition to Christianity also meant that new rules were introduced. Nutaraaluk from Iqaluit related, 'The hunters in the North really refrained from hunting on Sundays, even if they were hungry. When they did hunt, the whole animal had to be consumed right away.... An animal that was caught on a Sunday had to be consumed the same day. If there were leftovers, the leftovers had to be thrown to the dogs. Even the skin had to be cut up and fed to the dogs. The whole thing had to be consumed in one day' (quoted in Oosten et al. 1999: 140). The distinction between Sunday and the other days was honoured.

After the adoption of Christianity, it was accepted that only human beings had souls, and the word *tarniq* was accepted as a translation of the Christian concept of soul. After the conversion, most rules of respect were no longer observed. But even today elders emphasize the necessity to respect animals. If animals are not respected, they will retaliate. Emile Imaruittuq, an elder from Iglulik, stated:

From the time we were small we were taught to have the highest respect for all wildlife, even for the smallest bird. We were told to treat all wild-life with respect, even baby birds and animals. If we didn't do this they could take revenge on us. If we abused a certain part of an animal, that same part within us would be affected.... This is another story about a man who shot a caribou in the leg. The wounded caribou was still alive when he cut off its nose because he wanted to eat it. As a result of this, later in his life his nose became decayed and it fell off. This is what happens if you mistreat wildlife. (quoted in Oosten et al. 1999: 37–38)[19]

Noah Piugaattuq (IE 009) shared another incident he could recall:

In Repulse Bay, a young girl who was old enough to get married mis-treated a bird, an eider duck, by making it unable to fly and plucking some of its feathers and setting it free to the water. She made fun of it, since the bird easily headed for land because it couldn't fly and some feathers were missing. The bird was suffering and in a few short days after, her own brother's face started to peel off and he deteriorated and died. The bird had taken revenge by letting the girl see what can happen. Anything that can think is the one who can take revenge on someone.

Furthermore, if you respect animals, you can hunt them. Imaruittuq explained,

> If you legitimately hunt wildlife and don't cause them to suffer, if you respect them, then it is fine. There will be suffering on occasion but you have to try and minimize this out of respect for the animal. We should not even make nasty comments about wildlife. We shouldn't quarrel about them amongst ourselves. Wildlife has been placed on this Earth for us to use, but we must treat them with respect. (quoted in Oosten et al. 1999: 38)[20]

Piugaattuq (IE 009) related,

> It is said that when a conflict keeps occurring over a certain animal then that animal will soon start to disappear. ... This has always happened, when we were trapping we were told not to have conflicts so that we will have a better chance of finding them. Another thing, when someone was stealing something and the other person starts to find out but they never come out to talk about it, then the animals will stop coming to the area where there are traps since a disagreement is occurring regarding the animal.

Imaruittuq pointed out that *qallunaat* are not always aware that Inuit consider animals to be agents that will take action whenever people break the rules, the *piqujait*, relating to them:

> When we started dealing with land claims we had to talk a lot about wildlife. This created a lot of fear amongst the elders. They used to tell us not to quarrel about wildlife because this was a very dangerous thing to do. We explained to them that we had to quarrel about the wildlife because we were negotiating with the *qallunaat* and this was a *qallunaat* process. We explained that we were legitimately negotiating over the wildlife. This is a *piqujaq* that we must adhere to. We should not quarrel about wildlife or it will take revenge on us. (quoted in Oosten et al. 1999: 38)

Any misbehaviour or wrongdoing would have an impact on hunting. The moral behaviour of people directly affected their success in hunting. A death in the camp or of a relative might also affect hunting. Piugaattuq (IE 70) related,

> Sometimes we used to have a very difficult time catching a game before we heard of such death. This was apparently the result of a death from our own kinship, who had gone through adversity. ... My younger brother and myself used to live in one camp and one of our sisters was living in one of the distant camps as she was married off. When she was one of the victims of adverse death, I went through this phenomenon.

Respecting animals was always a matter of life and death. Although in the past the sea woman, the moon man and the spirit of the wind might punish people, usually the animals themselves were thought to retaliate when the rules were broken. This belief that animals will turn against you when you abuse, ridicule or otherwise mistreat them is still generally shared in Inuit society.

## Animals and Shamanism

In shamanism animals were often used as *tuurngait*, helping spirits. Aupilaarjuk from Rankin Inlet related, 'A *tuurngaq* could come from anywhere. It could even be a rock. It could be any object. It could be a living thing, it could be anything. It could be land, something alive, something that had died. It could be a dog' (quoted in Saladin d'Anglure 2001). Nutaraaluk from Iqaluit explained, 'The *angakkuit* used everything for their *tuurngait*, from insects to animals to *qallunaat*, even before anyone had ever seen a *qallunaaq* up here. They used everything including things you would find down at the tidal flats such as shrimps, krill and seaweed' (quoted in Oosten and Laugrand 1999b: 122). Tungilik described their appearance:

> Some of them would have twigs for hair. Some of them would have pelvic bones for a face, and they would seem to be dripping. Some of them would have pelvic bones for a face, others would have fire. It varied. Some of them would be animals such as polar bears or *nanurluit*, very big bears. There were different kinds of worms, and all kinds of animals from the land, from the sea, and birds that fly. They varied. (quoted in Oosten and Laugrand 1999b: 96)

*Tuurngait* could be ferocious. Boas (1901: 160) related, 'At night a piece of meat is placed in a dish near the child. If the child's guardian spirit should visit it at night, he would look for food, and, if he should not find any, would eat first the mother's vital organs, then the father's, and finally those of the other natives.'

According to Job Murjungniq (quoted in Oosten and Laugrand 2010: 172), '*Tuurngait* hunt non-human-beings, such as caribou and only eat adult female caribou. They hunt for those that are alone. We talked about caribou that were not really caribou but wolves and things like that. That is their food. Paungaalaaq [a deceased Aharmiut *angakkuq*] said that his *tuurngaq* would eat those animals that don't really exist, but he could see them. They also ate mushrooms.' According to the list of *tuurngait* collected by the missionary Reverend Peck in South Baffin in the beginning of the twentieth century, many *tuurngait* were thought to provide food.[21] This tradition is less widespread in the North Baffin and Kivalliq areas. But Rasmussen (1931: 307) related,

> People got to know Arnapak here at Netsilik, for once she had driven to Arviligjuaq (Pelly Bay) with her real husband, whose name was Qarsaitsiaq. On that journey, people say, a helping spirit cooked meat for them and, when the meat was ready, it was also a helping spirit that moved the cooking pots back from the lamp so the soup did not boil over. It was also the helping spirit who caught seals for them.[22]

The helping spirits might be ordinary animals such as bears, which were considered very powerful helping spirits, but they might also be giant bears known as *nanurluit*. Another powerful spirit was the sea ermine. Rasmussen (1929: 121–22) reports,

> Most dreaded of all helping spirits was imaap tEria, the sea ermine. This creature is fashioned like the land ermine, but is more slender, lithe and swift, and able to dash up out of the sea so suddenly that defence is out of the question. It has dark, smooth skin, and no hair save a little at the tip of the tail and on the lobes of the ears. When a man was out at sea in his kayak, it would shoot up swiftly as lightning from the depths and slip into his sleeve, and then, running over his naked body, fill him with such a shuddering horror that he almost lost consciousness.

Thus, the shamanic universe provided space for all kinds of creatures.

In the past, the shaman (*angakkuq*) was thought to be able to change into an animal. Shamans might show animal features in trance. Thus, the famous *angakkuq* Qimuksiraaq was known in Chesterfield Inlet for showing his polar bear fangs. The *angakkuq* also acted as a healer. Rasmussen (1929: 197) reported, 'A shaman is not allowed to hunt any kind of game during the time he is occupied in endeavouring to cure a sick person. Should he kill any animal in this way, he might easily happen to kill the soul of the persons for whom he is working at the same time.' Illness is often perceived as loss of the *tarniq*, and the *tarniq* of a human being might take refuge in an animal.

The crossing of boundaries was a central feature of shamanism. The *angakkuq* could travel up in the sky to the land of the moon man or to the bottom of the sea to the land of the sea woman when the rules of respect were transgressed and the animals no longer offered themselves to be killed. The *angakkuq* could travel to places where animals lived in human appearance, and he could see the *tarniq* and perceive the true nature of an *inua*. When he returned from his travels he would give an account of his experiences and relate how animals lived in their own communities just like human beings. Shamanism appears to have been a domain where the boundaries between animals and human beings could be crossed, and this is a recurrent topic in Inuit art.

## Conclusion

The sky, the sea and the land are populated by spirits and animals that have to be respected in various ways. All animals are sentient beings. Like human beings they have a *tarniq,* and they may appear as human beings. *Angakkuit* will discern that this human being is the *inua* of animal, not an *inuk,* a human person. A *tuurngaq,* helping spirit, may also appear as an animal, and sometimes non-human beings such as *ijirait* may appear as human beings. Hunters should be aware of the nature of the animals they encounter. Are they *silaat,* ordinary animals, *tuurngait* or other beings? They should assess the nature of a being before killing it and eating it. But whatever the nature of a particular animal, all animals have power and can retaliate if they are not respected, or if they are abused or ridiculed. Therefore the rules pertaining to each animal have to be respected. It is up to the hunter and his wife to take care of this. Whenever people make mistakes, the *angakkuit* have to intervene to propitiate the animals or their owners.

## Notes

1. Various versions of the myth of Aakulujjuusi and Uumarnituq exist (see, e.g., Rasmussen 1929: 252).
2. Bearded seals.
3. Kublu presents an excellent version of the narrative as related by her father, Michel Kupaaq from Iglulik (see Oosten and Laugrand 1999a: 153–66).
4. The story of the sea woman exists in many versions. A survey of variants and a discussion and analysis of the origins and meanings of the story can be found in Sonne (1990).
5. The myth is often told as part of the myth of the sun and the moon. See Rasmussen (1929: 77–81; 1931: 232–36) for detailed versions of the narrative.
6. For discussions of Sila, see Saladin d'Anglure (1980a, 1990a, 2006).
7. Randa (2002b) shows that when Inuit discuss animals, morphological resemblance is usually at the origin of relationships shaped by lexical derivation. Numerous zoonyms are derived from the names of anatomical parts showing the importance of the body as an essential reference for human and animal terms. For example, *tuktuvak,* 'the big caribou', also

designates the moose, and by lexical derivation the mosquito is called *tuk-tuujaq*, 'what resembles a mosquito', because of its long legs. *Umingmak* refers to both the musk ox and the bison (Paillet 1973: 60). According to Randa (2002b: 100–2), most animal names are constructed with infixes such as *-lik*, 'there is', *-jjuaq*, 'bigger', *-arjuk*, 'smaller', *-tuuq*, 'to possess in good quantity', or *-ilaq*, 'he has not'. They also use *-ujaq/-ruaq/-luaq/-suaq*, 'what resembles'.

8. Statement collected by Brody (1976), quoted in Freeman (2005: 65).

9. Annie Grey, 1987. Kativik Teacher Training and McGill Course; Quotes from Course Binder on Inuit Values; Interviews done by teachers on training; Course Instructor, Betsy Annahatak; Consultant from McGill, George Wenzel. Betsy Annahatak, personal communication, 5 July 2013.

10. Tomassie Kudluk, 1987. Kativik Teacher Training and McGill Course; Quotes from Course Binder on Inuit Values; Interviews done by teachers on training; Course Instructor, Betsy Annahatak; Consultant from McGill, George Wenzel. Document in the possession of Betsy Annahatak.

11. On the value of hunting, sharing and eating country food, see Dorais (1997: 89), who shows that in Quaqtaq and in most Nunavik communities, *maqainiq* (eating and sharing country food) is still perceived as the most complete manifestation of Inuit identity. Through *maqainiq* one can show one remains an *inutuinnaq*, a 'genuine Inuk'. See also Condon et al. (1995), who use the ambiguous notion of 'subsistence economy' in their study in Holman. Inuit do not perceive hunting in this perspective, and they often resent the notion of 'harvesting', which has a Western connotation of managing animals. See also Brody (1987).

12. Anglican missionary Julian Bilby (1923: 205) observed with respect to Cumberland Sound, 'The *Tarnuk*, or soul of a man, has the shape of a man, but is about one inch in height, and is to be discovered in the hand of a conjuror or in that of a new-born babe. The soul of a bear is like a bear; that of a walrus like a walrus; but the soul of a deer resembles a spider, and that of a salmon, a man!'

13. Bennett and Rowley (2004: 44).

14. See Blaisel and Arnakak (1993) for a detailed analysis of this myth. The Iglulik Oral Traditions Project database contains many variants of the myth (Piugaattuq, IE 172; Paniaq, IE 424; Quassa, IE 156; Imaruittuq, IE 161; Nasook, IE 159; Kunnuk, IE 160; Kappianaq, IE 168, IE 155; Kupaaq, IE 166, IE 172).

15. See Brightman (1993: 37) for that of the Rock Cree. According to R. Nelson (1983: 20), working with the Koyukon, 'this derives not so much from the animal nature of humans as from the human nature of animals', and Nelson gives the example of the wolverine and the bear, which in the past received funeral rituals similar to those of humans. Marie Mauzé (1998; quoted in Descola 2007: 8) indicates that many Northwest Coast Native Americans also believe that animals shared a similar substance with human beings, but that this substance was transformed when it came into contact with a different skin.

16. The word 'Inuit' means owners or inhabitants. Inuit derive their name and identity from the places they inhabit: Iglulingmiut are 'the people of the

place that has igloos', Nattilingmiut 'the people of the place that has seals'.
The relationship between people and land is strong. Creation myths relate
that people originate from the land itself. They are owners of the land as
well as owned by the land.

17. On the *siqqitiq* ritual, see also Laugrand (1997).

18. See Laugrand (1999a, 1999b; 2002) and Laugrand and Oosten (2010). See
    also various descriptions of this practice in the Iglulik Oral Traditions Pro-
    ject database.

19. The topic is often discussed in the Iglulik Oral Traditions Project database.
    See, for instance, Panikpakuttuk's story (IE 207). He relates how a man
    skinned a live snow bunting, leaving the skin on the head, the wings and
    the tail; he removed the skin from the rest of the body while the bird was
    still alive and then let it loose. As a result, his son got a small impetigo
    on his nose that eventually covered his whole face. He also related how
    a man cut off the snout of a caribou calf without bothering to kill it and
    started to eat it. As a result, later on 'his nose got impetigo which soon ate
    away all the skin right to the bone. He reached a stage where he would
    have so much difficulty breathing, he could not get any sleep on account
    of it. Whenever he started to fall asleep, he would stop breathing. So he
    would have to get up immediately, therefore he could not get any sleep.
    This was the way he ended in his advanced age.' Ijjangiaq (IE 94) related,
    'I once heard from Angutitaq that at one time he plucked the feathers of a
    snow bunting and an eider duck. He was just plainly making mockery of
    these birds. He removed all of the feathers except for the wings and soon
    he let loose the eider duck. He had a son of his own whom he loved dearly.
    I knew that he loved him so much, as his wife had never borne him a son
    before the birth of this son. Later on I heard that this son's skin started to
    peel off and just got damaged. It was easy to tell what had caused that. He
    was *akkiviujuq*. He lived for a long time and was so pitiful to look at with
    his skin all damaged. The cause was that the father was *akkiviujuq* by the
    snow bunting.'

20. See also Kappianaq (IE 330): 'It was strongly discouraged for animals to
    become the subject of conflict to other people. I believe most of us have
    heard about this. It is more so to fish, it is discouraged that they should
    not become the subject of conflict when they were fished in the weirs when
    there are a number of people involved. This would be the case when a cer-
    tain individual wants more than others. When the people start claiming
    a catch, for instance, if you start determining that certain fish belong to a
    certain individual, this usually caused conflict among the fishermen. It is
    said that once this is practised then the fish will not return the following
    year. I have heard this from all over the place.'

21. The list is published in Laugrand et al. (2006: 421–68).

22. The study of the sexual relationships between shamans and helping spir-
    its, first described by Sternberg for Siberia, was extensively developed by
    Hamayon (1990) in *La chasse à l'âme*. In Siberia, according to Willerslev
    (2007: 131, 198), sexuality was an important aspect of the relation be-
    tween the shaman and the helping spirit: 'The Yukaghir shaman does not
    differ from the common hunter in his quest to establish and maintain in-

timate sexual relations with spiritual beings.' He adds that 'many hunters claim to have one or more helping spirits with whom they copulate during their nightly dreams and who provide them with hunting luck in return'. In Inuit society we do not find this pattern. Rasmussen (1931: 198) refers to a rape of a shaman by his helping spirit: 'It also happens that tonrät seek sexual satisfaction with solitary men or women who while wandering have fallen asleep in the open. One never experiences this literally, but dreams of it. Afterwards one usually comes out in a rash and has stinking boils over the whole body.' Intercourse with a *tuurngaq* is by no means a beneficial act.

# CHAPTER 3

# The Making of a Good Hunter

Hunters should understand the movements and behaviour of animals. They need a thorough knowledge of anatomy and have to be skilled observers of animals' physiology. They should be able to assess the condition of an animal, if it is healthy or not, and they should know how to butcher animals' bodies, separating the various parts, muscles, bones, fat, skin and organs.[1] This requires instruction and training by elder hunters and, most of all, practical experience out on the land.

## The Hunting Cycle

The annual hunting cycle varied for each area. Inland people mainly concentrated on caribou hunting and supplemented their diet with other prey such as fish. Especially when the big caribou herds were moving north in the spring and south again in the fall, caribou hunting was very intensive. In the autumn the quality of the meat and the skins was at its best, and a successful hunt would ensure stocks that would allow the people to survive the winter.

Along the coast caribou hunting and sea mammal hunting were the most important sources of food. Inuit hunted caribou in the spring and the fall as well, and in summer they also hunted for sea mammals such as seals, belugas, walrus and bowhead whales in open water (see figure 3.1). After the sea ice had formed in winter they concentrated on seal hunting at the breathing holes. Annual cycles continually changed as people adapted to variations in the movements of the game and changes in the climate and the seasons. The dependency on game and its connection to the annual cycle is well illustrated by a calendar provided by Paniaq from Iglulik (quoted in Oosten and Laugrand 1999a: 126):

July: *iksuut* [Mittimatalik]. Because the rivers are melting, and people hear rivers melting. [Iglulik] *saggaruut.*

August: *saggaruut* [Mittimatalik]. When the land is not so moist any more, summer has come, and the thick hair of the caribou has been shed and is thin. [Iglulik] *akulliruut.*

September: *akulliruut* [Mittimatalik]. When the caribou hair is not too thin and not too thick, when it is in between. [Iglulik] *amiraijaut.*

October: *amialliruut* [Mittimatalik]. The caribou antlers are losing their covers. [Iglulik] *ukialliruut.*

November: *tusaqtuut* [Mittimatalik/Iglulik]. After the ice forms Inuit can travel to see other people and get news. Usually it was important to hear if they still had dogs or not because they were our means of survival.

December: *tauvigjuaq; taujualuk* [Mittimatalik/Iglulik]. Very dark; when it is very dark.

January: *qaummagiaq* [Mittimatalik]. When the sun is starting to return. [Iglulik] *siqinnaarut.*

February: *qangattaaksaq; qangattaarjuk* [Mittimatalik/Iglulik]. It refers to the sun going higher and higher in the air.

March: *ikiaqpavvik* [Mittimatalik]. The sun is higher in the sky but still not too high. [Iglulik] *avunniit.* Premature baby seals are born. Some make it, some freeze to death.

April: *natsijjat* [Mittimatalik]. When the seal pups are born. (Early April in Iglulik.)

Mid-May: *tirigluit* [Mittimatalik]. When the bearded seal pups are born. (Late April, early May in Iglulik.)

Late May: *tupiqtuut* [Mittimatalik]. Snow conditions make it difficult to stay in igloos, so people move into tents. (Mid-May for Iglulik.)

June: *manniit.* Birds are laying eggs. Or *nurrait.* Caribou are calving.[2]

Different calendars could be constructed for each area and for different periods.[3]

The distinction between summer and winter, *aujaq* and *ukiuq,* played an important role in ritual contexts such as the Sedna feast, when people defined themselves as ptarmigans, the people born in winter, and ducks, the people born in summer, deciding which season would yield a more successful hunt by a tug-of-war. The cycles of sun and moon also played an important role in divination. Piugaattuq (IE 246) observed,

> The moon always has been a determining factor. In the olden days it used to be said that the moon and the sun used to compete with each other when the sun was about to return after the dark period. When the sun did not come out even after the competing moon had been out and getting

**Figure 3.1.** Hunting scenes: shooting the caribou, bringing home the prey and returning with a seal. *Source:* Anglican Church of Canada/General Synod Archives/ Peck Papers, M56-1, series XXXIII, 4–6, 8–13.

large, this meant that the spring and the summer would not be as warm. It was termed as a weak summer (*aujjarluk*) because the sun was defeated in the competition with the moon. If the sun came out before the moon, that meant that we would see a warm spring right through to summer.

Knowledge of the seasons and the weather, however, was by no means sufficient to make one a good hunter. Young men were made good hunters by others. Often elders would help the younger men to become good hunters. Jimmy Taipanaaq from Qamanittuaq remembers how his grandfather made his baby a good hunter:

My grandfather was told that his bone was born (when a child is named after someone people say it's that person's 'bone').[4] We heard him coming towards our shelter, and he was carrying a rifle as he entered our shelter. I thought maybe he was going to shoot my son, but he took my newborn son and showed him the rifle and said to him, 'When Inuit are men, they usually hunt.' He pointed the rifle toward my son and said, 'Never be lazy with animals, do that.' I thought my grandfather was going to shoot my son, but I realized he was making him a good hunter. (quoted in Mannik 1998: 41–42)

## Amulets

The use of *arnguat*, amulets, played an important part in the making of a hunter. Amulets might be worn by the mother on behalf of her son or by the young hunter himself. The mother might already begin to wear the amulets before the child was born and the young boy would usually wear the amulets as a child, although adults might also use them, as recorded by Philipp Qipanniq (IE 198) from Iglulik:

There was another, an old man by the name of Kukik. He no longer hunted or anything like that due to his advanced age. He had made a harpoon head throughout the summer for me. He said that in his younger hunting years he was able to bring back game animals even when he went out alone on hunting trips. Once he had completed the harpoon head, he gave it to me for my use. And again, as this was in the spring when he gave me the harpoon head, we were hunting for young seals at the seal breathing holes. Again, I was the only one that kept harpooning seals at the breathing holes. I truly believe that the words of the elderly are powerful and can help if they so wish it to happen to someone in particular.

George Kappianaq (IE 188) recalled how his mother told him about the use of amulets to make someone into a good hunter with the necessary abilities:

In the case of the grandmother, they will ask their daughter-in-law to tie a muscle sinew of a wolf around the ankle of the newborn. This would make the boy a fast runner when he reached maturity. … These amulets will remain attached as long as they do not wear out. Once the sinew thread that is used to tie the amulet to the wrist is worn out and falls off, there is no longer a need for them to wear the amulet. Should it be the wish of the parents to replace the old thread they may do so, but under no circumstances should the amulet be removed. It will have to fall off on its own from wear. As for these types of amulets, that is, if the parents wish to have their newborn to be a fast runner or a fast igloo builder, there is no reason why that still can[not] be practised. We will not move away from the land, our feet are implanted to the land as it did in the past, so there is no reason why that still can[not] be practised.

Thus, the efficacy of the amulets depended on the mother, the animal and the way in which the amulet was attached and preserved.[5]

## Preparing the Hunter

Certain practices might also help to turn the young boy into a good hunter.

> For instance, should the boy go outdoors first thing in the morning, he will be asked to bring back a small piece of snow so that he could become a good hunter. Another is, if the parents wish the newborn boy to be strong when he grows up, the mother must swallow a piece of a caribou muscle. This is usually at the urging of the grandmother. She will ask her daughter-in-law to swallow a piece of caribou muscle that is a muscle from a bull caribou. There were also those that were made to swallow a muscle of a polar bear uncooked. I would have to guess that in swallowing a muscle of a polar bear they would have to remove some of the tissue in order for the mother to swallow the muscle, making sure some of the sinew of a muscle does not catch in between her teeth. It is said that those that were made in this manner usually grew up to be heavily built with a lot of meat. However, it is said that they would not get as strong as the one that were made to become strong by the mother swallowing a muscle of a caribou. (Kappianaq, IE 188)

Kappianaq (IE 265) also reported the practice of various games, notably pretending to be an animal. Someone would act like a polar bear and others would try to harpoon him:

> The people that are hunting this polar bear try to stay clear of the short whip. When you are whipped, it hurts especially if that person is much older than you are. Even when one is wearing caribou skin pants, you still get to feel the sting because the short whip being used is real and used for dogs. Even when one is trying to get away from the bear as fast as you can, the bear is going to rush you where you get a good whipping. One has to try and get away as fast as you can, but it is a lot of fun.

Another game was called *aivingnguujaq* and consisted of pretending to be a walrus. Kappianaq (IE 265) recalled how he played it as a boy:

> We used to play that a lot especially in an abandoned igloo ... they would hit me with a coiled rope where they would hold on to the other end. Once I was hit with the coiled end, they would have harpooned me. I had no other choice but to grab the coiled end because I had been harpooned. I had to rush to secure my footing before the line became taut when the others started to pull on the thong. There were all these games that were good for exercising to be a hunter.

Pretending to act like a seal was another game Kappianaq played with his brothers. It required the use of a miniature harpoon:

We used to play *nattiujaq* by making a play seal from a skin of a bearded seal and made it so that there are holes that we would try and loop with a *sakkuujaq* [toy harpoon]. We would use a seal pelvic bone for an *aglu* [breathing hole of a seal]. The head of a thighbone would be used as a pretend windbreak. Here we would pretend to have a hunter in position using the hollow part as your feet mat [*tutiriaq*]. I would pretend to make the water move as I headed for the opening. I would pretend that I would breathe air once, and dive right back in so that I would not get harpooned.

My older brother would loop the line to the holes so that he would pretend to harpoon me. I would immediately pull as hard as I can on this line, even trying to jam his hands into the hole in the pelvic bone. My older brother would instead get my hands jammed; then I would get upset and mad at him because he is trying too hard, that is, because I want to be stronger than he is. We used to make our younger brother cry when I would pull on the string before he did. It was more fun with him because he cried easily. (Kappianaq, IE 265)[6]

Children would first receive toys and later real hunting tools such as bows and arrows that would enable them to shoot their first ptarmigans and other small prey (see figure 3.2). After that they would be

**Figure 3.2.** Fishing with a fishing spear. *Source:* Anglican Church of Canada/General Synod Archives/Peck Papers, M56-1, series XXXIII, 4–6, 8–13.

taught to go after caribou and seals and their first catches would be celebrated.

## First Catches

Nutaraq from Mittimatalik recalled the joy of the first catch:

> Something that especially brought me joy was a first kill, any time I had a first kill. Of all of those, it was my first narwhal that brought me the most joy, although I did not kill it on my own. I only wounded it and my father killed it for me. It had quite a large tusk and it was still floating when he got it. He told me that it was my whale even though I hadn't killed it myself. I have always felt quite proud of that. I think it was the thing that gave me the most joy. Just like you, I have had a lot of things which brought me joy throughout my life. (quoted in Oosten and Laugrand 2001: 164)

In many accounts of first catches, the young hunter does not actually kill the prey, but only contributes to the hunt. The first catch should be consumed completely, and the young hunter should abstain from it. Imaruittuq from Iglulik related,

> When a person catches an animal for the first time it must be distributed and consumed completely. If any of the meat is saved it will stall the catching of more animals in the future. For this reason a first kill should be eaten as soon as possible. If you are named after a person and that person's wife is still alive you are obligated to give some of that meat to your wife through your name. This is a strong *maligaq* that should be followed.[7]
>
> If the parents of the person you were named after were still alive, you were obligated to give them meat also. If you didn't give meat to the people who should be receiving it, they would feel hurt. This is why you have to distribute a first kill in the community. (quoted in Oosten et al. 1999: 40)[8]

A first catch ritual often had marked sexual connotations. Mark Ijjangiaq (IE 191) from Iglulik recalled first catch celebrations:

> There was no particular ceremony or anything like that to mark my first catch. But I have heard that when a youth catches a game animal for the first time, they had to touch the sexual organ of an elderly woman. Kupaaq had to go through this ritual with the namesake of your *akkak*, Alaralak. He just put his hand in her abdomen section. But I personally did not go through that ritual *saqusiniq*, so therefore I am not as able at securing game animals. Yes, for those that had caught a game animal

for the first time there were no big celebrations or games, but they were asked to go through the ritual of *saqusiniq*, which might only be to touch the skin on the abdomen section, but it would have been considered to be *saqusiniq*.

The *sanaji* or *arnaliaq*, the midwife who had delivered the boy, was often considered the maker of the boy, and received a part of the first catch. As Uqsuralik from South Baffin related,

> A boy's first catch is always given to the *sanaji*, the midwife. That's how it is back home. If you were a boy that I delivered, you would call me your *arnaquti*. First catches should be given to the midwife. *Pijaqsaijuq* is the word for giving boys the skills to be a good hunter. There used to be ties to hold up women's pants called *unngiqtaq*. We would have the boy undo the tie of the pants so the boy would become a really good hunter. This was done after his first catch. Even though the boy would be shy to untie the pants, he would go ahead and do it because he wanted to be a skilful hunter when he grew up. This is true. That's how we made boys into very skilful hunters.[9] (quoted in Briggs 2000: 37)

Once the first catch had been made, the boy had opened a connection with the game.

## Gender in Hunting

In Inuit society men are raised as hunters. It is their task to kill game and thus provide meat and skins to their wives, who will prepare and distribute the meat as food and prepare the skins so they can sew them into clothing. Mythology suggests that men were primarily associated with the production of food, and women with the reproduction of children.

Men might have a dream of a beautiful woman before a successful catch. Jose Angutinngurniq from Kugaaruk related, 'A *niriujaarniq* is a good thing, especially the one I have about the woman, as I told you before. I know I will catch a caribou or another animal if I have that *niriujaarniq*. If I dream I am next to a woman, when I wake up the next morning I know I will have a good hunt' (Kugaaruk 2004).

The technique of hunting can also be modelled on the act of copulation, as in the case of Tungilik, who was advised to breathe like he were copulating when he was about to make a kill at a breathing hole of a seal. Thus, there is a suggestion that hunters relate to prey as men do to women, symbolically connecting the acts of killing game and having sexual intercourse with women.[10]

The gendering of the relation between hunter and prey should remain confined to the context of the hunt. Bestiality, an issue often discussed in the Iglulik Oral Traditions Project database, is absolutely prohibited.[11] Moreover, the game itself is obviously gendered, and gender often plays an important role in the selection of the game, as depending on the season a male or a female animal may be preferred as prey. Gender also determines people's relations to the animals. Men connect to animals by hunting and killing the prey; women should avoid direct contact with animals when they are menstruating or have delivered a child. Whereas immediately after a successful hunt men still often eat a part of a vital organ such as the liver or the kidneys (traditionally associated with the *tarniq*) raw, women must avoid the eating of raw meat when they are menstruating or have delivered a child.

Kappianaq (IE 174) from Iglulik recalled,

> At the time before the introduction of Christianity, women who were having their menstruation would never eat raw meat during their period. The only thing that they were allowed to eat was meat that had been placed in hot water. There is no need to fully cook the meat, but as long as the top layer was cooked, it needed not to be cooked all the way for them to eat for them to be *kilinngajunnirtuq*. So all through her menstruation she will not eat uncooked meat. There was no age restriction for this taboo. It is also applicable to young people. They will not eat uncooked meat during their menstruation. But now after the introduction of Christianity all the *kilinngajaujut* [taboos] are no longer applicable … This is also applicable when a woman miscarries, which is known as *allittuq*.

Thus, the adoption of Christianity freed women of a very strict regimen with respect to their food.

## Powerful Words

A hunter can only catch game if the game itself consents to the kill. Even the best hunters will be unsuccessful if animals decide to avoid them. If human beings showed respect to an animal, behaved themselves in accordance with the rules of the ancestors, maintained the important separations between land game and sea game, between everything connected with hunting and all things concerned with human birth, menstruation and death, the game might allow itself to be killed. A hunter should show an attitude of humility, imploring the game to come to him and to show itself to him. The hunter should also show great joy at the catch and respect the body of the animal once it was killed. Not killing the animal would imply slighting it. If the game did not feel welcome, it would not show itself again.

When hunting was difficult, hunters might take recourse to *irina-liutiit,* powerful words. Rasmussen (1929: 168) provides an example of such words:

> Words to call up game:
> Beast of the Sea,
> Come and offer yourself in the dear early morning!
> Beast of the plain!
> Come and offer yourself in the dear (early) morning.

As Piugaattuq (IE 248) related,

> There were all kinds of *irinaliut* that one could offer. This was also done when the hunters were desperate to catch a game animal. When they were hunting they would watch a game animal that was not aware of the presence of the hunters. It was absolutely essential that the hunter catch this game animal. Once in a long while someone would offer a *irinaliut* so that the animal would not become aware of their presence, thereby making it easy for the hunter to catch it. This type of *irinaliut* was known as *tirlisi.*

Shamanism went underground in the eastern Arctic when Inuit adopted Christianity and began to follow new rules. So did the use of *irinaliutiit.* Prayers and hymns replaced the shamanic formulas and powerful words of old. But the power of speech still remains very strong, and elders often compare words to bullets, warning the youths that they can kill a person (Therrien and Laugrand 2001).[12]

Christian hymns and prayers could be used much as *irinaliutiit* were used in the past. Tungilik from Naujaat recalled,

> I remember once we were totally out of food. We had a bit of flour, but there was no more meat at all. We were told that our father wanted to pray. While he was in Iglulik, he had started to follow the Anglican religion. He wanted to pray to be given some food from God. The next day after we prayed, we went down to the floe-edge. I was a child back then, and my brother was still alive. There were a lot of seals. He killed a lot of seals. He even got a bearded seal. He came up by dog team to show us. It was only afterwards that I realized that his prayer had been answered by God. (quoted in Oosten and Laugrand 1999b: 61)

Tungilik (quoted in Oosten and Laugrand 1999b: 61–62) recalled that his father prayed while singing a specific hymn. The text of the hymn was:

We sit on the highest throne,
With our father,
The one who loves us, the one who gives us food,
The one who is good to us.
Praise our God.
Praise our God.
Food, clothing,
They come from him
They come from him.

Tungilik related that his father was an *angakkuq* as well as a Christian:
'My father would be given animals through the help of God. He did
not think about the ministers or priests. My father would only make a
request to God when we were out of food' (quoted in Oosten and Laugrand 1999b: 75).

Saullu Nakasuk from Pangniqtuuq remembered that every time
someone caught a bowhead they used to sing the following song:

When we catch something
Holy, Holy, Holy
We will see Jesus
We say Holy
Holy, Holy, Holy. (quoted in Oosten and Laugrand 1999a: 137)[13]

Thus, prayers and hymns replaced the *irinaliutiit* connecting the hunter
and the game to God, who now came to be considered the source and
owner of all wildlife.

## Treating the Animals Respectfully

Respect for animals was organized by many rules that varied for each
animal. Some basic principles applied to all animals. An animal should
not be abused, or ridiculed. Unnecessary suffering should be avoided.
Kappianaq (IE 330) emphasized the need to make a quick kill so an
animal would not suffer:

> If we wound the animal and try to keep it alive on purpose, this is also
> something that was strictly discouraged. If at all possible, when condi-
> tions allow it, you should make your kill immediately. Once you wound
> the animal, then you must do whatever is necessary to kill the animal.
> One should never abandon a wounded marine animal. This is also appli-
> cable to land animals.

Mark Ijjangiaq (IE 94) emphasized that an animal should not be
mocked or abused in any way:

No one should ever make fun of animals in general. For instance you may have wounded an animal and deliberately kept it alive in order to mock it because you feel so much superior. This must not be allowed to happen. Or you now have a vehicle that is so fast that you can pursue an animal and try to tire the animal to exhaustion. This must not be allowed to happen. One must not do it to any land-based game animal nor should one make a mockery of marine animals. If a hunter has no desire to catch a game animal, then he should leave it alone. He should not pursue it. If a person feels that he is so much superior and can catch up to any animal with his fast machine and bump into the animal and just plain terrorize the animal in any way, even when the animal is fleeing, he should think before he acts. He must not do it. It must not be allowed to happen. Otherwise there is the possibility that he might have to suffer some physical ailments on account of it that could have been avoided had he thought before he acted.

In addition, hunters should never brag about their abilities. Aqatsiaq (IE 149) related a story about a hunter who boasted that he was not afraid of walrus. He added that walrus look like lemmings when walking on the ice. That summer he was stabbed by a walrus's tusks and pulled into the water.

Today, many elders think that animals are no longer respected sufficiently. They complain about the caribou carcasses left on the land and the bones found around the houses in their communities. Mariano Aupilaarjuk from Kangiq&iniq stated,

> There are times you would come across bones. For instance, bones from a caribou that had been killed by wolves. We were told if we came across bones on the ground we were to turn them around and then leave them. I still follow this practice today. I'll explain the reason for turning the bones. If I am in bed sleeping, I would become very tired if I just slept on one side. I would feel better if I were to move. In the same way, bones become tired from just lying in one way. It is in order for them to feel better that we have to turn them the other way. That is the *maligaq* concerning bones. I still follow this because I want to take away their tiredness. (quoted in Oosten et al. 1999: 34)

Aupilaarjuk prefers the old rules to the new laws.

> We just shouldn't be killing our wildlife without reason. We should only be killing them for food. There is no need to have new laws about wildlife for Inuit had their *maligait* about wildlife even though they were not written. The present laws about wildlife are not our *maligait*. The *maligait* that we follow are not seen because the Inuit *piusiq* [custom] is not visible. What I told you about the bones is a *maligaq* although it doesn't require a licence. It is a *maligaq* where respect is shown through wanting the bones of the caribou to feel rested. That way we show our gratitude

to the animal. This is an Inuit *piusiq* that is not being practiced anymore. In the past, all bones were carefully gathered together for this was one of the greater *tirigusuusiit*. (quoted in Oosten et al. 1999: 34)

Aupilaarjuk emphasizes respect and gratitude towards the animals. This was often expressed in the offerings the hunters made.

## Offerings

In the past, offerings played an important part in hunting. Offerings could be made to the deceased, to the owners of the game or to the animals themselves. Thus, the owners of the caribou demanded offerings of soles and lines before the beginning of the caribou season (Peck, quoted in Laugrand et al. 2006: 388–89), and in the *kiversautit*, a small offering was made to the sea woman before the beginning of the seal season.[14] These small offerings were required for successful hunting. Offerings were also often made to the deceased people so that they would give game.

Kappianaq (IE 453) from Iglulik recalled the importance of offering (*tunillai*):

We remember when we were encouraged to offer. The act of *tunillainiq* [offering] was encouraged, especially to the grave sites [of those] who had passed away at the time when they were craving for food that was not easily gotten.... If I caught a species that he had craved for, I would go and offer a small piece of the meat to the gravesite, or just throw it in the direction of the land where this person was buried.... It is said that a small piece of something is sufficient for the offering. It would have been something that this person, while alive, was craving for and never did get a chance to eat it when he passed on. That is the way we were told to give, even to a dead person, or to throw it to the direction of the grave, at the same time call out the name of the person that you are offering. Here is a piece of meat that you had wanted, then throw it to the direction of his/her grave.

Kappianaq (IE 453) also recalled how small offerings were made to Inukpaujaq, the woman who turned into stone at a place called Qariaq:

The site is located on a point, it has the view of the surrounding waters. She had apparently gone to the point and could not make the long detour back. So I would place a match or a piece of tobacco beneath the stone. Or it might be a small piece of meat, or something else, at the same time I would wish for a game animal by saying out loud the game animal that I wanted.

Piugaattuq recalled how people used to make offerings to the famous Christian preacher Umik, who was said to be craving *maktaaq*
(whale blubber) before he died. The same tradition existed with respect to Ataguttaaluk:

> It is the grave of Ataguttaaluk at Alarnniq. It is said that she passed away
> while craving *maktaaq*. So if a whale was caught close to that location,
> even though we know that she would not get it, but one should throw a
> small piece to the direction of the grave, then her soul will understand
> the intent, she would get it immediately. That is the case for those that
> had a craving but died before they could get it. That is what we were
> encouraged to do.
>
> This also is applicable to someone that wants to help others in se-
> curing game animals. Before a person passes on, he or she will make it
> known that in his death, one should make offerings to their grave and
> make known what they want. If it is practised, then there is no doubt that
> he or she would be able to assist the person offering with what they want
> in securing game animals. ...
>
> Indeed, offering was very common in those days, especially with
> something they were craving for in their deathbed. If a person passes on
> without getting what the person craved, then you can make the offering
> by throwing something to the direction of something that he or she was
> craving. One need not go directly to the grave to make the offer. (Piugaat-
> tuq, IE 453)

The data provided by Piugaattuq are particularly interesting, as it became well-known that in his old age he was craving *maktaaq* himself.
The hunters in Iglulik did not want him to die with this craving unful-
filled, and therefore they decided to organize an illegal whale hunt so
they could provide him with *maktaaq*.[15]

## Sharing and Meat Caches

Sharing is one of the fundamental values of Inuit society. It has been
extensively studied.[16] Sharing involved hunting partners, relatives,
namesakes and sometimes even the whole community. Patterns of
sharing varied in each area. Here we provide some examples from
the North Baffin area, as there are many elders' testimonies from this
area. The obligation to share applies especially to the animals caught
by the hunters. Rachel Uyarasuk (IE 436) recalled how sharing was
organized:

> At the time before I got married, our mother and fathers had their young
> people to hunt for them or do work for them, anybody that was younger

in their extended family, maybe their younger brothers or, if they had children, their sons. When these people had gone out hunting and returned with a catch, they would take their catch to their parents. The elders, who were the head of the family, when food was brought in from a hunt, ... would then look after the food that was brought in. ... That way, when younger people brought in food, they would bring their catch to their fathers' and mothers' household. I have never heard of an incident that raised questions where the catch was going to be distributed. Even when the hunters had returned from their hunting trip, no one ever seemed to have raised a question. ... It was the head of the household, the father and the mother, who would instruct their peers how to deal with the game animal that was caught. They would invite the community for a meal right after game animals were brought in. After the community was invited, they would then have a share of the catch. The head of the household, took the decision about the game animal that was brought in. ... Unlike today, we did not need to pay for what we got, as long as it was among the extended family members. Whenever one amongst us ran out, then those would be provided with, without paying for it. That was the way it was. This was mainly for food and clothing materials. We never needed to buy from someone.

Once the animal is killed, its remains have to be used and shared. The game is incorporated into society, respected, honoured and used. Thus, the obligation to give maintains the flow of game that nourishes the community and enables human beings and animals to reproduce. The hunter and his wife were obliged to make complete use of the remains of the animal. Its meat would be eaten or distributed. Its skins would be prepared and made into clothing and skin coverings.

Rachel Uyarasuk (IE 158) explained various forms of sharing relationships: (*tuq&luqarniq*):

> *Kikkariin*, or *avigiin*, these are derived from food. In the case of *avigiin* [share partners], when an animal that was not common was caught, one of the partners will give the other a part of the catch. And in a case where there is a gathering of people to share in food that is not a common diet, which is usually a treat to the camp, the person who has a *kikka* [a partner with whom she shares meat with bones] will cut a piece of meat with bone and will offer it to his *kikka*. That was the way it was. This was derived from the friendship bonds.

Superfluous food would be stored in caches to be used in times of need by the hunter and his family or other people in need. Piugaattuq (IE 22) explained how hunters would put a stone marker on a boulder on a spot that would not be covered by snow so they could find the caches when they needed them. As Uyarasuk (IE 436) recalled,

> Food was very valuable and we were strictly forbidden to waste any meat. The game animals that were taken back were cached; the ones that were not cached were dried, at least the surface would be dried so that they did not get rotten. ... [A]s for the bones, especially for those that lived in places where they did not hunt walrus, the bones were given to dogs where they would be gnawed by the dogs, so there were hardly any waste bones around the camp site. ... As for blubber that we would use to fuel our *qulliq* [lamp], the blubber would be stored in a skin that had been skinned without cutting up the skin ... even when it was fermented we still used them for fuel.

In caches the meat of the prey gradually fermented. Although usually fresh meat was preferred over cached meat, *igunaq* (fermented walrus meat) was considered a delicacy.

Clothes made from the skin of the prey would be used and reused as skin coverings or lining for the sled. Only at the end of the process would the rotten food or the worn-out clothing be discarded, and usually it ended up in the stomachs of the dogs.

The rules of distributing and eating the meat varied widely, but the general principle that the meat should be shared and no one should be left hungry still prevails in Inuit communities today. Zacharias Aqiaruq (IE 113) recalled that there was always a distribution system for walrus hunting: 'For the ones who had made the kill would get the fore flipper section, and the ones who did not make the kill would get the chest section, and those who came in afterwards would get the hind flipper section or the hunters who made the kill would get the parts that had more meat in them as their share of the catch.'

Imaruittuq (quoted in Oosten et al. 1999: 134) relates with respect to *ningirniq*, sharing, in the North Baffin area,

> Let's say there were several hunters that caught a walrus. The person that first hit it with a bullet or harpoon had the first pick. Then the second person, and anyone after that took meat back to their home depending on when they hit it. The first to harpoon or shoot it would take home the forearms. And the other people that hit it would take the middle section, the stomach and the chest. If there were a lot of people, they would have to split it. The last part to be given away was around the flipper area.

According to Imaruittuq (quoted in Oosten et al. 1999: 134), the hunter who killed the animal received the left shoulder and the lower part of the backbone for the women to eat. 'He also got the head. It was the women who would eat the *kujapik*, the lower part of the backbone.' Imaruittuq emphasized that each camp had its own way of distributing meat. Specific rules applied to big animals such as bearded seal, walrus, belugas and polar bear, whereas for ringed seal usually no specific method of distribution was followed. Nutaraaluk (quoted in Oosten et al. 1999: 135) relates with respect to South Baffin, 'It has always been the custom that hunters distribute and share the meat. The chest cavity area, the shoulders and the neck and also the back are shared. It was first come, first serve for the liver.' He relates that in Nunavik the ringed seal was cut up at home:

> If they caught more than one seal and they thought there would be enough for everyone, they would distribute the meat. ... They would feast inside an *iglu*. The women would have their meal up on the bed platforms. They would eat part of the ribs and also the backbone. The men would eat the hip area sitting on the floor. The shoulders were set aside for the person who caught the seal to set aside as cooked meat when meat was not scarce. (quoted in Oosten et al. 1999: 135)

The hunter gained prestige by success in hunting, his wife by distributing the meat generously. Emile Imaruittuq (quoted in Oosten et al. 1999: 84) relates, 'What I just told you, that when I had a wife I should be a good provider of food and not be stingy. That was the most powerful advice. The words that my mother told me, not to be stingy and to feed my spouse and any other family in need.' Nutaraaluk (quoted in Oosten et al. 1999: 138) made the same point:

> I used to be very proud of my wife. She always offered meat and tea to the people that came to our house, and to my in-laws, and to my father before he passed away. Anytime you had meat in the house, especially when you had a wife, you would just sit back and let the wife deal with the meat. It was the wife's role to make sure that people were being fed. I used to be very thankful to my wife for carrying out that role.

Of course, there were also stingy people. But they paid a price. Imaruittuq observed,

> People who are stingy about food, are probably always hungry. If you are a sharing person, you know you are always going to get more meat. The meat is going to be replenished immediately. That's what my father used to say. Stingy people think they are not going to get more meat so they are always hungry, which makes them stingier. But people who are really sharing are more successful hunters and have more meat to share, because they know the meat is going to be replenished. (quoted in Oosten et al. 1999: 137)

The people who shared knew that after they shared, more would come. As a consequence, there was little need to take action against stingy people. The game would retaliate in its own way. Stingy people would be poor hunters.[17]

## Preserving Wildlife

For thousands of years Inuit have survived by subsistence hunting. They developed sophisticated techniques that allowed them to hunt for land game and sea game, and an extensive knowledge of the land and its animals. Inuit society was completely oriented to hunting, and the beliefs and practices of the past all focused on sustaining a flow of life that allowed animals to be captured and used so Inuit could survive. Once Euro-Americans appeared in the Arctic, this lifestyle came under increasing pressure. They integrated Inuit hunters into their system of commercial whaling and depleted the whaling stocks. Contacts with the whalers brought benefits such as new materials and technologies, but also many problems such as diseases and impoverishment. When the whaling industry collapsed at the end of the nineteenth century, trapping became an important source of additional income in the first half of the twentieth century. It helped the Inuit to survive, but also made them dependent on outside agencies such as the Hudson's Bay Company. In the second half of the twentieth century the Canadian administration began to take control in the north. Their attempts to improve the situation of the Inuit often implied an undermining of their hunting existence. The move of the Inuit to permanent settlements terminated the nomadic existence of the Inuit and made continuation of a hunting existence much more difficult. The administration often considered the hunting mode of existence an anachronism and wished to integrate Inuit into a wage economy. Inuit were aware of this negative attitude towards their mode of existence. The relocations in the 1950s and the killing of the dogs in the 1970s (see chapter 6) were viewed as attempts to destroy Inuit people and their culture. In the second half of the twentieth century Inuit were also faced with the developments of external bans on whaling and the fur boycott. Although Western companies had made fortunes with whaling and the fur trade for centuries, these activities were declared immoral and prohibited by the time Inuit were beginning to take control of their own destiny. Even today it is hard to explain to Inuit why furs should be boycotted when the trade in leather from the animals slaughtered in the Western bio-industry is perfectly legitimate (see figure 3.3).

Today the management of wildlife is one of the central political issues in Nunavut.[18] The Canadian administration has tried to protect

**Figure 3.3.** Poster designed to turn the tables on anti-seal hunt activists. Used with the permission of Murray Angus.

wildlife by utilizing quotas, which caused great resentment among Inuit, who conceive of the management of wildlife as the foundation of the relationship between people and land. Philipp Qipanniq (IE 206) stated,

There should be no restriction on what a hunter can hunt. ... From time immemorial Inuit never wasted any of the game animals that they caught. They never killed game animals and just left them. ... What I have seen on television are fishermen who would be angling and once they got a bite they would reel in the fish and they would proceed to remove the hook from a beautiful-looking fish. If they cannot remove the hook by hand then they take what looks like pliers and pry the hook free. The fisherman have a good look at the fish for so long that it would seem the fish was dying when the fisherman would put it back into the water to release it. Sometimes the fish would be half dead and the fisherman pushes it away. This would never happen to an Inuk. Once he catches a fish he will keep it no matter what the size, maybe because he wants it for food and will eat. They would never release a fish because they felt it was too small. Why is it then those white fishermen are not getting attention and are told that they should not do that while restrictions on game animals are imposed on Inuit. ... Why then do they allow the white fishermen to abuse fish to such an extent when they would hook it, handle it and release them to their eventual death. I know that they are the ones that are killing the fish so uselessly because they handle the fish for so long.[19]

Although Inuit are critical of sport fishing, they are more open to polar bear sport hunting, since this activity not only provides a lot of money for families, but also facilitates sharing, which maintains social relationships.[20]

Like Philipp Qipanniq, Aupilaarjuk from Rankin Inlet feels that Inuit should be in charge of wildlife themselves:

It is the Inuit who should be in charge of their land because we do not try to hunt caribou until they are extinct. We have always tried to be careful with our hunting. This is what I think. There has been a quota placed on polar bears. In the past we had no quotas. Because there is a quota system in place in the communities today, it seems that the number of bears killed has increased because the people keep hunting them until the quota has been met. I believe if Inuit were free to hunt polar bear they would be killing fewer bears than they actually are. In the past I remember that we wouldn't even get five polar bears over the winter. Now because of the quotas they hunt them until they reach that number. (quoted in Kulchyski and Tester 2007: 36)

Similarly, Piugaattuq (IE 22) explained that hunting was better before the introduction of quotas. He argued that animals can only become extinct when they are not hunted:

At the time when dog teams were more widely used, game animals did not appear to be in danger of being hunted out of extinction. It is in more recent times when they started to have the Hunters and Trappers Organization that there started to be concern about the danger of game animals being hunted to extinction. At the time when they are no longer hunted as much, I believe that is the way it is. If they were continuously hunted there would be no danger of them becoming extinct. When they started to manage how much could be hunted, then it appears to me that there are less game animals that are protected.

He pointed out that animals, including birds, are always moving, 'following their leaders and elders' (Piugaattuq, IE 10), looking for food and quiet places to reproduce.

Michel Kupaaq (IE 128) emphasized that the abundance of animals depended on the availability of their food:

I believe they were given so that we could use them and they cannot be hunted out of extinction. Of course, there were times when game animals hunted were not as numerous, but the numbers depend on the availability of food that they eat. At least for the marine animals, which would include the seals who depend on arctic cod, when there is less arctic cod then the seals are not going to be as numerous, when there are more then the seals are in more abundance, it all depends on the availability of the food that they eat.

Like Piugaattuq, he thought that hunting was essential to the protection of animals:

Trapping was essential at the time. Sometimes there were more foxes than at other times but there were always some around. Now it seems there are not as many foxes as there used to be even though the foxes are no longer trapped as much. As the hunting for wildlife continues, there appears to be no sign of a decrease in numbers even when the hunting continues to be practised. In the days when there were no quotas on polar bears there were some areas that the polar bears did not venture to, but now there seem to be more polar bears around. As long as the animals continue to be hunted, the number will remain [stable]. Once certain species are no longer hunted the chances of extinction are increased. That's what I think anyway. We have heard that certain species may be on the decline but as long as they are hunted they will never become extinct. The only reason they were created was to serve a purpose, especially for food. As long as they are hunted they will never become extinct. As soon as they are no longer hunted the number seems to decrease. (Kupaaq, IE 128)

Peter Alogut, from Coral Harbour, and Simeonie Akpik, from Lake Harbour, stated:

The mussels, especially, multiply more when they are being harvested. Also I wish they could stop saying that the whales are decreasing in numbers. The Inuit people still believe that the animals will always show up even if you don't see them in a particular area for a long time. Inuit know about that, but the Renewable Resource people keep telling us that the animals are decreasing in numbers. They can even tell you how many animals there are, but nobody knows how many animals are really left. In our traditional knowledge, when you use the animals according to their purpose, they will always prosper and reproduce themselves as you need them. We can never believe it when we're told the animals are decreasing because we know the animals and environment work up here. We also know any living being will cease to exist when the time comes. Today our food is here for us to use as it was planned in the first place. (quoted in McDonald et al. 1997: 60)

Many Inuit, and particularly the elders, do not trust biologists (see George 2008b). They feel they interfere with their hunting[21] and have insufficient knowledge of the land. As Barnabas Peryouar from Qamanittuaq explained,

Biologists don't believe us when we tell them that they are making the caribou change their routes by bothering them. Biologists never grew up on the land with caribou, they never learned about caribou all their lives like the Inuit. People who grew up with caribou and lived by the rules of the seasons know more about them, they know what to do to keep caribou from turning back from the crossing, but they are not heard from. (quoted in Mannik 1998: 177–78)

According to Peryouar, caribou are not on the verge of disappearance but fleeing from human activities: 'Long ago, the herd used to winter down around the tree line, but they're starting to spend their winters where there are no trees because it isn't safe for them to roam around the trees any more. Mining, the sound of airplanes, and the foul smell of the mining stuff has made it so the caribou can't roam around the tree line any more' (quoted in Mannik 1998: 176).

Michel Kupaaq (IE 128) also stated that animal behaviour has changed:

When I was able to go along on hunting trips I remembered when the hunters used to have dogs on a leash as sniffers for the seal breathing holes under the snow. We used to enjoy doing it especially when we were covering areas that had already been covered and find a breathing hole that had not been found. Now since the dogs had started to be tied down even when one may pass a breathing hole with the dog on the leeway, they simply will not pay any attention to it or maybe they simply no longer can smell it. In the days when the dogs were not tied down they would run for the source as soon as they smelled it when they were on the leeway. The caribou behaviour has also changed from the time when they were hunted. In those days when one saw a caribou late in the afternoon, the hunters would let it be until the following day when the light returned. The caribou would still be around. But today the caribou seen in one location will have disappeared as if they never existed. ...

I do believe the behaviour of animals has changed on account of motorized hunting equipment. In the days when the hunting equipment were not motorized, we were able to see beluga whales even in the summer time, but now since most of the hunting equipment is motorized we do not get to see beluga whales until late in the autumn. And in those days the beluga whales were able to [go] right up to the shores, and when they fled, they used to go in the direction of the land as long as they were not bulls.

But now it is not possible for them to be made to flee towards the land, instead they will try to go to the deeper waters when they flee as a bull beluga whale would do.

Today, modern hunting equipment (snowmobiles, motorboats, guns, fishing gear, etc.) is expensive, and it has become very hard to survive by hunting alone. Many Inuit earn their livelihood through wage labour and hunt in their free time. But Inuit still identify as hunters and are very much convinced that the maintenance of their hunting lifestyle is essential to their survival as a culture. Sharing and respecting animals are thought to be essential features of this lifestyle. It is hard to predict the future, but the fact that Inuit have succeeded in maintaining their hunting identities despite many adversities for centuries gives hope for the future.

## Notes

1. On the extensive Inuit vocabulary regarding the body, see Bordin (2003).
2. See also Rasmussen (1931: 482) for an Utkuhigjalingmiut calendar.
3. See Bennett and Rowley (2004: part 2) for a discussion of the hunting calendars of various Inuit groups.
4. See also Guemple (1965) for the relation between bone and name.
5. See Oosten (1997) for a discussion of amulets and their use.
6. For many other games related to learning hunting skills, see Petit (2011).
7. See also Martha Nasook's (IE 159) discussion of the significance of namesake relationships for the first catch.
8. See also Rasmussen (1929: 179): 'A young man must never eat the flesh of the first animal of any species he kills. ... If a young man kills any animal for the first time the heart of that particular animal must only be eaten in

his house or tent, and nowhere else. Its blood must not be touched by any woman. The first time a young man makes a kill, he must give away the skin of the animal killed.'

9. See also Boas (1901: 161): 'After a boy had killed his first caribou, his mother gave a piece of the meat to each person, and along with it a few beads cut of from her clothing. He must give the skin to an old man for his clothing. By so doing, the favor of Nuliayoq is obtained, who will help the boy in future when hunting. After this, the mother is allowed to trim her clothing with white and black edging.' Nutaraaluk from Pangniqtuuq related, 'The summer I was seven, I shot three calves with it. Those three caribou that I caught for the first time were given to my *arnaquti* midwife, Pitalusi. Another time I remember, I had caught something else for the first time. They used to untie the belt of the *qarlikallaak*, short pants, when there was a first kill. I remember my *arnaquti* untying her *qarlikallaak*. Whenever a first catch was made they would untie their *qarlikallaak*. I remember my *arnaquti*, untying her *qarlikallaak* as I had made a first kill, but I don't remember what it was.' (quoted in Oosten et al. 1999: 106).

Similar traditions existed in Nunavik. Pernet (2013) explains that the wish of the animal to be killed by the hunter is taught very young to the child when the *sanaji*, the midwife, asks him to beat her as if he were killing his prey. Pernet (2013: 285) provides a few interesting examples of such a practice. One is given by Tuumasi Kudluk, from Kangirsuk: 'When a child caught his first animal, he should hit his *sanaji* as hard as possible on the cheek. The first ptarmigan a child caught was a sign that the child had become a hunter' (quoted in Avataq Cultural Institute 1984: 185, our translation).

10. Brightman (1993: 127) observes that among the Rock Cree, 'sex is a metaphor for hunting, and women are metaphors for animals' (see also Henriksen 2009: 41). Brightman (1993: 113) states that dogs, adolescent females and menstruating women should avoid the butchering site, which has to remain clean.

11. See Piugaattuq (IE 005): 'In the past some men used to commit bestiality with caribou or other animals. They would develop some sort of sickness in their buttocks or their private parts and this person would not mention this, although people would know he was hiding something.'

12. According to Feit (2000: 135), Cree can also send their demands to Chitche Manitu (God), and the hunters will then receive animals. Animals offer themselves if the hunter continues to respect his prey. Brightman (1993: 106–9) also refers to this power of words in hunting.

13. You have to stand with your hands in the air when you sing this song (C. Trott, personal communication, June 2013).

14. These offerings will be discussed in chapters 8 and 9, on caribou and seals.

15. See chapter 10 for a discussion of the revival of whale hunting in Nunavut.

16. See, e.g., Van de Velde (1956) for the Nattilik area and Wenzel (1991, 1995) for the *ningiqtuq* system of sharing in the Clyde River region.

17. Sharing is a marked feature of all first catch celebrations. See Saladin d'Anglure (2000), Pernet (2012, 2013) and Nutall (2000).

18. According to many Inuit, hunting has never been really understood by *qallunaat*. Inuit have much experience in resisting the new regulations introduced by the *qallunaat*. See Kulchyski and Tester (2007: chap. 4).
19. Similar conflicts erupted in Alaska, where Yup'it also complain about 'playing with the fish' (see Fienup-Riordan 1990: 185–87).
20. See Freeman and Wenzel (2006), Wenzel (2005, 2008), Wenzel and Dowsley (2008) and Dowsley (2010) on polar bear sport hunting and the value of a polar bear in such an activity.
21. This lack of trust in biologists is widespread in the Arctic. According to Fienup-Riordan (1990: 177), 'Nelson Island women also express concern that female biologists are doing irreparable damage to the goose population in the course of performing their scientific observations', since women are forbidden to touch any empty nest.

# PART II

# LIFE AND DEATH

# CHAPTER 4

# The Raven, the Bringer of Light

A mythological complex focusing on the common raven (*Corvus corax*) as a trickster and creator is widespread in the Arctic, extending far into Siberia and North America.[1] Extensive mythological cycles have been recorded among Native Americans.[2] E. Nelson (1899) and Lantis (1947) provided rich accounts of the mythological complex of the raven in the western Arctic. The creation of the earth and everything upon it is credited to the Raven Father (Tu-lu-kau-gûk), who is said to have come from the sky and made the earth when everything was covered with water. He created man and founded many cultural institutions. The raven is a creator as well as a trickster, at once very shrewd and very stupid.[3] He easily fools other beings and is easily fooled by them. He is a master of light, showing and hiding the light in various myths. He realizes all kinds of transformations by lifting his beak and/ or flapping his wings.[4]

Whereas in the western Arctic a complex mythical cycle of the raven developed, in the eastern and central Arctic we mainly find short myths about the raven. But the use of raven masks seems to be an integral part of Inuit culture, and Thalbitzer (1925: 240) already classified ideas pertaining to the whiteness of the raven as one of the characteristic features of Eskimo culture. Kleivan (1971: 10) devoted a case study to the myth of how the raven and the loon tattooed each other and demonstrated the continuity of the mythical theme from Alaska to Greenland.

String figures also testify to the ubiquity of the raven complex among the Inuit. According to Guy Mary-Rousselière (1969: 48–49),

> The raven is one of the widest spread figures among the Inuit. It has been found in Siberia; in Alaska, in Point Barrow and inland; in Canada, among the Copper Inuit, the Qaenermiut, and among the Iglulingmiut;

in Greenland, at Cape York, Upernavik and Ubekendt Island. Almost everywhere, the string figure representing a raven is followed, as in Pelly Bay, of three other figures: *teriganiarjuk* (the fox), *nuvuyanguaciaq* (what looks like a cloud) and *anaruaciaq* (excrement).

Mary-Rousselière then provides the corresponding words that should be pronounced with each figure. With the first figure, one has to make it move and say, 'The fox is winning, he follows the raven's footprints.' With the second figure, one has to say, 'A cloud is passing on top', and with the last figure, 'The excrement is rolling, moving further.' Mary-Rousselière concludes: 'It is remarkable that the words pronounced by this figure in Pelly Bay are almost identical to those heard at Point Barrow and at Cape York, as well as among the Aivilingmiut and Iglulingmiut.'

The fact that in the central Arctic mythological and ritual cycles are not found to the same extent as in the western Arctic does not imply that the organization of myth and ritual is less complex. The apparent flexibility of myths and ritual gives much space to the participants to combine stories and rituals and often obscures the fact that these rituals and myths are well organized and exhibit structural features testifying to the continuity and resilience of basic patterns in Inuit societies.

In this chapter we discuss the mythical complex of the raven as well as its ritual position, the use of (parts of) the raven in amulets, and various practices and beliefs relating to ravens. In the first part of the chapter we focus on the creative and destructive powers of the raven, and in the second part on his role in marriage and alliance.


## The Power of the Raven

The raven is a scavenger and of all birds he is the one most present in Inuit communities. The word *tulugaq*, raven, is derived from *tulu*, to hit (Schneider 1985: 418). It refers to an action of hitting or biting (see, e.g., *tulurpuq:* he/it gives him a blow of his tusk or a bite of his teeth; to hit an obstacle). It is probably related to *tuluriaq*, canine tooth.

In a song collected by Rasmussen (1932: 177) among the Umingmaktormiut, the expression *tuluriaqaqpaak* (has it a fang?) is used, and Rasmussen explains, 'Here is a reference to the fact that, unlike other birds, the raven is able to bite a thong through, and therefore it is jokingly asked if it has "fang" (carnassial tooth) – the teeth the dogs use to chew seal thongs when they eat them.' The word *tuluriaq* is also found in the name of Tulurialik, a helping spirit.[5] Both the raven and the bear are marked by their capacity to hit or bite.

According to Randa (1994: 312), there is no terminological distinction between the male and the female raven, but *tulugaarruluit*, young ravens, are distinguished from an adult raven, *tulugaq*, or a big raven, *tulugarjuaq*.

Parts of the raven were used for various purposes. His feathers were used for the feathering of arrows (L. Turner [1894] 1979: 247; Mathiassen 1928: 57; Holtved 1962: 71). His wings served as brushes (Bilby 1923: 97; 1926: 52, 94) and his skin for cleaning. Parts of the raven such as his legs and wings might also be used in the context of witchcraft and sorcery.[6]

According to Randa (1994: 313), the raven is primarily viewed negatively as a thief, *tigliktituinnaruluk*, from *tiglikti*, thief, but he is considered to have *isuma*, thought, sense. He is *isumalialuk*, the one who thinks much. He robs the traps of the hunters and may even rob the dogs of their food (see Bilby 1923: 259–61). A tale collected from Qajuina relates how he fooled a fox that had caught him:

> The red fox laid himself on the ground and pretended to be dead. The raven came too close to pick up his eyes and was caught in his mouth. The red fox brought him in a very uncomfortable position, to the place where he intended to eat him. But suddenly the raven asked: 'From what direction is the wind?' The red fox thought that the question was stupid so he opened his mouth to say 'No.' And the raven flew away. (Métayer 1973: 196–98)

Human beings are close to ravens. In Greenland, H. Egede (1818: 64) already described them as nearly domesticated animals: 'Raven seem to be domestic birds with them [Inuit], for they are always seen about their huts, hovering about the carcases of seals that lie upon the ground.' With respect to Nunavik, L. Turner (1888: 108; see also [1894] 1979: 262) explains, 'The raven is endowed with omniscience, valor and cunning.' Jenness (1922: 147–48) related, 'If the other hunter is some distance away the Eskimo sometimes croaks like a raven to put him on his guard.'

The voice of the raven is often marked. In Alaska, throat singing that 'consists of a series of guttural ejaculations' is attributed to the raven (Hawkes 1916: 123). In Greenland, Thalbitzer (1914b: 629) pointed out the use of raven whiskers for the drum: 'A drum provided with an amulet, says Kunnaq, is to improve the voice of the man when he is singing; the amulet consists of the "whiskers" of a raven (stiff feathers near the root of the beak) and is inserted under the lashing, by means of which the handle of the drum is fastened to the wooden rim.'

Hunters might make good use of the presence of ravens when hunting a polar bear. As Piugaattuq (IE 058) related,

> Ravens usually scavenge around polar bears and the bears are so used to the cries of the ravens. The bear would be fleeing slightly since it had been alerted earlier but unable to make out the noise it suddenly hears the 'caw' sounds and it would stop. Hearing that noise it would stop to investigate. The dogs would be able to get to the bear quicker because by stopping to investigate it has allowed the hunters to get closer. I have seen this technique being used on a hunt…. Hearing the usual sound of the ravens the bear would make the mistake to stop to investigate allowing the hunter to get closer…. The sound of the ravens does not scare or alarm the bear. That was the method that they used when hunting a polar bear.

Like most birds, ravens have divinatory connotations. In the story of Ataguttaaluk, who ate her husband and children, a raven approached her and said, 'There are Inuit coming.' And the next day Kadluk and Tagornak arrived. They put her on a sled and provided her with food.[7] But one should not always believe a raven. In a tale recorded by Mary-Rousselière from Ukkumaaluk (quoted in Laugrand and Oosten 2009: 90–91), a raven deceived a woman by informing her that her husband had caught a caribou.

### The Creator of Light

The *isuma* of the raven comes to the fore in the myths of the creation of light. An Aivilik story recorded by Rasmussen (1929: 253) from the old storyteller Ivaluardjuk relates that originally everything was dark, and light came to mankind only through the intervention of the raven.

> During the first period after the creation of the earth, all was darkness. Among the earliest living beings were the raven and the fox. One day they met, and fell into talk, as follows:
> 'Let us keep the dark and be without daylight', said the fox.
> But the raven answered: 'May the light come and daylight alternate with the dark of night.'
> The raven kept on shrieking 'qau, qau' (Thus the Eskimos interpret the cry of the raven, qau, roughly as qau, which means dawn and light. The raven is thus born calling for light). And at the raven's cry, light came, and day began to alternate with night.
> It is said that in the days when the earth was dark, the only creatures men had to hunt were ptarmigan and hare, and these were hunted by wetting the forefinger and holding it out in the air; the finger then became luminous and it was possible to see the animal hunted.[8]

In a variant of the myth recorded among the Umingmaktormiut, the fox is replaced by the black bear (see Rasmussen 1932: 217; Boas 1901: 306). Both versions of this myth preserve the role of the raven as master of light as well as the alternation of light and dark that is at the core of the raven complex in the western Arctic. The raven effectively becomes a master of periodicity.

The creation of light triggers a transition from a primordial stage where people live in the dark, have only limited food supplies, eat earth and find their children on the earth to a stage where human beings become numerous, hunt animals and eat and procreate as they do today. This way of life is only made possible by the creation of light, which allows mankind to discern between human beings and animals and enables the hunter to see his prey.

Whereas light allows good hunting, darkness is associated with the level of the *tarniq* (derived from the root *tar-*, dark), the miniature image of a being that survives after death. Boas (1901: 321ff.) provides an interesting version of the famous story of Arnaqtaaqtuq, describing how a *tarniq* might enter a being that ate its corpse: 'Once upon a time an old woman who had died was buried, and then a raven came and began to eat her. Her soul entered the body of the raven, and she became a raven. The raven laid its eggs; but a man came and shot the bird, took it into his house, and gave it to a dog to eat. Then the woman's soul entered the dog.' After many modes of existence it entered a seal.[9] Finally the soul of this seal entered the harpoon of the hunter that killed it. From there it entered the womb of the wife of the hunter, and thus the old woman was finally reborn as a human being. The story shows that the distinction between animals and human beings was precarious, and the boundary between people and animals could be crossed when the *tarniq* passed from one existence to the next. In this narrative the raven triggers a series of transformations allowing the *tarniq* to incarnate in various beings and move from one mode of existence to another. On the level of the *tarniq*, marked by darkness, the distinctions between different modes of existence are transcended as one existence is followed by the next. On this level darkness even seems to be a requirement for the process of transformation to take place. Boas (1901: 143) reports that a pregnant woman should not eat 'any part of the seal except the kidneys, because they make it dark for the child in the womb'. The implication may be that in darkness the child may transform into something else. Thus, darkness and light constitute complementary spheres of life.

Shamanism encompasses both domains, as the *angakkuq* performs in the dark, inside the house with all lamps extinguished, and requires

*qaumaniq*, enlightenment or shamanic vision, to see. In order to become an *angakkuq* a person had to obtain this *qaumaniq*. It enabled
the *angakkuq* to see hidden things such as spirits and shades, or transgressions of *tirigusuusiit* (things people had to abstain from). Rasmussen (1929: 113) described *qaumaniq* for the Iglulingmiut:

> The first time a young shaman experiences this light, while sitting up on
> the bench invoking his helping spirits, it is as if the house in which he is
> suddenly rises; he sees far ahead of him, through mountains, exactly as
> if the earth were one great plain, and his eyes could reach to the end of
> the earth. Nothing is hidden from him any longer; not only can he see
> things far, far away, but he can also discover souls, stolen souls, which
> are either kept concealed in far, strange lands or have been taken up or
> down to the Land of the Dead.[10]

According to Rasmussen (1929: 113), the *angakkua* or *qaumaniq* was
obtained from the moon spirit, but it could also be obtained from a deceased person among the *ullormiut* (the deceased in the upper world),
bears in human appearance, Pakitsumanga (the mother of the caribou)[11] or a white lemming. In addition, in South Baffin shamanic light
was often brought by *tuurngait*, helping spirits.

The Anglican missionary Peck collected a list of 347 *tuurngait*
during his stay in South Baffin from 1894 to 1905. Many of these *tuurngait* were described as owners of game or bringers of light. In his
list we find several ravens as well as birds that may have been ravens
or associated with them, and it is worthwhile to look at some of them
in more detail.

In Peck's list (Laugrand et al. 2006: 419–68), Soolutvaluk (sounds
like a bird's wing) is described as '(like) a raven having one wing', emphasizing another important feature of the raven, the sound of his
wings. Qutyarngnuk is 'one of the first torngaks. When the world was
made he was a great bird. Lived by the boundary of the earth. Black
head. Curved beak. Breast white. Beautiful to look upon. Good spirit.
Ready when invoked by the conjurors to help in various ways, viz.
heal the sick, give food of various kinds.' Although he is not identified
as such by Peck, the description suggests a raven. Audlaktak (departs
frequently) '[m]akes short flights to various places. Like a large bird.
Black and white. Good spirit. Brings light on the back of his head from
heaven, the world boundary, and the land. Light being considered a
means of life, a bringing light is the cause of healing and blessing.'
Audlaktak most probably refers to a raven, since ravens were said to
be the only birds able to 'pass the hole through which the spirits pass
to the true heavens' (Hawkes 1916: 153). The spirit also evokes the fea-

ture of bringing light. We have to take into account that in Peck's list the bringing of light usually refers not so much to ordinary light, *qau*, but more specifically to the shamanic light, *qaumaniq*, which enables the *angakkuq* to see everything clearly.

Ujarak, son of the shaman Aava, told Saladin d'Anglure (1988a: 66–67) that the raven had been a very effective protector of his father. When Aava was born, he was clothed in raven skin and feathers and he had preserved that first garment as an amulet. He was saved from death by a raven that he had invoked in despair after falling into the sea. Clinging to a piece of ice he heard the flapping of a wing and saw a raven. The bird came to him from the east at night when dawn lit the sky and circled above him. The piece of ice changed direction and floated to firm land. He was saved and at the same time obtained *qaumaniq*, shamanic vision, thanks to the raven, his protective spirit.

## The Raven as Trickster and Eater of Flesh

Other birds in Peck's list such as Aggevak, Milluksak, Eyekudluk (large eye) and Yavao'ow'luk evoke the raven in their description (see Laugrand et al. 2006).[12] Savikpiatak is described by Peck as 'a crow which calls out its own name viz. Savikpiatangmi'. The word *savik*, knife, evokes the equation of the beak of the raven and a knife. Siggook (beak) has a 'head like a crow, but a body like a human being, having wings. A good torngak, because he brings seals meat to the Eskimo with his beak.' The close association between the beak of the raven and the knife is preserved in a story collected by Métayer from Ivarluk:

> An orphan boy and his grandmother used to get some food from a rich man. The boy had been thinking about going away. He left for the mountains. He went right up on the top, wrapped himself in his sleeping skins and pretended to be asleep. A big raven came flying over his head, croaking over and over; he alighted close by and pricked the boy's feet and back with his beak to make sure he was dead.
>
> The happy raven sharpened his knife and came closer to the head. The orphan cried 'Haa aa aa!' and the raven flew away and forgot his knife. The boy took it and went home followed by the bird who asked for his knife. The raven went ahead of him, dug a hole in the ground with his left foot and waited for the boy. When he arrived, he said to him: 'Give me back my knife and all animals will be yours to hunt.'
>
> He saw many caribous in the ground but he did not give the knife back.
>
> The raven dug another hole with his left foot and the boy could see wolves, red foxes and some other animals but he still refused to give the knife back.

In the next hole, there were white foxes and the boy wanted them badly. He gave back the knife and took the foxes home with him.

The grandmother put the hides outside her igloo to dry. The rich man's wife saw them and told her husband about it. The man sent his daughter to fetch the boy: 'How is it that you are now so good a hunter?' 'I went up the mountain and pretended to be asleep. A raven came and I took his knife.'

The man was jealous and he left for the mountain; he wrapped himself in his sleeping skins and pretended to be asleep ... but he really fell asleep; and the big raven took his eyes out. (Métayer 1973: 679–83)

The young man exchanged animals for the knife and became rich.[13] In this story the raven emerges as an owner of game. His fondness for eating eyes was already noted by early ethnographers and is marked in many stories. Parry (1824: 134) already related, 'On the morning of the 8th the same wolf was found round the S. E. point, frozen quite stiff. A raven discovered the position of the carcass, by hovering over it, after having picked out one of the eyes.' A story by L. Qajuina relates,

The Inuit had set up their tents on a river's bank. They were worried about one of their hunters who had been away far too long. When a big raven started flying above their heads, a man cried: 'Let us catch him! He knows everything!' The raven answered right away: 'You want to know? I took out his eyes between the two rivers.' Everyone understood: their man had been attacked and killed. They searched for him between the two rivers and found his dead body. (Métayer 1973: 618–20)

The raven could use his *isuma* to trick people and obtain their eyes, as in a story told by A. Qavviaktok,

Following the advice of a raven, a group of Inuit went to meet some visitors and built their igloo at the foot of a high cliff to spend the night. While they were sleeping, after the lamps were extinguished, the raven started dancing and jumping on the iglus and on the cliff. He thus provoked an avalanche and all the people were buried under a huge snow bank. The raven remained close by and, when spring came back, he had a great time picking out the eyes of his victims. (Métayer 1973: 184–87)

The raven could cause fear. Ijjangiaq (IE 196; see also IE 192) describes how his family was pursued by a raven:

One time we were followed by a raven that might have belonged to that place. From that time on ravens scare me a little. We were trying to catch *iqalugait* [fish] ... when we saw a shadow of a large raven. When it landed near us, it was all wet and was jumping around and cleaning itself at the same time. We had to make a detour around it for we were scared of it.

Our tent was close on a rise. As we started to leave the lake, it followed us and landed right in front of us. At first we did not join hands as we started for home but we all joined our hands and proceeded on home yelling all at the same time. We started to head to the wrong way to the side of the tent as we continued to make a detour avoiding the raven. We all started to take our footwear off for some reason.

That late afternoon, my father arrived from his hunting trip on foot while the others still had not arrived. He had caught a caribou that day so as he was flensing the caribou he suddenly felt really tired and sleepy so he had lain down next to the caribou carcass that he was flensing and fell asleep. He felt something so he woke just to find a raven trying to take his eyes out. I think it was the same raven.[14]

The raven not only eats eyes, but also other parts of the human body, as well as all kinds of waste that cannot be eaten by human beings. But like human beings, the raven has to observe specific rules with respect to his food. Sâmik told Rasmussen (1931: 266) a story of a sick raven:

A shaman once came to a sick raven who had a bad leg. The raven said: 'It is not to be wondered at that I have a bad leg. I was bound to get a bad leg; I have eaten of the corpse of an infant and of a killed caribou at the same time.' The animals have taboos just like humans, and a raven must not eat of human flesh on the same day that it has eaten caribou. If it does, it will be sick. Now its neighbours had gone away hunting and it was left behind, but the shaman cured it. Then the raven thought over what to give in return, and gave the shaman a dog's turd. I suppose it was hard for it to find a proper game animal.[15]

The raven taboo in the story obviously does not apply to human beings.[16] The story marks various features of the raven: the raven as a provider of non-human food and the eating of human flesh. Boas (1901: 216–17)[17] related the following story of the raven and the gull:

Once upon a time a hunter came to the house of the Raven. He entered, and saw an old man who said, 'Haak! Surely you are hungry. We are generally hungry when we wander away from home.' Now he asked a boy to bring in some human flesh. The boy brought it in. The old man cut off a piece, and gave it to the hunter. The latter said, 'I do not like that kind of flesh'; and the old man retorted, 'Give it to me, I can eat it.' After he had finished eating, he said to the boy, 'Bring in some whale-skin'; but it was really fowl's dung. He gave it to the Eskimo, who said he could not eat it. 'Give it to me', said the old man, 'I can eat it.' Then he told the boy to bring in scrapings of whalebone. He offered this to the Eskimo, who, however, said he could not eat it. The old man said again, 'I can eat it, give it to me'; but after he had finished eating, he said, 'My stomach aches', and he vomited everything he had eaten. A short distance away there was the house of the Gull. The hunter was invited to enter. He went in, and the Gull gave him dried salmon, which he was glad to eat. Then he left and went home, and told how the birds had fed him.[18]

Thus, the food of the raven should not be accepted and may be poisonous. The story of Atungai relates that two raven women offered poisonous food to him, but he perceived the trick and forced them to eat it themselves (see Boas 1901: 228–30).

The man-eating raven is a recurrent figure. In a dialogue between an Inuk and a raven related by Itqiliq (Rasmussen 1931: 412), 'A human cried: 'Raven, what have you in your beak?' The raven answered: 'A human's thigh! Because I like it I have it in my beak! Frozen meat – I am pecking at, frozen meat – frozen meat! Frozen meat!' The topic can also be found in modern Inuit art. Alasuaq, an Inuit artist from Nunavik, told Saladin d'Anglure (1978: 73), 'I carved a history related by Livai Qumaaluk, the history of a big raven who changed himself, his wife and his children into a human being. He holds the thigh of a human being between his claws.' According to Bilby (1923: 168), Inuit on Baffin Island did not object to their corpses being eaten by ravens:

> The people much dislike to have their dead bodies devoured by dogs, lest their souls have to wander over the ice and land on vain hunting trips; but they do not object to wolves on the same score, since the wolves also devour the souls, and the departed, thus disposed of, will always hunt deer successfully and live on the meat. Neither do they object to the carrion-loving raven, as the soul in this case is also absorbed by the bird and provided for in perpetuity.

Everywhere, the raven is considered inedible. A story by Boas (1901: 227–28) relates that a boy who was only fed on raven meat changed into a raven himself (see also Boas 1907: 227). But a raven can be killed. Boas (1901: 303) recorded the following tradition from South Baffin:

*The Song of the Ravens.*
The father of a man named Apalok killed a bear; and a Raven which was near thought, 'Shall I not try to eat the blood by putting my head into the wound?' But while the Raven's head was in the wound, the hunter came up and killed the Raven by twisting its neck. The Raven, while dying, cried, 'I am taken by the neck in the hole (wound)! Oh, where is the light now? My dear little children! I think of them only. They are wandering about unfledged, unprotected from the cold. O Aimakta, Nuimakta, Atsenaktok, Tokoyatok, Ovayok, Makkongayok, Akpayok!'

The dying raven asks for the light and names the children he can no longer protect.

The raven is a trickster that can be tricked as in the story told by Ivarluk. In that story he is forced to become a giver of game. An eater of inedible food, he offers it to people. Essentially a non-social being, he still cares for his children when he is killed. Always ambiguous he is a bringer of light as well as an eater of eyes.

### Using the Power of the Raven

Parts of the raven were used to strengthen the child and transfer the qualities of the raven to it. Mathiassen (1928: 186, 189) related, 'The first garment of the infant child is a cap of fox or bird skin, usually a raven skin; it must not be of caribou skin; one of these raven-skin caps is given to the child even at birth.' According to Boas (1907: 515), 'Skins of ravens are used for making garments for infant boys, because it is believed that this will give them the power to discover game easily.' This is confirmed by Rasmussen (1929: 177): 'Newly born male children are often given, as their first garments, a dress of raven's skin with the feathers outside. The ravens always manage to find something; this gives good hunting.' According to Randa (1994: 315), an *atigi* (skin parka) made of raven skin would give strength to the baby. In other contexts, it would facilitate polar bear hunting. Philipp Qipanniq (IE 197) recalled that his first hat was made from a skin of a raven, but he was never told why.

In addition to raven skin giving newborn boys good hunting skills, Rasmussen (1931: 43) related that a raven's head and claws ensured good shares during a hunt, because the raven has the peculiarity of always being present where the quarry is brought down (see also Weyer 1932: 311; Thalbitzer 1914b: 633).

Raven skin might also have healing properties. The *angakkuq* Aava related,

> My father had got a walrus with its unborn young one, and when he began cutting it out, without reflecting that my mother was with child, I again fell to struggling within the womb, and this time in earnest. But the moment I was born, all life left me, and I lay there dead as a stone. The cord was twisted round my neck and had strangled me. Ardjuaq, who lived in another village, was at once sent for, and a special hut was built for my mother. When Ardjuaq came and saw me with my eyes sticking right out of my head she wiped my mother's blood from my body with the skin of a raven, and made a little jacket for me of the same skin. 'He is born to die, but he shall live', she said. (quoted in Rasmussen 1929: 116–17)

Rasmussen (1929: 175) related that when a new mother came home after her residence in the birth hut (*kinirvik*) the child received new clothing. The old garments, the child's first clothes, should be placed either in a raven's nest or in a gull's nest, or put on a small island in a stream.

Raven skins were also used in *aarnguat,* amulets. Rasmussen (1929: 149–50) related,

> A woman in childbirth for instance must use a raven's claw as toggle in the strap which fastens her *amauti* (carrying bag for a child) at the bottom. It is afterwards given to the child as an amulet, and brings vitality and success in hunting. But even though these powers of good luck do not emanate from the claw itself, but from the soul of the raven, an amulet made from another part of the raven's body would be of no avail.

The raven claw is often mentioned as an *aarnguaq.* Rasmussen (1930: 96) depicts a complex *aarnguaq* used by the Caribou Inuit (see figure 4.1).

The Nattilingmiut had a rich *aarnguat* tradition. The boys Tertaq and Nânaoq had raven skins to make them invisible to the caribou at their crossing places (Rasmussen 1931: 271–72). The old woman Kagtârssuk wore two raven heads, bringing good hunting shares, sewn to her amulet belt for the benefit of her little adoptive son Ûnaq (Rasmussen 1931: 275–76). The little girl Qaqortingneq wore an amulet belt on the outside of her coat for the benefit of her future sons. The claw and stomach of a raven were sewn to it. They would bring luck to his hunting companions, so that he would get many hunting shares when he did not make a kill himself (Rasmussen 1931: 276). Moreover, a woman with an infant son would wear a raven's claw or a piece of hardwood used as a toggle on the *amauti* strap. 'When the boy grows up he will use this strap as a belt, and the raven's claw or the piece of wood as a belt buckle; this will give him a strong life' (Rasmussen 1931: 277).

**Figure 4.1.** Amulets, composed of a raven foot with the claws, insects sewn into small skin bags and two ermine skins. *Source:* Rasmussen 1930: 96.

One cannot only get access to the power of the raven by amulets, but also by *irinaliutiit*, powerful words. Rasmussen (1929: 47) presents an *irinaliutiit* by the *angakkuq* Aava to protect a child on its first journey.

> Aua [Aava], who as the angakoq had to see that all needful rites were properly observed, went up to the child, bared its head, and with his lips close to its face recited a magic prayer as follows:
>
>   'I arise from rest with movements swift
>   As the beat of a raven's wings
>   I arise
>   To meet the day
>   Wa-wa.
>   My face is turned from the dark of night
>   To gaze at the dawn of day,
>   Now whitening in the sky.'

Elsewhere, Rasmussen (1929: 114–15) related,

> When one sees a raven fly past, one must follow it and keep on pursuing until one has caught it. If one shoots it with bow and arrow, one must run up to it the moment it falls to the ground, and standing over the bird as it flutters about in pain and fear, say out loud all that one intends to do, and mention everything that occupies the mind. The dying raven gives power to words and thoughts. The following magic words, which had great vitalising power, were obtained by Angutingmarik in the manner above stated:
>
>   Earth,
>   Earth,
>   Great earth,
>   Round about on earth
>   There are bones, bones, bones,
>   Which are bleached by the great Sila
>   By the weather, the sun, the air,
>   So that all the flesh disappears,
>   He-he-he.
>   Spirit, spirit, spirit,
>   And the day, the day,
>   Go to my limbs
>   without drying them up,
>   Without turning them to bones
>   Uvai, uvai, uvai.

According to a few elders, the raven is able to transfer its capacity to move fast to human beings. Kappianaq from Iglulik stated, 'I was told that if I wanted to get the ability to *qiluriaqsiuqtuq* [to create folds in the land], I was to make a raven fall, and catch it before it touched the ground. When you had this ability you could cover ground in one day that would have taken others two or more days' (quoted in Kolb and Law 2001: 153).

The raven is a bringer of light and an effective helping spirit. He has *isuma*, yet he is an eater of man, preferably of his eyes, and even though he is wise, he cannot be trusted. People try to acquire his powers through *aarnguat*, amulets, or *irinaliutiit*, powerful words.

## Alliance, Competition and Transformation

Before we discuss the role of the raven in alliance, competition and transformation we must position the raven within the wider categories of birds.

Although some birds are eaten (such as geese and ptarmigans), they are not considered important prey. Many migratory birds, however, are treated with respect due their prediction of the weather and the seasons, as related by Noah Piugaattuq (IE 246):

> When sea gulls were seen it meant that melting of the snow will now resume without any freeze ups. When old squaws come to our land, that meant the spring is here and will continue on. My father once composed a song about the old squaw ducks. The past winter had seen hard times where they had experienced death. As the old squaws start to arrive the danger of starvation is no longer imminent as the seals will now start to bask on top of ice so that the hunters would now be able to find it easier to catch seals even if they had to depend solely on harpoons. His song goes: Tasuumaktiluta agiarjuili makua tikira&alirmingmatta. That meant that they will now be able to catch animals for their food on a regular basis. When the old squaw ducks had started to arrive, there still will be times when they will run short on food, but now they will be able to hunt any game animals much easier. So birds were used to tell time. There would be a prolonged period of good warm weather so the women would take advantage of that to dry skins. At this time the loons[19] had started to come. When a loon cries out, 'qaqqaqaa', it is said that wet weather is on its way, so the cry of the loon was used to determine the forecast. This was more so at Tununirusiq because there are not as many birds in that area. I believe they used the loon much more to determine the forecasting of wet weather. When determining the foul weather without the loon, they would say that the west side is getting bad. That meant that the women must make certain that all the skins that they had laid out to dry must be stored in a dry place, because they knew that the bad weather was coming from the west and it was going to be a long spell. Loons could also be heard, loons do not cry out 'qaqqaqaa' too often.

These were the things that were observed to tell forecast. As for Arctic terns, when one is sighted before a full ground thaw out, it is said that from now on the ground is going to continue thawing out because Arctic terns have arrived. When the summer is going to be weak, sometimes you will see that the temperatures are not as warm than normal, so when you see an Arctic tern even when it does not appear to be spring, that meant that the summer was going to be weak; sometimes there was not even an ice breakup.

The divinatory nature of birds played an important part in the traditional Inuit winter feasts as described by Boas (1888: 603ff.). The outcome of the tug-of-war between the ptarmigans and the ducks, the people born in winter and the people born in summer, decided the hunting fortunes of summer and winter. The ptarmigans and the ducks competed with each other and made derisory songs about each other. Thus, birds seem to constitute a suitable medium for the discussion of alliance, competition and transformation.

A tug-of-war might also play a part in the first catch of a bird. Tivi Etok (quoted in Weetaluk and Bryant 2008: 167) from Nunavik discussed his first catch of a ptarmigan:

A boy's first catch of a bird was always torn apart by very excited people. It was ripped apart in celebration of the momentous event. The breast, the thighs, the back, every piece of the ptarmigan that could be separated was torn off. That was our tradition. All members of the families ripped apart the bird. Although my mother and father could not partake. I could, and I did. When a bird was being torn apart someone had to hold the head, and it was always the person who had made his first kill. So I got the ptarmigans head, It was tiny and meatless. The only thing you could do was gnaw at it. … Since it was my first kill, I had to hold the head and our neighbours grabbed whatever there was to grab. They ate every edible part. Any game bird, such as a seagull or a loon,[20] was ripped apart like that. Every first kill was shared that way and always with laughter and joy. Sometimes the tugging came down to two individuals. The person who caught the loon held onto the head and another person held the neck, which was very strong. When two grown men tugged against each other, they could cause one another to lurch forward. Spectators would almost die of laughter. Some were so hysterical that it seemed they were crying.[21]

In mythology birds may become alliance partners of human beings, as in the story of the young woman who married a stormy petrel or fulmar and thus became the sea woman, the mother of the sea game, or in the myth of Kiviuq, who married a goose and made a long journey to recover his wife after she left him. When he finally found her, he entered a hole where the animals were having a songfeast. The raven and the gull were deriding each other (Rasmussen 1931: 371–73):

> The raven's song of derision:
>> You dirty-white gull,
>> Where do you think?
>> You are plumping yourself?
>> You are no match for me,
>> So leave me in peace!
> The gull's reply:
>> When the ice breaks up
>> In the rivers,
>> I take my salmon-leister,
>> And so easy is it
>> To spear salmon!
> Thus the gull mocked the raven, because it cannot catch salmon; but the raven replied:
>> Where do you get to?
>> When the icy cold comes
>> to the one who can endure being out?
>> Turd and scum!
>> Nothing impossible
>> To the one who can!
> The gull could not reply to that, and so the raven had won. When the feast was over Kivioq went home with his wife.

The song shows how the two birds competed in a songfeast, just as human beings do.

Even though Kiviuq recovered his wife, alliance relations between human beings and birds usually did not last. However, a temporary transformation of a human being into a raven might save a marriage, as in a story of a woman who became a raven (Boas 1901: 303–4):

> The husband of a woman named Peqaq was angry with her. She left her home and went away, walking on the ice and weeping bitterly. Her husband followed her on his sledge; and when she saw him, she said, 'Oh that I might become a raven!' She was turned into a raven, and flew to the top of an iceberg. Her husband drove along by the side of the iceberg, but, since he did not see his wife, he returned home. As soon as the man had returned home, the raven flew away, and in the evening alighted on a rock near Niutang. The people were surprised, and said to each other, 'What is that on top of the rock? Is it the moon?' – 'No', said some, 'it is a man.' Now these people went to sleep, and while they were asleep the raven came down. She peeped through a hole in a tent and saw a man in the rear. She thought, 'Oh that he might come out and ease himself!' She

had hardly thought so, when the man put on his garments and went out to ease himself. The raven had resumed the shape of a woman; and when he saw her, he took her for his wife.

Similarly, the relations between different birds as spouses usually did not work out either. Rasmussen (1930: 86) presents a story about a snow bunting who is courted by an owl but rejects her suitor.

Although all animals may figure as potential spouses for human beings, birds appear to have a special position in this respect. Especially in the context of ritual, where different groups or genders compete, people often represented birds. Sometimes this representation of birds was related to the use of the little bird skin that was used to wipe the newborn clean. Rasmussen (1929: 171) relates, 'A newly born infant is cleansed by being wiped all over with the skin of a sarvaq, a small snipe; water must not be used.' With respect to the Nattilingmiut, Rasmussen (1931: 259) states, 'As soon as a child has been born its whole body is wiped with the skin of an eider duck, snipe, or with a piece of the skin of a wolverine, caribou, bear or musk ox.'

The bird skin was an important amulet, and at specific ritual feasts concerned with the competition for women and meat, a man might identify with the bird whose skin he had been cleaned with as a newborn infant. In a description of the winter feast, Captain Mutch (quoted in Boas 1901: 140) relates,

> On this day all the people have attached to their hoods a piece of skin (koukparmiu'-tang) of the animal which their mothers used when cleaning them when they were born. The skins of ptarmigan, golden plover, Stercorarius sp., goose, owl, and others are used for this purpose. If they should not wear this piece of skin, they would be subject to sickness; and severe punishment would be inflicted upon them if they should wear the skin of any other kind of animal. Their souls would become light, and would leave the body. It is said, that if they wear this piece of skin, they are 'made new'

A person might even transform into a bird in a shamanic context. Pisuk (quoted in Kolb and Law 2001: 142–43) related how two *angak-kuit* transformed into an *ukpigjuaq,* a big owl, and a *naujaa,* a seagull, and competed with each other.

Thus, birds appear to be a category with which human beings can easily identify in the context of ritual, shamanism or on the level of the *tarniq.* This identification also seems to be important in the context of rituals pertaining to alliance and sexual competition.

### *The Raven as a Husband and Suitor*

The raven is an apt subject for the topic of alliance, as ravens often live in couples (see Parry 1824: 177). Yet the raven is often depicted as an unfaithful or incompetent husband. A story related by B. Ivarluk (quoted in Métayer 1973: 707–10) depicts him as an unfaithful husband:

A raven and his wife had two children. He was a good provider and never came back from a hunting trip with an empty bag. He got sick and died asking that his bow, quiver and tool-kit be put in his grave. His wife brought his body halfway up a cliff. It was hard work, and while she was pulling, she farted. The two children said, 'Daddy nearly laughed ... how come a dead man can laugh?' The children were acting silly!

Later on, while they were gathering berries to eat, a red fox came towards them. 'What are you doing?' he asked. 'We have nobody now to hunt fox for us', the woman answered. 'Your husband is not dead: he took a seagull for a wife', declared the fox.

The real wife got mad, left her children behind and started searching for the seagull and finally found her house. She went in and offered to clean her ears by taking out the wax but she pierced them right through and killed her.

She placed the body up outside as though it was looking at a returning hunter and put a mitt full of lice in the bed.

Soon a raven came in sight; he was dragging a seal on the ice and called out to the seagull for help. As she did not move, he pushed her on the back and she fell down on her face. Inside the house, everything was full of lice. He was itching all over even when he was in his bed. He cried loudly, put his pants on and went out. But he had put them the wrong way round and was always tripping on his tail. He fell head first at every step he made.

Rasmussen (1929: 280–81) related a story by Ivaluardjuk of a raven who married two geese. It emphasizes the contrast between water and land (see also stories depicting a raven and a loon) as well as between migratory (geese) and non-migratory birds (ravens). The geese advised the raven not to come with them on their migratory route, because they were afraid he could not make it:

But the raven was so fond of its wives that it would not part from them, and when the day came for them to set out, it went with them. Off they flew towards the south. Soon the wild geese were so far ahead of the raven that it could not see them at all, then again it could just make out where they were. Sometimes they flew away from him, sometimes he would overtake them a little, and when at last the wild geese grew tired and sat down on the surface of the sea to rest, the raven managed to come up with them, but had to keep hovering in the air above them, and could not get any rest itself. As soon as the geese had rested, they went on again. The raven followed after. Then again the wild geese grew tired and sat down on the water to rest, and once more the raven hovered in the air above them. As soon as the wild geese had rested sufficiently, they flew on again. This happened four times; four times they sat down on the water to rest, and four times they flew on again when they had rested enough. Then, when they settled down on the water for the fifth time, the raven had grown so tired that it could do no more, and said to its wives:

'Wives, place yourselves close together.'

And the wives placed themselves close together on the water, and the raven sat on top of them. But it was afraid of the water, and kept on saying:

'Dear wives do keep close together.'

After a short rest, they flew on again, and when the wild geese once more wanted to rest, they did as before; the raven's two wives placed themselves close together, and the raven sat down on top of them. But it clutched at their necks so hard that all the feathers were worn away. Their brothers noticed it, and were afraid their sisters might freeze to death if they lost their feathers, so they said to them later on, when the raven had dropped behind and was far away:

'Next time he comes and begs you to sit close together so that he can sit on top of you, wait till he has settled himself comfortably and then swim suddenly apart.'

It was not long before the raven came, and cried pitifully to his wives:

'Place yourselves close together, wives, place yourselves close together.'

And the wild geese placed themselves close together, but the moment the raven sat down on them, they suddenly swam apart, and the raven fell into the sea. It called after the wild geese in despair:

'Oh, come and help me, come and hold my chest above water.' But, no one heeded the raven's words, and so it was left behind far out at sea.

Rasmussen (1931: 400–1) also collected a Nattilik version of the story by Manelaq that ends with a dialogue between the raven and his wife:

The raven fell into the water and at once began to sink. And while it sank deeper and deeper into the sea, people say, he and his wife talked:

The snow goose: 'Where does it reach you now?'
The raven: 'Right to my feet!'
The snow goose: 'Where does it reach you now?'
The raven: 'Right to my ankles!'

The dialogue continued as the raven sank deeper and deeper. Finally,

The snow goose: 'Where does it reach you now?'
The raven: 'Right to my mouth!'
Bubble! Bubble! Splash! And the raven sank to the bottom and drowned.

This type of dialogue is a recurrent feature of raven stories.[22] The contrast between the water and the raven is often seen in the raven complex.[23] Randa (1994: 316) relates that if storms prevent the hunting of sea mammals, a raven is killed and thrown into the sea. As the raven cannot land on water, the sea will become smooth. A tradition related by Pitseolak (quoted in Pitseolak and Eber 1993: 119) also evoked such a procedure:

> When I was growing up I also heard that when the weather was very, very bad in the summertime and the waters were rough for many days, the men would go looking for a raven. They would hope for a raven that was very, very fat ... a raven with a lot of fat in the stomach. That was the best. They took the fat and pounded it with a rock. Then they threw the fat into the sea and hoped for calm waters.

A similar procedure is followed if one wishes to speed up the formation of the floe edge (Randa 1994: 316). One may also mix fat taken from the intestines of a raven with part of the crop from a ptarmigan (*aqiggiq*) and throw the mixture into the water. Drowning a raven, however, may have serious repercussions. In a course at Nunavut Arctic College, Aalasi related an interesting example to the students:

> There was another man who caught a raven in a trap. He tied a rock onto its claw, put it in a bag, and put it in the water. The man who did that was mentally deranged for approximately a year. All he could talk about were the claws. That is all he saw. ...
>
> We were also advised never to put land animal bones into the water. God created the animals and we have to dispose of them properly. Our parents taught us to treat animals with respect as they were given to us for food. That raven sought revenge towards the man who had put him in the sea. (quoted in Therrien and Laugrand 2001: 240–41).

Thus, the raven belongs to the land. He often eats carcasses of caribou, ptarmigan and other land animals. All attempts to ally himself with birds associated with water are bound to fail, either by his own incompetence, as with the geese, or by his wife when he starts an affair with a sea gull.

## Nunagiqsaqtut

The raven can make marriage alliances and break them. A widespread myth related that a man married a fox in human appearance. When the raven wanted to exchange wives with him, he told him not to make any reference to the foxy smell of the woman. Of course, the raven did not heed the warning, and as a consequence the woman changed into a fox again (Boas 1901: 225–26).[24] Thus, because of the raven's actions the man lost his wife.

A man with a raven mask played the role of a matchmaker in the Inuit winter feasts in South Baffin. Here the Sedna feast was celebrated each year in the late fall. It varied in different areas, but one of its main recurrent features was the pairing of married men and women that had to spend the night with another partner than their spouse. The missionaries took great offence at it. Substantial information on this feast was provided by Boas (1888, 1901, 1907). Already at the end of the nineteenth century the feast was declining, and it probably disappeared completely at the beginning of the twentieth century, when it was replaced by Christmas. The Anglican missionary Julian Bilby was probably one of the last to witness a celebration of the feast, which he described vividly in various publications. The pairing of men and women was usually done by two masked shamans, one of them representing a raven, the other one cross-dressed as a big woman.

Bilby (1926: 37) described how he saw the pair coming out of the tent of Sukkenuk, one of the shamans performing in the ritual:

> The minor conjurer had dressed himself to resemble a raven. He wore a tight coat and trousers, and had fastened sticks to his feet to represent the feet of a bird. A close-fitting cap was drawn low down and furnished with a long peak as a bird's bill, and in his hand he carried a short whip. Sukkenuk was even more awe-inspiring. His face was covered with a mask with the usual tattoo marks. His body was clothed in a woman's loose jacket tied round the waist, and his legs were encased in loose trousers and his feet in very large boots. Fastened to his shoulder was a sealskin float filled with water, with a line attached. In his right hand he carried a walrus-spear as representing a man, and in his left a skin scraper to indicate a woman. These two beings shambled and hopped up and down between the human lines, the Raven indicating with his whip, according to previous arrangement, a man and a woman alternately. The couple immediately paired off, and advancing to the chief conjurer drank of the water and received his benediction; then, with cries of joy, they went to their tents, playfully pursued by the Raven. And so the ceremony continued until all had been paired off, and then the conjurers returned to their own tents to examine their gains at leisure, and feel grateful or otherwise towards the donors. Sounds of mirth and song came from every tent, except Seorak's, until late at night.

Apparently the raven played a crucial role in the ritual in connecting the pairs. An important feature of the feast is that the two *angakkuit*, as well as the other participants, attempted to make the pairs laugh. If they did so, their lives would be short. Therefore, they had to control themselves. The raven thus plays a central role in the feast in creating temporary sexual relationships that benefit society.[25]

During the Sedna feast performed in South Baffin, a special category of shamans referred to as *nunagisaktut* performed in raven dress. Bilby (1923: 222; see also Laugrand et al. 2006) related,

> He dresses himself up in a medley of garments and dons a close-fitting cap made from the skull of a ground seal. This cap has a peak, to represent a bird's bill. He binds upon his feet some of the sticks used for beating snow from clothes, so that they resemble a raven's, and hops about in imitation of that bird. As often as the people come up and accuse themselves of wrongdoing, he betakes himself to the beach, to tell Sedna, and returns with forgiveness.

The late Aksaajuq Etuangat mentions that this ritual was performed to provide a good hunting area to the Inuit hunters:

> *Nunagiqsaqtuq* is when the shamans would try to perform a ritual in order that people in the land and in the camps could have good weather and good hunting area. They would try to make the area nice for the hunters so that people could get food. When food and animals were needed and when they would get it, they would also perform *nunagiqsaqtuq*. (Laugrand 1997)

A similar explanation was given by Kappianaq from Iglulik with respect to the Tivajuut feast celebrated in the North Baffin area (McDonald 1998: 40).[26] Thus, the *nunagiqsaqtut* prepared the land by taking the confessions of the people and conveying them to the sea woman. In doing so they placed the imprints of the raven claws on the land with their feet. The raven prepares the land for hunting.

Petitot (1981: 155–56) provided an interesting description of a man imitating a raven:

> He (Kreyouktark) stood up in his umiak, having turned his kayak over to his son Manark. He took his drum and entertained us first with an Eskimo boat song, the rhythm of which the women followed with the strokes of their oars.
>
> Then he passed on to a singular theatrical performance in which he imitated the stance, the hops, the bizarre contortions, wing beats, even the calls, of a raven, to perfection. He was so comical we had to hold our sides laughing. The song that went with this fitted the dance. It sounded like a raven being answered by others. Indeed the Eskimo language lends itself to this because of the frequency of the dipthongs *kra* and *ark*.
>
> Seeing himself admired and applauded, master raven shed his plumage and changed his song. With admirable ease and perfect mimicry, he varied the theme of his dance to represent a white whale hunt or that for

the much larger bowhead whale. Though I had never seen one of these hunts, I could easily recognize his representation, the approach of the kayak, throwing the harpoon, the movements of the wounded whale, his blood-stained blowings.

The performance may well have referred to the preparation for whale hunting.[27] In that case it would follow the pattern that the raven plays a central part in the rituals preparing the hunting season. By transforming themselves into ravens, *angakkuit* acquired their power to clean the land.

### Tattoos, Kakiniit

Manêlaq told Rasmussen (1931: 399) the story of the raven and the loon who tattooed each other:

> In times gone by the raven and the loon lived in human form, and so one day they agreed to tattoo each other. The loon was to be tattooed first and all the fine little patterns of its plumage (*kukualarniuit*, actually: the little fire sparks) are the tattooings that the raven gave it. But then the raven became impatient and took a handful of ashes and threw them over the loon. That is why its back is grey. At this the loon became furious and gathered the soot from its cooking pot and threw it all at the raven, with the result that its whole body became black. Before that time, it is said, all ravens were white.

This myth exists in many versions (see Kleivan 1971; Hawkes 1916: 160). In several versions it is related that the raven threw an object such as a drip pot (Spalding 1979: 78) or firestones (Rasmussen 1929: 278–79) on the loon (see also Rasmussen 1930: 87). Since that time the loon cannot walk properly. In a variant published by Boas (1901: 220–21),[28] the owl and the raven were the main protagonists. All versions emphasize that the raven is unable to sit still and continually hops from one foot to the other. His mobility and agility contrast with the awkwardness of the loon. Kleivan also (1971: 34–37) emphasizes the contrast between land (raven) and water (loon) in her analysis. Various oppositions are at play. The cry of the raven is associated with light, whereas the cry of the loon is associated with laughter. Kleivan also contrasts the sound of a weeping child with the cry of a human being. The raven acquired gleaming eyes when the loon threw soot at it (see Kleivan 1971: 34), whereas the loon's eyes are swollen from crying (Kleivan 1971: 36). The story may be an origin myth for the practice of tattooing.

The practice of tattooing women when they began to menstruate disappeared in the beginning of the twentieth century[29] but was still quite strong in the middle of the nineteenth century. Hall (1864: 523) reported,

> The women, generally, are tattooed on the forehead, cheeks, and chin. This is usually a mark of the married women, though unmarried ones are sometimes seen thus ornamented. This tattooing is done from principle, the theory being that the lines thus made will be regarded in the next world as a sign of goodness. The manner of the operation is simple. A piece of reindeer-sinew thread is blackened with soot, and is then drawn under and through the skin by means of a needle. The thread is only used as a means of introducing the colour or pigment under the epidermis.

Boas (1888: 561) related that the women were tattooed when they were about twelve years of age. Tattoos were mainly inserted on the face, the arms and the legs. The hands of women were extensively tattooed with the exception of the fingers. Horizontal lines seem to separate the fingers from the hands and the hand from the arm. In a drawing of the tattoos of Pakak, two lines marked the first joints of the fingers. Thus, the tattoos may well have referred to the origin narrative of the sea woman and may have been intended to be seen by the sea woman as well as the game animals. The meaning of most of the designs is not known.

A marked feature of the raven complex in the western Arctic is his representation in marks and tattoos. E. Nelson (1899: 324) relates, 'The raven totem or mark is represented by an etched outline of the bird's foot and leg, forming a tridentate' and he provides a figure (see figure 4.2).

The mark was used on objects as well as bodies. E. Nelson (1899: 324–25) related, 'At East cape, Siberia, I saw numerous arrow- and spear-heads of bone or ivory bearing the raven mark, and the same mark was seen tattooed on the forehead of a boy at Plover bay.' He (E. Nelson 1899: 325, fig. 115) explained that these marks were 'frequently seen on carvings, weapons, and implements of almost every description. On clothing or wooden utensils it may be marked with paint.'

Thalbitzer (1914b: 630) observed, 'The mark of proprietorship in Alaska – the three-forked figure known as the raven totem – seems to be found again in the Y-shaped patterns for ornamentation (on bone implements, e.g., needle-cases) and in the patterns for tattooing of the Hud-

**Figure 4.2.** Raven's print. *Source:* E. Nelson 1899: 324.

son Bay Eskimos.' The three-forked raven foot may have represented the imprint of the raven foot on the skin of the woman. This mark is quite clear on Atuat Ittukusuk's body, a woman from Iglulik who was famous for her tattoos. Atuat explained that tattooing 'was not exactly painful but it felt like your skin was burning' (D'Argencourt 1977: 58, 61). The practice may have served a similar purpose as the imprint of the raven foot on the land: preparing a woman for the reproduction of children, analogous to the preparation of the land for hunting.

Today, Inuit elders remember the practice well. Tattooing was closely associated with sewing (D'Argencourt 1977: 61). Arnatsiaq (IE 258) related,

> They would make the tattoo just as they would when they are sewing. They would pierce the skin with a needle and run the thread just below the skin leaving the soot in the skin. They would use some fat with the soot. Some tattoos came out very clearly which were applied just beneath the skin, those that were deeper did not come out as clearly.

Panikpakuttuk (IE 227) described the process of tattooing in detail:

> The main reason was for them to be beautiful, to show that they were women. They would use soot to mark the skin. ... They endured pain just to become beautiful. It is said that the area at *qipaluk* [corner of eye] hurt the most. ... The only reason why they used tattoos was because they wanted to show that they were women and wanted to be beautiful. They would only get tattoos when they became adults. Part of the designs ran along the jaws and the end was formed like an arrowhead, the one that ran on the chin was called *talluruti,* the one that ran across the jaw was called *agliruruti.*

Tattoos appear to have provided women with beauty and protection, 'signs to show that you are becoming a woman', as Atuat pointed out (D'Argencourt 1977: 58). According to Rasmussen (1929: 148), the Iglulingmiut attached great significance to tattooing, especially in the past, 'for the woman who had handsome tattooing always got on well with Nuliajuk when, after life on earth, she passed her house on the way to the land of the dead'. The fact that a special land of the dead existed for lazy hunters and women who were not tattooed (Rasmussen 1931: 316) suggests strong cosmological sanctions for people who failed in their most important roles.

The raven and the moon spirit were not tattooed, but were instead covered with soot, the raven because he was impatient and could not sit still, the moon spirit because of an incestuous relationship with his sister. The marking of the moon by the sun is also a recurrent theme in Native American mythology. In some Native American myths (e.g., among the Arekuna), it was related that the moon spirit was marked with red paint or menstruation blood (see Kretschmar 1938. Vol. 1: 178). This would make sense, as the periodicity of the moon is connected to that of the menses. In a version of the myth of sun and moon from the Lower Yukon reported by E. Nelson (1899: 482), the waxing and waning of the moon is explained:

> The girl then became the sun and the boy became the moon and ever since that time he pursues but never overtakes her. At night the sun sinks in the west and the moon is seen coming up in the east to go circling after, but always too late. The moon being without food, wanes slowly away from starvation until it is quite lost from sight; then the sun reaches out and feeds it from the dish in which the girl had placed her breast. After the moon is fed and gradually brought to the full it is then permitted to starve again, so producing the waxing and waning every month.

Thus, a relation between menstruation blood and soot may exist, and the periodicity of the moon may be a consequence of the marking he received from his sister. A young woman is tattooed when she starts to menstruate, complementing the internal process with an external marking.[30]

Soot is the final product of the lamp, considered a representation of the sun by Saladin d'Anglure (2006: 131), which is managed by the women. He interprets the process of tattooing as a symbolic cooking effected by the soot introduced under the skin. However, successful hunters also wore tattoos, and some tattoos were related to the killing of a man. A *kigjugaq* was a tattoo mark between the eyes worn by someone who had killed a human being. It would act as a protection against *ijirait* (Saladin d'Anglure 2001: 60–62, 240).

Thus, tattoos marked a transition or a transformation and provided protection, but more research is needed to explore the full range of meanings of tattooing in the Canadian Arctic. The raven, a master of light, is continuously associated with final products such as soot, excrement, inedible food and human bones. The marking with soot seems to refer to non-social behaviour, whereas tattooing marks the cultural transition of a young woman to womanhood, or a young man to a killer of men and/or *ijirait*. In tattooing itself a connection is suggested to the raven as a master of time and transformation.

According to Hawkes (1916: 108), the fact that the trifurcated line, 'the raven's foot' of E. Nelson (1899), was also found on an old woman from Nachvak indicates that the raven could also be a suitable candidate to help humans in protecting themselves against non-human beings. 'A story which the old woman mentioned above told me in connexion with this mark throws some light on its possible origin. She said that whenever an Eskimo approached the abode of Torngarsoak, "the great Torngak", who lives in a cave in the high mountains near Cape Chidley, one hung upon one's breast a raven's claw for protection.' And Hawkes (1916: 108) concludes, 'This may have led to the adoption of the "raven's foot" mark as a constant protection against the Tornait.' The fact that the raven himself is marked by soot underlines his ambiguous position. He is not just a master of periodicity, but is also subjected to it.

## Discussion

In the eastern Arctic the raven shares many features with his counterpart in the western Arctic. He is not a cultural hero who created mankind as well as the cultural and social organization of the world, but he is still considered the creator of light. In the eastern Arctic light is valued as a condition for hunting. Rasmussen relates that in a distant past when the earth was still dark the ancestors could hunt by making light with their fingers. Light also played an important part in the shamanic complex as *qaumaniq*, the shamanic light and visions that enabled a shaman to see what was hidden. *Qaumaniq* implied true vision and knowledge, and the relation between light and knowledge is still emphasized in modern concepts such as *qaujimajatuqangit*, 'traditional knowledge that is still useful today'. According to Peck's *tuurngait* list, the raven could bring the shamanic light, but it is by no means exclusively connected to him. A third form of light is provided by the *qulliq*, the lamp that lit the igloo and often seems to be connected to the *tarniq*, the small miniature image of a being that could be hidden in the lamp. The raven is not directly associated with the *qulliq*, but he is covered with the soot produced by the lamp. The raven thus appears to encompass the beginning of light and the end product of the lamp, just as he encompasses day and night by setting up their alternation. The raven may bring the light, but he cannot be identified with it. Neither can he be identified with knowledge. He may have *isuma*, intelligence, but just as his counterpart in the western Arctic, he appears as very shrewd in some tales and very stupid in others. In that respect his intelligence appears to be closely associated with his capacity to see and find meat caches.

The masked raven plays a central part in the western Arctic. The raven can transform himself by taking off or putting on his mask. In the eastern Arctic we find the masked raven in the Sedna feast, either as the masked dancer creating pairs of men and women or as the *nunagiqsaq-tut* who cleanse the land and leave the imprints of the raven on it. The motif of the raven claw as a tattoo, which is also known from Alaska, at least suggests an analogy with the raven imprints on the land. The imprints of the raven claws cleanse the land and the women and prepare them for hunting and childbirth. The question of to what extent the tattoo itself represents a mask protecting women from non-human beings can be raised. The raven is effectively involved in crucial temporal transitions: the annual renewal of the land for hunting and the transition of a girl into a young woman. Meletinsky (1973, 1980) emphasized the temporal dimensions of the Asian raven myths. He was not a migratory bird, and his temporary alliances with migratory birds such as the geese failed miserably. Temporal dimensions were also acknowledged in Greenland: 'Whenever they believe that something they are waiting for will not happen within reasonable time they use the expression: "when the raven gets white" (tulugkat qaqortigpata)' (Kleivan 1971: 38). Thus, the whiteness of the raven is at the beginning and at end of time and encompasses his blackness, associated with the tattooing of women. He also plays an important part in another process of transition: the birth and development of the hunter. Raven *aarnguat* were worn by mothers on behalf of their sons and by young boys to protect them and make them into good hunters. *Aarnguat* established lasting relations between the boys and the raven, who could come to protect them in times of need. *Irinaliutiit*, powerful words, derived from the raven also gave protection and strength.

The raven's role in the Sedna feast highlights his complex position. Incapable of a social alliance or marriage himself, he initiates the asocial relations between temporary non-married partners that allow society to establish good connections with the sea game and the sea woman. In many respects he is responsible for society without being part of it. This position reflects contemporary conceptions of the bird: the raven is still living in Inuit society without being part of it. He can only be a predator and a scavenger, eating dirt, excrement and human flesh. And yet he created light, enabling people to see, and invented the art of tattooing that transforms girls into nubile young women.

## Notes

1. On the raven, see Charrin (1983) and Mathieu (1984a).

2. See, e.g., Swanton (1909) for the Tlingit and Bogoras (1904, 1913) for the Siberian people.
3. See R. Nelson (1983: 80) for the Koyukon people.
4. See Oosten and Laugrand (2006) for a more extensive discussion of Alaskan traditions.
5. Tullorealik is 'like a small bear, very long teeth, lives upon seals'; Tulloreak is 'like a man, large canine teeth like a bear (so-called *tulloreak*)'. Both are listed in Peck's list of *tuurngait* (quoted in Laugrand et al. 2006: 421).
6. See the various examples provided by Qalasiq and Pisuk in Rankin (personal interviews) as well as Sonne (1982: 28).
7. Mary-Rousselière, Okomaluk: Tape VI, no. 2, min. 33–36, Tape VII, no. 1, min. 1–5.
8. Many stories describe the origin of the ptarmigan. Mary-Rousselière collected a variant of this myth from William Ukkumaaluk from Iglulik. It relates how a child transformed into a ptarmigan when it was tickled too much (see Laugrand and Oosten 2010: 95–96).
9. The story describes extensively the life among the seals, constituting an interesting variation on the seal boy myth discussed by Fienup-Riordan and Mary Meade (1994) among the Yuit.
10. See also Boas (1907: 133): 'When a person becomes an angakok, a light covers his body. He can see supernatural things. The stronger the light is within him, the deeper and farther away he can see, and the greater is his supernatural power.'
11. Also known as Tugtut Igfianut.
12. Ravens appear to have been effective helping spirits. Annie Kilabuck from South Baffin made a tapestry that depicts a raven frightening sea spirits that might attack human beings (Von Finckenstein 2002: 110–11).
13. In an Alaskan version of this myth (E. Nelson 1899: 475–79), the young man refused the exchange and died as a consequence.
14. On the revenge of a raven, see also Piugaattuq (IE 009).
15. See also Rasmussen (1931: 416).
16. Rasmussen (1931: 266) states, 'There are many examples of the fact that there is not much difference between man and animals, and that the animals, perhaps as a memory of the time when they were sometimes animals, sometimes humans, have to keep quite the same taboos as humans.'
17. See also Rasmussen (1929: 265–66).
18. Ravens and gulls are often paired. Rasmussen (1929: 265) refers to villages of ravens and gulls. Rasmussen (1929: 175) reports that the first clothes of a new-born child should be placed 'either in a raven's nest or in a gull's nest, or out on a small island in a stream.' Rasmussen (1931: 257) noted, 'Only the great gulls and the great ravens eat humans.'
19. For the importance of the loon in dance and ceremonial clothing among the Copper, see Driscoll-Engelstad (2005: 44). She connects the return of the loon to the renewal and regeneration of life.
20. The *qaqsauq* (the red-throated loon) was used in Nunavik for healing and in conversion rituals (Laugrand 2002).
21. See also Naalak Nappaaluk, Kangiqsujuaq, 2006 in Pernet (2013). In an interesting myth recorded by Rasmussen (1929: 278–79) from Ivaluardjuk,

we find the theme of the tearing apart of an owl: 'An owl was out hunting one day when it caught sight of two hares sitting close together. The owl came down on the hares from above, gliding down slowly and noiselessly on its wings, and when it was just over them, it grabbed at them both at once. The hares leapt up in a fright and ran opposite ways, but the owl had got its claws fixed in their flesh and could not get them out again. And such was the strength of the hares that they tore both thighs from the owl as they ran their different ways, and the thighs went with them as they ran away. So it came about that the owl caused its own death.'

22. See also the dialogue between the raven father and son in Boas (1901: 301–2).

23. Lévi-Strauss (1971: 201) identifies the raven as always thirsty in North American mythology. Among the Inuit of the eastern Arctic such a feature is not marked.

24. See also Rasmussen (1929: 223). Father Guy Mary-Rousselière also collected a variant of this story from William Ukkumaaluk from Iglulik (see Laugrand and Oosten 2009: 235–38).

25. In Greenland, some shamanic performances also implied raven symbolism. Freuchen (1935b: 135) describes such a séance: 'Krisuk, went out of his head. Unable to contain himself to the regular rhythm of the service he leapt to his feet, crying like a raven and howling like a wolf. He ran amuck, and the audience had to defend itself against his attacks.' The combination of wolf and raven can also be found in a game described by Jenness (1922: 217–18): 'Similar to our "tag" are the games of "wolf" and "raven". One child is made the hunter; the others run off, flapping their arms and croaking like ravens or leaping and howling like wolves. Whoever is caught first then becomes the hunter. Adults as well as children sometimes play this game, especially at halts during a migration, when exercise is needed to keep up the circulation of the blood.'

26. See Laugrand et al. (2006) and Laugrand and Oosten (2010) for extensive discussions of the winter feasts and their transformations in Inuit society.

27. Soby (1970: 49) reports that raven amulets are good to be used on boats.

28. See also Boas (1988), Kroeber (1899: 174) and Von Finckenstein (2002: 106).

29. A new interest in tattooing can be observed among Inuit women. Recently Alethea Arnaquq-Baril from South Baffin and Aaju Peter from Iqaluit (originally from Greenland) decided to tattoo their face in the old tradition.

30. The timing was important. Atuat related, 'Angutiannuk said to me: "My sister-in law, get yourself tattooed, because girls without tattoos look like men. Do it!" But, at the same time, I was being told by another person that I was not allowed to be tattooed. Somebody had caught a bearded seal at that time, and I was told it was a taboo for a young girl like me to be tattooed' (D'Argencourt 1977: 60). The prohibition to tattoo when game was caught may be connected to similar rules applying to menstruating women.

CHAPTER 5

# *Qupirruit,* Masters of Life and Death

The life of small beings such as the *qupirruit* (insects and other small life-forms) has not received the attention it deserves. Biologists acknowledge that the insect fauna of the Arctic regions is not yet adequately surveyed. Yet, more than 2,200 species of insects and their relatives have been reported from north of the tree line in North America, and many more probably remain to be discovered (Danks 2004: 85).

An excellent paper by Vladimir Randa (2003) in a book devoted to the place of insects in different cultures is probably the only substantial contribution that can be found on the subject. Randa rightly argues that the concept of *qupirruit* is much broader than that of insects, since it encompasses quite a range of subcategories, including some crustaceans, spiders and worms. Randa (2003: 453) conducted extensive fieldwork in Iglulik and published a preliminary list of the various species that fall under the *qupirruit* category (see table 5.1).

The notion of *qupirruit* as used by the Inuit does not constitute a clearly defined zoological category. Louis-Jacques Dorais (personal communication, 4 April 2007) pointed out that, for instance, a crocodile is referred to as a *qupirrualuk,* big insect, by the Inuit of Ungava Bay (except in Kuujjuaq) and Kuujjuaraapik. According to the Schneider Inuktitut-English dictionary (1993: 238), *pamiulik,* 'has a tail', refers to a crocodile in Kangiqsujuaq and to some species of water insects in Kuujjuaq. An account by Kunnuk (IE 093) about a place named Qupirurtuuq, 'place of plenty of bugs or snakes', shows the connection between snakes and insects. 'I am not certain as to why it is called by that name but … it is said that the river used to have snakes but I am not exactly certain, and the land around the river usually has all kinds of little bugs or insects.'

**Table 5.1.** Randa's (2003) list of *qupirruit* known by Inuit in Iglulik.

| Inuktitut Name | Latin Name | English Name |
|---|---|---|
| *Kikturiaq* | *Aedes sp* | Mosquito |
| *Tagiut* | *Cephenemyia trompe* | Worm infesting nostrils of caribou |
| *Kumak* | *Oedemagena tarandi* | Louse |
| *Milugiaq* | *Tabanidae sp* or *Syrphidae sp* | Black fly |
| *Ananngiq* | *Calliphora sp* or *Empididae sp* | Dung fly, house fly |
| *Tuktuujaaq* or *tukturjuk* | *Tipulidae sp* | Long-legged, long-winged water fly |
| *Iguptaq* or *iguttaq* | *Bombus sp* | Bee, Arctic honey bee |
| *Tarralikitaaq* or *tarralikisaq* | *Boloria sp* | Butterfly, moth |
| *Kumak, kumait* | *Pediculus sp* | Louse, lice |
| *Minnguq* | *Pterostichus sp* or *Amara sp* | Land beetle |
| *Tulugarnaq* | *Dytiscus* | Diving beetle |
| *Aasivak* | *Alopecosa asivak* | Spider |
| *Ulikapaaq* or *ulikappaalik* | *Lepidurus arcticus* | Kind of shrimp |
| *Kinguk* | *Gammarus locusta?* | Sea louse, shrimp |

*Source:* Randa (2003), with additional details from Spalding (1998).

Inuit concepts and perceptions of *qupirruit* do not aim at the construction of a zoological system but at the construction of a meaningful symbolical system encompassing land and sea animals. Thus, *putjuuti*, the crab, is referred to as the spider of the sea (Schneider 1993: 273). Similarly, a bumblebee exists on the land as well as in the sea.

In this chapter we will examine the symbolism of these small animals, which are often thought to transform into each other in narratives. We show how the fear of these animals is embedded in a cosmological framework. These small animals are masters of life and death and control the transformations from life to death and vice versa.

We first deal with Inuit perceptions of insects, their role as *tuurngait* and their use in *aarnguat,* amulets. Then we examine their role in the Kiviuq stories in which many distinctive features of *qupirruit* come to the fore. Next we move to a more detailed analysis of various kinds of *qupirruit.* In the final part we identify some structural patterns in the perceptions of *qupirruit.*

# Inuit Perceptions of *Qupirruit*

## *Agents of Revival and Rejuvenation*

Insects are a very visible feature of Arctic animal life, especially in the summer, when the tundra is swarming with mosquitoes. They also play an important part in cosmology, especially in the context of shamanism. Thus, the caribou are referred to as *kumarjuait,* the lice of the earth, in the language of the spirits and the shamans. But all animals might be referred to as very small beings on a cosmological level. Nutaraaluk from Iqaluit related, 'When the people in the camp were unhappy or abusive towards wildlife, the wildlife used to move away from the camp.... The animals would flee to Sedna's shed where they were so numerous they seemed like maggots. It was because they had gone there that the hunters couldn't catch them anymore. That was when the *angakkuq* had to go and get them' (quoted in Oosten et al. 1999: 190).

Although small, *qupirruita* denote a notion of abundance, and this abundance might also have negative connotations. Franz Boas (1888: 586) reported that the sea woman might withhold the sea mammals from the hunter: 'The reason for thus withholding the supply was that certain filthy obnoxious parasites fastened themselves upon her head, of which she could only be relieved by an angakoq. Then she could be induced again to send out the animals for the benefit of man.' Insects were thought to stop the flow of animals that were essential for the survival of the Inuit.

Another key feature in the symbolism of insects is their survival in winter. According to Randa (2003: 451), Iglulingmiut assume that insects freeze in winter and return to life the following summer. Lizzie and Ollie Itinnuaq from Rankin Inlet provided similar statements in 2008. This capacity of revival is important and may explain the use of insects in *aarnguat,* amulets. Boas (1907: 505) already noted the qualities of insects in this respect:

> Bugs and bees sewed to the under-garment are believed to prolong life. It is said that once upon a time an old woman sewed a number of bugs and bees in her boy's clothing in the belief that, if he should die, he would afterwards come to life, as these animals come to life in spring. The child grew up to be a man, died, and was buried, but in a few days came to life again.

Thus, insects often appear to be masters of life and death. Marc Ijjangiaq from Iglulik related how insects enabled Qamukkaq from Arviligjuaq to come to life again when he was a child:

When he was all alone trying to gather seagull eggs in the springtime he fell down a cliff. This was the time when the shoreline was all ice, as the snow had melted from the sun. He died instantly. No one went out looking for him. He awoke to discover that one side of his face had melted through the ice. Apparently he had been dead for a long time and returned to life. From that time on he had physical disabilities. Had he been with someone else at the time he fell down he would surely have passed away, but because he had insects as amulets he returned to life. (quoted in Bennett and Rowley 2004: 49)

The rejuvenating capacities of insects appear in a South Baffin story published by Boas (1901: 226–27) dealing with a woman and her daughter who were left behind.

The people had left nothing for the women to eat, who gathered insects (Ea-kan) for food. One day while they were out looking for insects, the old woman was attacked by an ermine, which bit her on several parts of her body. Her skin fell off, disclosing a fresh, new skin underneath, such as a much younger person might have. The insects had taken compassion on the poor old woman, and had asked the ermine to bite off the old skin, that she might be rejuvenated. The daughter was grateful to the insects for doing so much for her mother.

After a time the people sent for the two women to come to their new camping-place, but, as they had never sent them any food since they had been away, the women did not go. They went instead to live with the insects, and both took husbands from among them.… The next year the women went to the camping-place where the people had gone. They told them how kind the insects had been to them, – how they had given them food, and had asked them to come and live with them; how the old woman had remarked to them that she should look much better if she could only be made younger-looking, and how they had told an ermine to bite all her old skin, and cause it to fall off.

In this story the women effectively joined the insects, taking a husband among them and living with them. They were rejuvenated, but also ate insects, adopting the non-social and cannibalistic behaviour of insects.

### Small but Powerful

Today, many Inuit elders agree that all small life-forms have to be treated with respect. Kappianaq (IE 330) from Iglulik explained, 'This [small animals] includes insects like house flies, spider or other living things. We used to be told that we should leave these alone, including spiders and other insects and birds.'

Josie Angutinngurniq from Kugaaruk related that despite their size insects are like human beings; they have souls: 'Even insects underground, and things in the water, even small living things, they all have a soul. There is another part of them somewhere. That is why we are not to abuse them. Their souls are very strong. That is why we should not mistreat them' (Arviat workshop, 2003).

Nevertheless, many ethnographers observed that Inuit exhibit a strong distaste for insects. The Oblate missionary Emile Petitot (1981: 123–24), who travelled in the Canadian western Arctic in 1868, observed,

> And these people who fear no man, who mock God and invoke the devil, cry out in alarm when a blue fly stings them or a dragonfly's wing brushes their face. You will then see them pursue the innocent insect to the death and sing out in triumph when they have destroyed it; a burlesque parody of bravery. From the fear betrayed in their faces and the glory which overtakes them when they have killed the paltry insect, one can deduce that they attribute immense malignity and power to these creatures.

Inuit women are particularly sensitive to insects. Petitot (1981: 149) observed,

> While we were having a bit of a siesta, the wind having dropped, she uttered a piercing cry as if a bear or a wolf had leapt on her, and getting up at a bound, she ran off crying out in horror, 'Mana, mana.' 'What is it now?' I asked, 'What is bothering the woman?' 'Illatkroutchitortork' said Krarayalok with ill-concealed fear. Illatkroutchitortork? A name as long as a centipede meaning what? One of the elegant aerial neuroptera which during the summer make war on other insects. Yes, a dragonfly with diaphanous wings like a ray of sunshine, had persisted in circling Aoularena's face to rid her of mosquitoes. She yelled every time its wings brushed her face. She fought with both hands what to her was a new kind of harpy, to which childish superstitions attributed a sinister and malign influence. Gravely superb in his indignation and bravely – Krarayalok got up. He seized his fur parka, pursued the ill-fated insect and did not sit down again until it lay dead at his feet.

Insects are usually not eaten by Inuit except for the *kumak*, a larva living under the skin of the caribou. The fear of insects might be related to a fear of being eaten by them. A painting by Victoria Mamnguqsualuk in the 1980s of a giant insect eating a human being illustrates this fear (see McMaster 2011: 176). Qanguq (IE 144) also emphasized that insects and larvae eat dead corpses. Rasmussen (1931: 316–17) relates that insects may serve as the food of the dead who did not fulfil their social roles adequately:

The other land where the dead go to is called nuqum·iut, and it means: those who always sit huddled up with hanging head. Their land is quite near to the crust of earth we walk on, almost just under the surface of the earth (nunap atätqä·uane). There go all the men who were lazy, all those who are bad hunters because they are too indolent to hunt, and there go all the women who are not tattooed, all those women who do not care to suffer a little in order that they may be pretty. There was no energy in them when they lived, and that is why they now, after death, hang their heads and their chins are pressed right down on their breasts. They are always hungry, for their only food is butterflies. They always sit on their haunches with bowed head and closed eyes; only when a butterfly comes flying over them they lift their heads slowly and snap at it, just as young birds open their red mouths after a fly. And when they do, yellow dust flies from their neck bands as from a bursting puff-ball. Thus they always squat down with drooping head.

Thus, those who do not know how to handle life eat insects after death. People fear to consume *qupirruit* or *pamiulik* of the lakes, so they do not drink stagnant water, but boil it first. Apparently, consuming insects implies becoming like dead people or like insects, as in the South Baffin story recorded by Boas.

## Qupirruit *as* Tuurngait

*Qupirruit* also served as *tuurngait,* helping spirits of the shamans. In Peck's list of 347 *tuurngait,* several maggots are described. They are all very swift and ambiguous. Peck describes Puttokãaluk as "a maggot (centipede) that goes quickly and is a good food supplier" (quoted in Laugrand et al. 2006: 441). Qalloaãlik is a land animal, very swift and with legs like a maggot, indicating that it is a bad spirit ('a demon') that does not wish to give but rather desires to kill (Laugrand et al. 2006: 459). Qîlegonyak is described as another maggot that moves very quickly and is considered a good spirit disposed to giving (quoted in Laugrand et al. 2006: 458).

Kupak from Naujaat mentioned various insects among the helping spirits he recalled in 2001: 'Just to name a few *tuurngait: nanujak,* spider; *qukluriak* the caterpillar. Some shamans will have *tuurngait* from the ocean, a worm or a bumblebee from the land.' Pisuk, from Rankin Inlet (quoted in Oosten and Laugrand 2002: 180), also stressed the use of insects as a means to help a person:

A *pisuqsauti* was something that enabled you to do something. My father had a small *niviuvaq,* a dung fly, to help him get home. Three days after we buried him, my brother Aattaaluk was visiting Kanaaq and saw my father knocking on the door. He recognized him through the window. My father had said if he wasn't taken right away, he wasn't going to keep trying. He had told us he was going to go to Kanaaq's, and not to our house. People don't seem to be using *pisuqsautit* any more. In the past, people used to come back. *Tarralikitat*, butterflies, were also used as a means of helping you to come home. Someone would wipe the butterfly on the back of the parka of a young girl or boy. This was different from using house and dung flies.

The size of these small life-forms places them on the same level as the *tarniq*, the miniature image of a being contained in a bubble of air. The *tarniq* was the seat of health and life, and it could be attacked or captured by a shaman. To defend themselves against dangerous spirits, such as *tupilait*, spirits of the dead that had turned against humanity or spirits sent by evil shamans, shamans defended themselves with miniature weapons, *qalugiujait*, attached to their shamanic belts. The *tarniq* and the body represent different levels of reality, contrasting in terms of visibility. Whereas the human body is visible to everyone, the *tarniq*, like the *tuurngait*, can only be seen by the *angakkuit*. The root *tar-*, meaning dark, can also be found in the word *tarralikitaaq*, butterfly. Armand Tagoona from Qamanittuaq said this about his drawing of a butterfly: 'Translation of *tarralikitaaq* is "quickly shadowing". When they fly very near the ground the butterflies can only be seen like shadows on the ground' (Tagoona 1975: plate 21).

The fate of the body depends on the *tarniq*, which will survive at death. The *tarniq* can be destroyed by evil shamans, and if that happens, a person will inevitably die. The shift from one level to another is indicated by a difference in scale. But whereas for the larger life-forms there is a distinction of scale between the level of ordinary life and the miniature level of the *tarniq*, this does not apply to the small life-forms. Their bodies already operate on the level of the *tarniq*. But they can increase in size, and narratives about giant worms or bumblebees play an important part in Inuit oral traditions. Like *angakkuit*, *qupirruit* operate on different levels of reality, connecting them and mediating between them.

### Qupirruit *as* Aarnguat

The problem of scale also applies to *aarnguat*, amulets. Usually only a part of an animal can be integrated into an amulet so that a part/whole logic operates in the functioning of the amulet. But most *qupirruit* can be wholly integrated into an amulet, and often more than one specimen can be contained in one amulet.

Bilby (1923: 233–34) refers to the use of a spider or beetle sewn up in a piece of skin and worn on a boot or breast. The bumblebee, the spider and the fly were often used in amulets. Rasmussen (1931: 43) found in a collection of amulets 'a fly, which gives invulnerability because a fly is difficult to hit, and a water-beetle, which gives strong temples'. Today, many elders remember the use of *qupirruit* as amulets. Julie Hanguhaaq Tuluqtuq from Qamanittuaq recalled that some people used to sew worms onto a piece of clothing or fringes of clothes (quoted in Mannik 1998: 204).[1]

This connection between *qupirruit* and amulets is by no means accidental. An Iglulik myth recorded by Rasmussen (1929: 110–11) explains that before the coming of shamanism, healing was associated with a sea urchin (*itiq*), a small sea animal belonging to the category of the *qupirruit:* 'The first amulet that ever existed was the shell portion of a sea-urchin. It has a hole through it, and is hence called iteq (anus) and the fact of its being made the first amulet was due to its being associated with a particular power of healing.'

The *itiq* clearly connected the level of the human body to the level of the *tarniq*. Indeed, farting played a part in traditional methods of healing (Rasmussen 1929: 111, 182). The anus was the channel through which, on one side, people could break wind, a healing procedure, and, on the other side, through which *qupirruit* might enter the body, a procedure that could easily be fatal, as shown in the Kiviuq stories. The notion of the hole and the anus suggest transition and transformation associated with healing. Rasmussen's report suggests that *qupirruit* were present at the origin of shamanism, as well as of amulets.

### Qupirruit *in the Epic Tradition of Kiviuq, the Great Traveller*

Kiviuq narratives are well-known in the central Arctic. Kiviuq was a hunter who got lost in his kayak in a storm and encountered many non-human beings. Famous stories relate how he escaped from a cannibalistic woman called Ivigtarsuaq, the big bee, and various other dangerous beings, how he married various non-human wives and how he finally returned to his homeland. In a narrative told by Imaruittuq, from Iglulik (quoted in Oosten et al. 1999: 194), it is related how Kiviuq punished his unfaithful wives by filling up his mitts and his slippers with worms.

> When they became full he took a caribou skin that was drying and emptied the worms onto the skin. His wives were there watching and he asked one of them, 'Which is scarier, worms or a harpoon head?' One of the wives replied, 'Since you can squish worms they are not as scary.' He

emptied all the worms from his mitts and slippers onto the skin and told his wives to sit down on the skin after removing their pants. When they tried to sit on the tail flap of their parkas, he cut the flaps off. The worms started crawling inside them. Lemmings started coming out of their mouths. After he became a widower, he went out caribou hunting again.

In a variant of the Kiviuq story presented by Boas (1901: 223–24), the vermin consists of insects such as spiders and beetles. The power to kill through *qupirruit* also played a part in a story by Nakasuk, collected by Rasmussen (1931: 292):

There was once an old woman who asked for water to be brought her. Her daughter-in-law made as if to fetch water for her and brought the old woman her own piss. The old woman was blind, and therefore she was not afraid of her. The old woman took a draught of it and then said to her daughter-in-law: 'Lice or sea scorpions, which of them do you think would tickle your body most?' 'One only has to crush lice, and one can break the back of a sea scorpion' answered her daughter-in-law. This she said, but at the same moment she drew a sea scorpion out of her genitals, and she pulled one sea scorpion out after another until she fell down dead.

A Nattilik version of the Kiviuq story relates how Kiviuq encountered Ivigtarsuaq, the big bee (Rasmussen 1931: 336–67). He entered her house without a roof and saw the sorceress tanning a human skin. She was a cannibal. He escaped with the assistance of his helping spirit, a snow bunting. The big bee pursued him and threw her *ulu* (woman's knife) at him. 'It skidded over the top of the water and finally turned to ice, to an ice floe. People say that all winter ice comes from that troll-woman's ulo; and the sea began to freeze over in winter. Before that there had always been open water.' After Kiviuq had escaped from the big bee, he still had to deal with her helping spirits, who all belonged to the category of *qupirruit*. The first ones were 'two enormous ausiva·luit, two giant caterpillars, that came running on their hairy legs to steal his kayak.' But Kiviuq outran them, reached his kayak and escaped out to sea. Paddling out over the sea, Kiviuq heard a voice behind him warning him about a giant mussel. It was his own helping spirit warning him. He managed to get away from the giant mussel and arrived at a village where two spider women in human form were standing alone while their husbands were out hunting. He stayed with the women and lay with them both and took all their beads from them. 'They had so many beads that they filled both his pualut (mittens) and his pinerqät (short outer kamiks). And both the small spider-women wept.'

The big bumblebee is replaced by a spider woman in a version of the Kiviuq myth recorded by Boas (1901: 193; see also 1888: 264). The spider woman 'took up a knife and cut off one of her eyebrows, and ate it. She continued cleaning the skin while the blood was dripping down. Then she took up some object and drew it across her eyebrow. Suddenly the blood stopped, and the eyebrow looked as though it had never been cut.' Kiviuq wished to enter the house, but the passage was too small for his head. The spider woman told him to open his mouth and then he could enter. When she approached him, he cut off her head. Her body dwindled until she became a spider. 'When he was outside, he looked in at the window again, and saw her the same way as before, cleaning the caribou-skin.' This version of the story emphasizes the capacity of *qupirruit* to come back to life again. Kiviuq managed to survive all his encounters with *qupirruit*.

Boas (1901: 225–26) presents an interesting variant of the Kiviuq narrative. It relates that after the hero had avenged himself on his unfaithful wife, he married a fox in human appearance. He made a wife exchange with a raven, who complained about the smell of the fox woman. She was ashamed and ran away, and Kiviuq went after her. He followed her to a small hole in the stones of an old hut.

> He stamped with his foot over the hole and called her. Although she knew it was her husband calling, she spoke as though addressing her children: 'Go out and see who is there.' Then an insect came out of the hole. When it appeared, the man said to it, 'Smoke is coming out of your head.' In this way quite a number of insects and worms were sent out of the hole, and to each of them he said the same. Finally his wife asked him to come in. She told him to shut his eyes, to turn both sides of his jacket inward, and to come in back-ward. He complied with her instructions, and backed into the fox's hole. When he got inside, he saw a large dog in one corner of the room. It was his wife's son. His wife appeared to him again in human shape as he had known her. The fox's hole seemed to him like a hut. What he believed to be a dog was really a spider.

The usual sequence is that various animals come out and offer themselves as wives to Kiviuq, but he refuses them all. Then he enters the hole, which turns out to be a big house. He witnesses a songfeast celebrated by animals (see chapter 4 of this book), and recovers his wife (see, e.g., Rasmussen 1931: 372–73). In the story presented by Boas (1901: 225–26), the insects do not offer themselves as wives, but the hero still sends them away, referring to the smoke coming out of their head. He is probably referring to the *pujuq*, the vapour unclean women were thought to emanate during their menstruation.

The whole setting suggests a shift of scale: the hero would have to become very small to enter the hole. This shift in size is also suggested by the fact that the dog was in fact a spider. The miniature house with the woman and the dog evokes the context of the shamanic trip to the house of the sea woman.

The Kiviuq narratives show that many of Kiviuq's adventures take place on the level of the *qupirruit*. According to the Nattilik version, Kiviuq did not die; in fact, he is still alive.

> Later, people say, Kivioq went to the land of the white man. He had killed a man among the inuit in his native village and therefore did not come back. But the white men made him a great isumatAq: a great man with great possessions. It has been said that he has five ships, and sometimes he comes to Ponds Inlet.
>
> It is said that Kivioq has had many lives and that he is now at last living his last one. Formerly when he came to the end of a life he fell into a deathlike sleep, and when he awoke out of it he began a new life. But this did not mean that he began every time as a young man; he continued his age and become older and older – indeed his face looked older and older with every life. People say that he is ghastly to look at now. The last time he was seen by the inuit they had been almost scared to death merely by his appearance. And so he now goes about with his face covered up, for it is quite black, moss-grown and hard as granite.
>
> Since Kivioq settled among the white men we know no more to tell about him. All we know is that he is still alive and that before he ends his last life he will once more see the Inuit, his countrymen, and his native land. (Rasmussen 1931: 376–77)

Like the *qupirruit*, Kiviuq himself turns out to be master of life and death. But he is not completely successful: like the *qupirruit*, he can revive after death, but unlike the *qupirruit*, he cannot do this indefinitely, and he ages with each new life. He cannot escape death completely and has become a non-social being, living in the land of the white man and ghastly to look at.

## Different Kinds of *Qupirruit*

All *qupirruit* transcend the boundaries between life and death, but each *qupirruk* has its own specific symbolism. Therefore, we will now examine them in more detail.

### Bumblebees

The role of bumblebees was first explored by Lydia Black (1983, 1987). Black (1983: 16) related that she became aware of the significance of the animal in the Aleutian Islands when 'Aleut acquaintances be-

gan to warn me, ostensibly in jest, of the danger in that locality from
man-eating bumblebees: giant creatures who would leave nothing but
our bleached bones, if we were not careful'. She concluded, 'the bumblebee is apparently a symbol for the power to kill, associated with the
image of the killer whale' (Black 1987: 23).

In the eastern Arctic, bumblebees also have aquatic connotations,
and the bumblebee of the sea plays an important part in shamanic
initiation. Nuliajuk from Gjoa Haven related,

> There is a bumblebee and a lemming in the sea. I have never seen these
> living beings in the sea, but I have heard about them from older people.
> When a person is becoming an *angakkuq*, this has to come from the bee
> in the sea. This is what I have heard. The one who wanted to become
> an *angakkuq* was a fisherman. The bee went up through his sleeve and
> sucked everything out of his body, in order for him to become an *angak-
> kuq*. After sucking out all the deep places in his body, the bee would go
> down toward the earth. (Kugaaruk workshop, 2004)

Thus, the bumblebee sucks the body of the shamanic candidate empty.
Angutinngurniq from Kugaaruk added,

> I have never seen anyone initiated as an *angakkuq*, but I have heard my
> grandfather, my father, and my uncle telling stories about becoming an
> *angakkuq*. The *iguptaq*, the bee, is actually a person. The bee would go
> inside your sleeve and suck your body right through. An *angakkuq* could
> help somebody else become one. This seems like a fairy tale, but it was
> real. The *angakkuit* would put something up to block the view when they
> were performing. The *angakkuq* who was helping someone else become
> one would take him right under the sea, and the bee would go through
> his sleeve and suck his body. He would grab it like this to throw it in the
> hole. There was a place that had a platform right beside that hole. You
> had to go through that hole or nothing would happen. After they went
> through the ice for just a few minutes, they came out again. It seemed
> that they didn't remember anything about what happened down there.
> (Kugaaruk workshop, 2004)

The bumblebee thus played an important part in shamanic initiation.
Kupak from Naujaat related how he was once attacked by an *iguptaq*.
It may have been a shamanic calling.

> There were two of us in the fall. It was just beginning to freeze beneath
> the sea. You could tell that there was a bumblebee flying around. It
> wasn't loud, but we could hear it. We were down at the shore. I went in
> the tent. There were two of us, and it came into the tent. The noise got
> closer and closer. You could tell it was a bee from the sea. I went to the
> tent to get away from it. I knew this other person would be scared so I

went there. I didn't know what to do once I was in the tent. The earth around me became alive. I know it doesn't sound believable, but the bee became so loud that the earth was shaking because of that noise. It didn't do anything to me. I was inside the tent, but the earth moved every time I heard the noise. I didn't know what to do. I didn't have any weapon to protect myself. There was an old bone from the shoulder of a caribou, a *kisiaq*. I found somebody's old dog harness. I put it around this caribou bone. The earth started to tremble and make noise, right through the sea. I could tell. There were just two of us. This other person didn't say anything. I knew this person was very scared. I was becoming scared myself. I grabbed the *kisiaq*, this bone, and threw it away, along with the dog harness. I could tell that the bee was going toward the sea. I could tell because the earth was moving. You know that bees are not big. They are small, like flies, but this was very loud, similar to thunder. If I hadn't paid any attention to it, I don't know what might have happened. If I had just stayed there, and I hadn't done anything, I wonder what would have happened. It would have come to the land. It was not completely on the land. It was on the shore ready to come out on the land. You could hear it because the earth was responding to that noise. Even me, I was afraid. My partner, who is easily frightened of things, was calm. I was the one who was afraid. I threw that *anu*, that dog harness, towards the land.

I found something on the ground. It looked like an *unaaq* [seal harpoon]. I don't know what it was exactly. I stabbed the air all around us and the noise became fainter and fainter and eventually it went away. If I hadn't done anything, the bee would have come to the land where we were. It was the bee of the sea. I worked hard to fight the noise, as I was scared. (Kugaaruk workshop, 2004)

The sound of the bumblebee is clearly a distinctive feature of the animal. Apparently Kupak knew how to defend himself by using a *kisiaq*, a caribou shoulder bone, and an *anu*, a dog harness. A dog harness often served to protect a person against danger. Even though Kupak never saw the bumblebee, his description of the sound suggests a huge being. If the context was that of a shamanic calling, Kupak clearly refused to answer it.

Kappianaq (IE 458) related how his mother was approached by an *iguptaq*:

She said that once an attempt by a sea bee was made to become her helping spirit, as she was afraid of it. She could hear it but could not see it. It was on the ice while they were hunting seals by *mauliq*. She had walked to another community in the company of an older woman. As they walked, they kept hearing a bee. All along they were walking on the ice late at night. Sometimes the sound would go around her, as it turned out it was looking for a place to enter her. If it had gotten into her, then it would have become her helping spirit. It has the same sound as an ordinary bee buzzing. When she mentioned that, she told her companion that it was an ocean bee. As soon as my mother mentiôned that, it immediately left.

The sound of the bumblebee is again strongly marked in this account. Apparently the appearance of the bumblebee was a shamanic calling that would have been answered if it were allowed to enter the body of Kappianaq's mother. She countered this by identifying the animal.

The bumblebee could be a strong helping spirit. A tradition collected by Rasmussen (1931: 196) from the shaman Sâmik relates how the bumblebee punished two women who refused to have intercourse with men other than their husbands.

> Two men, Oqortoq and Tinaoq, had one evening agreed to exchange wives. When night came and they were to retire to rest they each bade his wife to go to the tent of the man whose wife he awaited. But then the strange thing happened that both women, whose names were Arnangussaq and Tinôreq, declared that they would not sleep with any other than their own husbands. Nevertheless the husbands compelled them to go out, but neither of them would go into the other tent; they remained standing outside. Then suddenly a spirit came over them, the spirit that is called Ivigtarssuaq, 'the big bee'. Ordinarily it is only a common bee; but when its anger is aroused it can turn into any form, become big and dangerous and frightful. In this case it came over these two disobedient women as an enormous and shapeless figure. Arnangussaq at once fell swooning outside the tent she should have been in, whereas Tinôreq fled out into the dark night. With great difficulty Arnangussaq was called to life again, after which they started to look for Tinôreq. At length she was found by Oqortoq, for he was a shaman. She lay like one dead, stretched out on the ground and chilled through and through, and her heart beat so faintly that it could scarcely be heard. She was carried home as if dead, and only towards morning did they succeed in bringing her to life again.

Sexual intercourse between non-married partners might be required in ritual contexts such as the Sedna feast, a shamanic healing or a wife exchange between ritual partners. Rasmussen related that after this the women willingly lay with others whenever their husbands required them to do so. Rasmussen (1931: 297–98) emphasizes the violent nature of this helping spirit in another tradition about Tinôreq and his helping spirit Ivigtarssuaq:

> Tarraijuk was a handsome young man, a skilful hunter, and was said to have long enjoyed the favour of Tinôreq when her husband, Tinaoq the shaman, was out hunting. At this his [Tinaoq's] helping spirit Ivigtarssuaq, a bee in human form, was offended and punished Tarraijuk by possessing him and making him wild and senseless whenever it did so.

And then the peculiar thing happened that the helping spirit found such great spiritual gifts in Tarraijuk that, in the end, it became reconciled to him and became his helping spirit too, but without leaving or failing Tinaoq. Ivigtarssuaq came to Tarraijuk, it is said, one summer while be was out alone hunting caribou, and so violently did he possess his body that it took several men to hold him; he struck out so furiously and raged so violently against his surroundings.... The reason was stated to be that Ivigtarssuaq on such occasions was filled with anger because, as a holy man, he had eaten of white man's provisions. Tarraijuk rushed about and shouted like a madman, frothing at the mouth, until some strong men at length overpowered and bound him.

The bumblebee interfered when Tarraijuk meddled with sexual relationships or food that were no concern of his. The bumblebee is a ferocious spirit. Women especially fear it. Uqalik (IE 432) from Iglulik expressed her fear of bees, stating that if a bee would come in, she would flee immediately.

Arngnasungaaq from Qamanittuaq related how long ago his mother had protected him in a healing ritual against a bumblebee:

My mother helped me once when I was sick for a long time.... My mother said someone or something must be trying to get me. My mother rolled a bit of the skin bedding at the back of the iglu, and facing the back edge of the iglu she was saying things to get my spirit back. A large bumblebee was trying to enter from behind the iglu, but didn't go in, so I guess that thing was trying to get me. Days after my mother did her ritual I started getting up and felt well, and today I am still alive. Those kinds of rituals were helpful. (quoted in Mannik 1998: 217)

Thus, people could protect themselves against bumblebees, as Kupak did with a caribou shoulder bone and a dog harness, or as Kappianaq's mother did by identifying the bee trying to become her helping spirit.

Kappianaq (IE 458) also explained that the tusks of small *airujjait*, fairy shrimps, from the lakes can be used during a shamanic incantation. They can be fitted into the mouth, and the mouth is stretched. As the *airujjait* are associated with light and transparency, the stretching of the mouth appears to create brightness. His account evokes Black's description of the bumblebee (Black 1987: 23), and there may be a connection between the *airujaq* and the bumblebee, which is still represented by the Aleuts as a giant man-eating beast, with a gaping jaw and ferocious fangs.

The bumblebee, however, was not only a ferocious animal. It could also be beneficial, and was often used as an amulet. According to Rasmussen (1931: 43), 'A bee with all its progeny sewn into a piece of skin and fastened to the hood gives a strong head.'[2] The connection between a bee and its offspring in an amulet suggests a connection between the bee and life and vitality. Manelaq stated (quoted in Rasmussen 1929: 221–22), 'Perhaps it has also helped me that as an amulet I have a bee, which is also said to give vital power. That is why I still look young, in spite of my great age.' Similarly, Rasmussen (1929: 170) relates, 'A live bee must be rolled over the back of a pregnant woman and afterwards kept; when she gives birth to her child, this bee will become an effective amulet; fastened on top of the head in a hair band, it gives long life.' The connection to hair confirms the relation to life and growth. According to Boas (1907: 515), 'To help the growth of hair of a girl, her hair is washed with blood; or a bee is attached to her hood, but this is believed also to produce lice.'

Peryouar, originally from Qamanittuaq, recalled how an old woman made amulets with bumblebees: 'Before sewing them on she would put the dead bees in a piece of caribou hide. She would sew them on, not too close together, and there got to be many on the belt' (quoted in Mannik 1998: 158). According to Aupilaarjuk from Rankin Inlet,

> But we do see what is in the stomachs of bearded seals and ring seals. We can find what we call *Igutsaup siggungit,* because they resemble bumblebee stingers. This is what my father put on the back of my nephew's parka so that, if he was going to die before his time, he would come back to life. This was taken out of a bearded seal's stomach, and placed on the back of my nephew's parka. They have a beak exactly like a bird, I don't know what they are, but we call them bumblebees. (quoted in Saladin d'Anglure 2001: 29)

Inuksaq from Arviat recalled, 'I had mittens when I was a child and I had a pouch in each mitten. There were two adult bees in each, and a baby bee was put there as well. These were there so that when a woman in labor had complications I could help ease the delivery' (quoted in Bennett and Rowley 2004: 202).

The bee can also serve as an amulet for dogs. Jenness (1922: 169) relates with respect to the Copper Inuit, 'Higilak once wrapped the body of a live bumble bee in a shred of cloth and tied it round a pup's neck to make the animal fierce and bold like the bee.'[3]

The bee can also play a part in dreams. Alain Ijiraq (IE 231) related,

> At the time when we had to sleep at the bottom of the fiord at Avvajaq before we went back to our tent, I had a disturbing dream. The dream I had was about a bee that had come to us. This particular bee was different from any other bee that I have seen. It had a real mouth and it was after

me. I had a knife in my hand and hacked it with it into two. As it turned out there was another bee which went right to the one that I hacked and it immediately proceeded to lick the downed bee. Both bees had real eyes. As soon as the other started to lick it, the other started to get back together and regain its full size, at once they started for me again but I woke up. The dream was short but I woke up my partner and told him about this strange dream that I dreamed and I told him that I had lost hope. As it turned out, in the very near future I was going to fall into the water through the ice.

Although the dream testified to the regenerative power of the bees, it spelled bad news. But bees could also be a good sign. Randa (1994: 392) reports that a lone bumblebee on the seashore is a sign that the fish are returning.

As in Alaska, bees are associated with cannibalism and the power to kill. The notions of cannibalism and killing merge in the shamanic calling that implies a symbolic rebirth. In most cases, when people felt threatened by bumblebees a shamanic calling may have played a part. Bees operate on different scales. Although very small, they can increase their size and become very dangerous. They can punish wrong alimentary or sexual behaviour, and women seem to feel especially threatened by them. However, they are associated with life vitality, mobility and regenerative powers when used as amulets.

### Spiders

In the eastern Arctic spiders are numerous. Father Van de Velde, for instance, once found a big sea spider in Pelly Bay (Kugaaruk) in 1956 (see figure 5.1). We did not find an origin myth for the spider, but Rasmussen collected a complex origin myth in north Alaska (quoted in Ostermann and Holtved 1952: 226–28) evoking features of shamanic accounts of travels to the lands of the sea woman and the moon man. A woman who did not want to marry finally married a head. When he was stabbed in the eye by her father, the husband disappeared and she went out to find him. She first travelled to the bottom of the sea. When her husband rejected her, she went up into the land of the sky and met the moon man, who tried to kill her. Thanks to the help of a little woman dressed in animal guts, she escaped and killed the moon man. Then she descended from the sky along a thread made of sinew, but because she opened her eyes too late she was transformed into a spider. All spiders are descended from her.

The story shows that the spider connects different levels of the world, the land at the bottom of the sea and the land in the sky. Her

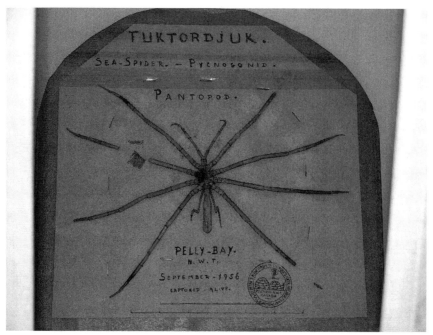

**Figure 5.1.** Tuktordjuk, a sea spider found by Father Van de Velde in Pelly Bay (Kugaaruk), in 1956. The specimen is preserved at the Eskimo Museum (Churchill). Photo: Frédéric Laugrand, 2008.

thread makes the connection. The girl should have opened her eyes the moment she touched the ground, but as she was too late, she was transformed into a spider. Thus, seeing something can prevent a transformation.[4]

In the eastern Arctic we find various stories about spiders in human appearance. We already referred to the spider woman in a version of the Kiviuq myth recorded by Boas. Métayer (1973: 804) related a story about an orphan and a spider family:

> An old lady used to beg some food for her grandson from a rich man. The orphan boy used to stay outside while his grandmother was sleeping. One night he saw a light in the darkness and went to it. It was a spider's house. The spider told his wife to bring some food for their visitor. She brought in some pieces of wood and told him to eat. The boy did not know how to eat wood … so the woman showed him, and he found it good: it was fish that looked like wood. They also gave him some of that food for his grandmother. She also liked it and brought some of it as a gift to the rich man's family.

Later on, the orphan boy told his grandmother, 'I would like to have a good time with the rich man's daughter. Go and fetch her!'

She went. Upon seeing her, the rich man thought that she wanted some food for her grandson. When she told him what the boy had asked for, he told his daughter, 'Follow her!'

The boy had a wife and they lived on friendly terms with the spider family. They worked together and exchanged their wives.

The spider woman gave a knife to the boy's wife. They used to exchange all kinds of gifts.

In this story the spider and his wife provide food and gifts and enable the boy to marry the daughter of a rich man. Just as in the Nattilik version of the Kiviuq myth (Rasmussen 1931: 368), spiders are rich.

Lizzie Itinnuaq (quoted in Oosten and Laugrand 2007: 131) related that she had been threatened by a spider wishing to get a name. She stated, 'There is a spider that has human flesh that has tried to get one.' The notion of a spider with human flesh evokes the origin myths of the spider recorded by Rasmussen about a girl transformed into a spider. Lizzie Itinnuaq also referred to the use of spiders as helping spirits. 'One day I found a spider. I went to spray it and it disappeared. I thought maybe this spider belonged to someone who did not like me who was using the spider as a helper' (quoted in Oosten and Laugrand 2001: 84).

Spiders could predict a death. Rasmussen (1929: 51–52; see also Rasmussen 1927: 146) provides an account by Orulo of such a prediction at Admiralty Inlet:

Then one day I remember we were startled to hear a woman from one of the tents calling out: 'Here, come and look, quick, come and see.' We all ran to the spot, and there we saw a spider letting itself down to the ground. We could not make out where it came from; it looked as if it were letting itself down from the sky. We all saw it, and there was silence among the tents. For when a spider comes down from the sky it means someone is going to die. And true it was; when people came up from the coast, we learned that four men had perished in their kayaks.

This idea of the spider bringing death may be connected to Balikci's (1970: 70) description of a Nattilik *iviutaq* in the context of seal hunt: 'The indicator was a device used to signal the arrival of the seal at a breathing hole. The down indicator was the most commonly used. It was an extremely delicate device, consisting mainly of a piece of hard caribou leg sinew, split so as to resemble a small spider with two claws. A bit of swan's-down was attached to this by a sinew thread.'

Aqattiaq (IE 149; see also IE 267) related how, a long time ago,

[i]n the winter I saw a caribou hair that was shaped in a round position and part of it stretched out a bit, it was falling from the ceiling from our *qarmaq* as would a spider making its way down. I told her [her grand-mother] that the caribou hair was acting like a spider making its way down in its web. She was alarmed and asked to see it, so I showed it to her and she said ... 'Oh my! Something is terribly wrong somewhere, someone might have drowned, we will be getting some news about a dire consequence in the future!'

It turned out that a person had drowned.[5]

A spider could also be used as an amulet. According to Rasmussen (1931: 270), 'Four amulets [were] worn by Naujâq: ... a spider: makes the wearer a good craftsman; is especially effective if sometimes it is used for stroking in between one's fingers.'

The spider can replace the bumblebee, and like the bumblebee it can be used in divination. Randa (1994: 407) related how some Iglul-ingmiut believe that killing a spider brings strong winds.

The most striking feature of spiders is that they predict death. They can connect different worlds, and in stories they are described as rich. They can be used in an amulet to make someone a good craftsman.

### Beetles

Kolb and Law (2001: 58) relate that Qalasiq from Rankin Inlet did not believe that her father Anarqaq was an *angakkuq* until he showed her his ability in handling a beetle (*minnguq*):

He put his hand over his mouth. When he removed it, there in his hand was something walking. It was a *minnguq*, something like a beetle and it was walking in his hand. I never believed him before. I looked and there it was walking about on the palm of his hand. He said, 'You don't believe me, so look at this.' He gave me his hand, and I looked at it. He put his hand over his mouth again. He opened his mouth and I looked to see where the *minnguq* was. He didn't seem to have swallowed it. It just dis-appeared. I believed more then, after he showed me this. Up until then I always thought that he wasn't really an *angakkuq*.

In an interview with Laugrand in 1999, Qalasiq added that she real-ized it was one of his helping spirits. The handling of small insects may have been a feature of *angakkuuniq*. At a workshop in Arviat in 2003 Anautalik from Arviat, who according to his sister and his wife had been an *angakkuq*, often showed his skill in handling these small animals (see figure 5.2).

**Figure 5.2.** The late Luke Anautalik playing with an insect in Arviat. Photo: Frédéric Laugrand, 2003.

The beetle was often used in amulets. Rasmussen (1931: 274) stated that a *minnguq* (specifically a water beetle) 'sewn on to a boy's hood band opposite the eyes and temples gives strong temples and powerful eye sockets'.

The Kiviuq narratives relate that small life-forms have song contests just like human beings do. Rasmussen (1931: 355) presents a dialogue in a song contest between a water beetle and a blowfly. The blowfly told the water beetle that he would not be able to respond, as he was belly-less, but the water beetle retorted that belly-less or not, he should answer back, and turned his back on him. A variant referring to a worm and a fly[6] can be found in Rasmussen (1931: 354–55) as well. He rendered a dialogue by Niaqúnuaq in which a worm told the fly it had no coat of hair, and the fly responded that all the same, it should retaliate. These songs illustrate that these small life-forms should never be underestimated, since they always have the capacity to get back at you.

### Mosquitoes

According to a tradition recorded in the journal *Inuktitut*, mosquitoes (*kikturiat*) originated from the body of a giant. A young man went into caves where giants lived. The Inuk shot a giant in the heel. He fell and became smaller and smaller until he was the same size as the Inuk. The young man went out to inform the people, who flocked towards the cave. Then they saw the body of the giant was on fire. 'All the Inuit looked at the fire; then they looked at the sun. There, flying up from the fire, were thousands and thousands of mosquitoes. The giant, as he burned, was being changed into mosquitoes' (Anonymous 1985: 50–52).[7]

According to a narrative collected by L. Turner ([1894] 1979: 100), lice, instead of mosquitoes, are derived from the body of a dead giant, whereas mosquitoes are derived from a human mistake and disrespect. A woman never cleaned her husband's garments properly. Finally, he took some of the dirt from it and flung it after his wife. 'The particles changed into mosquitoes, and now (in spring), when the warm days come and the women have the labor of cleaning clothes to perform, the insects gather around them, and the women are thus reminded of the slovenly wife and what befell her.'

Rasmussen (1929: 271) relates a version of the story of 'How the Mosquitoes First Came' by Inugpasugjuk, connecting the origin of mosquitoes to the eating of lice.

> There was once a village where the people were dying of starvation. At last there were only two women left alive, and they managed to exist by eating each other's lice. When all the rest were dead, they left their village and tried to save their lives. They reached the dwellings of men, and told how they had kept themselves alive simply by eating lice. But no one in that village would believe what they said, thinking rather that they must have lived on the dead bodies of their neighbours. And thinking this to be the case, they killed the two women. They killed them and cut them open to see what was inside them; and lo, not a single scrap of human flesh was there in the stomachs; they were full of lice. But now all the lice suddenly came to life, and this time they had wings, and flew out of the bellies of the dead women and darkened the sky. Thus the mosquitoes first came.

Rasmussen (1930: 21–22) also presents another version of this story, relating that the wife of the cannibal Igimarahugjuk was killed to assess whether she had only eaten lice at the time he had eaten his children. 'But afterwards no one would believe that Arnahugâq had only eaten lice, and they killed her and cut open her stomach and saw that it was full of lice. But all the lice came alive again when the men cut the stomach open and became kikturigjät: mosquitoes, which flew out over the land. And from them, it is said, all gnats come.' Here we have a double transformation, mosquitoes coming out of lice and gnats from mosquitoes.

Mosquitoes are associated with the heat of the summer. Aava's famous song, published in Rasmussen (1929: 18), states, 'Cold and mosquitoes, These two pests come never together'. Killing mosquitoes may change the weather. Angutinngurniq from Kugaaruk explained,

One time I remember I was walking around and there were a lot of mosquitoes. I hated them and I wanted to get rid of them. I removed the wings while they were still alive. I put one down on the ground and did the same thing with other mosquitoes. I was going after them because I hated them. Later on that day, it was a hot day in the summertime, it started to snow. It started to get cold. If I had been alone I would not have kept going. The weather turned suddenly cold. I was able to survive because there was someone else with me. That was the time I learned that all living things, even mosquitoes, do have a soul. They have a spirit. (Arviat workshop, 2002)

Thus, mistreatment of mosquitoes results in a change of the weather. Mosquitoes would also retaliate when they were not respected. Ijjangiaq (IE 094) related,

I also have heard about a person that would take off the proboscis of a mosquito and release it afterwards in a tent. After that experience the following year when the mosquito came alive again, this person had to be protected by others from the mosquitoes.... The mosquitoes were so numerous that it appears as smoke was coming out of them above the two people that were returning to the camp. This was the way he was *akkiviujuq* by the mosquitoes. This happened very recently when we were already alive. When this individual was taken inside the tent, all the holes were secured so that no mosquitoes could enter. Above the tent it was swarming with so many mosquitoes that it appeared as if it was smoking.

Paillet (1973: 32–33) reports that in Qamanittuaq, the only inland community of Nunavut, 'two types of mosquitoes are recognized, the *kikturiaq*, the noisy and greedy ones which have become the emblem of Qamanittuaq, and the *tuktuujaaq*, said to be less obnoxious'. At Qamanittuaq a special ritual could be performed to protect a baby against mosquitoes. According to Annie Haqpi, babies were exposed to mosquitoes so that later on they would not be devoured by them (Baker Lake workshop, 2005). Rose Iqallijuq from Iglulik also recalled such a practice:

I was kept informed that I was fed to the mosquitoes when I was born. When I was born even before I suckled I was placed face down and was left alone to be stung by the mosquitoes despite the fact that I was crying until I was all 'eaten up', so I was fed to the mosquitoes.... So from that time on I do not get mosquitoes bites, hardly ever. It was said that when newborns were fed to the mosquitoes that they would be all 'eaten up'. (quoted in Piugaattuq, IE 150)

Teresi and Mark Ijjangiaq (IE 019; see also IE 196) also described this *nungutaujuq* practice in detail:

In the spring when there are a lot of mosquitoes around, when a child is born during a hot weather, the newborn would be placed outside with a mat placed under him, which may be a caribou skin. The newborn is crying and cold because it had just been born. The newborn would get covered completely by mosquitoes; then after a while the mosquitoes will start to leave; it is said that the newborn is 'devoured' [*nungutaujuq*]. When this child reached his adulthood then the mosquitoes are not going to bother him. The word *nungutaujuq* is used only to pretend that the child had been devoured when in fact it is not.

Boas (1901: 213) related a story about a man and a woman who were warned by a *tuniq*, a people that had preceded the Inuit as inhabitants of the land, not to pursue their trip because of the mosquitoes. The woman stayed with the *tuniq*, but finally the man decided that he did not want to stay in the house of the *tuniq* and went out with his stick, assuming that he could deal with the mosquitoes. When he did not return, the *tuniq* went out to look for him and found him dead with his stick in his hand. Many mosquitoes were lying dead beside him, but they had sucked out all his blood. Thus, mosquitoes are considered a great nuisance and can be dangerous to Inuit.[8] Zacharias Aqiaruq (IE 113), for instance, recalled,

At that time I went out in search of caribou alone I almost got suffocated by the mosquitoes, my nostrils were constantly plugged by them as I walked home as the day was getting warmer and there were no winds at all. I had to cover my face with my hands so I could breathe through my mouth as I could not breathe through my nose. I agonized over the heat at that time so much, it looked as if I was going to get suffocated by the mosquitoes. I made it back and it passed as all misfortunes will pass.

Mosquitoes also had a predictive value. According to Arngnasungaaq, an elder from Qamanittuaq, mosquitoes are a sign that the caribou are coming (quoted in Mannik 1998: 217). In the Kitikmeot region, Inuit indicate that caribou hate mosquitoes and that when there are too many, they gather and go in circles to get rid of them: 'Sometimes when they shook the flies off, it would make the sound like thunder' (quoted in Thorpe 2000: 86). Randa (1994: 400) relates that in Iglulik, when the first mosquitoes appeared in spring, people would know that the bearded seals were about to enter the bays. Pisuk from Rankin Inlet stated that a big mosquito appearing in his dreams would predict a death (Oosten and Laugrand 2007: 112–13).

In origin narratives, mosquitoes originate from a giant, human filth or lice in the stomach of a dead woman. Today, elders do not always agree on their origin. Thus, Ollie Itinnuaq thought that mosquitoes come from the ground, whereas his wife Lizzie Itinnuaq (interview, 2008) assumed they come from the sky. Mosquitoes are considered a plague, but they should not be mistreated, as they can retaliate and kill you. When killed, they may change the weather. Like other *qupirruit*, they announce specific events. In addition, mosquitoes and lice appear to be closely related, so it is lice that we turn to next.

## Lice

In a story collected by the botanist Lucien Turner ([1894] 1979: 100) in the Nunavik area, '[l]ice are supposed to drop from the body of a huge spirit, dwelling in the regions above, who was punished by having these pests constantly torment him. In his rage to free himself the lice dropped down upon the people who condemned him to his punishment.' For the Canadian western Arctic, Maurice Métayer (1973: no. 62, p. 772; see also no. 40 for a variant) presents the following origin myth of lice (*kumait*):

> A man who hunted deer in the summertime, built a shelter by a lake. Some beetles and caterpillars across the lake were waiting for him to get asleep. Then they crossed the lake in their kayaks to see him. They raced to see who would be the first ones to arrive. By the time they were in the middle of the lake, the caterpillars were still ahead, but they broke their paddle and the beetles finally took the lead. They were the ones to arrive first. They went inside the shelter to see the hunter and were turned into lice. Before that, man never had any lice.

In this narrative, competition plays an important part. The lice originated from beetles, just as in other stories mosquitoes originated from lice.[9]

Lice are also connected to health. Joamie from South Baffin (quoted in Therrien and Laugrand 2001: 200) reported, 'Elders today, including myself, think that lice help to control and remove illness from our bodies. People always got fresh blood when the lice sucked out the old blood from our bodies. We elders like to think that lice remove illnesses.' Atagutsiaq from Arctic Bay related (quoted in Therrien and Laugrand 2001: 14–15) that lice were also used to cure eyes and especially to alleviate blindness:

> I have heard that they were very useful for people who had eye infections that were not caused by snow blindness. A head or body of a louse was tied to a strand of hair, and put in the eye that had become infected. The louse would walk around in the eye. After it was removed, the louse's legs

were covered with the infected matter, which it removed from the eye. A person who was going blind was then able to see.[10]

According to Ootoova from Mittimatalik, lice were killed with the teeth, but not eaten. She used to squash lice with her teeth and then spit them out (quoted in Therrien and Laugrand 2001: 23–24). Peter Freuchen (1935b: 142) related,

> They can be disposed of easily by having the women look you over. It is considered quite elegant and in the height of fashion when one feels a louse biting to indicate the spot with his finger, bend over, and let a woman pick it out. It is also possible for her to reveal her emotions towards the man in so doing. If she crushes the insect between her fingers or drops it in the lamp flame, she is merely being courteous. But if she cracks it between her teeth and eats it, that is a sure sign she looks with favor upon the man.

However, Freuchen might not be the most reliable source in this respect, and there may be more at stake. According to a story related by Rasmussen (1932: 208–9; see also Rasmussen 1931: 412–13), a louse that is eaten can still escape through the anus, but once it is cracked between the fingernails, it is definitely destroyed.

> A louse once asked for his mittens, saying: 'Bring my mittens and my axe. The ones who are going to "The land of the Neck" are getting ready to go'. His wife is said to have replied: 'They will only crack you', to which he answered: 'If they put me in their mouths I can get out through their backsides, so I'll come home all right. But if I am squeezed between fingernails I won't be able to come back.' It is said that he never returned, so presumably he has been cracked between finger-nails.

According to L. Turner ([1894] 1979: 89, fig. 51), lice were sometimes removed from the body with a specific tool, a back-scratcher called *ku-mé-u-tik*, 'that which removes lice'. In Wachowich's stories of Inuit women (1999: 194–95), Rhoda Kaukjak Katsak from Pond Inlet relates how she was struck by the negative attitude of nurses towards lice: 'The nurses, they taught us that we weren't supposed to have lice in our hair. We had never thought that lice in our hair was necessarily a bad thing! When I got to town that very first day, they found lice in my hair, they took me to the nursing station and cut my long hair off.'

Stories about lice also refer to the shifting of scales. In a story recorded by Rasmussen (1932: 258), an Inuk adopted by a giant referred to the lice of the giant as lemmings. Rasmussen (1932: 109) relates that in the shamanic vocabulary, caribou are said to be the lice of the land:

'A very large herd of caribou is seen moving over the ground, they are compared with lice swarming on the scalp.' Thus the term *kumaqjuaq*, the big louse, for caribou in the shamanic vocabulary indicates another shifting of scales.

Lice are attributed to Indian people as well as some non-human beings. Rasmussen (1931: 122) related with respect to Nattilik views of Indian people, 'We call them Itqilît (those with many louse eggs) because they are full of lice.' According to the Umingmaktormiutaq Netsit, Amaligjuit, non-human cannibals who steal children by putting them into their *amauti*, are infested with lice (Rasmussen 1932: 202–3).

Lice originate from a giant being or beetles, they are marked as non-human food and they are able to circulate through the body. They operate on different scales: as *qupirruit* in relation to human beings, as lemmings in relation to giants and as caribou in relation to the earth. They can be used in healing. As masters of transformation from one scale to another they continue to fascinate, and today many Inuit artists enjoy representing these very small beings in carvings and drawings (see figure 5.3).

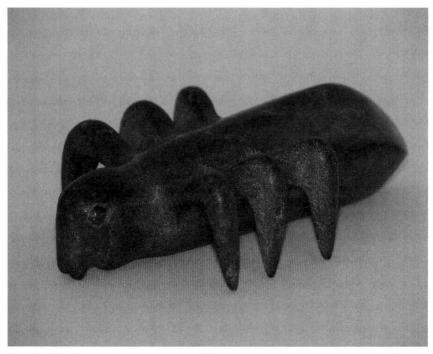

**Figure 5.3.** Anonymous carving from Naujaat representing a louse preserved at the Eskimo Museum (Churchill: C68.19.1). Photo: Frédéric Laugrand, 2008.

### Worms, Caterpillars and Maggots

In Inuit narratives, worms and caterpillars are closely connected. In the nineteenth century, Captain Lyon (1824: 408) reported, 'I discovered at this period that the women had a great dread of caterpillars, for I could persuade none of them to touch some which I had spinning in a box. The bare pretence of having thrown one into the jacket of a young girl almost alarmed her into fits.'

Rasmussen (1929: 268–69) relates a story by Ivaluardjuk about a woman who adopted a larva and nursed it in her armpits so it grew on her blood. She treated it as a son, took it on her lap and sang nursery rhymes for it: 'Little one that will bring me snow when you grow up, little one that will find meat for me when you grow up!' But as the larva grew, the woman became more pale, and people became afraid of it. One day when she was out visiting they threw it out into the passage of the house and it was torn apart by dogs. It was completely filled with blood. When the woman returned, she cried, 'Oh, they have thrown my dear child out of the house.' And she burst into tears and went into the house weeping (see also Rasmussen 1930: 33–34, 90; 1932: 227–28). The figure of the larva is also represented in the string figure tradition (see Rasmussen 1932: 136).

In a version of the story recorded among the Caribou Inuit from Kibkârjuk by Rasmussen (1930: 90), the larva does not suck blood, but the breasts of its adoptive human mother. In a Nattilik variant told by Nakasuk (Rasmussen 1931: 401), the woman adopted a caterpillar. She put it into her stocking so it could suck her blood. It was thrown to the dogs by her grandchildren. Rasmussen (1908: 171–72) also recorded variants of these stories among the Polar Inuit. In one version a woman adopts a caterpillar that is eventually killed by the men of the camp after it eats a little baby. In another version she adopts a worm that is finally torn apart by the dogs. All these narratives emphasize the parasitic nature of these beings. They can be adopted, but they can only live as parasites on the living human body. They are insatiable beings fed on blood and milk and ultimately killed by the men of the camp. The fear of these beings is also expressed in the Kiviuq stories. In a Copper version of the Kiviuq narratives told by Tatilgäk, a caterpillar woman replaces the bumblebee as a cannibal woman trying to eat the hero (Rasmussen 1932: 237–38).

The eating of the human body is especially attributed to the maggots, *qitirulliq*. Among the Copper Inuit we find various references to the fear of being devoured as a corpse. Rasmussen (1932: 136) presents a dead man's song collected among the Umingmaktormiut describing the fear of maggots entering through the hollow of the collarbone and the eyes. Inversely, maggots can be eaten by human beings, but they are not considered edible by the Inuit.

Therrien and Laugrand (2001: 258–59) quote Aalasi Joamie from Iqaluit: 'I have heard that you can gain weight from eating maggots. There is no way I can eat them. I ended up in the hospital once because I was afraid of a maggot. I fainted when I saw a maggot, while I was eating *mattaaq*. Maggots are like ghosts for me. I really fear them.' But maggots would be present in aged cached meat. Aalasi related, 'I have heard of maggots in aged cached meat being so numerous that you could hear them swarming. People scooped them up and ate them.' She adds that people sometimes survived by eating them. Rasmussen (1931: 59–60) reports an experience he had in Qeqertaligârssuk where maggots were eaten:

> Right alongside the spot where we pitched our camp we found an old cache of caribou meat – two years old I was told. We cleared the stones away and fed the dogs, for it is law in this country that as soon as a cache is more than a winter and a summer old, it falls to the one who has use for it. The meat was green with age, and when we made a cut in it, it was like the bursting of a boil, so full of great white maggots was it. To my horror my companions scooped out handfuls of the crawling things and ate them with evident relish. I criticised their taste, but they laughed at me and said, not illogically: 'You yourself like caribou meat, and what are these maggots but live caribou meat? They taste just the same as the meat and are refreshing to the mouth.'

Thus, the vitality of the maggots is derived from the meat, but obviously meat is to be preferred.

The fear of being eaten by maggots, worms or caterpillars seems to be at the root of a practice to become an *angakkuq*. Boas (1901: 153–54) relates that a person could become an *angakkuq* by having the flesh of his arms eaten by worms.[11] Such a practice was reported by Suvaksiuq from Arviat:

> If you wanted to become an *angakkuq* you would put the moss that contained all kinds of living things such as insects and caterpillars and whatever else was under the earth on your skin. You had to be able to stand this when it was on your arm. You had to be able to stay still when these living things started sucking on your arm, on your blood. (Arviat workshop, 2003)

Bilby (1923: 222) relates a practice performed by the *tuniit*, the predecessors of the Inuit, on Baffin Island, who would obtain their lightness in order to run very fast 'by filling their boots with all kinds of insects and caterpillars, which gnaw the flesh from the bones'.

*Qupirruit* may also bring life, however. Rasmussen (1931: 11) relates that the son of the *angakkuq* Orpingalik had an accident when he was travelling with his father. Orpingalik carried him up to the bank and tried to call him to life with a magic song. It was not long before a caterpillar crawled up on the face of the corpse and began to go round its mouth, round and round. Not long afterwards the son began to breathe very faintly, and then other small creatures of the earth crawled onto his face, and this was a sign that he would come to life again.

In the western Canadian Arctic, Métayer (1973: 762) related a story about a woman who exchanged clothing with a woman she met while travelling. Then she began to change into a caterpillar. Nobody wanted to marry her, except an old man. After some time she asked him to make a drum for her, and when he did so both of them regained their youth and beauty. Thus, the transformation into a caterpillar turned out to be an intermediary stage in a process of rejuvenation.

Worms or caterpillars could serve as helping spirits as well. The Anglican missionary E. J. Peck (quoted in Laugrand et al. 2006: 421) relates that Nemereak was a being living in the sea, 'like serpents but become like men to the conjuror'. As serpents do not occur in the area, the term worm seems more to the point. Rasmussen (1929: 208) presents a picture by Anarqaq of Nimeriarjuaq, the hairy worm, commenting, 'Moves by writhing its body sinuously; lives both on land and sea; smaller and narrower than the bearded seal, is very fast and only has hair on back and belly; acts as helping spirit, heals the sick; can also be used as defender.'

In Peck's *tuurngait* list, Têtêtak is described as a hairy caterpillar that calls out 'têtêtak'. Peck refers to the story of the woman who adopted a caterpillar and fed it from her blood. He reports that Têtêtak is considered a good spirit, 'said to suck away from a sick person the cause of pain. A kind of leech' (quoted in Laugrand et al. 2006: 440).

Like other *qupirruit*, worms and caterpillars operate on different scales. Arctic ethnographers provide many examples of this variation of scales, when small animals are more powerful than bigger ones. Rasmussen (1931: 300) provides a drawing of 'Âfserssuaq, the giant caterpillar, enormous and frightful'.[12]

Today, *qupirruit* play an important part in dreams. They may enter the body of the dreamer,[13] or the house. Ujarasuk from Iglulik (Oosten and Laugrand 1999b: 34) related,

In the dream we lived in an *iglu* that didn't have a *katak,* an entrance. There was a porch beyond it, and the porch was not covered. It was very dark. There was no light at all. It seems that this was the very first dream I ever had. There were snakes and caterpillars coming in through the entrance. They came in without touching the floor. They came in and they headed straight towards me. I was so scared that I started crying. That woke me up. I told my mother that when this thing opened its mouth there were teeth. I woke myself up crying out of fear. My mother said it was because I didn't listen to her words anymore that I had that kind of a dream.

Contemporary Inuit artists do not represent *qupirruit* as often as other kinds of animals such as bears, walruses, dogs and seals.[14] But when they make these representations, there is usually a spiritual meaning connected to them, as in the case of Nick Sikkuark, who represented many *qupirruit* in his carvings preserved at the Musée national des beaux-arts du Québec. In a recent book published by Kardosh (2003), we find three worms created by Nick Sikkuark, emphasizing their capacity to move in time and space. His first art piece is made out of whalebone and caribou antler and represents a shaman transformed into a worm. In the second one, Sikkuark indicates that by changing into a worm a deceased person travels beneath the earth and sea ice 'so fast that he burns the land'. With respect to the last piece, he comments that an *angakkuq,* by turning himself into a worm through his shamanic power, enjoys himself by travelling in the land and sky (see Kardosh 2003: 56–57, fig. 16; 74, fig. 24; 84, fig. 29).

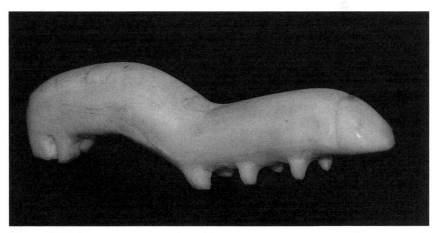

**Figure 5.4.** Anonymous carving from Naujaat representing a caterpillar preserved at the Eskimo Museum (Churchill: C55.11.1). Photo: Frédéric Laugrand, 2008.

Worms, larvae and caterpillars are all considered to be parasites living on the human body, but they can also give life. Worms are particularly associated with transformation, able to transform a human being into an *angakkuq*. They are powerful helping spirits, capable of moving at great speed and operating on different scales. Like lice and other insects, they are often represented in Inuit art (see figure 5.4).

## Discussion

*Qupirruit* encompass different species of small animals. From an Inuit perspective, they are closely related, and all these small animals appear connected. They all have the power of transformation, and tales relate how they transform into each other. A beautiful art piece by Pudlo represents a spider that turned into a dog while he was drawing (Pitseolak [1978] 2003: 116, fig. 30). *Qupirruit* can increase and reduce their size, and often there are equivalents of different species in the land and the sea. Thus, bumblebees and spiders also exist in the sea.

They are very powerful helping spirits, and especially the bumblebee seems to be at the centre of the shamanic complex, playing an important part in shamanic initiation. *Qupirruit* are associated with vitality and regeneration, and if respected, they may provide life and rejuvenation. In Inuit traditions the Western taxonomy of insects makes little sense and distinctions between the various *qupirruit* often collapse. Mosquitoes may originate from lice, and lice from beetles. *Qupirruit* often live on the land as well as in the sea, like the bumblebee, or have their counterparts in the sea, like the spider and the crab. A lack of clear distinctions marks the non-social nature of *qupirruit*, a feature they share with non-human beings (see also Oosten and Laugrand 2010).

All *qupirruit* are ambiguous and potentially dangerous. They appear to be masters of life and death, able to come to life again, and they can convey this quality to human beings through amulets or in other ways. Biologists point out that Arctic insects have no fur, are often cold-blooded and cannot withstand cold by generating heat, but still manage to cope with the long, cold winters and short summers in the Arctic. Inuit think that insects are able to adapt and transform better than any other being. But according to Inuit views, insects do not survive the winter; instead, they return to life again. In a shamanic context, they are powerful because of their capacity to kill, particularly when they enter the human body. Various tales relate how people were killed by *qupirruit* entering the anus or vagina. With the exception of the larvae that live under caribou skin, they are not considered edible. This becomes clear in stories about the women who lived on lice. *Qupirruit* may eat a corpse, suck empty a human body or devour its entrails. In the Kiviuq narratives, we see how the bumblebee, the spider and the caterpillar can take shape in cannibal women who attempt to eat the hero.

*Qupirruit*, however, are not just repulsive. They are effective helping spirits, used in amulets, predictions and dreams. Anarqaq proved that he was an *angakkuq* by the way he handled a beetle. During a workshop in Arviat in 2003, Anautalik, who according to his sister and his wife had been an *angakkuq*, was carefully manipulating a small insect in his hands. This scene greatly intrigued the Inuit who were watching it.

Today, shamanism has gone underground and Inuit have adopted Christianity, but *qupirruit* are still very present in Inuit discourses. With respect to the Arctic climate changes, Inuit point out that today *qupirruit*, especially bugs and mosquitoes, are not only increasing in numbers but are also present for longer periods of time (Thorpe 2000: 63; Community of Kugaaruk 2005: 19). Many Inuit are also scared to see that new *qupirruit*, such as black flies or horse flies or even some water worms, are now appearing in some northern communities. In July 2011, Niore Iqalukjuak from Arctic Bay reported to CBC his unexpected discovery of a wasp-like insect that had never been seen in the Arctic before (CBC News 2011). In Cambridge Bay, Inuit observed the appearance of mosquitoes that were bigger than the usual ones in great numbers (see Gagnon 2011). But even if global warming favours the increase of chlorophyll and thus the mass of food available to insects, the appearance of new and bigger insects may be mainly due to the increasing number of commercial ships transporting equipment, food and insects from the south (Community of Naujaat 2005: 1–17).

In modern Inuit society, fear of *qupirruit* such as the bumblebee, particularly among women, is still widespread.[15] The symbolism of *qupirruit* does not seem to have changed much. Metonymically, they connect different levels. Their size positions them on the level of the *tarniq*, image, soul or shade, itself a miniature being. It is on this level that matters of life and death are decided. *Qupirruit*, as masters of life and death, therefore, remain a matter of serious concern.

## Notes

1. See also Tataniq, quoted in Mannik (1998: 231).
2. See also Rasmussen (1929: 275): 'A bee and its young sewn into skin and used as a brow band: gives a strong head, especially in fisticuffs.'

3. See also Angutinngurniq, quoted in Oosten and Laugrand (2002), and Thalbitzer (1914b: 627).
4. A similar principle is at stake when a person kills a dwarf, an *inugarulligaq*. The moment he does not watch it, the dwarf will come to life again.
5. The belief that a spider predicts death may explain customs described in Greenland that one should kill a spider that lets itself down. Birket-Smith (1924: 412–13) relates that specific words have to be pronounced: 'He who wants to have deft fingers, should crush a spider, when it lets itself down, saying: *"Púsūka pikit, púsûtit piláka!"* i.e. you get my fingers, I get your fingers.' Ostermann (1938: 194) states, 'If a spider is seen descending from its web, it must be pinched to death with the words: "You can have the fingers I pinch with, then I can have your fingers." This is done in order to become as clever as the spider.'
6. According to Randa (2002b: 98), the fly is often referred to as *ananngiq*, 'that is obsessed by excrements'. Another fly is referred to as *milugiaq*, from *miluk*, the action of sucking.
7. In this myth of the origin of the mosquitoes, they are associated with death. Césard et al. (2003: 392–93) observe in their study of insects in Amazonia that although insects lack blood, they desire the blood and vital energy of others, which make them attractive for the indigenous peoples.
8. Mosquitoes as a plague are a common topic in Inuit art. Artists often represent mosquitoes bothering humans (see the drawing by Pitseolak Ashoona or the camp attacked by mosquitoes by Janet Kigusiuq in McMaster [2011: 161, 173]) or animals (see the mosquitoes attacking dogs or geese by Pudlo in Pitseolak [(1978) 2003: 124, 103]).
9. This competitive aspect also comes to the fore in a tradition from the Egedesminde district in Greenland recorded by Birket-Smith (1924: 442) attributing the origin of death to lice: 'According to another tradition a worm and a louse were to run a race towards man. If the worm came first, man was to live; if the louse came first, man was to die. The worm fell down a rock and was killed, and so man must die.'
10. See also Philippe (1951) and Black (1977: 84).
11. In the western Arctic, Lantis (1938: 454–56) discusses extensively how worms, preferably from dead bodies, were used in whaling. She points out that 'when a young person was being made ill by dreams in which spirits appeared, one sure sign that he was becoming a shaman was a dream about a mass of worms' (Lantis 1946: 315). Rasmussen (quoted in Ostermann and Holtved 1952: 130) related, concerning shamanic initiation, 'The old shaman gradually teaches him his art, beginning by putting him through the hole to the worms in the *agdlupâq* (the largest breathing-hole), where his "flesh" is eaten up. He becomes light and "shining" as a shaman ought to be.'
12. Birket-Smith (1924: 221–22) refers to a giant maggot in Greenland: 'There is a huge caterpillar, *auseq*, which is also dangerous for man.' In Alaska, E. Nelson (1899: 443) refers to TiÅå-si˘kh-pûk, the great worm or caterpillar that lived in the days when animals had the power to change their form to that of human beings at will. And in Siberia, Bogoras (1904: 13) not only refers to a Chuckchee tradition about a giant worm living in the land

of the dead that lives on big game such as caribou, but also to another giant worm that lives in the sea and that is so strong it can kill a whale by squeezing it between its coils (Bogoras 1904: 307).

13. See the representation made by Leah Qumaluk from Povungnituk (Povungnituk 1966: 20, no. 285).

14. *Qupirruit* are more and more represented in carvings and drawings: see the blue insect created by Pudlo (Pitseolak [1978] 2003: 27), the bees and flies carvings in Seidelman and Turner (1993: 25) and the water bugs by Helene Kalvak (Wight 2001: 46).

15. In 1998 the Kuujjuarmiut were alarmed when they found their trees being eaten by hordes of hungry insects known as sawfly larches (George 1998). This may have been nothing new, as scientist Louise Fillion pointed out that major infestations had already occurred in 1905 and 1940.

PART III

# FELLOW HUNTERS

# CHAPTER 6

# The Dog, Partner of the Hunter

## 'When They Killed the Sled Dogs in Nunavik'

The *Nunatsiaq News* of 26 March 1999 (George 1999) reported a discussion at a meeting of the Makivik Corporation of the dog killings in Nunavik in the 1950s and 1960s: 'Many elders can still remember how a way of life abruptly changed when government officials killed their Inuit husky dogs.' The killings, to control canine diseases and reduce numbers of loose dogs, are still viewed as an injustice, almost a ploy, to make the Inuit dependent on the government. The president of Makivik Corporation, Pita Aatami, said, '[I] would like to see Inuit receive an apology and compensation similar to that offered to those Japanese interned in Canada during World War II.' An elder stated, 'It looks like there was an attempt at genocide when our dogs were killed, an attempt to annihilate us.' Other elders expressed similar views. 'All the men lost their dogs', said Josie P. Tullaugak. 'I remember women beginning to cry as if they were losing their own kin. It was a painful experience.' 'They were pretty close to shooting human beings', said another. 'I am not kidding you.'

The killing of the dogs was experienced as an attack on kinsmen or the Inuit people themselves. It was thought to have lasting effects. A young man said, 'Take a look at the young people today. I have a brother who is frequently in jail, but if a lot of dogs hadn't been killed, I'm sure he would have had a healthier youth.' Inuit remember that they often relied on their dogs for survival. 'Tookalook can remember subsisting on dog meat when there was nothing else to eat. In those days, dogs provided everything from transport, to fur, to friendship.' Another elder, Paulusie Weetaluktuk from Inukjuak, added, 'In the past, a man without a dog wasn't a man.' And Kaudjak Tarkirk from Salluit observed, 'We had all six of our dogs killed. When our dogs were killed it was like as if our loved ones passed away from us. The dogs to us were like human beings as they were our only means to get something. It seemed as if we became little children' (Anonymous 2005).[1] Clearly, eating the dogs and friendship with the dogs are by no means incompatible in these statements. The affection felt for the dogs does not exclude that the dogs are eaten if necessity requires doing so. There is no contradiction there. It only strengthens the bond between human beings and dogs.

Silas Kalluk from Baker Lake considers dogs and humans to be close partners who depend on each other: 'Dogs learn from older dogs and they learn as well when people teach them. Dogs are our protectors, as they can hear what we cannot hear, but we are really their protectors, since we feed them and care for them. They used to help us to get things from far away, so we used to want them to eat well' (quoted in Mannik 1998: 92). Mark Uninnak from Aupaluk feels indebted to dogs: 'The *qimmiit* ... were survival tools. In a blizzard, where you can't see anything, they could bring their master home. They are the real reason why people survived ... the *qimmiit* were the first ones to realize when the ice was dangerous, the first ones to recognize danger ... the *qimmiit* are the reason why I am alive today' (Anonymous 2005).

Resistance against killing dogs was already noted by Peter Freuchen (1935b: 179). He reports, 'A Hudson Bay Eskimo ... will never kill a dog. Even in case of rabies dogs are not killed. When a hunter wants to get rid of puppies he will leave them behind in the snow just as he would do in the case of an infanticide. He will not kill the puppy himself.' Birket-Smith (1929: 1:96, 171) also refers to the aversion of the Caribou Inuit to killing dogs.

A close association between an attack on the dogs and an attack on the community at large emerges from these recent statements of the Nunavik elders. It is congruent with ethnographic data collected earlier in the twentieth century. In this chapter, we will explore the position of dogs in Inuit traditional culture. To what extent are dogs seen as members of human society and what role did they play in preserving it? Then we will discuss Taylor's study of canicide as an Inuit killing ritual in Labrador. We will argue that the healing practices of killing or mutilating dogs can be explained in terms of the close relationship that exists between the dog and its owner within a logic of part-whole relationships.

## The Dogs as Animal Partners in Human Society

### *The Cosmological Position of the Dog*

Inuit have always relied on their dogs (s. *qimmiq*, pl. *qimmiit*) as their companions in hunting and travelling. In the past, they helped the hunter to trace the breathing holes of the sea game. They were useful in hunting down polar bears or caribou (see figure 6.1). Before the extensive use of snowmobiles, they enabled the Inuit to travel great distances on their sleds (*qamutiit*) (see figure 6.2) and to find their way in difficult terrain and bad weather (see Ekblaw 1928; Freuchen 1935b). They warned people in case of danger. There was a real symbiosis between dogs and men that might result in strong affectionate bonds.[2] Applying an ethno-linguistic approach, Therrien (1987b: 128–29) gives many examples of concepts expressing this symbiosis between dogs

**Figure 6.1.** The dog as a hunting companion. Dogs were often used to hunt polar bears. *Source:* Anglican Church of Canada/General Synod Archives/Peck Papers, M56-1, series XXXIII, 4–6, 8–13.

**Figure 6.2.** Charlie Inuaraq attaching his dogs to his *qamutik* (dog sled) before going out hunting in Mittimatalik. Photo: Frédéric Laugrand, 1995.

and humans. Thus, *qimuksiit* refers to the collective action of dogs and humans when they are pulling the sled together. Many words also apply to dogs as well as people: *iqiannguruittuq* refers to a brave person or dog; *angajuqqausiqpuq* to a person or dog trying to abuse its power or leadership position; and *itaapuq* to a pilfering person or dog.

The dogs helped the Inuit to live, but without their human masters the dogs themselves would not survive. Inuit fed their dogs well, and often the feeding of dogs had priority over the feeding of people, since dogs were indispensable to hunting. Only in times of need and scarcity were the tables reversed. Dogs might be eaten in times of starvation, but this was a last recourse.[3] Once the dogs were eaten, only cannibalism might save starving people from death (see, e.g., Mary-Rousselière 1980: 123). In considering the position of the dogs, we have to consider that in the Arctic dogs cannot survive outside society. They are no match for wolves. While Inuit were the human members of society, dogs were its animal members.

Dogs were on the borderline between the inside and the outside. They were not tolerated inside the houses and would sleep outside, but in times of harsh weather they might take refuge in the entrance of the igloo. In this respect the dog mediated between the outside and the inside. He did not live off the land or in the house, but in the intermediate zone around the house and in the entrance of the house. Dog-like features were attributed to some non-Inuit people, notably the Indians. Like dogs, they were halfway between human beings and wildlife.

We do not know when dogs were first domesticated, but the hunters who thousands of years ago migrated to the Arctic tundra to hunt the abundant caribou were probably already accompanied by their dogs. Freda Kretschmar (1938) has shown how the peoples of Europe, northern Asia and North America share a common cultural heritage with respect to dogs. In her study *Hundestammvater und Kerberos* she focuses on the two positions taken by dogs in the mythologies of these peoples. On one side the dog is often represented as the first ancestor of human beings, and on the other as the guardian of the realm of the dead. Those who enter the world of the dead have to get past the dog that is guarding the entrance. Thus, the dog is at the beginning and at the end of human life.[4]

These cosmological and mythical themes are shared by the Inuit. The myth of the dog husband relates how Indians, white people and other non-Inuit people or spirits originated from the marriage between a girl and a dog. The dog and the girl were transferred to a little island.[5] Each day the dog swam to the mainland to bring food from the father to the girl and her offspring. When the father became fed up with this he tricked the dog by loading the saddlebag with stones covered with a thin layer of meat. The dog drowned when he tried to swim to the island and he became the guardian of the world of the deceased under the sea. After her marriages to the dog and the stormy petrel the girl became the sea woman living in a house on the bottom of the sea.

Kappianaq (IE 096) described how *angakkuit* visiting the sea woman's house would have to face this dog:

> When they make their journey to the one known as Kannaaluk, there is a *qarmaq* down there without any roofing.... Once the *angakkuq* is about to enter, he will see a dog gnawing human bones. Once the dog has chewed up all the human bone, the skeleton of a human will all be chewed up thereby making it not possible ever again to be human. As the shaman is about to enter, the dog will be fierce. However, the shaman will enter without being touched by the dog. It is said that this dog belongs to Uinigumasuituq [the woman who did not want a husband, the sea woman].

Dogs also might serve as *tuurngait* for the *angakkuit*. The *tuurngaq* of a giant dog resembles that of the polar bear. According to Boas (1888: 597),

> Another spirit of which the natives are in great fear is Qiqirn, a phantom in the shape of a huge dog almost without hair. Like the bear which has

been alluded to, it has hair only at the mouth, the feet, and the points of the ears and the tail.

If it comes near dogs or men they fall into fits and only recover when Qiqirn has left. It is exceedingly afraid of men and runs away as soon as an angakoq descries it.

In Peck's list of *tuurngait* (Laugrand et al. 2006: 419-468) we find fourteen dogs described *as tuurngait*. Moreover, eleven more *tuurngait* have dogs as companions. Most dogs are considered good *tuurngait*. Only Qêkoot (no. 37) is evil. Pongoāk (no. 25) and Qingoatseak (no. 35) do not appear to be favourable to hunters. These spirits call to mind the dog at the bottom of the sea that was married to the *inua* of the sea. All other dogs are good helping spirits, tending to 'give freely'. Poutyukak (no. 170) and Taktôalik (no. 227) give freely. Nessalik (no. 177) gives seals; Ooyamêtok (no. 213) heals and gives food; Ooyameralalalak (no. 276) is swift and catches many reindeer. In some cases a *tuurngaq* brings game or goods through his/her dog, such as Tikgoangnuk (no. 175) and Siggalāk (no. 272).

The symbolism of the dog comes to the fore in procreation as well. Rose Iqallijuq from Iglulik related her prenatal memories in the womb to Saladin d'Anglure (1977). She recalled that the womb resembled a small house and through the entrance a dog came in and vomited white food. Thus, the penis of the father was represented by a dog. In her memories Iqallijuq echoes the myth of Akuulukju and Umernitu, where the same theme is recorded with respect to the first normal birth. Thus, we meet the dog at the origin of life as well as at the end of life, as described by Kappianaq. He encompasses human life. In the origin myth of the sea woman, as a *tuurngaq* and in the memories of Iqallijuq, he acts as a bringer of food.

### The Social Identity of Dogs

The dog in Inuit society has a peculiar feature that distinguishes it from other animals. It has a name (*atiq*) by which it can be addressed and to which it responds. From that perspective, each dog has a social identity. Moreover, each dog has an owner, the *inua* of the dog. Dogs and their owners (Inuit) were named, whereas other animals traditionally had an *inua*, its person or owner, but neither the *inua* nor the animal itself were usually named.

No systematic study has yet been made of the names of dogs. It appears that they can have all types of names, even the names of deceased human beings. Parry (1824: 521), who visited Iglulik in the early 1820s, observed, 'Their names are frequently the same as those of the people, and in some instances are given after the relations of their masters, which seems to be considered an act of kindness among them.' This was confirmed sixty years later by Franz Boas's (1888: 612) statement that 'dogs are called by the name of a friend as token of regards'. However, Mathiassen (1928: 84) no longer found the practice of naming dogs after friends and acquaintances in the 1920s.[6]

Rasmussen (1931: 150) provides much detailed information on the naming and significance of dogs in the Netsilik area. His findings corroborate the data provided by Parry and Boas. 'Dogs are named either after dead dogs or living people. And they should have many names, for they have a name-soul just as people have, and many names therefore shield them from sickness.' Their names operate very much like human names, protecting them from illness. Rasmussen gives the names of the five dogs of the *angakkuq* Qaqortingneq. Like humans, most of them have several names. Three are named after dead people, one after a shaman who is still alive. One dog who is named after a dead person also bears the name Qaqortingneq and is thus the shaman's namesake (Rasmussen 1931: 150). Birket-Smith (1929: 1:172) observes of the dogs of the Caribou Eskimo: 'Not uncommonly they are called after human beings, alive or dead.'[7] Fifty years later, in Kangiqsujuaq (Nunavik), Bernard Saladin d'Anglure collected similar testimonies from the famous Inuit writer Salumi Mitiarjuk Nappaaluk. According to Mitiarjuk Nappaaluk, a person may even give his own name to a dog. 'Dogs are taken as namesake…. When a very young child is given a dog and is asked what he is going to name it, he wants simply, out of affection, his [the child's] own name; so he receives as a namesake his own dog. Children do this because they are very infatuated [with their dogs]' (Mitiarjuk Nappaaluk 1994: 79). Then the child will become very fond of the dog and the dog will behave well: it will not steal and will always love its master and family. However, even though the dog would become a very good dog, it was not common practice to name a dog after oneself. Although the consequences are beneficial, the act of naming the dog after oneself appears to be a weakness (being infatuated with the dog).

One may also name a dog after an enemy:

When an Inuk has a dog, which is a rotten animal and does lots of thieving, it cannot really be considered as a good dog. So the Inuk may give it the name of someone that he has a grudge against. So having linked the dog to that person, without the dog knowing it, the Inuk will make it suffer and will feed it badly. It is as if he wants to make it waste away by giving it the name of someone that he has a grudge against. (Mitiarjuk Nappaaluk 1994: 79)

In this case it is the weakness of the dog, not of its owner, that is at the root of the namesake relationship.

Finally, the namesake relationship can be based on reciprocity. No weakness appears to be involved.

> An Inuk can give a dog the name of the person from whom it was acquired, even if he does not have a grudge against that person, because the Inuk, not knowing the name of the dog, often gave it the name of its previous owner. The dog was not an object of resentment, this was simply a way of naming it. So a name can be given out of affection, out of discontent, or out of ignorance of its name. Because of the great friendship uniting us, my late cousin Nutaraaluk Kristina and I each gave the other's name for fun to one of our dogs. My cousin had a dog [named] Mitiarjuk, and I had a dog [named] Nutaraaluk. We did that for fun, perhaps because we liked each other so much. (Mitiarjuk Nappaaluk 1994: 79)

In this case, the dog is named after a friend. An element of play is involved. Mitiarjuk Nappaaluk suggests that naming a dog after its previous owner was a common custom.

Rasmussen (1931: 150) also notes that in the Nattilik area a dog might be called after a relative for reasons of affection. An old woman had a dog named after her daughter, who lived in a distant village. She explained,

> Every time I feed my dog I persuade myself that now my daughter is also being fed. I am afraid of her being in want, and so I feel that I give her food every day. And when I call my dog by my daughter's name, it is as if my daughter, whom I love, is near, and so I believe, too, that if I always have my dog Qipajuaq beside me, I will often see Qipajuaq my daughter.[8]

The naming of a dog thus varies from a simple reference to its colour, such as 'the little black one', or a particular property of a dog, such as 'the hungry one', to the use of names that evoke relationships with human beings up to the point of emotional and affective identification. People may also be named after dogs. Winnie Tayak Putumiraqtuq reported that her brother-in-law was named after a dead shaman's dog spirit (Mannik 1998: 11). At the annual CIERA (Centre interuniversitaire d'études et des recherches autochthones) meeting in 2013, Nunavut commissioner Edna Elias also recalled being named after a dog.

People took great care to bring up puppies in such a way that they would become useful members of society. According to Piugaattuq (IE 60), puppies that had been fathered by a wolf were more attentive than other dogs and would not become elusive. To enhance the qualities and capacities of dogs, amulets could be used. Rasmussen (1931: 149) reports that among the Nattilingmiut a seal tooth round the neck gives a dog a powerful bite when fighting, and '[t]he big sinew at the front of the foreleg of a caribou ... round the neck of a pup ... gives strength and health'. Rasmussen (1932: 49) relates with respect to the Copper Inuit, 'The small snails one finds in the country are hung round the necks of dogs as amulets. A dog with an amulet of this kind will notice at once when the bad weather is approaching; it will become restless and warn its master.'

Today, Angutinngurniq recalls,

Back then when pups were born, their characters were also made. I think when they were being born there was something placed in their mouths but I can't remember what it was. It was only, I remember, if they were born in the summer; a mosquito or a shrimp, they are called *uqumiut*, was placed there. Because when they became adult dogs, they would be the ones that were good at finding seal holes. I think we call them *iqurniit*. They [*uqumiut*] are a little bit yellow and a little bit long, not that long. I remember one being placed around the neck so that this dog would have long legs. I have seen this but I don't know if it was considered as *aarnguat*. Also, so the dog wouldn't have a big stomach. (Kugaaruk workshop, 2004)

Philipp Qipanniq (IE 019) also recalled various techniques to improve a dog's qualities:

So in order for the dogs to have tough paws they would use a polar bear paw to hit the dogs while they are still pups, or hit them with a polar bear's *iquliniq*, fur around the anus area, so that when they mature they can be aggressive towards game animals. Or when I am eating cooked polar bear meat, I should not use a knife but strip the meat with my teeth. So I used to have good aggressive dogs. I would think that this was true as it was done at the urging of the elders. I know that the elders knew what they were saying as they would have gained all that knowledge from personal experience.[9]

A widespread procedure to improve the qualities of dogs was cutting their tails off, especially when they were still puppies. Freuchen (1935b: 184) reports,

Many people among the Central Eskimos have the idea that cutting a dog's tail off when young makes it faster. Others cut them off because the dogs are inclined to collect lumps of ice in the tail hairs, although some merely cut away the longest hairs. I once met a man who had four dogs minus their tails. He declared frankly that he had cut them off as the result of a dream.[10]

Freuchen (1935b: 162) states that sometimes the carnassials were also removed to prevent a dog from eating its harness. Usually it was done while the dogs were still puppies. However, a fully grown dog could be made unconscious for a few minutes by hanging, and then the carnassials were removed with a hammer.[11]

Observing specific rules might also enhance the qualities of a dog. Rasmussen (1931: 149) reports that a female pup should be given the gulped-up food of an owl. Then it will become a good mother with big pups. Its nostrils should be sucked now and then so that it will have a good sense of smell and easily get the scent of seal breathing holes. A puppy is provided with a small saddlebag with two firestones so that it will be a good at carrying burdens in summer. Every time it has eaten it must be blown into its anus with the mouth so that it will be able to go for a long time without getting hungry.

Dogs were not allowed to eat anything that pleased them such as hare meat or bones of caribou caught with a kayak at a crossing place. That would offend the souls of the caribou and bring about bad hunting. They were not allowed to eat the flesh of a hare, for then they will become thin and their coat poor (Rasmussen 1932: 40). Dogs were often fed with wolf meat or fox meat (Mannik 1998: 14).[12]

When Christianity was adopted by the Inuit of the Canadian eastern Arctic, dogs as well as humans were involved in the process. In the Iglulik area, at Ingnertok, the Christian leader Umik requested that all visiting people had to shake hands with the dogs (Mathiassen 1928: 235). Freuchen (1935a: 435) reports that dogs in Naujaat had to wear a crucifix on their necks.

The Nattilingmiut had to observe ritual rules with respect to dogs: 'No man may eat dog flesh, and their skins must never be used for clothing or sleeping rugs; a sick dog must never be killed, it must die itself, and if it is dead, it must be dragged some distance away from the house and left with a stone at head and hindquarters. Small dead pups, however, are sometimes buried under stones' (Rasmussen 1931: 150).[13]

Various practices such as naming, the use of amulets and the presence of social rules suggest that the dog is a member of society. However, even if the dog is a social being in many respects, it remains a non-human being and is treated as such.

## The Ambiguity of Dogs

Although dogs were the partners of human beings in society and the only animals to be given names, dogs were also fairly ambiguous when it came to eating (dogs eating humans as well as humans eating dogs) and sexual intercourse.

Dogs ate human faeces and sometimes even human corpses (see also Freuchen 1935b: 152). In the past, Canadian Inuit did not bury their dead but placed them on the frozen ground, surrounded by stones. From the ethnographic records it becomes clear that the dead were often eaten by the dogs. Captain Lyon (1824: 371) observed, 'The Eskimaux are quite regardless of the body when it has once been covered (with snow); and the nearest relations will not cover it again, even if they see that the dogs have dug up and are devouring it: this we have known to be actually the case.' In December 1901, Peck stated after the death of Kappeyok, 'Often these wretched people leave the bodies of the deceased to be devoured by dogs' (ANC/GSA/Peck Papers M56-3).[14] Boas (1888: 613) observed, 'It is strange that, though the ceremonies of burying are very strictly attended ... they do not heed the opening of the graves by dogs or wolves and the devouring of the bodies.' He notes that during funerals, 'dogs are not fed until 3 days after the death have passed' (Boas 1907: 486). 'After returning from the burial, the relatives must lock themselves up in the old hut for three days. ... After they leave the hut forever, the dogs are thrown into it through the window and allowed to devour whatever they can get at' (Boas 1888: 614). Thus, it is left to the dogs to get rid of the remains of the deceased as well as his edible possessions. Rasmussen relates concerning the Iglulik area that at the end of the mourning period, one of those who assisted in disposing of the corpse at the burial site took a piece of a dog's excrement and carried it around the house of the deceased in all directions (Rasmussen 1929: 199). We may infer that a dog's faeces were associated with human faeces as well as the flesh of the corpse. In this respect the faeces of dogs represent the end of the cycle of life and death.

Various other rules applied to dogs after a death. With respect to the relation between dogs and sleds, Boas (1888: 613) noted, 'Dogs are never allowed to drag the sledge on such an occasion [burial].' Moreover, 'For three or sometimes even four days after a death the inhabitants of a village must not use their dogs' (Boas 1888: 614). Instead, they should walk to their hunting grounds. 'On the sixth day they are at liberty to use their dogs again' (Boas 1888: 615). Rasmussen reports concerning the Copper Inuit that after a death dogs should only eat flesh and never gnaw the bones of game animals.[15]

Eating dogs might be a last recourse in case of starvation, but dogs were not considered as food. Freuchen (1935b: 178–79) states that Inuit in Canada will not eat dog flesh. He connects it to cannibalism, noting that '[s]ome people at Iglulik said they ate neither dog nor bear meat because it reminded them too much of human flesh'.[16] Rasmussen (1931: 150) observes that no man may eat dog flesh.[17] Olive Mammak Innakatsik from Qamanittuaq remembers how in a context of starvation she was afraid of eating dog meat even if it was cooked (quoted in Mannik 1998: 61).[18]

Freuchen (1935b: 178) reports that Inuit dogs should not be overfed. Otherwise, they would be less effective as sled dogs. However, they may attack and eat human beings when they get hungry. Freuchen (1935b: 178) relates a case of dogs that had been well fed but then attacked and ate the seven-year-old daughter of their owner. Regilee Ootova (2000: 20) related that in the old days, particularly in winter, the afterbirth 'would be carefully hidden from the dogs as they easily could develop a taste for human flesh'. Thus, dogs were considered potential eaters of human flesh.

As in most societies, alimentary and sexual symbolism are closely connected in Inuit culture. Both the eating of dogs and sexual intercourse with dogs were matters of controversy. The notion of sexual intercourse with a dog was not only a central theme[19] in the myth of the sea woman who married a dog, but also a topic of interest in Inuit society. Rasmussen (1931: 197–98) related that among the Nattilingmiut it was viewed as a common practice and that no shame was attached to it. Even respectable hunters might be involved in it. Specific rules had to be observed, however:

> Intercourse with dogs must take place when they are in heat; the natural instincts of the animals must be respected and it is considered to be dangerous to attempt it out of season. Aqatsuaq, a man up in years, one of the best salmon fishers, was mentioned as a particularly ardent votary of this means of obtaining sexual satisfaction; 'But', they say, 'he once got a bad collarbone because he sought intercourse with she-dogs out of season. A *torngaq* has struck him with sickness of the collarbone to punish him for seeking love with a dog out of season.'
>
> Copulation with dogs must always take place out under the open sky, never indoors.

Intercourse between dogs and women was also reported, and in one case it was related that after having intercourse with a dog a woman 'had given birth to young, some of which were dogs with human hands and hairless bodies. She had been confined in the open air in the shelter of some stones, but her fellow-villagers had been ashamed of her and pushed the stones down over her so that she and her young were killed' (Rasmussen 1931: 198).[20]

Even today, bestiality is often referred to in the Iglulik Oral Traditions Project database, and various elders, such as Emile Imaruittuq, referred to it extensively (quoted in Oosten et al. 1999: 152–53).[21] However, despite Rasmussen's reports of the Nattilingmiut, it is usually considered to be shameful, affecting the health and well-being of the perpetrator or his loved ones. Obviously most reports of bestiality are based on hearsay, and it is hard to say to what extent intercourse with dogs really took place to the extent that ethnographic sources suggest. But it clearly played an important part in the discourse on sexual relations. The dogs were not only viewed as social partners through their names; they were also potential sexual partners.

While dogs could become sexual partners, some human beings were also considered to be like dogs. Inuit attributed dog-like behaviour to *itqilît*, or Indians. Narratives relate that their women were supposed to behave like bitches in heat. The notion suggests a strong aversion to marriages with Indians.[22] The term 'dog' could also be used as a pejorative for sexual partners within Inuit society. Father Jean Philippe (1947: 3) noted that Inuit women could be referred to as dogs by their husbands: 'A woman was often called a dog by her husband even when he was not provoked to anger.'

Thus dogs were considered inedible, and yet people could take recourse to eating dogs in times of starvation. Sexual intercourse with dogs was not allowed, yet it was an important topic of discourse and played an important part in the origin myth of the sea woman. Therefore, dogs were ambiguous as food and as sexual partners.

### Dogs as Protectors of the Community

As stated previously, dogs constituted an intermediate category with respect to the outside world, unable to survive in the wild but not invited into the home with the human beings. In this position as a mediator between the inside and the outside, they also protected the community from human enemies as well as dangerous spirits. Freuchen (1935b: 181–82) reported, 'As in Greenland, the Canadian Eskimo dogs yap when anything unusual approaches, a circumstance which is often taken by the Eskimo to mean that they can see mountain spirits or other ghosts, as the dogs often give a warning at the approach of things which men are unable to see.' When dogs are seized by unexplainable panic it is 'put down to supernatural causes, visible only to dogs and shamans'. Rasmussen (1932: 36) gives similar information for the Copper Inuit: 'If a house is visited by evil spirits and the dogs start to bark, which is always a sure sign of the presence of spirits, they put two pieces of wick-moss up against the window, and all the people gathered in the threatened house to exorcise the spirits.' Kappianaq from Iglulik recalled, 'Sometimes we would know from our dogs who would be spooked if they smelled wolves. It is *tuurnginngujuq*, being spooked by a *tuurngaq*. That is when the dogs are aware of a *tuurngaq* being close by, they are spooked' (quoted in Oosten and Laugrand 2001: 62).[23] The dogs thus play a part in protecting the community against dangers that cannot be perceived by ordinary people.

Indeed, when a dog cried, something was seriously amiss. As Luke Anautalik from Arviat related (quoted in Oosten and Laugrand 2010: 185–86),

> There was another incident that happened when this dog started crying like a person. That dog was able to speak Inuktitut. It was crying like it was evil. It turned into a dog that could speak. I took it outside, and it kept crying. You have heard people cry very loudly and that's how the dog cried. The dog told me to look around for something. That dog could speak. I started looking for something but I didn't see anything. I got tired so I went to bed. I could hear the dog crying, and I feel asleep. When you have been crying for a period of time you make a certain kind of noise. The dog was making that kind of noise. While it was still crying I went to sleep. When I woke up, the dog was frozen.

Nutaraaluk from Iqaluit related how his kinsman Miqqualaq committed murder (quoted in Oosten et al. 1999: 110):

> He was hearing bad things inside his head. He travelled to his grandparents camp to talk about this. He told them he shot at his dogs but they wouldn't die; they only cried out in pain. He removed the cartridges from his gun and the cartridges were still whole. He told them his intention was to kill the dogs and then to kill his parents but he was unable to kill the dogs. He used his father's dogteam to visit his grandparents. This experience that he went through triggered his attempt to wipe out the camp.

Miqqualaq effectively murdered his parents, but his attempt to wipe out the whole camp failed, and Miqqualaq was killed by his own kinsmen.

The dog was the animal partner of human beings in human society. Dogs had to observe ritual injunctions like human beings. They should not be eaten, and there were even burial rules applying to dogs. They were named like human beings, and their names could evoke relations between human beings. As animal partners of human beings, they were potential sexual partners as well as potential food. But the use of dogs as sexual partners or food was controversial and ambiguous. Sexual intercourse with a dog was the first step to bestiality, and eating dogs was the first step towards cannibalism. In cosmological terms, dogs could be at the start of life (as ancestors of human or human-like beings) or at the end of life (in their role of cleaning up the remains of human corpses and the possessions of their deceased owners and as guardian of the land of the dead under the sea). Like shamans they were aware of the spirits, and their barking or whining might prevent a conjunction of spirits and Inuit or a collapse of heaven and earth. Thus, dogs seem to be always between: between animals and human beings, between spirits and human beings. They constitute a transitory category and in ritual terms they appear everywhere the boundaries between distinct categories may collapse. The dogs then provide remedies to prevent those collapses and preserve the separation of categories.

## The Killing of Dogs

In the *Nunatsiaq News* the killing of dogs was described as an attack on human society. But ethnographic sources testify that the killing of dogs occurred in the past in Inuit societies and might even be a remedy against illness. In the second part of this chapter we will examine in more detail how this apparent contradiction between the killing of dogs as an attack on society and the killing of dogs as a remedy for disease can be explained. We will begin the discussion with an examination of Taylor's important study of canicide in Labrador.

### *Sacrifice or Exorcism?*

John Garth Taylor (1993: 4–6) described three cases of canicide as healing rituals in Labrador at the end of the eighteenth and the beginning of the nineteenth century.

*1. Hopedale, 1796*
An Inuk named Lucas became ill and had one of his dogs that was not worth much brought into his tent. 'He stabbed it and washed his hands in the dog's blood. This was supposed to help save him from death and the dog should die instead of him' (Taylor 1993: 4).
*2. Okak, 1804*
After the wife of the shaman Uivernuna had died, the shaman wished to depart with several people in a boat.

> After the sick and the healthy got into the boat, he (Uivernuna) once more stepped ashore. He ordered that a dog (which of course had a lame leg) be captured and stabbed it quickly in the chest.... He washed his hands with

its blood and let some run on the land which they were just about to leave. This was intended to prevent and hold back the bad disease so that death would not follow them. (Taylor 1993: 5)

### 3. Hopedale, 1811

When an epidemic raged at Hopedale, people tried to avert illness and death by stabbing a dog and cutting off the ears of several other dogs. Later, people compared their action to slaughter of the Passover lamb. A widow also requested her son to cut off the ears of one of his dogs so that she would recover, but he refused to do so. She specified that the dog should not be 'livelier and healthier than herself' (Taylor 1993: 6).

Taylor first proposes that the dog is sacrificed as a substitute for a human being. The notion of sacrifice was already used by the Anglican missionary Peck when he referred to the sacrificial dimensions of the killing of a dog in Nunavik (quoted in Lewis 1904: 23):

> 'I have known', writes Mr. Peck in this connection, 'a sick man who was scarce(ly) able to crawl, and who had no angakok at hand, managed to load his gun and with great difficulty shot his dog, hoping to recover by merit of his sacrifice, though the sequel to his act was not a cure, for he died of the malady of which he was suffering'.[24]

The notion of sacrifice seems to be derived more from the Reverend Peck's vocabulary than from an Inuit notion. Taylor uses the notion of sacrifice as an explanatory concept. He is well aware of the problems raised by applying this notion to Inuit culture. He relies mainly on Siberian data provided by Bogoras and Jochelson with respect to Chuckchee and Koryak traditions. But even here the notion of sacrifice is problematic. The sacrificial interpretations referred to in the Hopedale case by Taylor, such as the reference to the Passover lamb, were derived from a Christian tradition, not from an Inuit tradition. Taylor does not make clear what is gained by qualifying these ritual killings as sacrifice. Inuit culture did not have a sacrificial tradition. Ritual rules focused on bringing animals into the community, not transferring animals from the community to the spirits. Even though we cannot exclude the sacrificial hypothesis completely, we should approach it with caution, as the notion of sacrifice itself is complex, tangled and open to conflicting interpretations. The qualification of a killing as a sacrifice explains little unless it is embedded in a specific theory of sacrifice. Such a theory is not presented in Taylor's paper.

Taylor then proposes a second interpretation of the ritual killing of dogs. He compares the mutilations of the dogs to the ritual fights with *tupilait*, evil spirits, that might imply wounding the *tupilait* and shedding their blood on the earth. He argues that *tupilait* might take the shape of animals. He gives the example of a dog that was killed by some Inuit at Nain in the early 1870s because it was considered to be Satan. The influence of Christian ideas again appears to have played a part. The dog was axed and buried. Taylor concludes that it is more likely that dogs were seen as the causes of disease than as mere sacrificial offerings.

Neither interpretation is convincing. The second interpretation does not answer the question of why specifically dogs are killed. One would expect that any animal representing a *tupilaq* would be liable to be killed, unless there is a specific reason for *tupilait* to adopt the appearance of a dog. Taylor does not give any proof of such a preference.

In the killings described by Taylor the shedding of blood plays an important part.[25] In this respect it contrasts with killings described by Jensen (1961: 58), who stated that hanging, *qiminitseq*, was the most common method for killing dogs, whereas nowadays dogs are killed with a .22-calibre rifle.[26] It is worthwhile to note that strangling was also practised in the Nunavik area.

Strangling also occurred in the case of human suicide. Old people wanting to commit suicide were often assisted by kinsmen. Apparently this was not conceived as murder, and no revenge from the shade was feared. In this respect it is noteworthy that Jenness (1922: 171) refers to the dangers of killing a dog named after a human being. The shade of the namesake may take revenge on the killer. Inversely, a dog may avenge a human being; the dog was also capable of revenge. Rasmussen (1932: 47) reports that used as an amulet, 'bones of a dog have the effect that, if one is murdered by men, revenge will be taken by the soul of the dog' (Rasmussen 1932: 47).

The Swiss missionary Samuel Waldmann relates that in northern Labrador dogs were not always killed to heal the sick:

> One also wounds an animal to appease the sufferings of the sick; thus, in the winter of 1906–1907, I found close to me a dog that was wounded by a bullet. When I asked the owner of the beast why he had wounded it, he answered me that his dog always escaped in the night to disturb the fox traps. He lied. One of the children of that man had a faint during the night. On the advice of his uncle he had wounded the dog to save the sick person.
>
> I saw another dog that had the tendons of the hind legs cut. With some trouble I found out that a young boy had committed this cruelty to save his sick mother. (Waldmann 1909–10: 440, our translation)

If the dog is not necessarily killed to cure a sick or dying person, the explanations by Taylor become even less convincing.

Mutilation of dogs also occurred in cases besides sickness. L. Turner relates the following concerning beliefs in Nunavik ([1894] 1979: 36):

> A great spirit controls the reindeer. He dwells in a huge cavern near the end of Cape Chidley. ... The spirit is informed that the people have in no way offended him, as the shaman, as mediator between the spirit and the people, has taken great care that the past food was all eaten and that last spring ... none of the young (or fœtal) deer were devoured by the dogs. ... So long as the people refrain from feeding their dogs with the unborn young, the spirit of the deer will in time return again to his guardianship.
>
> Certain parts of the first deer killed must be eaten raw, others discarded, and others must be eaten cooked. The dogs must not be allowed to taste of the flesh, and not until an abundance has been obtained must they be allowed to gnaw at the leg bones, lest the guardian spirit of the deer be offended and refuse to send further supplies. If by some misfortune the dogs get at the meat, a piece of the offending dog's tail is cut off or his ear is cropped to allow a flood of blood.

Apparently the mutilation of the dog restored the relation between human beings and the spirit of the deer. It seems that not the killing of the dog but the shedding of its blood is the crucial feature connecting all these rituals.

However, it is by no means clear why this shedding of blood should be effective. Mitiarjuk Nappaaluk related that, in Kangiqsujuaq, Nunavik, Inuit could cut dog's ears to protect themselves from being attacked by the *aqsaqniit*, the northern lights (Mitiarjuk Nappaaluk 1993: 16). In this case, the goal of this action seems to have been to protect the owner of the dog against harm.[27]

The killing and mutilation of dogs should not be understood in terms of sacrifice or the killing of *tupilait* but in the context of healing.

### Healing

Elders today still see a connection between the health of people and the health of dogs. According to Tipuula Qaapik Atagutsiaq, a healer from Tununirusiq (Arctic Bay), 'People were relieved when it was the dogs that died instead of them. It was said that if it wasn't the dogs that were sick it would have been humans instead, so they were relieved. It was better if the dogs were dying instead of people' (quoted in Therrien and Laugrand 2001: 123). Peck (ANC/GSA/M56-1, XXXV no 19) reports that west of Hudson Bay, 'The *angakkuq* questions the sick man of his past life and deeds. After confession the conjuror orders one of the sick man's dogs to be shot.'[28]

When a child was attacked by a dog, its recovery was closely connected to the well-being of the dog that had attacked it. Paulusie Angmalik from Pangniqtuuq observed, 'If they [dogs] killed somebody they were supposed to be destroyed seven days later. They were not supposed to be killed right away, because it was feared that they would take revenge' (quoted in Oosten and Laugrand 1999a: 119). Ilisapi Ootoova from Mittimatalik stated, 'I have heard that if a child was attacked by dogs and was seriously injured but still alive, the dogs were not supposed to be killed. They had to wait for the child to recover and only then could the dogs be destroyed so they wouldn't attack again.' This was confirmed by Tipuula Atagutsiaq. Tirisi Ijjangiaq from Iglulik related that Kupaaq from Mittimatalik was bitten by a dog and that his stitches opened again when the dog that had bitten him was punished by its owner (quoted in Therrien and Laugrand 2001: 123).[29]

The central role of dogs in healing is well illustrated by a magic song recorded by Rasmussen (1931: 281–82) among the Nattilik Inuit:

A woman, it is said, turned back for a dog that was lame,
A magic song, it is said, it then uttered, and she heard it:
    My dog's down there
    Its skin down there
    Its foot-sole down there
    My gift, my present,
    The one without a pattern, ajai
    There, there, yonder
    A skin boat put off from land
    At (the spirit) Manilik's he was born
    aijauna uwfale-una
    ufvatitaujaq
    niklatitaujaq
    poq poq poq!
The last lines are special dogs words that cannot be turned into comprehensible human speech, but they are of powerful effect, driving out evil spirits, when uttered by a sick person.

The healing song comes from a lame dog, who provided it to an old woman. The song itself contains dog words, confirming that dogs have their own language. These dog words drive out evil spirits, emphasizing the importance of dogs as guardians of human society against evil spirits.

Various substances derived from the dog such as urine, saliva and faeces were credited with strong healing powers. According to Salumi Ka&&ak Qalasiq from Kangir&iniq, the urine of old dogs was used to cure patients. Felix Pisuk, from the same community, had to try the remedy as a child, but he immediately threw it up. Pisuk also stated, 'I have heard that some people when they are sick cut themselves a little, then get the dog to lick them because of its healing power.'[30] Manelaq, a Nattilik woman, told Rasmussen (1931: 221–22):

> When I was a girl my grandmother took me out with her and found old dog turds for me. Every single turd I had to wet with my tongue, and when it was softened I had to rub myself with it all over my breast and stomach. That made me vigorous for the old shaman told me that dog turds, used in the right way possess magic powers and are a kind of fountain of youth.

Rasmussen also observed for the Copper Inuit that the saliva of a dog is good for certain ailments, especially those of long duration. The saliva must be swallowed, and then something must be given to the dog in payment, for instance, a handsome collar of skin (Rasmussen 1932: 49). Jenness (1922: 172) also refers to the healing qualities of the saliva of a dog. He relates how his dog was thought to restore the lost souls of sick people. A white caribou fur was attached to its neck in recognition of its healing. The white caribou fur, the *pukiq*, was also the preferred material for a *tapsi* or *angaluk,* a shamanic belt.

The head of the dog could also be used for certain purposes. In Mittimatalik a dog's head was given to a boy to eat when he was one year old, so that he would have a strong head (Boas 1907: 514).

In the Kitikmeot area, it was thought that dogs could take away a sickness. The Oblate missionary Lucien Delalande related that someone pressed on a boil and transferred the pus to a dog, and so the illness was cured (Delalande 1958: 154; see also Jenness 1922: 173).

Dogs' names might also be used for healing. Boas (1888: 612) reported, 'When a person falls sick the angakut change his name in order to ward off the disease or they consecrate him as a dog to Sedna. In the latter's event he gets a dog's name and must wear throughout life a harness over the inner jacket.'[31] Boas (1907: 510) stated that on the west coast of Hudson Bay a young *angakkuq* should not whip his own dogs for a whole year after he has accepted the calling. The notion of whipping is intriguing in this respect. In the story of Kaujjakjuk it is related that an orphan grew into a very strong man by being whipped by the moon spirit. In normal circumstances one would whip a dog, not a human being. The story may imply that Kaujjakjuk became strong by being treated as a dog of the moon. Becoming a dog may thus be a means of becoming healthy and strong.

## Discussion

Eating a dog, having sexual intercourse with a dog and killing or wounding a dog are usually controversial acts. Only the cutting of the tail to improve a dog's qualities seems to be generally accepted. The other acts imply a dangerous balancing on the borderline between animal and human behaviour. They are central to Inuit discourse but do not seem to have occurred frequently in practice. Taylor (1993) presents only a few cases of the actual killing of a dog. Yet, the close relationship between dogs and the health of Inuit is still acknowledged by elders today. Clearly, there are great inhibitions in performing these acts. Several factors contribute to this.

First of all, the dog has a name. In the past, human beings could be killed without problem if they had not yet been named. Once a child had been named, the killing was no longer allowed, as now a relation to a namesake was implied. In the central Arctic, a dog's name was traditionally often related to a human being, a friend or a relative. Any action towards the animal implied an action towards the namesake.

In the past, it was assumed that each animal had an *inua* or owner. That *inua* appeared as a human being and many stories relate how people arrived in places where animals lived in human appearance. For dogs such places did not exist. The Inuit were their owners.[32] Dog and owner constituted a pair, just like an animal and its *inua*. This may be the reason why in the central Arctic, according to Freuchen, it was not the custom to sell dogs: 'In fact, the two men explained to me that if they purchased dogs of others the sellers would always feel that they had done a benevolent action, and, no matter what had been paid for them, the sellers would always consider they had the right to take them back again' (Freuchen 1935b: 144).[33]

The bond between owner and dog would be even stronger if the dog was named after its master, as in the cases referred to by Mitiarjuk Nappaaluk and Qaqortingneq. Eating one's dog, killing it or having sexual intercourse with it was considered repulsive, but it might be required in times of need.

The wounding or killing of dogs took place in cases of disease. Unfortunately, we have no information about the cause of such illnesses, so we do not know whether the cause of the illness affected the nature of the cure. Neither do we know how the mode of killing affected the cure.

The *inua* of a dog and his dog belonged together. The closeness of the relationship is expressed in the account of Iqallijuq, where the dog

represents the penis of the man. Thus, the dog and his owner constitute a physical whole. Dogs and human beings also constituted a social
whole, as indicated by the accounts of the *Nunatsiaq News* in which
an attack on the dogs was perceived as an attack on the community.
Killing the dogs implied an attack on their owners, hence the reference
to a kind of genocide by one of the elders. Obviously, the community
as a whole consists not only of people, but also of the dogs they own.

In explaining the symbolism of dogs we have to take into account
the relationship between various part-whole relationships. First, the
relationship between a person and the cosmic order; second, between
the dog and its owner; and third, between a dog and its parts.

Illness was usually perceived as a disintegration of a whole: the shade
or *tarniq* of a person might have become separated from his body. If it
did not return, the patient might die. A person might also have transgressed a ritual injunction and so antagonized the owners of the game,
or the spirits of the dead. In all these cases relations had to be restored.
A confession of transgressions was usually required. Only when the
relationships between the people of the community or between people
and spirits were restored could healing be successful. A healing process can therefore be considered as a restoration of a whole, be it the
unity of the body and the *tarniq,* or the relations between the person
and the spirits and other people, that is, the society at large.

In this respect, the contrast between the two modes of killing dogs
considered above is relevant. In the case of strangling the *anirniq,*
breath, is retained in the body and the whole of the body is preserved.
In the case of stabbing or mutilation a separation between the body
and the blood or a part of the body and the rest of the body is effected.
The latter procedure is followed to heal an illness. Healing procedures
might include a separation between a dog and his owner, that is, the
dog is killed, or a mutilation of the dog, that is, part of the dog might
be cut off (ears, tail, etc.) or the dog might be made to bleed. Why are
these procedures thought to be effective?

Healing through manipulating parts and wholes is a widespread
phenomenon. In an excellent paper on the healing gift in Halmahera,
eastern Indonesia, Jos Platenkamp (1996) provides a stimulating theoretical framework for the analysis of part-whole relationships in
healing techniques. He argues that the manipulation of part-whole
relationships focuses on the transfer of relationships. A part may be
separated from a whole, and a new part-whole relationship may be
constructed that serves to transfer the properties from the original
whole to the person. In this way we do not need the idea of the transfer
of an element to explain the practice. The whole procedure is embed-

ded in a logic of relationships. We may apply this approach to the case of Manelaq, in which the faeces of a dog were rubbed on the body of a human being. The implication would be that now relevant others (spirits, people) would attribute to her the properties of a dog and not harm her. The logic of this operation may imply that through such an operation the person herself is referred to as a dog. This can indeed be the case, for example, when a person who wears the harness of a dog is transformed into a dog of Sedna.

A second aspect should also be taken into account. The dog functions as a pars pro toto. If society is afflicted, it is better that the dogs die first; if a human being is afflicted, it is better that his dog dies. Even part of the dog may suffice, either to save a human being or to save the dog. It is hence by destroying a part that the whole is improved or restored.

Illness cannot only be viewed as a disjunction, between a human being and his *tarniq* or between a human being and other human beings, but also as an undesirable conjunction with death. In that case a ritual is required that effects a disjunction and separates a person from the disease and eventual death that may befall him. The dog is a whole that is divided. When the separation of life and death is at stake and the life of a human being becomes tenuous, the mediator between life and death, the dog, who is always on the borderline between life and death as well as between animals and human beings, is separated into parts. By dividing the mediator the separation between life and death is restored and a sick human being becomes well again. The separation between the person and the socio-cosmic order of which he is part is replaced by a separation between the dog and its blood. The cure implies a separation of the dog from its owner, and in most cases is effected by a stabbing, which results in the mutilation or the killing of the dog. The person restores the relation to his community or the spirits by dividing the dog into parts. The procedure can only be effective because there is such a close relationship between the dog and his owner. If we apply the logic proposed by Platenkamp, we might argue that by killing the dog, or destroying part of the dog, significant others (spirits, enemies) will consider the person dead, and there is no need to kill him anymore. The destruction of the part is the only way to save the whole.

The same logic may have been at work in the killing of the dogs in the Parousial movements, where this was a recurrent feature (see Blaisel et al. 1999). Thus, the religious leaders in Kangirsuk, Home Bay and the Belcher Islands required that the hunters killed their dogs. The killing of dogs was thought to be an effective means of realizing the

Parousia. By killing the dogs the hunters destroyed part of themselves and their community and became part of a new and other world. In all cases the killing of dogs appears to be a last resort, for the individual as well as for the community, in times of great need to effect a transition from a state of utter hopelessness to a new life.

## Notes

1. See the report submitted by Makivik to the minister of Indian Affairs and Northern Development for the government of Canada entitled *Regarding the Slaughtering of Nunavik 'Qimmiit' (Inuit Dogs) from the mid-1950s to the late 1960s.* Since the Qikiqtani Truth Commission was created by the Qikiqtani Inuit Association to enquire about dog killings in Nunavut between 1950 and 1975, several studies were conducted on this topic. See Lévesque (2008, 2010, 2011) and Tester (2010) for the dog killings in Nunavut and Nunavik.
2. The literature on dogs in North America is considerable. An interesting and recent study by Delâge (2005) deals with dog rituals. On the history of the Inuit dog, see McRury (1991) and Cummins (2002). See also Kishigami (1993) for the Nattilik area and Tumivut (2000).
3. Dog meat was never easy to eat. See the testimonies of elders who experienced eating dog meat in starving conditions in Mannik (1998: 11, 17, 49) and Patridge (2009: 102, 142).
4. Among the Innu, the dog is sometimes described as the grandfather of human beings (Clément 2012: 486), whereas among the Koyukon it is the reverse. The person who owns dogs is called their 'grandfather' or 'grandmother' and the animals are referred as 'grandchildren' (R. Nelson 1983: 191).
5. Weyer (1932: 101–2) points out that some Inuit groups in Labrador and Greenland used to banish their dogs to a small island to fend for themselves. In the myth of the woman who did not want to marry, the father kills the dog when it proves to be unable to provide for its family and has to collect food from its father-in-law, whereas the norm would be that a son-in law provides food for his parents-in-law. In this respect it is striking that in the list of *tuurngait* (helping spirits) of Peck, the dogs figure primarily as bringers of food (see Laugrand et al. 2001: 81–82).
6. He collected lists of dog names from Igalik and Southampton Island: 'The names of a sledgeteam from Igalik were: Iglulingmiutaq – the one from Iglulik; Qernerkuluk – little black one; Qingmikuluk – the little dog: Tunuserut – the one from Admiralty Inlet; Tabakert – tobacco; Qernialuk – the big black one; Nakateq – the one who does not get what he goes for; Kaktoq – the hungry one; Taguarbik, Ququngmiaq, Paqbiseq, Ajakaluk – "only names"' (Mathiassen 1928: 84).
7. Among the Copper Inuit naming followed a similar pattern. Whittaker (1937: 202) reports, 'The puppy may be named for any relative of its mas-

ter or mistress.... The name of a dead relation is most often used.' In Greenland the situation is less clear. See Jensen (1961: 51) for the naming of puppies.

8. See also the case of Katsarsuk in Rasmussen (1929: 281).

9. The use of amulets for dogs is also well documented in Greenland. Jensen (1961: 50–51) reports on their use in Umanaq. An informant first tried a shrimp as amulet, but the dogs just devoured it. Then he tried caribou hair tied around the neck of a bitch. When she got puppies they were very big and grew fast, but suddenly they all died. 'When a bitch next came on heat I sewed together a feather, leg and bones of a ptarmigan, *aqigsseq*, and tied them round the dog's neck. The puppies were born and grew up like other puppies. When they learned to walk they accompanied us when we went to cut peat. They ate the flowers on the mountain, ate everything other dogs could not eat. They were always in the same condition, summer and winter' (Jensen 1961: 50).

10. See also Mathiassen (1928: 89). The cutting of tails was common in eastern Greenland as well as western Greenland. Holm reports it in Ammassalik (Holm 1887: 32) and Nansen (1891: 21; quoted in Jensen 1961: 57) in western Greenland. According to Jensen (1961: 56), 'When puppies begin to die one after the other. ... The hunter cuts off a piece of the living puppies tail, where after the animals stop dying, say a large number of informants.' It is also thought to be a good 'remedy against laziness', *eqiasungnavêrsârut*, in dogs (Jensen 1961: 56). In the southern Disko Bay area it was practised to help a dog to get rid of its indisposition when moulting. Moreover, 'in the old days some sledge drivers were of the opinion that the dogs became more alert when they had not so much blood. Therefore they removed the tail or a piece of it and thereby the superfluous blood' (G. Nellemann, personal communication, 1959; quoted in Jensen 1961: 57). The practice of ear and tail cutting was still continued by an old hunter in the Umanaq district in 1959 (Jensen 1961: 57). From other Arctic areas to the west, there are also examples of a shortening of sled dogs' tails, though the reasons for so doing vary (Jensen 1961: 58).

11. See also Weyer (1932: 101) for data on Greenland.

12. Among the Yup'ik in Alaska, various rules applying to dogs were also recorded. E. Nelson (1899: 438–39) reported, 'Dogs are regarded as very unclean and offensive to the shades of game animals, and great care is exercised that no dog shall have an opportunity to touch the bones of a white whale. Should a dog touch one of them the hunter might lose his luck – his nets would break or be avoided by the whales and his spears would fail to strike. One of the best hunters at St Michael once let a dog eat a portion of a white whale's head, and the people attributed to this the fact that he took no more in his net during that season. When the bones of a white whale have been cleaned of the flesh, the hunter takes them to some secluded spot, usually on cliffs fronting the seashore, where dogs do not go, and places them there with several broken spear-shafts.'

13. With respect to Greenland, Victor and Robert-Lamblin (1993: 339) observe that when puppies were about to be born or a puppy was stillborn

the inhabitants left the house, just as they would have done in the case of a human being.

14. Fienup-Riordan (1988: 11) reports that during a religious upheaval in Alaska, on the Kuskokwim, Brother Hooker was convinced he would ascend to heaven after having been torn to pieces by hungry dogs.

15. Rasmussen (1932: 40) notes, 'Under ordinary circumstances there is otherwise no taboo against dogs gnawing the bones of caribou, even if killed with the bow and arrow; the head is the only part the dogs must never have.'

16. See Delaby (1993) for the relation between dogs and bears among the Ghiliakh.

17. According to Saladin d'Anglure (2006: 111), the Inuit of Belcher Island consumed the meat of puppies. He also relates that according to Frobisher, the Inuit on Baffin Island used big dogs for sleds and small ones for consumption.

18. Although resistance against eating dog meat is widespread in the Arctic, Jensen (1961: 61) reports that in the Umanaq district in Greenland it was quite common, but 'there was once a certain ban on the eating of dog flesh'.

19. See also Weyer (1932: 101) and Sonne (1990) for the dispersal of the mythical theme.

20. Freuchen (1935b: 180) also refers to sexual intercourse between people and dogs, involving men as well as women.

21. Jensen also reports on sexual intercourse between human beings and dogs in Greenland: 'Lynge has noted down the following statement: "We know that men lay with dogs on a mound. This was a very serious offence that was punished with death" (Lynge 1955: 185; quoted in Jensen 1951: 61). Hans Egede (1729: 118, quoted by Birket-Smith 1924: 441) related that the first dogs originated from a mound of earth. This suggests a common origin from the earth for both human beings and dogs. Rasmussen notes with respect to the Iglulingmiut that sexual intercourse with the earth itself was strictly forbidden (Rasmussen 1929: 98).

22. See the myth of Navaranaq in Holtved (1943) for disastrous effects of marriages between Inuit and Indians.

23. See also the story of Winnie Tayak Putumiraqtuq in Mannik (1998: 9) and the statement of Martha Tikivik in Patridge (2009: 56), who explains that dogs howl when *tuurngait* are around but are invisible to humans. Egede and Crantz (1767) already reported on the meaning of whining or barking of dogs at specific occasions in Greenland. 'During moon eclipses cries are heard from old graves. Poul Egede relates how on the same occasion water and urine tubs were likewise to be covered, as otherwise one ran the risk of seeing the horrible moon dogs put their heads out of the tub, and thus being frightened to death. At the same time some old dog was ill-treated. If it did not whine (which as a rule it certainly did!) it was a bad omen, for … if once the beasts begin to lose sense and feeling, then it may later on be the turn of the humans' (Birket-Smith 1924: 437).

24. In an account of the same incident in an unpublished document, Peck notes that people in Cumberland Sound had the same beliefs (ANC/GSA/ M56-1, XXXV no 19).

25. In Alaska we find a report by Phillips of a bloody killing of a dog: 'The St. Lawrence Islanders practiced a ceremonial greeting in which a dog was sacrificed. Three baydares, with ten men in each, approached us within ten paces, where they stopped, chanting in a pitiful voice; one of them, rising, spoke some words in an energetic manner, and while holding up a small black dog in his hand, drew forth a knife, with which he stabbed the animal, and then threw it into the sea' (Phillips 1819: 41; quoted in Weyer 1932: 102). The dog was evidently killed by shedding blood and then thrown into the sea. Victor and Robert-Lamblin (1993: 339) observe with respect to Greenland that dead dogs were never thrown into the sea, but put under stones.

26. See Jensen (1961: 41) on western Greenland: 'An old, worn-out dog is killed by hanging. The dog is hoisted up on a drying stand with a rope tightly round the neck behind the ears. A man holds its hind legs so that it can not wriggle loose at the moment it is hoisted up.' Peary (1898: 1:506) stated that at Smith Sound a man's 'favourite dogs, harnessed and attached to a sledge, are strangled to accompany him. In case of a woman one dog was killed' (see also Rasmussen 1908: 113). Jensen (1961: 61) notes that in the past in western Greenland it was tradition 'when a hunter died to kill all his dogs and lay them by his side in the grave', but he does not specify how they were killed. Various sources indicate that in Greenland the custom existed to bury a dog's head with a child 'so that that animal may show the way to the shade of the child to the land of the dead' (Crantz 1767: 1:237; cf. H. Egede 1925: 376; P. Egede 1929: 49). Weyer (1932: 102) refers to the killing of dogs at burials: 'The Diomede Islanders kill a dead man's "best-friend-dog" and place it with his body.'

27. Like the Inuit, the Innu would sometimes cut the ears of their dogs, as it is said that it improves their hunting performance (Clément 2012: 484).

28. Birket-Smith (1924: 424) also reports that in Greenland dogs could be killed as part of a cure: 'In the Julianehaab District … a dog belonging to the patient is hung on the house post. Elgström mentions the same treatment from the Sukkertoppen District.' He also refers to a cure in which '[a] dog is given of the expectoration of the patient, and when it shows symptoms of illness, it is killed at once, after which the patient is supposed to recover' (Birket-Smith 1924: 424).

29. Similar beliefs are documented for the Yup'ik in Alaska. 'Dogs are never beaten for biting a person, as it is claimed that should this be done the *inua* of the dog would become angry and prevent the wound from healing. During my stay at St Michael a little girl four or five years of age was brought to me to dress her face, which had been badly torn by a savage dog. I told the father that he ought to kill such an animal, to which he replied in alarm, "No, no; that would be very bad for the child; the wound would not heal"' (E. Nelson 1899: 435).

30. Salumi Ka&&ak Qalasiq and Felix Pisuk, interviews with H. Kablalik and F. Laugrand, December 1999.

31. For dog names, see also Spencer ([1959] 1976: 465ff.), who reports that if several children died in succession, the one surviving might be given a

dog's name to break the sequence. It was said that this always worked and saved the life of the surviving child.

32. Thalbitzer (1930: 89) points out that in Ammassalik dogs had no other *inua* than their owner.

33. See also Freuchen (1935b: 179) on the selling of dogs. For example, a man refused to sell his dog because it had been named after his grandfather.

# CHAPTER 7

# The Bear, a Fellow Hunter

In Western society the polar bear has always been an icon of the Arctic. The word Arctic itself is derived from the Greek word *arctos*, bear. For the Inuit the polar bear, or *nanuq* as they call him, represents altogether something else: a fellow hunter as well as an animal of prey. Like Inuit, polar bears hunt on the land as well as in the water. But Inuit also have a long tradition of hunting the polar bear, and today this is becoming more and more difficult as the polar bear has become a protected species. The United States and Canada just added polar bears to a list of species of special concern. Nunavut Inuit are deeply concerned today about the new regulations adopted by these governments. There is much discussion of their efficacy. It is estimated that there are about seventeen thousand polar bears in Nunavut (George 2011a, 2011b), and many Inuit hunters think that there are more polar bears today than in the past.[1] Today, the Nunavut government is taking new initiatives to improve its management of polar bear hunting. It is well aware that polar bear management needs more input of Inuit knowledge, a policy defended by Gabriel Nirlungayuk, the director of wildlife at Nunavut Tunngavik Inc. (Rogers 2011).[2]

Inuit have been hunting polar bears for many centuries, and they do not share the view that a restriction on polar bear hunting will result in the preservation of more polar bears.[3] They think that polar bears are threatened by pollutants and pesticides coming from outside, not by hunting. They resent any restriction on their traditional hunting rights. In this chapter we will explore Inuit views of this powerful animal that is at the same time a fellow hunter and a highly valued animal of prey.

In 1926, Hallowell published an extensive study on bear symbolism in the northern hemisphere, arguing 'that a bear cult was one of the characteristic features of an ancient Boreal culture, Old World in origin and closely associated with the pursuit of reindeer. Later it became intercontinental in its scope, extending from Labrador to Lapland' (Hallowell 1926: 161–62).[4] Paproth (1976: 11–12) distinguished two central features in the ceremonial bear complex: the hunter should propitiate the animal so that its soul will not avenge itself on the hunter, and care should be taken that the bear can be reborn and killed again by the hunter. Paproth (1976: 13) pointed out that the ceremonial complex of the bear is less specific along the coast of the Bering Strait and the North American Arctic coast. In this area these specific features of bear hunting apply to all game animals.[5] The bear still has a marked position in Inuit cosmology, and may have had such a position for a very long time.[6] Various studies of the polar bear (*Ursus maritimus*) and its symbolism in Inuit culture have been published, notably by Larsen (1970), Saladin d'Anglure (1980a) and the well-documented study conducted by Randa (1986; see also Randa 1994). Most literature on polar bears deals with hunting strategies and knowledge.[7]

Saladin d'Anglure and Randa emphasized the resemblances between the polar bear (*nanuq*) and a human being: the polar bear can stand on its hind legs, hunts like a human being at seal breathing holes, kills seals and walruses with blocks of snow or stones, and hibernates in snow holes evoking Inuit igloos. Like human beings, the polar bear hunts on land as well on sea (Saladin d'Anglure 1980a: 72–73). Saladin d'Anglure (1980a: 74) quoted Ujarak from Iglulik, who pointed out that the bear is an ancestor of human beings.[8] Saladin d'Anglure concluded that the bear is a symbol of male power in Inuit society. This position was also taken by Randa (1986: 304), who stated that the bear symbolizes the masculine qualities upon which the Inuit value system is founded. Randa argued that for men the bear represents a realization of an ideal, a superior level of humanity, whereas for women the bear represents a threat as a capturer of women and an eater of human beings (Randa 1986: 305).

The identification of the bear with masculinity raises several problems. What is the symbolic position of female bears? That question is especially important, as the gender of the bear is important in rituals and amulets. Trott (2006: 106) presents an intriguing perspective, arguing for a homological relationship between the symbolism of the polar bear and the categorization of gender among Inuit. Inuit themselves usually do not emphasize the masculinity of the bear, but its humanity. Various stories exist relating how human beings, especially women, transformed into bears to avenge themselves on those who had done them wrong.[9]

Ethnographic sources do not always distinguish between the polar bear (nanuq) and the land bear (aklaq), but they appear to have had different meanings and connotations in Inuit traditions. More research is required here. In this chapter we examine the complex symbolism of the bear and explore his position as a fellow hunter in the animal world.

## Bears and Human Beings

As stated above, polar bears and human beings are thought to resemble each other. Bears have many human features and may transform into humans. For example, a tapestry signed by Malaya Akulujuk from Pangnirtuuq represents two bears dressed like humans (see Von Finckenstein 2002: 58).

Inuit have an extensive knowledge of polar bear behaviour and distinguish between various categories of bear. As Felix Alaralak (IE 208) relates,

> *Angujjuaq* is a full-grown large male polar bear. *Nukauq* is also a male polar bear but it is still not matured, or it might be a young male about the same size as an *angujjuaq*. It is younger, therefore it is called *nukauq*, as we would say for someone younger *nuka&ik*, but for a polar bear it is called *nukauq*. *Arnaq* is a female polar bear that can be without a cub (*atittaittuq*) or with a cub. I am not certain as to what age they might be, but they are called *arnaq*.
>
> *Tiqittuajjuit* are bigger than *atittaq* (cubs). This is applicable to both sexes. Polar bears have slow growth unlike other species of animals. When a cub is lost and gets separated from the mother, which usually happens when the polar bears are mating, so this cub is called *avinnaajjuk* while it is still small. This term is used to describe a cub that has been separated from the mother (*avutijuq*) by various reasons.

According to Alaralak, polar bears are referred to in kinship terms: the big male as an elder brother and the young bear as a younger brother.[10] Some references to polar bears are derived from their behaviour. The notion of *atittaq/atirtaq* means 'a polar bear cub' (*nanukuluk*). *Atirtalaalik* designates 'a she-bear with newly born cubs', whereas *atirtalik* designates 'a she-bear with cubs' (Spalding 1998: 13). These three terms are derived from *atirpuq*, which refers to the travelling of the bears when they leave the inland area where they spend the winter hibernating in their dens to go down to the coastal areas. Thus, like Inuit, polar bears have seasonal movements. Each year, beginning in mid-winter and spring, they move northward following the shore ice to hunt seals, and males precede females during the move.

Several myths collected by Métayer discuss attempts to create alliance relations between bears and human beings. In a myth told by L. Qajuina (quoted in Métayer 1973: 439–44), a female polar bear visited human beings. When she was discovered, bear hunters started chasing her. But as she was a fast runner, by the end of the day there was only one pursuer left. She took off her hood and showed him her human face. She said, 'We are both fast runners. Tomorrow, you shall go back home among humans and I will go back home to my parents, among the bears. Let us sleep here first in order to be well rested for our trip back tomorrow.' The man was scared, but the next morning, the she-bear told him, 'Go back to your wife but be careful now. Don't take your clothing off for the next four nights.' The hunter went back home, but he did not tell his wife the taboo he had to follow. As his wife did not understand why her husband was avoiding her, the third night she insisted on making love with him. Soon, her husband became sick. He started losing his skin and died. The text underlines the connection between clothing and the skin.

Qajuina indicated that the word used by polar bears for human beings is *ulrunnapiat,* meaning 'those who are shaky on their legs when they walk' (quoted in Métayer 1973: 444). According to Savard (1966: 161), bear cubs use the term *aja* to designate humans. *Aja* means 'aunt' and it is often used to name the friends of one's mother.

A story from A. Qadlun (quoted in Métayer 1973: 11–14) relates that while a young girl was left alone with her dog, a few polar bears visited her hoping to take her away as their wife. But the dog managed to kill them all, and the bears were thus transformed into food for them. Another story told by E. Qarqajaq (quoted by Métayer 1973: 86–102) relates that every time bears come to take a girl away, a young dog with not an ounce of fat on his body always manages to kill them and turns them into a pile of meat to eat. Thus, the alliance between a bear and a human being is prevented by dogs, marked as killers of bears.

Adoption is also a central theme in bear stories. Hall (1864: 2:240) related how an Inuk woman adopted a bear cub and raised it as a very good hunter (see also Rasmussen 1929: 267–68). Other Inuit became envious of him and threatened to kill him.[11] Therefore, the old woman told the bear to flee. He fled, but continued to provide for her. Ollie Itinnuaq (interview, 2005) from Rankin Inlet related that in the past people might adopt a bear cub after they had killed its mother. They would feed it, and it would sleep with them in the igloo. It might assist them in finding seal breathing holes. When it grew too big they would send it away, but would never kill it or eat it. Rachel Uyarasuk (IE 049) also recalled how polar bear cubs were used as pets:

As for ourselves we had a cub for a pet which we kept in the porch. This cub would dig a hole through the wall so that it could get out. Once that started, a big wooden box was made to keep the cub in so that it no longer went outdoors. When the weather conditions were foul, it would shriek and pace around restless; in addition, it did not want meat but ate a lot of blubber. When the cub got used to us, it no longer made any attempts to get away. So it no longer needed to be tied, and we would play with it outdoors and go out walking with it when the dogs were taken out on a hunting trip. Whenever the cub saw someone running, it would immediately go after that individual as if it wanted to get to the person as quickly as possible.... When the cub first started to stay outdoors, there was a need to protect the cub from the dogs, but in time the dogs got accustomed to it so there was no longer a need to protect the cub but just let it roam free. When we moved camp, the cub was fitted in with a harness like a dog so that it could help pull the load with the rest of the team. Unfortunately it would not follow the rest of the team but walk in any direction it desired. In the spring as the ice surface water puddles started to form on the shores, it would play in these puddles. It was at this time it was taken away to the place of the white people.

Polar bear cubs adapt to human presence quite easily. They like to play around. We use to slide down a hill so this cub would come with us and slide down with us.

Lucaatsie Nowdlak from South Baffin also remembered having a bear cub as a pet, but he only kept it for a week before selling it to a *qallunaaq* (Patridge 2009: 25).

The adoption of bear cubs evokes the catching of bears among Siberian peoples such as the Nivkh. Among the Inuit the bear was well treated and the fact that, in contrast to dogs, it slept inside the igloo suggests that it was treated like a human being. But whereas among the Nivkh the bear was ritually killed, among the Inuit the bear was not killed but sent away. The adoption may have served to establish or maintain good relationships with polar bears.

Inuit also have traditions of polar bears adopting people. Rasmussen (1929: 274–76) related the story of Kakuarshuk, who was adopted by polar bears. His foster father took him to a village where polar bears live in human form. He protected him against a dangerous bear. After Kakuarshuk had wounded that bear, they became friends, and Kakuarshuk continued to live among the polar bears and was greatly appreciated for his hunting skills.

In these stories, the adoption of a male bear in a human community and the adoption of a man by bears are not without problems, but ultimately the result is satisfactory. However, in a story told by Ivaluardjuk of a woman visiting bears, the relation is more ambiguous (Rasmussen 1929: 271–73). A woman with her little son visited the house of the bears and hid behind a curtain. When the bears came, the child began to cry, and the woman strangled it to prevent them from being detected. Once the bears had left, she managed to escape. When the bears found the dead child they fled, because they knew that human beings would come after them. When the hunters arrived they found the lair empty (see also Rasmussen 1929: 276–77).

## The *Isuma* of Bears

The bear was considered the most intelligent of all the animals. Like ravens, bears are said to have *isuma* (the capacity to think like humans). The following story told by Angmalik from Pangnirtuuq is instructive:

> I lived in Qikiqtarjuaq area and I helped to chase bears away especially around this time of the year, when it was still boating season. There were shacks around that could be entered and used by anyone. There were a number of shacks out there. When we were in one, we were approached by three bears. Even though there were attempts to chase them away during the night, the next morning while our canoes were pulled up on land, I saw a bear hanging around the end of the canoe where the outboard motor was. The bear went up to the starter that you had to pull. I have heard that bears think like humans. I heard that a long time ago. He bit it and started pulling at it. My belief that polar bears have the capability to think like humans became stronger after I saw for myself how the bear pulled and released the starter repeatedly. (quoted in Oosten and Laugrand 1999a: 121–22)

Bears employ ingenious strategies to reach their goals. A case in point is the hunting technique of killing a walrus with a stone or a piece of ice. This technique is well described in the ethnographic literature. A carving made by L. Akpaliapik in 1965 (Brandson 1994: 182) depicts a polar bear killing the walrus: 'The bear surprises the sleeping walrus on the ice. Picking up a piece of ice he crushes the head of the walrus. If the piece of ice is too light to kill the walrus, the bear will dip it in and out of the water until the size is increased.'[12]

Human beings are said to imitate bears in many respects (see Randa 1986: 149). Inuit tested the snow and built their igloos the same way bears built their winter shelter, named *apitiq*.[13] Brody (1976: 214) pointed out that the den is kept very clean, as the she-bear neither eats nor defecates once the cub is about to be born.

Hunters imitate bears by adopting some of their hunting techniques. This is particularly obvious in hunting at seal breathing holes.[14] Waiting at the seal breathing hole, the bear lures the seal to its death by scratching with its claws on the ice to arouse the seal's curiosity. The animal is then dispatched with a blow of the bear's paw. Inuit elders say that hunters just imitate this technique. They replace the claw with a small implement that produces the same effect and use a harpoon instead of the paw (see also Saladin d'Anglure 1990b: 183).[15] According to Giesecke, the bear taught men how to use the shooting screen when hunting at breathing holes, for they habitually crept up on the seal under cover of a clump of ice (quoted in Birket-Smith 1924: 328).

Bears also resemble Inuit in their behaviour. Comer (1921: 243–44) reported that polar bears also follow hunting rules:

> When a bear kills a seal and eats it, it would be supposed that the skeleton would be torn apart, but this is not the case. I have seen such a skeleton on the ice and have wondered how it could be preserved in a perfect condition, but the natives say it is the custom of the bear never to break the bones apart. They think this is done by the bear so as not to offend the seal's spirit or Nude le a uke [Nuliajuk], the goddess who is the mistress of life.

Thus, bears respect the sea woman Nuliajuk, just as human beings do.

Bears are also said to understand the language spoken by human beings (see, e.g., Rasmussen 1908: 176).[16] In return, Inuit hunters are able to judge whether or not bears are hungry or in a bad mood by watching the animal's ears; 'the more of the ears that were showing, the more dangerous it was likely to be' (Brody 1976: 214). Bears also talk to their prey.[17] Hall ([1867] 1970: 533–34) reported,

> From the polar bear, too, the Innuits learn much. The manner of approaching the seal which is on the ice by its hole basking in the sunshine is from him. The bear lies down and crawls by hitches toward the seal, 'talking' to it, as the Innuits say, till he is within striking distance, then he pounces upon it with a single jump. The natives say that if they could 'talk' as well as the bear, they could catch many more seals.

Wenzel (1983: 94) related an interesting anecdote about the position of the bear in Inuit contemporary traditions. When he came back from a polar bear hunt with a few Inuit from Clyde River, he commented to several members of his group on the foolishness of the bear in allowing the snowmobiles to approach so closely before it began to flee.

> Two Inuit, one in his mid-20's and the other about 35 ... advised me that it would be best if I did not speak in such a manner. Then they turned back to the bear. Two days later ... the camp *isumataq* briefly

mentioned to me that he had overheard my words on the ice and that he had thought I knew better, but that since I was a white man it probably would not have any serious effect.

Similarly, in 1965 Jean Ayaruar from Chesterfield Inlet (quoted in Brandson 1994: 181) related,

> I recall that our elders taught us never to make fun of polar bears; polar bears understand us, they used to say, and whoever makes fun or speaks ill of 'Nanook' will always suffer the consequences. Should you not believe me, listen to the story of Igalialuk (Father Prime Girard). One night, at Chesterfield Inlet, Igalialuk was smoking his pipe and joking about polar bears. 'Never yet have I seen a bear', said he. 'I would enjoy seeing a polar bear!' As it happened, the next morning, just as the Mass, which I was attending was about to start, the dogs outside started to howl, but to howl in such an unusual way that Igalialuk wanted to know what was going on. He opened the door only to find himself face to face with an enormous polar bear standing on his hind legs.

Thus, bears and human beings both have *isuma*. They are hunters and predators of both land mammals and marine mammals, employing the same techniques. Randa (1986) quotes a statement collected by Malaurie (1976: 186): 'After having killed a bear, a Polar Eskimo once said: "He's the one closest to us"' (see figure 7.1).

**Figure 7.1.** A polar bear in the tundra. Photo: Robert Fréchette/Avataq Cultural Institute.

## The Dangers of Polar Bear Hunting

When one of the students in the 1996 oral traditions course asked Pauloosie Angmalik whether he had ever killed a polar bear, Pauloosie answered, 'Of course. I am a man.' But women might also hunt polar bears. Rachel Uyarasuk (IE 049) related how she killed a polar bear. For the Pelly Bay area, Van de Velde (1957: 14–15) reported,[18]

> More than one Eskimo may take pride in having killed a bear. I present the most recent case.... Lucie Imingak was staying alone in her tent with her little boy of two years. Lucie, who was severely incapacitated by an attack of polio, was expecting a baby. Anxious, she managed to go outside, hoping to see the sled of her husband coming in the distance. But outside on the ice she perceives something quite different: a bear has smelled the camp and is running towards it. Lucie takes the old gun that is available.... When the animal is only a hundred feet away she puts it to her shoulder.... Mortally wounded, the bear collapses like a rock. Lucie goes back into the tent; the baby has not even woken up. (our translation)

Piugaattuq (IE 50) gave very detailed and instructive information on polar bear hunting:

> When a hunter spots a polar bear he would release the dogs so that they can pursue the bear, it would not be long before the dogs will stop the bear.... You can tell the behaviour of the polar bear quite easily. A hunter usually keeps a close watch to the behaviour of a polar bear especially when the hunter is apprehensive. In the case when the bear is being intimidated by a pack of dogs, the bear will get settled not being bothered by the dogs but its attention is focused to the hunter. When the bear starts to look backwards it means that the bear will attack the hunter. When the bear changes its attention so that it appears to shy away from the hunter and starts to face backwards, it is a sign that it is getting ready to plunge at the hunter. This is the way you can tell that the bear is about to attack.

Thus, the dogs keep the polar bear at bay. If the polar bear is aware that the hunter constitutes the real danger, the hunter has to be extremely careful. Piugaattuq related:

> The hunters who spend time hunting bears know the behavior of the bear so that they know how to dodge the bear. A dog, though well trained, cannot dodge the bear effectively in the areas where there is deep soft snow, as it deliberately annoys the bear as part of the hunting procedure. As the dog dodges towards the rear section of the bear, the bear will quickly strike with his head. If it misses the first try, in succession the bear will

strike again with accurate effectiveness. The bear is very effective when striking backwards. If it tries the strike in this direction, the bear cannot turn; that is why the hunter is able to dodge the bear relatively easily. The hunter will observe the bear as it attacks. The hunter focuses his attention on the fore leg of the bear. When the bear pounces and the hunter knows that the bear will not set another step in its final plunge, the hunter knows that the bear cannot turn and ... has its mouth open with the head tilted, so the hunter quickly dodges the bear on the side where the jaws of the bear are positioned.

Dodging the bear might also be necessary when the hunter is using a rifle. Piugaattuq recalled,

> I waited, as I was right on the route the bear would take as it started for the floe edge. I immediately knelt down on one side and took aim at the polar bear but the rifle I had did not fire. At this time there was only one step the polar bear would need to reach me. When the rifle failed to fire, I immediately got up to my feet while there was time for me to dodge the bear. As soon as polar bear got close to me, I immediately jumped to the side trying to stay clear from it. The polar bear landed where I had been and stopped. At this time I was trying to get my rifle to load up and cleared it so that I can give a shot away. The polar bear was right in front of me standing up on its hind leg. All this time I was trying to get the mechanism to work and free it from the jam. The dogs had caught up, immediately attacking the polar bear. This gave me time to fire a shot, which hit the bear.

Piugaattuq (IE 60) recalled how dogs were trained not to be afraid of bears:

> My uncle trained his dogs to be aggressive (*nakujjaksaijut*) for the dogs that had just started to get experience. By wounding the polar bear at the jugular vein, the blood will start to flow through the wound. When the dogs approach the polar bear on the side where there is the wound, the bear will not make attempts to bite the dogs. Some dogs are experiencing bear attacks for the first time. They will participate in keeping the bear at bay. This was the way they were made to get a pleasure and desire to hunt polar bear.

A good hunter was not afraid of a polar bear, but knew he had to exercise extreme caution. Even though the strength of the bear is always acknowledged, he is not necessarily considered the strongest of all animals. In a story related by Ivaluardjuk (Rasmussen 1929: 279–80), a bear was beaten by a caribou in a contest of strength. The skinny-looking front leg of the caribou proved stronger than the paw of the bear. Thus, appearances may deceive bears as well as human beings.

A hunter might take recourse to *qilaniq* (divination by head lifting) to assess whether a bear hunt would be successful. Abe Okpik (quoted in McComber 2005: 228) recalled,

> I spent fifteen days in Igloolik when Johanasi Uyarak was already an old man then. He said one time, as a young man, he and another guy were out polar bear hunting beyond Fury and Hecla Straits, in the Committee Bay area. There are a lot of polar bears around there in the springtime. After they camped, they saw some polar bears, and that same morning they followed the two polar bears' tracks. Johanasi said he was just travelling with the other hunters.
>
> One of the hunters said to another, 'Take off your parka.' The man took his parka off, and he put it on the ground and lay on it. The first man tied his whip around the other man's head and said, 'Face toward the polar bear tracks that are going that way.' So the hunter started chanting and tried to lift the man's head. The head moved off the caribou parka, so he took the parka and put it on the other tracks. He put the man's head back down and started chanting again. This time, the first hunter couldn't lift his friend's head! 'Now', he said, 'we're going to catch a polar bear.' In a short while, they saw a polar bear that had just caught a seal. It was full and was sleeping when they came to it, and they got it.

Aava related a story of a successful hunt to Rasmussen (1929: 238):

> He was out one day hunting walrus with his brother Ivaluardjuk, when they caught sight of a huge bear, a male. It came forward at once to attack them, running at full speed, looking delighted at the prospect of fresh meat, almost like a cheerful dog that comes running up at a gallop, wagging its tail. And so assured did it seem of the inferiority of its prey that it appeared quite annoyed at having to take the trouble of turning when Aua sprang aside. And now commenced a hunt that lasted the whole day. Ivaluardjuk had clambered up to a ridge of ice and was shouting at the top of his voice to frighten the bear away. So swift and fierce was the bear in its movements that Aua was unable to harpoon it, while Aua himself was so agile that the bear could not get at him. At last the great fat bear became so exhausted that it sat down in the snow, growling like a little puppy in a nasty temper. Then Aua ran up and thrust his lance into its heart. Ivaluardjuk stood up on his ridge of ice a little distance from the scene of the combat and waved his arms delightedly. He was so hoarse with shouting that he could no longer speak.

Bears might attack camps as well as individuals. Uyarasuk (IE 49) related,

> The case where a baby was mauled by a polar bear happened in this area when a polar bear came right to the camp. In our case we made Aggu our home when it was reported that there was this incident. Polar bears

that are known as *avinnajjuit* have a habit of getting right into the camp.
They are also known to roam around more than other polar bears, so
they tend to get right to the places where people make their homes. I
have not heard too much of incidents where people were mauled by polar bears. This particular case, which is an isolated incident, happened
when the woman was trying to protect her children from a polar bear
while she had an infant tucked in her *amauti*. What happened was that
the polar bear may have torn her *amauti*, which caused her infant to
spill out from her *amauti* while the polar bear was still after her. She
crawled over to her child and tucked her in through her front section. It
is amazing how she was able to get to her child when the polar bear was
still harassing her. The other woman managed to shoot the polar bear,
though it was only a wound, the bear was able to let go of the woman.
That is the way I have heard about the incident.[19]

A story collected by Métayer (1973: 568–74) from A. Qavviaktoq relates that in the old days, polar bears were everywhere in the country
of Puipleq. They attacked people often, using their tracks to find them.
Once an old couple heard their dogs fighting on the porch. The man
took a stick and went naked onto the porch to beat his white dog. As
the night was dark, he could not see well, but when he struck a white
body he could see, he discovered it was a polar bear. He and his wife
were then severely mauled.

Bilby (1923: 164) related how a hunter attacked a bear that had
taken possession of the sleds and the provisions stored on them:

> Crouching with poised weapon low on his haunches, he suddenly sprang
> up and began to sing and dance about, on this side and on that, but
> drawing nearer all the time to his astonished adversary. The bear became
> more and more bemused by the noise and the agility of the oncomer,
> until at last the latter was able to rush close in and strike him one fatal
> blow with the practised spear.

Unfortunately, Bilby does not provide the text of the song, but it is
said that magic words could be used in polar bear hunting. Nakasuk
(quoted in Rasmussen 1931: 282) used magic words to bring luck when
hunting musk oxen and bears:

> Your flanks,
> A little old woman's
> Breathing with that you shall breathe
> Well up into the wind, properly up into the wind.

Angutinngurniq from Kuugaarruk pointed out that if a polar bear fled,
an *irinaliuti* (powerful word) called an *avalaqsiut* could be used to sur-

round the bear. Interestingly, the same *irinaliuti* could also be used to surround an adult or a child: 'I would use my grandfather Paksikkaq's *irinaliuti* as a deflector. I could deflect polar bears as well. I know these, but I have never used them' (quoted in Oosten and Laugrand 2002: 105).

In hunting bears one had to be aware that the bear one hunts is not necessarily a real bear. It might be a helping spirit, a *tupilaq* (evil spirit) or another being appearing as a bear. According to Boas (1901: 153),

> The Aivilik believe in a monster called tupilak [see figure 7.2], which is said to look somewhat like a bear.
>
> The Netchillik of Boothia Felix are believed to be able to make out of snow an artificial monster in the shape of a bear. They put bear's teeth into its mouth, and the figure is believed to come to life, and to kill the enemy of the maker. At another place Captain Comer says that the Netchillik are believed to be able to transform a bear's skull into a tupilak, but that some people have the power to make the tupilak turn back and destroy its maker.

Boas (1907: 507) related how two hunters met a bear that was really a *tupilaq*:

> Two other men one day fell in with a polar bear. One of them attacked the bear with his spear; but the bear turned, and struck his assailant, lacerating his head and face. Finally they succeeded in despatching the bear. When they came back to the spot where the hunter had been struck

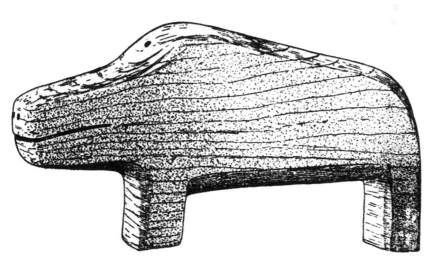

**Figure 7.2.** Model representing a *tupilaq* that resembled a bear. *Source:* Boas 1901: 153.

by the bear, they saw a bear's paw lying on the ground, although the skin of the bear itself was complete. Thus they discovered that the bear was a tupilak made to destroy them.

The bear may be a formidable opponent, but an experienced Inuit hunter knows how to deal with him. A *tupilaq* is obviously another matter. Here, extreme caution is required. But all bears should be respected. One should not talk about them lightly, and many rules of respect concerning the bear had to be observed.

## Rules of Respect

Many rules for hunting and partitioning bears exist and they are well described by Randa (1986: 190–96). Hall ([1867] 1970: 325, 332) related that during a bear hunt from a boat the women were completely covered with caribou skins. Most rules refer, however, to the distribution of the prey and the treatment of the bear after death.

Bilby (1923: 253) reported, 'In bear hunting, the rule is for the skin to go to the first hunter who sights the prey (not necessarily the first to kill it). The best part of the body goes to him who deals the fatal blow.'[20] Piugaattuq (IE 50) related that the first one who wounded the bear would be considered the hunter who had made the catch. Boas (1901: 211 n1) observed, 'The Eskimo say, that, according to the custom of the Tornit, the game belongs to the hunter who sees it first. According to the custom of the Eskimo, the game belongs to the hunter who hits it nearest to a vital part. The bear belongs to the hunter who is the first to wound it.'

According to Boas (1888: 591) and Rasmussen (1952: 117), the bear's soul is very dangerous. Many rituals had to be observed after killing a bear. Boas (1901: 147) related, 'No work must be done for three days after a bear or ground-seal has been killed. The women must not comb their hair.' According to Rasmussen (1929: 195), 'At Tununeriseq: Admiralty Inlet, no work must be done for three days after caribou or bearded seal, narwhal, walrus or bear have been caught. During the same three days it is forbidden to break the soil, or to break fuel.'

In Iglulik a period of three days was also observed. According to Rasmussen (1929: 184),[21] 'When a whale, a bearded seal or a bear is killed, no man's or woman's work must be done for three days. It is also strictly forbidden during these three days to cut turf or gather fuel from the earth. Clothing may, however, be mended; and distinction is here to be observed between ordinary needlework and actual mending.'

In other areas the length of the taboo period after the killing of a bear depended upon the animal's gender. The Nattilik and Copper Inuit observed a taboo against working for five days for a female bear, four for a male bear; work of all kinds was strictly forbidden (Rasmussen 1931: 184; 1932: 40).

A special temporal rule applied to women among the Iglulingmiut. According to Rasmussen (1929: 195), 'Women are not allowed to eat bear's meat or walrus meat during the time when the sun is low in the heavens. If they eat walrus meat, then the walrus will disappear; if they eat bear's meat, all the bears will become very shy.' Birket-Smith (1929: 139) reported with respect to the Caribou Inuit, 'In the winter they must not eat the meat of walrus or bear at all.' The story of the couple who fought over a bear leg collected in Nunavik by Nungak and Arima (1988: 145) warned people against the danger of bear meat. The myth relates the story of a man and his wife who spent their time fighting each other over bear meat. Every time the man brought bear meat home the woman wanted to take it all for herself, and her husband had to take it from her by force, or his child would have been left with nothing. One day, the man got a leg of polar bear as his share of the kill. Thinking that it would be equally divided up among all his family, he brought it home. But after he went out for a short while, he found the leg behind his wife.

The liver was especially marked. Hall ([1867] 1970: 325, 332) stated that the liver of a polar bear was never eaten. Rasmussen (1929: 189) specified a number of additional rules for the Iglulingmiut:

> When a man has killed a bear and returns to his house he must take off all his outer clothing, including outer mittens and kamiks, before entering the house, and for a whole month he must not eat of the meat or blubber of the bear.
>
> In a house where oil made from bear's fat is used for the lamps, it is forbidden to eat marrowbones. The souls of bears are very dangerous, and will not allow marrowbones to be eaten while bear's fat is burned.
>
> People who have eaten human flesh never eat bear's meat; this because it is said that bear's meat is like human flesh.

Boas (1901: 149) also related that the taste of the flesh of a human being and bear meat is similar: 'A person who, during a famine, has eaten human flesh, should never afterwards eat bear-meat, because it is believed that bear-meat resembles that of men, and that to eat it will keep alive the desire for human flesh.' The rule that a man who has eaten human meat should not eat bear meat suggests a structural equivalence between the two kinds of meat. A similar rule exists with respect to raven's meat. Freuchen (1935b: 432) reported, 'The natives in Hudson Bay do not like to eat bear meat because they think it looks and tastes like human flesh. Which would seem to indicate that many of them know whereof they speak. They also say bear meat produces moles.' Elsewhere, Freuchen (1935a: 179) stated that bear and dog meat were not eaten by some Iglulingmiut because they resembled human flesh.

Interestingly, an opposition between bear meat and dog meat is suggested by the origin myth of the sun and the moon. The (grand)mother of the blind boy did not give him meat from the bear he had shot, but told him he had failed to hit his target. She killed a dog and gave the boy dog's meat instead (see Rasmussen 1929: 77–81; 1931: 232–36). The myth contrasts the delicious bear meat with dog meat, which is considered hardly edible and only eaten in times of dire need. The substitution of bear meat by dog meat implies a substitution of meat from outside by meat from inside; meat of an animal killed by a man by meat of an animal killed by a woman. But the two types of meat also have something in common: they share a relationship to human flesh. Human flesh should not be eaten, but at the same time it is often suggested that once a human being has eaten human flesh, he can no longer stop. It has become the only attractive food to him. Thus, human flesh encompasses the qualities of both bear meat and dog meat: objectionable as well as delicious.

After a bear was killed, he received cultural objects as gifts. Boas (1888: 501) reported,

> After a polar bear has been killed, it is cut up on the spot, the intestines are thrown to the dogs, and the rest of the body is taken home. A piece of the tongue and other small parts are hung up in the hut; and knives, saws, drills, and other small objects, are attached to them as presents to the bear's soul. It is believed that then the soul will go to the other bears and tell them how well it has been treated, so that the others may be willing to be caught. At the end of three days, the man who killed the bear takes down the objects, carries them out into the passage-way, and then throws them into the house, where the boys stand ready to get what they can. This symbolizes the bear spirit presenting these objects to the people. The boys must return the objects to their owners. During these three days, the women are not allowed to comb their hair.

The soul reports its good treatment to other bears. But what is the good treatment? Apparently, parts of the bear are associated with cultural implements. The fact that the entrails of the bear are eaten by the dogs is apparently consistent with this good treatment. But the story does not end there. The bear is clearly identified as an owner of the cultural objects and ends up giving these objects to the boys through the mediation of the man who killed the bear. Whereas human beings after their death are supposed to become givers of meat to their descendants and namesakes, the dead bear becomes a giver of cultural objects.

Hall ([1867] 1970: 332) reported that special attention had to be given to the bladder:

> Now we have a Ninoo, of course the Innuits will inflate the bladder, and attach it, with several peculiar charms, to a staff; which must be kept in a prominent position – in the boat while we are voyaging, and on the tupic while encamped. In accordance with Innuit custom, it must be thus exposed for three days and three nights.

Boas (1888: 596) reported a similar custom for the South Baffin area: 'When a bear is caught the Nugumiut and the Oqomiut are accustomed to fasten its bladder to a stick which is placed upright near the hut or encampment for three days.' According to Hall ([1867] 1970: 536), specific instruments were added to the bladder: 'If the captured bear be a male, his bladder, with certain instruments belonging to the men, must be placed for three days on the top of the igloo or tupic. If the bear be a female, her bladder, with one of the women's brass head-ornaments and some beads, must be hung in like manner.' Rasmussen (1929: 188–89) reported that similar rules applied among the Iglulingmiut:

> When a bear has been captured, its bladder, penis, maᵛsAq (spleen) and part of the tongue are hung up inside the house together with men's implements. This arrangement is to hang for three days.
>
> At the end of that time, the man who got the bear must take it out into the passage and throw it down on the floor; the children in the house must then try which can be first to get hold of the implements and give them back to the owners.
>
> When a she-bear is captured, sewing thread, needle and a woman's knife are hung up together with the bear's nakasuk, or bladder, its sungAq, or gall, and maᵛsAq, spleen; this ceremony is called naciblugo, and means: 'in order to wait for the time to pass'. The soul only remains there on the spot for three days.

In the funerary rites the gender of the bear was also acknowledged, and its cultural identity was gendered through the objects it received.[22] Jenness (1922: 181) reported,

> According to Milukkattak the usual custom is to lay a miniature bow and arrow beside only the male bear or wolf; beside the female the hunter places a strip of sealskin or deerskin which the shade of the animal can use as a needle-holder. They are like human beings, Milukkattak went on

to say, and have need of the same things, the male of his hunting weapons, and the female of her needle-case.

The bear was provided with a cultural gender through the funerary gifts. According to Rasmussen (1929: 189), the souls only remained on the spot for three days. Apparently the *tarniq* moved from a part of the body such as the bladder or another vital part to the cultural implements. A similar movement was referred to in seal hunting, when the *tarniq* of the seal was thought to reside in the harpoon head after the kill (Rasmussen 1929: 185). The necessity to free the *tarniq* was emphasized by Father Mary-Rousselière (1957: 18), who related that in the Iglulik area bears – like humans and dogs – were supposed to be shot or hung so their *tarniq* could leave their body if they were not killed with a harpoon, as had been the tradition in the past.

## Pairings

In oral tradition polar bears are often paired with other animals in terms of differences and similarities. These pairings inform us about the complex symbolism of the bear.

Dogs and bears can be described as cousins. Nakasuk told Rasmussen (1931: 283) the magic words to be said over dogs that are to be trained as strong and enduring bear hounds:

> Little child like a Tuneq,
> Little dog, little dog,
> See, its heart
> Tastes of luscious blubber
> Your cousin, leap on him,
> Your cousin, fight with him!

According to Rasmussen (1929: 176),[23] bears and dogs were cross-cousins of the same sex (*illuriik*). *Illuriik* competed with each other in song-feasts and drum dances. The relationships between *illuriik* also had sexual connotations. They might exchange wives, and often a son and a daughter of two *illuriik* were preferred marriage partners.[24] Peter Arnatsiaq relates that bears themselves refer to dogs as their cousins (Bennett and Rowley 2004: 44).

A story recorded by Boas (1888: 636–37; [1888] 1964: 228–29) relates how a bear hunt resulted in the origin of the constellation Udleqdun (*ullaaktut*), a bear pursued by dogs and men. Three men went bear hunting with a sled and took a young boy with them. When they approached the floe edge, they saw a bear and went in pursuit of it. Though the dogs ran fast, they could not get nearer, and all of a sudden they observed that the bear was lifted up and their sled followed. At this moment the boy lost one of his mittens, and in his attempt to pick it up fell from the sled. There he saw the men ascending higher and higher, finally being transformed into stars. The bear became the star Nanuqdjung (Betelgeuse); the pursuers, Udleqdun (Orion's belt); and the sled, Kamutiqdjung (Orion's sword). The men continue the pursuit today; the boy, however, returned to the village and told how the men were lost.[25]

The close association between dogs and bears also comes to the fore in Jenness's (1922: 188) account of the sea woman among the Copper Inuit: 'But Kannakapfaluk's hut is at the bottom of the sea, and her dogs are two bears, one brown and one white.' The sea woman is often viewed as a gigantic figure. The substitution of dogs by bears emphasizes a change of scale. In contrast, her husband is depicted as a dwarf.[26]

According to Randa (1986: 220–21), the land bear (*aklaq*) and the polar bear (*nanuq*) constituted an opposition. He quotes Spencer's ([1959] 1976: 302) statement that some shamans in northern Alaska could transform into land bears and others into polar bears, but never into both types of bears. Warriors wore the amulets of the land bear on the right arm and those of the polar bear on the left arm (Spencer [1959] 1976: 272).[27] Spencer also observes that the brown bear was thought to be stronger and more dangerous than the polar bear. A famous story relates that a land bear drank so much water from a river that it burst, causing the origin of fog (see, e.g., Boas 1901: 308–9). Thus, the land bear also seems to have an association with water, and more research is required to explore the relationship between the two types of bears.

A structural equivalence between bearded seals and bears is suggested by some ritual injunctions. Rasmussen (1931: 242–43) reported for the Nattilingmiut,

> Bears and seals are always thirsty. Consequently it has a favourable effect on their souls to give them drinking water when they have been killed and brought into the house. But it has to be done in a particular manner:
> A small piece of ice is taken from the ice window of the house; this one melts in the mouth and then allows the water to drip down either into a fold in the skin of drip down into the mouth of the animal, at the same time saying:
> 'qilaipagluse qagliniArpagluse: If you are thirsty, just come near to us'.
> Bears and seals are the only game animals that are given water. But on the other hand one must not neglect to give it them.

This rule of giving water to the dead animal is described in minute detail.[28] One should not just give water, but it should come from the windowpane of the house (a cultural origin), melted in the mouth of a man (mediation and transformation), poured on a part of the animal and finally dripped into the mouth of the animal itself. Thus, the human body and the animal skin both acted as mediators between the house and the animal.

Pairings do not focus on natural features of animals but place them in a cosmological perspective. In this perspective, connections (between the bear and the dog, the bear and the sea mammals) and distinctions (between land bears and polar bears) are made that position the bear in the wider cosmological framework of Inuit culture.

## The Bear in the Shamanic Complex

A close relationship between the shamanic complex and bear symbolism is well attested. In the shamanic language, a bear is called *tulurialik*, the one with a fang, *uqsuralik*, the one with fat, or *pihuqahiaq*, the one who walks. Bear fangs are said to be an important visual sign of an *angakkuq* when a bear *tuurngaq* enters his body. Iqallijuq as well as Taparti (quoted in Oosten and Laugrand 2002: 39) related that Qimuksiraaq was able to appear with bear fangs (see also Jenness 1922: 199; Rasmussen 1932: 35). In many areas bear fangs were recognized as a feature of the shaman. Jenness (1922: 193) reported that among the Copper Inuit some shamans could transform themselves into bears. Rasmussen (1932: 35) related,

> Thus Ilatsiak said that when his grandmother was a child there was a shaman named Makettak who could change into a polar bear. He would bend down to the floor of the dance-house, resting his hands on the ground. Slowly his hands would change into polar bear's feet, then his arms become legs, and finally his whole body and head would assume the shape of the bear. In this state he would go out of the dance-house and visit the neighbouring houses, saying to the children in each as he entered, 'Stand up against the wall beside the door and then I shall not eat you.' ... Higilak's father could change into a polar bear, but only when he was alone. Uloksak claimed the power of transforming himself into a white or a brown bear, a wolf and a white man. ... Even Higilak, according to her daughter Kanneyuk, had the same power; Kanneyuk had seen her change into a polar bear.

Bears were powerful *tuurngait*, helping spirits. Ava and Qinngaq had a bear and a giant bear (*nanurluk*) as a helping spirit. Balikci (1970:

231–34) reported that several shamans among the Nattilingmiut had polar bear *tuurngait*. Boas (1888: 591–92) related for South Baffin,

> The bear seems to be the most powerful among these spirits. ... The bear tornaq is represented as a huge animal without any hair except on the points of the ears and of the tail and at the mouth. If a man wishes to obtain a bear for his tornaq he must travel all alone to the edge of the land floe and summon the bears. Then a large herd will approach and frighten him almost to death. He falls down at once. Should he fall backward he would die at once. If he falls upon his face, however, one bear out of the herd steps forward and asks him if he wishes him to become his tornaq. He then recovers and takes the bear for his spirit and is accompanied by him on the return journey. On the way home, they pass a seal hole and the bear captures the animal for his master. The Eskimo is now a great angakoq, and whenever he wants help he is sure to get it from his bear.[29]

Bear *tuurngait* protected the *angakkuit*. Boas (1888: 598–99) reported that a mighty *angakkuq* paid a visit to the moon and faced the dance of the entrails-eating spirit:

> The man joined her dance and their attitudes and grimaces looked so funny that the angakoq could scarcely keep from laughing. But just at the right moment he called to mind the warnings of the man in the moon and rushed out of the house. The man cried after him, 'Uqsurelik-taleqdjuin' ('Provide yourself with your large white bear tornaq'). Thus he escaped unhurt.

Kiviuq also had a bear as a helping spirit who saved him from a cannibal woman (see, e.g., Rasmussen 1929: 287–90). Boas (1907: 154) reported that during a famine a shaman could only reach Nuliajuq when his bear *tuurngaq* defeated the *tupilaq* that blocked his way. In Peck's *tuurngait* list, many bears emerge as *tuurngait*. Whereas dogs function as bringers of food in this list, polar bears are marked as masters of sea game.

An interesting variant of the bear *tuurngaq* is presented in Peck's list of *tuurngait*. Qattenuk (no. 96) 'is like a creature split in two, one portion being like a man, and the other like a bear'. It is here important to note that in the past, Qattenuk was apparently a bear but 'because he ate a man he turned into the form mentioned above' (quoted in Laugrand et al. 2001: 149).

L. Turner ([1894] 1979: 36–37) described a spirit controlling the caribou appearing as a bear:

> A great spirit controls the reindeer. He dwells in a huge cavern near the end of Cape Chidley. He obtains and controls the spirit of every deer

which is slain or dies, and it depends on his good will whether the people shall obtain future supplies. The form of the spirit is that of a huge white bear. The shaman has the power to prevail upon the spirit to send the deer to the people who are represented as suffering for want of food. The spirit is informed that the people have in no way offended him, as the shaman, as a mediator between the spirit and the people, has taken great care that the past food was all eaten and that last spring, when the female deer were returning to him to be delivered of their young, none of the young (or foetal) deer were devoured by the dogs. After much incantation the shaman announces that the spirit condescends to supply the people with spirits of the deer in a material form and that soon an abundance will be in the land. He enjoins upon the people to slay and thus obtain the approval of the spirit, which loves to see good people enjoy an abundance, knowing that so long as the people refrain from feeding their dogs with the unborn young, the spirits of the deer will in time return again to his guardianship.

Similarly, Hawkes (1916: 124ff.) described a spirit called Torngarsoak (great *tuurngaq*) in the shape of a bear:

He lives in a cave in the great black mountains at the northern extremity of the peninsula, which they call the Torngait, or Spirit mountains. The scenery here is wild and impressive. Torngarsoak takes the form of a huge white bear when he appears to angekok novices. He devours them limb for limb, and then spews them out again, when they become endowed with superhuman power. ... He lives in the water, and all creatures that live in the water are subject to him. It is he to whom the Labrador Eskimo appeal when in search of whales or seals.

The symbolism of shamanic initiation suggests that the shaman was initiated by a reversal of roles from hunter to prey and became food for the bear or Torngarsoak. Once the *angakkuq* had passed through the ordeal, the bear could become his helping spirit. The bear was no longer a monster threatening to devour him, but an ally who allowed him to function as a shaman.[30]

In addition, various non-human beings were dressed in bear clothing. Saladin d'Anglure (1983: 80–81) connected the moon spirit with the bear. He referred to Gessain (1978), who shows a picture of the moon spirit completely dressed in bear clothing. Elders in an oral traditions conference in Rankin Inlet in 2002 suggested that bear clothing was associated with *tuniit* (see Oosten and Laugrand 2010). Lyon reported for the Iglulingmiut that the husband of the sea woman, Nappayook, 'has only one arm', the hand of which is covered by a very large mitten of bear skin (Lyon [1824] 1970: 231–32). Kupaaq (quoted in Oosten and Laugrand 1999a: 159) mentioned that the father of the sea woman wrapped himself in a polar bear skin before reaching his daughter at the bottom of the sea. Bear clothing is thus often associated with figures that played a central role in the shamanic complex as helping spirits or initiators of shamans.

## Discussion

Bears resemble humans. They have *isuma* and are skilled hunters. They have taught the Inuit many hunting skills. But they are not part of human society, as dogs are. Unlike dogs, they have their own villages where they live in human appearance. Human beings can visit them, or bears in human appearance can visit people. Lasting alliance relations cannot develop between bears and human beings, although bears can support human beings and human beings can live with bears for a while. The power of the bear is particularly emphasized in the shamanic complex. In Greenland the shaman was often initiated by a bear, and in the central Arctic shamans could transform themselves into bears. Bears were powerful helping spirits able to transform people into shamans.[31] Today, the image of a standing bear holding a drum has become quite popular. It may well express the old tradition of the transformation of the *angakkuq* into a bear.

Among the Copper Inuit, bears were the dogs of the sea woman. Saladin d'Anglure (1983) pointed out that bears were perceived on different scales. Foxes, lemmings or ermines were considered bears by dwarves. Giants had their own bear in Nanorluk, the giant bear. The bear was present at all levels of the scale, from giants to dwarves.

The funerary rites show that in contrast to other animals, the gender of the bear was quite important. Bears were gendered just like human beings. Thus, the conclusion by Saladin d'Anglure and Randa that the polar bear represents masculinity does not sufficiently cover the complexity of bear symbolism. Kappianaq (quoted in Kolb and Law 2001: 91) remembered, 'In the days when I would hunt, if I dreamed about this woman, a beautiful woman, then I knew I was going to get a bear.' Thus, the bear was perceived as a woman in the context of the hunt.

Women rejected by society could turn into polar bears or land bears and avenge themselves on people.[32] This transformation does not imply a change of gender. Trott (2006) is well aware of the gendered nature of the bear, but we found little evidence in the ethnographic data for a homological relationship between the symbolism of the polar bear and the categorization of gender among Inuit.

The complexity of the symbolism of the bear is well illustrated by the use of various amulets. Bear amulets can support men as well as women. According to Kumlien (1879: 45–46), 'Another charm of great value to the mother who has a young babe is the canine tooth of the polar bear. This is used as a kind of clasp to a sealskin string, which passes around the body and keeps the breasts up. Her milk supply cannot fail while she wears this.' According to Rasmussen (1929: 182), 'A whip with a handle made from the penis of a bear is good for frightening away evil spirits.' The whip was an important ritual instrument of transformation. In the myth of the orphan boy, Kaujjajjuk, the moon spirit transformed the boy into a powerful man by whipping him. The Nattilik *angakkuit* tamed the wind with their whips. In addition, Rasmussen (1931: 273) reported, 'The genitals of a she-bear sewn behind the trousers at the band: a young man will be lucky at bear hunting, he will always be on the path of bears; for just as genitals of the she-bear are the certain way along which its urine will go, the young man will be sure to go there where bears come.' Thus, these amulets mark the sexual nature of the bear, ensuring milk for the mother, protection from evil spirits and good hunting. The genitals of a she-bear are closely associated with femininity, yet they are instrumental in becoming a good bear hunter. The humanity, not the masculinity, of the bear is at the core of the bear complex; the bear is always gendered, just as human beings are.

Although the bear shares many qualities with an Inuk, it is still an animal that should be killed and eaten. After his death, however, a male bear does not just turn into an object of exchange, where his meat is distributed among the members of the community; he may also become a giver of objects. He is supposed to report on his fate to other bears. This pattern corresponds very much with patterns reported in Siberia. But whereas among the Nivkh the bear is socialized before he is killed and then reports his good treatment to the spirits, among the Inuit he is socialized after his death.

The bear thus appears to be an animal encompassing contrasts (land vs. sea, hunter vs. prey, human vs. non-human). He is the most intelligent of all animals, but still remains an animal, serving as food. In the shamanic complex he can become the transformer of the shaman, killing him and bringing him to life again and turning into an ally, a helping spirit. Thus, Randa correctly qualifies him as a great mediator, and in this role he is comparable to the dog. But whereas the dog is part of human society and derives his name and identity from his owner, the bear remains an unnamed human partner, outside society. He is an intelligent hunter, but unlike a dog he cannot be socialized during his life, only after his death.

## Notes

1. Calculations of polar bear populations are an issue of debate, as the situation varies in each region. Recently, Nirlungayuk, the director of wildlife at Nunavut Tunngavik Inc., reported that Nunavummiut and especially hunters are seeing more polar bears in the territory than ever before. According to him the polar bear population has not diminished, but rather has grown from eight thousand animals forty or fifty years ago to more than fifteen thousand today (George 2011b). For more information on these debates, see Bell (2007, 2008a); Bird (2008a, 2008b, 2009); George (2010); Thompson (2007a, 2007b); Watt-Cloutier (2007); and Windeyer (2010a, 2010b).

2. On bear hunting and the conflicting views of Inuit and biologists, see Tyrrell (2006), Freeman and Wenzel (2006), Foote and Wenzel (2008) and Clark et al. (2008). For a broader perspective and a discussion on the sustainability of polar bear hunting, see Freeman and Foote (2009).

3. They also are critical of Western notions of preservation. On 20 May 2011, Nick Arnalukjuak, an Inuk from Arviat, submitted a paper to the *Nunatsiaq News* entitled 'Polar Bears Shouldn't Be Kept in Zoo'. He strongly opposed polar bears being kept in captivity for amusement or as a showcase by the zoos, arguing that much cruelty and suffering was caused by the preservation of bears in an unnatural environment and climate.

4. In his analyses and conclusions, Hallowell (1926) relied particularly on Siberian data. The bear feast among the Nivkh or Giljak is extensively documented, and a film was made by Taksami of a modern celebration of the feast. Bear ceremonies have also been extensively documented in other Siberian societies such as the Tungus (e.g., Paproth 1976), the Gold, the Oltscha and the Orochi. Bear rituals were also documented among the Ainu of northern Japan (Ikeya 1997; Kimura 1999) and among Finno-Ugric people, such as the Ostiaks, the Voguls (Rombandeeva 1993) and the Samoyeds. See Hallowell (1926), Mathieu (1984b), Kwon (1999) and Sokolova (2002).

5. On the bear feast in Siberia, see de Sales (1980).

6. Larsen (1970: 32) argues that a carving in walrus ivory of a hanging polar bear skin from the Dorset culture (approximately AD 500) near Iglulik represents 'a polar bear skin hung up in the same way as done by the Netsilik Eskimo'.

7. See, e.g., Sandell (1996) for Greenland; Keith (2005) for King William Island; and Wenzel (2005).

8. In that respect, Inuit seem very close to North American indigenous traditions (e.g., Ojibway, Tsimshian) or some Siberian societies (e.g., Tungus, Yakut) that consider the bear to be an ancestor, whereas other societies such as the Menomini consider him 'an elder brother', a reference that is also used by the Iglulingmiut for a big male bear.

9. See Boas (1901: 251–252, 'The Woman who transformed herself into a Bear'; 252–254, 'The Woman who became a Bear and killed her Enemy'; 307–308, 'Origin of the Black Bear'); see also Rasmussen (1929: 267–259). In the Western Arctic grizzly bears are also mentioned. A story recorded by Métayer from B. Ivarluk (Métayer 1973: 694–699) relates how a woman

avenged herself on her husband, who wished to take another wife. The wife as well as her two children changed into bears and killed the husband. After that they could not resume their human shape. See also Fienup-Riordan (1994: 61):, 'The bear is an unpredictable person, a trait attributed to the woman who was transformed into a bear in her search for her unfaithful husband.'

10. Randa (1994: 119) gives other examples of kinship terms used for bears, such as *anaana* (mother), *ataata* (father), *qiturngaq* (child), and *irniq* (son).

11. When polar bears cubs were adopted by Inuit, they would call them *tiguaq* (adopted, taken), which is also a term used for humans. Mary-Rousselière collected a story from William Ukkumaaluk from Iglulik about a young orphan adopted by bears. The orphan had an enemy among the bears but managed to win him over, and they became hunting partners. See also the variant provided by Solange Atagutsiaq from Mittimatalik (quoted in Laugrand and Oosten 2009: 99–100; 222–25).

12. Similar versions of this story were recorded from the Iglulingmiut a century before by Captain G. F. Lyon (1824: 375) and Hall ([1867] 1970: 534), and from the Caribou Inuit by Reverend D. Marsh (1987: 76).

13. See Mary-Rousselière (1957: 18) for a very instructive illustration of an *apitiq* built by a bear; see also Randa (1986: 162).

14. See also the art piece and comments by Joseph Suqslak in Seidelman and Turner (1993: 104): 'When stalking seals near their breathing holes, a hunter must imitate the infinite patience of the animal without a shadow. He must enter the spirit of the polar bear.'

15. See also Hall ([1867] 1970: 534–36) on techniques copied from bears.

16. See also Fienup-Riordan (1994: 114): 'Bears, like seals, could hear what people said about them.'

17. Clément (2012: 279) relates that among the Innu, black bears, like many other animals, are said to be able to speak the human language and can understand the songs of the hunters. However, their eyesight is weak. Brightman (1993: 104–6, 115) also refers to hunters speaking to bears in their den before killing them or of other hunters using drums and songs to catch their prey. See also Preston ([1975] 2002: 198–200) and Scott (2006).

18. See also the myth of the old woman who killed a bear collected by Nungak and Arima (1988: 107–9) in Nunavik. One moonlit night, an old woman killed a big male bear with her walking stick. Turning her mitts inside out, she put them on the end of her cane and jabbed the stick in the bear's mouth. The mitt stuck in its throat and the bear died. The next morning, when she came back to her prey with her son, they discovered an enormous dead creature. After this event, the old woman, who had not been allowed to go on the sled and had often been very hungry, was taken good care of and invited to go on the sled.

19. See also the story of Qanguq's wife, attacked by a bear while she was alone in a tent with her baby on her back and her daughter. Piugaattuq (IE 58) explained that she threw an axe at the bear and finally managed to kill it with a .22-calibre rifle. When the hunters returned they only had to butcher it. An attack by a bear on a man named Urulu was also described by Piugaattuq (IE 50): 'As he was putting his footwear on, at once the bear

broke through the walls of the igloo just over the meat platform. He had set up camp for the night with his wife so their dwelling was small. When the bear broke through, it immediately got its paw to the meat platform. He still had not put on his footwear but he was now faced with the bear right there. At once he grabbed hold of his footwear and cried out, 'Angaaraalungunaak', hitting the bear with his *kamik* right on the face. The bear did not make a move at once but soon it started to back off and blew out air. He found the smell of the breath of the bear awful. The bears behave almost like humans, they do not like their faces meddled with. This applies to most of the animals.'

20. According to Hall ([1867] 1970: 536), 'It is a custom among the Innuits, dating from time immemorial, that whoever first sees a Ninoo is entitled to the skin, no matter whether the fortunate person be man, woman or child.'

21. See also Balikci (1970: 220) for the Nattilik area.

22. See Soby (1970: 63–64) for cultural objects and gender in Greenland: 'Thus, the Eskimos at Augpilagtoq in South Greenland carried a dead bear's head into the house and placed it on the edge of the lamp stand – ipat – facing southwards, the very direction from which the bear came, namely, along with field ice around the southern tip of the land. One put fat into the bear's mouth "to please it, for it loves all kinds of smelly grease". The crown of the animal's head was decorated with all sorts of small objects: Cut-out boot soles, knives, glass beads, and so on, in the belief that the bear's ancestors had sent it to fetch these things. The bear's head remained like this for five days (Rink, S.: 1896, p. 99; Nansen, F.: 1891, p. 185). When a Polar Eskimo bear hunter came home with game, its scraped skin was placed in a chest used for dog food – qingmerfik, and its head was placed on the window sill with its muzzle pointing inwards. Given a male bear, it was customary to hang a harpoon line, a harpoon head, and a harpoon on its muzzle, as well as a little blubber and meat and a few bits of skin; all these objects were meant to please the dead bear's soul. If the bear was female, one simply put a piece of sealskin and a little meat and bits of skin on its hide. The skin and the head, and these gifts, usually remained in place for five days. As a bear's meat gradually was consumed, its bones were collected and placed on the windowsill beside its head.'

23. See also Mary-Rousselière (Tape 4 IV C-g-TIV-10T1.doc).

24. Saladin d'Anglure (1980a: 77–78) qualifies *illuriik* as 'sporting opponents and real adversaries'.

25. See also Jenness (1922: 179). 'Long ago a polar bear was being hunted by a man and his dogs. It fled into the sky, and its pursuers followed after it. We can still see the bear, *nannoryuk*, in the sky, and behind it the hunter and his dogs, always pursuing but never overtaking it. One native pointed to the Pleiades and called them the bear, while Aldebaran and some stars near it were the hunter and his dogs, *agleoryuit* "The pursuers"; but the more usual name for the Pleiades is *Agietat*, the meaning of which I did not discover.' Rasmussen (1929: 263) also provides a variant of the origin of the Pleiades.

26. Hawkes (1916: 126) reports a special bond between Sedna and the polar bears in northern Labrador: 'The belief in Sedna, prominent among the

Baffin-islanders, is not unknown in northern Labrador. At Cape Chidley, an Eskimo informant spoke of an old woman whose home was at the bottom of the sea. Sometimes she came up to breathe across the strait, near the shores of Resolution island (Tutjarluk). She controls everything that swims in the sea; the fish, the seals, and especially the polar bear. She must be appeased, else she would drive the polar bears northward to Tutjarluk (Resolution island) where there are no hunters, or she might send a shark to eat their seals and cut up their nets, or make the codfish refuse to bite.'

27. Like polar bears, who used their left paw to fight against other bears, shamans used their left hand. For shamans, it was also forbidden to use polar bear fat while performing a healing séance (Rasmussen 1930: 108–9).

28. Mary-Rousselière recorded a story from William Ukkumaaluk from Iglulik about a woman who was visited by a bear needing a drink for her cubs. The bear asked the woman not to tell her husband about the visit, but the woman did not heed her advice. The result was a disaster, as the man went after the bears, killed the cubs and then was killed by the bear (see Laugrand and Oosten 2009: 96–97).

29. The text suggests an initiation ritual evoking similar traditions in Greenland. A central part of the initiation of the shaman was the rubbing of a stone on the beach. After some time a bear would appear that would devour the shaman. Thalbitzer (1923: 475) related, 'The angakok pupil should get up to the twofold enormous and aggressive bear appertaining to the inland ice; the terribly growling (bear) which has "a peculiar face".'

30. H. Egede (1818: 191–2) reports that if a Greenlandic shaman wanted to become a very powerful *angakkoq*, an *angakkoq pugdlit*, the lamps would be extinguished and his hands and feet would be bound. Then a white bear would appear and bite the *angakkoq* in his big toe and draw him into the sea. Here a walrus would grasp his genitals and together they would devour the shaman. A short while later his bones would be thrown on the floor where he was lying. Then his spirit would join with his bones and he would revive and be healthy again. Then he would be an *angakkoq pugdlit*.

31. Bears could also transform if necessary. Thus, a story recorded by Boas (1888: 639) relates how bears escaped a hunter by transforming into stones. 'At Qognung, near the head of Nettilling Fjord, there is a large white stone on each side of the fjord, somewhat resembling a bear. It is said that these stones have been bears which, being pursued by an Eskimo in the water, escaped to the land, but were transformed into these stones.'

32. See Boas (1907: 251–52, 252–54); Jenness (1922: 87, n90); and Holtved (1951: 309–12, no. 126).

PART IV

PREY

CHAPTER 8

# The Caribou, the Lice of the Earth

Caribou hunting has always been important for survival in the central Arctic, and today it is still very important for Inuit, who greatly appreciate the meat, skins and bones of the caribou. Most Inuit hunted for caribou, *tuktu*,[1] in the spring and the autumn, and some groups in the Kivalliq, such as the Ahiarmiut, depended almost completely on the caribou for survival (see figures 8.1 and 8.2).

Simon Tookoome (1999: 28–29) from Qamanittuaq related,

> The caribou used to gather in a very large herd to migrate. You could hear them coming for two days, walking over the frozen tundra. We would sit where they would pass and wait for them. It would take three or five days and nights for the herd to pass our camp. The land would be all torn up. They were not afraid in such big numbers. We would walk among them and pick out the fat ones. We would kill them carefully without frightening the herd. If we did not hunt caribou, they would multiply and there would become too many of them. Then they would suffer and starve until the herds were the right size again.
>
> Inuit would never set up camp in the path of the caribou. We wanted them to go their proper way. If someone put up a tent near a path, the caribou would change their route. When the mines started, the caribou were frightened and they changed their path. The Kabloonaq thought that the caribou were being hunted too much and that they were only a few left. But the caribou had just taken a different path.
>
> The caribou did a lot for us. They gave us clothing and food. And we used them for our boats and sleds. The sinew made rope. The antler was used to make hooks. The bones were good for needles. Nothing was wasted. Blood was used for clothing dyes; tendons for thread. Their skins made our tents. The lighter skin was used in the tent to let in light. The bladder was used for bags to hold lard. Even the fat could be chewed to make candles or burned in a stone lamp. We did not even need to eat vegetables or grains. The raw meat and organs of the caribou provided everything that a body needed to live.

**Figure 8.1.** A hunter approaching the caribou herd. *Source:* Anglican Church of Canada/General Synod Archives/Peck Papers, M56-1, series XXXIII, 4–6, 8–13.

When Inuit kill an animal in the traditional way, they give it a drink of water or, if there is no water, they melt snow with their mouths. The water is very helpful. Water eases the animal's suffering even after it is dead.[2]

We also removed the sinews before we cracked the leg bones. This was also to ease the dead animal's pain. The spirit of the animal was

**Figure 8.2.** A caribou near Mittimatalik. Photo: Frédéric Laugrand, 1995.

grateful. We respected the animals and the animals allowed us to catch them. After we killed a caribou, the tradition was to point the skin towards your home or tent. It sent more caribou that way.

Peter Suvaksiuq from Arviat related,

What I know is that when there is loud thunder[3] far away when there are no clouds or rain, the caribou are coming towards us. They say that there would be a large herd coming towards us because there was thundering far away. …

In the springtime, we didn't want to catch females with calves; we would try to get the ones that had antlers. We tried not to get bulls in the fall because the smell of them is awful, and it is not good for food during the winter. Caribou that had just had their babies were the good ones for food in the fall. …

When there is a herd of bulls together they are scary. When they are on top of a hill lying down, the younger males stand around the bulls and walk around them in slow motion. The young ones would keep the mosquitoes away from the bulls. Then they go a little way out, shake off the mosquitoes and go back to the bull caribou again. Even though they do not communicate like us, they know what they are doing.

This connection between the thunder and the caribou is rather ambiguous. In a version of the story of the origin of thunder and lightning, Rasmussen (1929: 162–63) relates: 'The two girls fled to the white men's country, where they now live; only now and then in summer do they visit their own country. They are never in want of food now, for whenever they like they can kill a caribou with lightning and eat it, and it is said that they grew to be very old.' Thus, the thunder evokes the coming of the caribou as well as the killing of the caribou.

The caribou is still conceived by elders as a gregarious animal living in such numbers that they can be compared to lice when they are seen moving from afar. Even if some hunters venture to kill some of them in the big herds, most of the time Inuit only hunt them when they are scattered in small groups. The caribou was hunted for its meat as well as its fur. Caribou skins were the favourite material for clothing because of their insulating qualities. Caribou sinew served as the favourite thread that was used to sew skins.

## The Origin of the Caribou

Different traditions with respect to the caribou exist. One tradition says that the caribou came out of the earth. Another tradition has it that the caribou and the walrus were created as a pair by the mother of the caribou, who is sometimes equated with the owner of the sea mammals. Boas (1907: 536–37) relates,

> In the beginning the people lived on small game. One man only would bring in a caribou every day. One of the natives followed him, and saw how this man lifted up a large flat stone, and how a caribou jumped out. The man killed it and put the stone back in place. After the stranger had left, the man who had followed him turned over the stone, and out came a caribou. While he was trying to catch it, more caribou kept coming out, until they had scattered all over the earth.
>
> At that time the caribou would gore the hunters with their antlers. Then the man who had first obtained the caribou singly from the hole struck them on the forehead, and thus made a depression, which all the caribou have at the present day. When the caribou turned round, he kicked it from behind, and thus broke off its tail.

The caribou coming from the earth evokes the idea of a multitude, and this idea is also preserved in the term for caribou in the language of the *tuurngait:* the word *kumarjuait,* meaning 'big lice', indicates a shift in scale, denoting the caribou as lice crawling the earth. The connection of caribou with the earth is always strong.

Rasmussen (1929: 202–3) relates that *silaat* that turn into caribou are called the children of the earth:

There are in the earth large white eggs, silaat, as big as the bladder of a walrus. They turn to silat or silAraluit: these silAraluit are, when fully developed, shaped almost like caribou, but with large snouts, hair like that of a lemming, and legs as tall as tent poles. They look as if they were as big as an umiAq, but they are not dangerous, they have the nature of the caribou. Their footmarks are so large that two hands with outstretched fingers will not cover one. If it is killed, and one wishes to cut it up, it will take several days, so great are these animals, and that even if one only tries to deal with one side of the carcase. When one of these giant beasts is seen among caribou, it appears like a white mountain of snow; when it takes to flight and treads the ground, rain falls, pouring, drenching rain, and a thick mist covers the earth.... They are called silaq, plural silat, and this means something of sila, of the earth, of the universe, of the air, of the weather. It is said that they are the children of the earth. Anyone killing such a silaq must observe the same taboo as a man who has lost his brother.[4]

Thus, the *silaat* are giant animals associated with rain and mist. Kappianaq (IE 100) from Iglulik recalled how a hunter caught a young caribou that was to become a *silaaq* and the whole region was covered with snow as a result. The famous Iglulik leader Ittuksarjuat told Iqallijuq that there were also black *silaat*. It was strictly forbidden to catch caribou *silaat* that were all black, because if one were caught it would make the weather bad for a long time. In those days it was believed that the earth and Sila were very protective of their eggs (Iqallijuq, IE 91). Thus, *silaat* were connected to Sila as well as to Nuna.

The second origin tradition connects the caribou and the walrus. According to Rasmussen (1929: 67), among the Iglulik some people believe the sea woman also owns the caribou, whereas others think the caribou have their own owner. Rasmussen (1929: 67–68) provided an account of the origin of the caribou as related by Orulo, the wife of the *angakkuq* Aava:

This is what is told of the Mother of the Caribou, of 'tuktut ikviat': 'the one with whom the caribou are':
    It is said that at the time when the sea beasts were first made, there were no caribou on the earth; but then an old woman went up inland and made them. Their skins she made from her breeches, so that the lie of the hair followed the same pattern as her breeches. But the caribou was given teeth like other animals; at first it had tusks as well. It was a dangerous beast, and it was not long before a man was killed while hunting. Then the old woman grew frightened, and went up inland again and gathered together the caribou she had made. The tusks she changed into antlers, the teeth in the front of the jaw she knocked out, and when she had done this, she said to them:

'Land beasts such as you must keep away from men, and be shy and easily frightened.'

And then she gave them a kick on the forehead, and it was that which made the hollow one can see now in the forehead of all caribou. The animals dashed away, and were very shy thereafter. But then it was found that they were too swift; no man could come up with them, and once more the old woman had to call them all together. This time she changed the fashion of the hair, so that all did not lie the same way. The hair of the belly, under the throat and flanks, was made to lie in different directions, and then the animals were let loose once more. The caribou were still swift runners, but they could not cleave the air as rapidly as before, because the hair stood in the way, and men could now overtake them and kill them when they used certain tricks. Afterwards, the old woman went to live among the caribou; she stayed with them and never returned to the haunts of men, and now she is called, the Mother of the Caribou, 'tuktut ikviat' or 'the one with whom the caribou are'.[5]

Thus, the caribou were made out of the breeches of a woman, inverting the pattern of breeches being made out of caribou skin.

Boas (1888: 588) related that in Cumberland Sound, among the Akudnirmiut, the walrus and the caribou were thought to be created by a woman from her breeches and boots:

During a famine a woman (I could not learn whether she was identical with Sedna or not) carried her boots to the hills and transformed them by magic into deer, which spread all over the country. Then she carried her breeches to the sea, where they were changed into walrus. The first deer, however, had large tusks and no horns, while the walrus had horns and no tusks. The Eskimo soon found that this was very dangerous for the hunter, as the deer killed pursuers with their tusks, while the walrus upset the boats. Therefore an old man transferred the horns to the deer and the tusks to the walrus.

It is very probable that this woman was Sedna, as the Eskimo affirm that the observances referring to walrus and deer are commanded by Sedna and as the first tradition accounts for her dislike of the deer.

This time, the caribou were made out of the boots and the walrus out of the breeches of a woman. This story exists in many variants and establishes a connection between the walrus and the caribou. This connection may be evoked by the fact that walrus are also gregarious and often can be found in multitudes basking in the sun.

Lyon (1824: 361) distinguished between the sea woman and Pukimna, the owner of the caribou. Boas (1888: 588), however, could not find any trace of the tradition 'of a being to whom he [Lyon] refers by the name of Pukimna (derived from *pukiq*, the white part of a caribou skin), who lives in a fine country far to the west and who is the immediate protectress of deer, which animals roam in immense herds around her dwelling'. Captain Low (1906: 169), who visited the area in the early 1900s, stated, 'There is a goddess of the land-animals called Pukimma, who appears to be closely identified with Nuliayok, and may be the same personage under a different name.' She may also be related to the Pinga, a spirit located in the sky by the Padlirmiut in the Kivalliq[6] (see Laugrand and Oosten 2008: 25–32). Rasmussen (1929: 113) also provides the name Pakitsumanga for the mother of the caribou, relating that she can provide *angakkuit* with *qaumaniq*, shamanic vision.[7] But Rasmussen (1929: 70) also stated that most Iglulingmiut considered the mother of the caribou and the mother of the sea game as the same being.

Peck (quoted in Laugrand et al. 2006: 369) was told that the caribou were owned by 'Tikkertserktok, the goddess of the land (noonaut innunga)'. Peck assumed that she was even more powerful than Sedna.

Thus the mother of the caribou was a powerful being. She could be distinguished from the sea woman but also be identified with her. She created the caribou and was their owner. She required gifts at the start of the caribou hunting season.

## Caribou Hunting Rituals

Oosootapik, one of Pecks main informants, related,

> That the land had an owner, a woman possessing a house on a hill in the centre of the land. She owned the deer. She wanted small soles of boots and lines used for carrying loads in the summer from the men. Only then was she prepared to make the caribou appear so that they could be killed.

If soles and lines were not given, people would become sick. Peck (quoted in Laugrand et al. 2006: 369) related,

> Tikkitserktok is said to have the power to cause sickness to those who did not give the things mentioned, they were pained in various parts of the body, and they suffered both while they were inland, and during the autumn; the conjurors who also had communion with Tikkitserktok could cure the sickness of those who were afflicted, taken away when the sufferer confessed that he had not given the articles named to Tikkitserktok.

The Iglulingmiut also had to make a gift when they started caribou hunting. Rasmussen (1929: 195) observed, 'People hunting caribou in kayaks on a river or lake must, while hunting, lay out a piece of sealskin under a stone as a sacrifice to Tugtut Igfianut, the Mother of the Caribou.' The value of all initial gifts appears to be small, but the success of the hunt depended on them. All gifts were intended for the owners of the game, who would then give the game to the hunters. Rasmussen (1931: 15) also refers to the initial gifts that open the caribou season in his discussion of the Nattilingmiut:

> Wild caribou, land louse, long-legs,
> With the great ears,
> And the rough hairs on your neck,
> Flee not from me.
> Here I bring skins for soles,
> Here I bring moss for wicks,
> Just come gladly
> Hither to me, hither to me.

Among the Nattilingmiut the caribou themselves instead of the mother of the caribou appear to be the receivers of the gifts.

Not only the mother of the caribou or the caribou themselves received gifts. Rasmussen (1929: 194) relates, 'When a caribou killed with an arrow is cut up, care must be taken not to break any of the bones, and when the animal has been cut up, a small piece of meat or suet is placed under a stone – qingaluklune – as a sacrifice to the dead – nErErquvlugit – piʃäkʃalik – manisinialungmat – it is desired that the dead shall eat, in the hope that they will procure game.' Michel Kanajuq from Qamanittuaq related how the deceased would interfere on behalf of their descendants:

> Some said that the mother of the caribou lived in heaven, and they thought that she was Nuliajuk. Our ancestors thought that all the people who died went to the underworld instead of up above, and that they went to Nuliajuk the mother of the caribou. When the caribou did not want to leave, their faces would change into human-like faces, and the people there would whip them so that they would go to where people were living. An elder would make a small whip, and whip the land, and give it to Nuliajuk and say, 'Here is your whip. Now let us have some caribou'. That is what they used to do to get the caribou to go where they lived. (quoted in Laugrand and Oosten 2009: 79)

Kanajuq is our only source for these rituals, however. Apparently, the deceased would use a whip to drive the caribou to the land. The whipping of the land probably prepared the land for the caribou hunting and evokes the use of the whip in rituals to calm down the wind. The gift of the whip to Nuliajuk appears to be an initial gift preceding the hunting season.

Thus, relations with the mother of the caribou, the caribou themselves and the deceased all come into play in the initial gifts required
for caribou hunting. In addition to these gifts, ethnographic data suggest that in the eighteenth and nineteenth century elaborate rituals
were connected to caribou hunting. In a short but rich publication,
John G. Taylor and Helga Taylor (1986: 237–38) described a summer
ritual observed by the Danish surgeon Christoph Brasen (1738–74) in
Nain, Labrador, in the year 1772:

> First they set up two poles about a hundred steps apart. On the top of
> each was an old caribou hide stretched on a four-cornered frame. At each
> pole were six Eskimo men, each with their wives. The wives were beauti-
> fully dressed, according to their manner, with their caribou clothing and
> were mostly young women who have had only one child or no children,
> or who wished to have more children. Therefore, Tagluina was here with
> his wives. Mikak and her sister, his second wife, so that according to their
> imagination they will become fruitful sooner. When both the women and
> the men were standing in a line to the side of each pole, one party of
> women went all in a row to the other women who stood in line at the op-
> posite pole. In front of these latter stood an Eskimo man with a knife in
> his hand, who sang with them and swung or made blows with the knife
> in hand and stamped his feet up and down during the singing. When the
> other women came to him, this man stepped in front of them with his
> knife in hand and went around them. The men at the same end stood
> next to these women and kissed them one after another. Then the Es-
> kimo again placed himself in front of the women, where he had formerly
> stood, and the approaching women had to stand in a line in front of him.
> He continued singing and swinging the knife in his hand. The women
> standing behind him helped with the singing. The other women were
> silent but during the singing they were kissed by the men and touched
> with hands in a bad way. After this had lasted for 10 to 12 minutes, these
> women went all in a row back to where their own husbands were stand-
> ing and placed themselves in a straight line. When they had returned,
> their husbands started to shoot arrows at the other pole or target with
> their bows and arrows. Each had 6 or 8 arrows. The shooting also took
> place in a certain order. After they were lined up in front of their pole,
> as soon as one had finished shooting the next had a turn and so forth.
> This continued until all the arrows were shot off. During the shooting,
> the Eskimo with the knife in his hand and his row of women, as well as
> their own wives, continued singing. The women who had gloves of snow-
> white rabbit fur, stood and swung back and forth with the hands as did
> the man with the knife in his hand. This usually continued until someone
> hit the target with an arrow. The arrows were collected by one Eskimo
> man and were deposited in a heap at their standing pole. Then every man
> went there and picked up his portion. While this was happening, their
> wives went all in a row to the women who were with them last. In front
> of the latter was also a man with a knife in his hands, who made the

same motions as the other one. And when the women arrived he walked around them a few times. Then they lined up. The kissing and touching [by] hands were done as before. Afterwards they returned. Then the men started shooting the arrows back to the pole or target. The singing and swinging with the knife and with the women's white gloves [continued] until someone hit the target. Generally they hit the target seldom. In like manner this game continued alternately until sunset. Then the men tested who was strongest, namely two at a time, one from each party. Whoever could throw the other one down had to try against a new man and the one who was strongest had won for himself and his party. We do not know whether this game ends in a whoring game, as it does among the Greenland heathen.

The connection of these games to caribou hunting is not explicit, but in 1777 the German missionary Beck connected such a game to caribou hunting:

Today the Eskimos, of whom there are with us more than 200 in 37 tents, wanted to perform a game, according to their custom, so that they could be jolly with each other. They like to play this game before leaving for the caribou hunt so that they might be fortunate in the hunt inland. (quoted in Taylor and Taylor 1986: 240)

In 1772 Drachart had already observed a kissing ritual at Amitok where nine young men kissed nine women. When he asked for the meaning of the ritual the men answered, 'They cannot get children but now they believe that they will get a child' (quoted in Taylor and Taylor 1986: 235). The reports on the ritual suggest a close connection between the stimulating of the fertility of the women and the caribou hunt. Skills such as success in shooting, and not marriage relations, organized the sexual relations between the genders in the ritual.

L. Turner ([1894] 1979: 196–97) refers to the ritual use of a pole to attract the caribou in Nunavik:

In order to cause the deer to move toward the locality where they may be desired the shaman will erect, on a pole placed in a favorable position, an image of some famous hunter and conjurer. The image will represent the power of the person as conjurer and the various paraphernalia attached to the image assist in controlling the movements of the animals.[8]

Turner does not refer to any rituals, but they may not have taken place, as he decided after a few days to add the object attached to the pole to his collection, and he suggests the *angakkuq* then had to invoke the help of another one.

Ludwig Kumlien (1879: 19) provided a description of a ceremony at the end of winter or the beginning of spring in the South Baffin area:

They have an interesting custom or superstition, namely, the killing of the evil spirit of the deer; some time during the winter or early in spring, at any rate before they can go deer hunting, they congregate together and dispose of this imaginary evil. The chief ancoot, angekok, or medicine man, is the main performer. He goes through a number of gyrations and contortions, constantly hallooing and calling, till suddenly the imaginary deer is among them. Now begins a lively time. Every one is screaming, running, jumping, spearing, and stabbing at the imaginary deer, till one would think a whole mad-house was let loose. Often this deer proves very agile, and must be hard to kill, for I have known them to keep this performance up for days; in fact, till they were completely exhausted.

During one of these performances an old man speared the deer, another knocked out an eye, a third stabbed him, and so till he was dead. Those who are able or fortunate enough to inflict some injury on this bad deer, especially he who inflicts the death-blow, is considered extremely lucky, as he will have no difficulty in procuring as many deer as he wants, for there is no longer an evil spirit to turn his bullets or arrows from their course.

They seldom kill a deer after the regular hunting season is over, till this performance has been gone through with, even though a very good opportunity presents itself.

The 'evil' caribou was represented by an *angakkuq*, who was symbolically killed. The killing of the caribou made the caribou available to the hunters. This act may have been equivalent to the killing of Sedna at the start of sea mammal hunting as described by Boas, who assumed Kumlien was referring to the Sedna feast here (Boas 1888: 606).

The description also evokes another ritual performance in the Cumberland Sound area recorded by Captain Mutch (quoted in Boas 1907: 489–90):

The angakok takes a ground-seal spear and a line down to the ground-ice and sets it up, with the harpoon-point upward. When the performance opens in the house, the angakok stands up, and near him are his assistant spirits. Then he goes down to the ground-ice, and soon he sees a walrus-spirit, which enters him. As soon as this spirit enters his body, he loses all knowledge of himself. Then his spirit assistants discover him, and harpoon him in the same way as a hunter harpoons a walrus. The angakok believes he dives. As soon as he dives, he sees the snow-houses of the village, which his spirit assistants have so far not noticed. The walrus rises, and moves in the direction of the snow-houses. It enters one of them, and then goes from house to house, frightening all the people. They see the harpoon-heads of the spirit assistants protruding from its body, and blow on them. Finally the walrus goes back to the ground-ice where it was first seen. The people take a little water and pour it over their feet, which is symbolic of drinking water. This helps them to recover from their fright. When the angakok gets back to the water, it appears to the spirit assistants as though the walrus had just risen again, and they throw it with a lance. When the spirit assistants have killed the walrus, they drag it out to the ice and pull out the harpoon – not, however, like human beings, who turn the harpoon-point between the splices of the warp, but by pulling it out through the body with all their strength. Then the spirits cut up the body. As soon as they gather the meat, the walrus revives, and becomes a man again. The spirits are particularly careful to put those parts together properly where the harpoon-point has been pulled out. Then the angakok goes back to the house, and his spirit assistants stay outside, ready to do his bidding any time during the following year.

In this description a walrus spirit enters the *angakkuq,* who transforms into a walrus and is harpooned by his helping spirits. Then he is cut into pieces and revived again. Whereas in the feast described by Kumlien the *angakkuq* is killed by other Inuit, in this ritual the *angakkuq* is killed by his helping spirits. The text may well refer to an opening of the winter hunting season. Unfortunately neither Mutch nor Boas provides an explanation of this performance. The parallelism between the two rituals is particularly striking considering the close relationship between the caribou and the walrus in the origin myth of the two animals.

Recurrent features of the caribou feasts appear to have been the division of the camp into two groups competing in an archery contest as well as a division of the camp into men and women. Clearly the success in the archery contest anticipates success in caribou hunting, as well as in the procreation of human society. Taylor and Taylor (1986: 243) refer to Saladin d'Anglure's (1984: 496) conclusion that the domains of hunting and procreation were explicitly fused. Another feature of the feast is that people dress in their best clothing and the women wear gloves. Thus, they manifest themselves as social beings having made the best possible use of their catches.

The close connection between the fertility of the women and the hunting of caribou evokes the Sedna feasts, where a similar relation existed and the exchange of women played an important part in the feasts, preparing the camp and the land for the hunting of the sea mammals. Indeed, Taylor (1986: 243) refers to Boas's description of an exchange of women in a ritual during the Sedna feast in South Baffin. Boas (1888: 608–9) relates,

Sometimes the latter ceremony takes place the night before the feast. It is called suluiting or quvietung. When it is quite dark a number of Inuit come out of their huts and run crying all round their settlements. Wherever anybody is asleep they climb upon the roof of his hut and rouse him by screaming and shouting until all have assembled outside. Then a woman and a man (the mirqussang) sit down in the snow. The man holds a knife (sulung) in his hand, from which the feast takes its name, and sings:

Oangaja jaja jajaja aja.
Pissiungmipadlo panginejernago
Qodlungutaokpan panginejerlugping
Pissiungmipadlo panginejernago.

To this song the woman keeps time by moving her body and her arms, at the same time flinging snow on the bystanders. Then the whole company goes into the singing house and joins in dancing and singing. This done, the men must leave the house and stand outside while the mirqussang watch the entrance. The women continue singing and leave the house one by one. They are awaited by the mirqussang, who lead every one to one of the men standing about. The pair must reenter the singing house and walk around the lamp, all the men and women crying, 'Hrr! hrr!' from both corners of the mouth. Then they go to the woman's hut, where they stay during the ensuing night. The feast is frequently celebrated by all the tribes of Davis and Hudson Strait, and even independently of the great feast described above.

The day after, the men frequently join in a shooting match. A target is set up, at which they shoot their arrows. As soon as a man hits, the women, who stand looking on, rush forward and rub noses with him.[9]

Boas's description raises considerable problems. The description of the feast very much evokes the descriptions of the caribou feasts. Furthermore, Boas observes that the feast could also be celebrated independently of the Sedna feast. Dealing with the caribou hunt, Peck (Laugrand et al. 2006: 336) does not provide a description of the feast but clearly refers to it:

[The Netseraktut – men who shoot with bow and arrow at deer skins]. As regards the singers, Netseraktut who sing in the open air (not in singing houses), they have two deer skins (fixed on a pole) at which they shoot (with bow and arrows) from some distance. If the man (shooter) misses, then he commences to sing, and then goes towards the other skin (at which he shoots) still singing, and the women (also) sing together with the shooters.

Bilby (1923: 240) provides more details for the South Baffin festivities. He relates that in the summer, different groups meet. After a general meeting of the elders to decide upon the direction and the details of the prospective hunt,

A special feast house was set up.
    The Kagge, or singing house, of the summer deerhunt is, like that of the Sedna ceremony, a big round house, similarly tenanted by the people

in circles around the walls. The summer Kagge is built of sod and stones. The women wear skin gloves – the backs black and the palms white – and take their station behind everybody else, with the children. The men come next, and the Angakooeet, as judges, sit in the front circle. The centre of the house is left vacant for the performers.

The first part of the entertainment consists of songs describing the exploits of the dead and gone heroes and hunters of the tribe, each song having a refrain which is taken up by the women, who sway their bodies from side to side as they sing, so raising and lowering their arms as to show first a circle of waving white and then a circle of waving black hands. Many of these songs are old-established favourites, extemporised at first by some individual as his own contribution to some occasion, which 'caught on' and became part of the tribe's collective musical tradition.

After these come the extempore efforts of the current evening. Each man contributes a song of his own, turning upon some event in his career, or some more or less poetic fancy which has occurred to him. The songs have probably been composed and polished, and possibly practised, in private for some time, but the contest is the occasion of their publication to the musical world. They are most attentively received, and judged by the Angakooeet. (Bilby 1923: 243)

After these festivities, the different groups split up to take up caribou hunting.

Further north, a similar feast was described by Rasmussen (1929: 243–44):

Another festival, only celebrated when there are many people, is called qulungErtut. It opens with a challenge between two iglɔreˑk, first to all manner of contests out in the open, and ending with a song contest in the qagge. The two rivals, each with a knife, embrace and kiss each other as they meet. The women are then divided into two parties. One party has to sing a song, a long, long song which they keep on repeating; meantime, the other group stand with uplifted arms waving gulls' wings, the object being to see which side can hold out the longer. Here is a fragment of the song that is sung on this occasion:

> See they come,
> gaily dressed in new fur garments,
> women, women, youthful women.
> See, with mittens on their hands,
> gulls' wings they are holding high,
> and the long, loose-flapping coat tails
> wave with every swaying motion.
> Here are women, youthful women,
> No mistaking when they stride
> forth to meet the men awaiting
> prize of victory in the contest.

The women of the losing party then had to 'stride' over to the others, who surrounded them in a circle, when the men had to try to kiss them.

After this game an archery contest was held. A target was set up on a long pole, and the one who first made ten hits was counted the winner. Then came ball games and fierce boxing bouts. In these, it was permissible to soften the effect of the blows by wearing a fur mitten with the fur inside. The combatants had to strike each other first on the shoulders, then in the eyes or on the temples, and in spite of the glove, it was not unusual for a collarbone to be broken, or for a blow in the face to do serious damage. I have at any rate seen a man who had had one eye knocked out in the course of one of these tests of strength and manliness. After all these sporting events, which in the respective games required the two iglɔreˑk to be unceasingly up to the mark and to show themselves at their very best, the conclusion took place in the qagge, where the two rivals had again to finish off their duel by a song contest lasting as a rule the whole night.

This feast is clearly a variant of the feasts discussed for Labrador in the late eighteenth century by Taylor and Taylor and for South Baffin in the late nineteenth century by Boas. The swaying movements of the women are identified with the movements of gulls.

Iqallijuq (IE 29) recalled a feast in which song cousins competed. She refers to it as *tivajuut*.

> They used to build a big igloo that was used for the 'Qaqiq'. There were two people that were to build the igloo … there would be a piece of walrus meat and a bull caribou body hanging from the ceiling. The two who were dressed up before would put their clothes back on when the spectators started to enter the igloo, every now and then a platform or mat would be laid in front of a person entering. The person had to imitate a certain bird, then went to the meat hanging [from the ceiling]. He or she would have to hit the meat with the left hand a few times. When this was over the meat would be prepared and cut up; then the feast would take place.

In order to obtain the meat, the men would have to identify with birds. In another interview, Iqallijuq recalled:

> It was at that time when men poke their knife at the meat and crying out the sounds of their particular Tiguti. So there would be qa'qa'qaa (loon), ah'a'ngiq (old squaw), qaviq'pip'pii (ptarmigan) and other species of bird in which each one was wiped as new born with its skin. So with the skin of a bird that they were wiped with, they would imitate the sound of the species of their Tiguti. (Iqallijuq, IE 204)

Thus, it was not only women who identified with birds (by waving gulls' wings). The men also identified with birds, notably the bird with whose skin they were wiped clean when they were born.

Among the Nattilingmiut, Rasmussen (1931: 82–83) witnessed a celebration called *arssautissut* in late October. It was celebrated because
Oqortoq's little foster son had taken his first step. Oqortoq's son-in-law
Tarraijuk, together with his mother-in-law Arnangussaq, walked out
onto the ice of the freshwater lake.

> Tarraijuk carried the shoulder and neck of a caribou. The frozen piece
> of meat had been hewn and shaped into a round lump, with no corners
> at all, so that there was nothing to get a grip on. Arnangussaq had a big
> pun-ErnAq: an enormous round piece of melted caribou fat also shaped
> like a sphere in order to make it difficult to grasp. This was the opening
> ceremony. The two meat-bearers were called the ivajA-rsiutErtut (those
> who bring out something that others are to fight for).

Then all the women threw themselves at Arnangussaq and the men at
Tarraijuk to get hold of the prize. The winner was the one who succeeded in holding on to the prize, pressing it with two arms to the
breast. The women fought for more than half an hour and the men
took even longer.

> At last Qaqortingneq was declared to be the winner. They gave up trying
> to get the meat from him, but undoubtedly he was the strongest and the
> most dexterous man in the tribe. As soon as the others had given up he
> lifted his booty at arm's length and shouted 'Hoy! Hoy! Hoy! Hoy!', just as
> Simigaq had announced her victory. The winner was called a-nigtoq (the
> one who takes the booty from the others and keeps it).
>
> When the contest had been settled the women lined up on the ice
> about fifty metres from the huts, where the men had taken up their po-
> sition. At a given signal all the men ran to the women, who stood in two
> rows facing each other; in front of all was the winner Qaqortingneq, and
> he went first round the whole row and kissed all the women one by one,
> placing his arms round their necks and nuzzling violently at their noses.
> After him it was the others' turn, and it is no wonder that the noses of
> many of the women were bleeding after this wholesale nose-rubbing.

A feast connecting the abundance of caribou and the fertility of
women was thus widespread from Labrador to the Nattilik area. In the
feasts the men showed their prowess and skills in shooting, and the
women their skills in dancing. The feasts were supposed to enhance
the fertility of the women as well as the success of the caribou hunt.
The hunters competed as rivals, whereas the women appear to have
represented birds, notably gulls. These birds appear to be associated
with a change of scale. Rasmussen (1929: 213) relates that on the level
of the dwarves, a gull changes into a caribou.[10] The gull can also take a
giant shape, as in the story of the monster gull related by Boas (1901:

195). A symbolic transformation of a human being into a gull may allow people to function on the level of the *tarniit*. Rasmussen stated, 'The wing of a gull was fastened to the pole as a sign or symbol indicating that the pupil should in time acquire the power of travelling through the air to the Land of the Dead up in heaven, or down through the sea to the abode of Takanakapsaluk' (1929: 111). Thus, the gull connected different worlds. Rasmussen (1931: 318) also related the story of a shaman transforming into a gull in the land of the dead in order to escape from danger.

Pisuk from Rankin Inlet (quoted in Kolb and Law 2001: 180) recalled,

> I was sick once for around two years. I was told in a dream that my *tarniq* was getting too far away from me. That was why I was not feeling well. In this dream it got on the back of a bird that looked like a seagull. I saw something that looked like high hills. Sometime later, I saw the area around the Fox Four Dewline site on television, and recognized it as the place I had been. The seagull swooped down. I could see my body sleeping. It touched my body slightly. I could feel the air rushing past my face. Since then, although I still get sick, I feel much better.

Thus, the gull seems closely associated with the travelling of the *tarniq*, the seat of vitality.[11] Considering the fact that on the level of the dwarves a gull changes into a caribou, the symbolism of the women representing the gulls may imply that, since on a smaller scale gulls become caribou, the women thus represent the caribou and can then attract the caribou to the community. In that case, the seductive behaviour of the women was not only directed at the men, but also at the caribou.

## Preparing for the Hunt

Hunters would prepare themselves carefully for the caribou hunt. They might use *aarnguat*, amulets, *irinaliutiit*, powerful words, and songs to be successful in hunting. Pisuk related that his father would 'put on what was called an *angaluk* [shaman belt] to get caribou. He put it around his neck. It was made from the white belly of a caribou skin' (quoted in Oosten and Laugrand 2002: 148).

Dreams might also predict hunters' fortunes in hunting. Angmaalik (quoted in Kulchyski et al. 2003: 283) related, 'I remember I dreamed of a huge police officer and that day I caught a male caribou with lots of fat. That was my interpretation. If I had a dream of a female non-Native with children, I probably would have seen caribou like that....

If people knew that I had a dream of Non-Natives, the other hunters would expect to see caribou that day.' Pisuk from Rankin Inlet (quoted in Kolb and Law 2001: 4) recalled, 'If we were out somewhere where there were no caribou, and I dreamed about a little rainbow, then I would know that we were going towards caribou. Sometimes it would be a one-day trip from camp, so we would have to sleep along the way. We would be able to go where there were caribou based on my dream.'

Other signs might also predict a catch. Kappianaq from Iglulik (quoted in Kolb and Law 2001: 91) remembered, 'If my middle finger were to twitch, I used that as a *niriujaarniq* for caribou. If it twitched or was tingling then I knew I was going to get a caribou.'

## Aarnguat

Especially among the Nattilingmiut, *aarnguat* were frequently used. Rasmussen (1931: 271) relates that various parts of the caribou could be used to make one into a good caribou hunter: 'Caribou front teeth, worn sewn on to the breast of the inner coat, give general luck on caribou hunts.[12] A caribou ear would make one a lucky caribou hunter.' Several *aarnguat* helped to make someone a good kayaker: 'The snout skin of a caribou: makes him just as sure as a kayak man as the caribou is a swimmer' (Rasmussen 1931: 272). Rasmussen (1931: 277) also reports on the use of '[a] caribou bull or male seal without a penis; by this is meant animals of the size, appearance and figure of male animals but genitals like female animals; the uterus of such an animal is dried and folded up inside the kayak and gives it a very high speed'. Often the selection of materials to be used in an amulet was quite specific: 'The great foot sinew of a caribou (qarᴌiuʃaq): will make him a good runner; a caribou antler which, after having been shed by the animal, has been gnawed by another caribou, and also a caribou's forehead skin used for wiping the blood from the boy when he was born: luck when hunting caribou' (Rasmussen 1931: 275).

Parts of other animals could also be used in amulets for caribou hunting. Wolves were excellent caribou hunters, and parts of their bodies used as *aarnguat* would enhance one's capacities as a caribou hunter: 'Wolf hair sewn into a piece of sealskin, on which the hair is inside: makes him good at chasing caribou down to the crossing places' (Rasmussen 1931: 272). 'Wolf hair sewn on to the back of the inner coat close to the right armhole was called un/c/rs/ugs/autit and was especially effective as a beater's amulet, scaring the animals in the right direction, i.e. towards the crossing places where they were awaited by the kayaks' (Rasmussen 1931: 179). In addition, a raven skin and raven head would make the hunter invisible to the caribou at their crossing places (Rasmussen 1931: 271).

Sometimes a caribou amulet might provide protection against non-human beings. Among the Iglulingmiut, 'A small doll, made from the extreme hard point of bone in the penis of a walrus, skillfully carved with arms and legs, is sewn into a boy's inner jacket, and he will then, when out alone after caribou, never encounter the dangerous mountain spirits called ijErqat' (Rasmussen 1929: 155).

The use of caribou parts in amulets might also help a man to hunt other animals. For example, the 'head of a red-throated diver with its stomach hanging to it and with white fringing of caribou skin, worn over the shoulders: luck when fishing for salmon; twelve caribou ears sown over back and shoulders: luck in hunting' (Rasmussen 1931: 272). 'On the left sleeve band a piece of skin from a caribou leg killed by the father: makes him a fast runner' (Rasmussen 1931: 272). 'The "gristly bone" of a caribou heart: strength and accuracy with the bow' (Rasmussen 1931: 272).

*Aarnguat* made from caribou parts might also help to produce certain qualities in a person. 'Caribou hair, turned into caribou fat by a shaman: health and old age' (Rasmussen 1931: 272). 'If it is desired to give a child long hair, the outer integument of a caribou antler is sewn into the hood' (Rasmussen 1929: 176). 'If it is desired that a little girl shall become a rapid and skillful needlewoman, then, as soon as she is old enough to begin sewing, a sewing ring is made for her from the muzzle of a caribou; this sewing ring may also be fastened to her inner jacket' (Rasmussen 1929: 177; see also Rasmussen 1931: 276).

Caribou amulets could also be used to influence the gender of a child. Dufour (1988: 59) relates that if one wanted a girl to bear boys, a puppet was made out of caribou bone that looked like a human being. The little girl would later have many boys. It was considered a dangerous practice, as these boys tended to die from accidents. An anonymous Inuk related, 'My grandpa used to tell me that if I have those nukiks (tendons from the bull) from the certain part of the male caribou ... I would have only boys. He wanted me to have them' (quoted in Thorpe 2000).

### Irinaliutiit

The use of *irinialiutiit* might also help the hunter. In 2003, Murjungniq from Arviat informed the other participants in a workshop in Arviat that he possessed an *irinaliuti* to obtain caribou. It had come to him in a dream. He had used it only twice. He had told his hunting companions Anoee (the Anglican minister in Arviat) and Ollie about it:

They kept asking me to perform. Everyone got up so I had no choice but to show them how my *irinaliut* worked.... I told them they would have to give me what I wanted later on and they agreed with me. We went to sleep that night. Our minister got up first and made tea. He said, 'Murjungniq did his *irinaliut*.' ... That morning we had tea and Anoee went out. He said he couldn't wait to go out because Murjungniq did his *irinaliut*. It was a beautiful day in the fall. He opened the tent and he said there were caribou all around us. He said, 'Get up. Get up. There are caribou all around. Get dressed. Go after them.' (Arviat workshop, 2003)

Murjungniq explained that he could exchange his *irinaliuti*, but specific conditions had to be met. In his dream he was informed that there had to be three people present at the transfer, and that they would have to give him the front and hind legs of a caribou.

Rasmussen presents various *irinaliutiit* he collected among the Nattilingmiut. The first one is from the *angakkuq* Orpingalik.

Magic words to bring luck on a caribou hunt.
kumaruaq niutɔ·q
You, louse-like, you, long legs
siuktɔ·q tiŋajo·k
You, long ears, you with the long neck hair,
ataunaŋa·t
Run not past below me
atuŋägʃautit, iperägʃautit
Skin for soles, moss for wicks
quiakluɡit
You shall look forward to.
ma·uŋa qai, ma·uŋa qai!
Come hither, come hither. (Rasmussen 1931: 279–80)

The *irinaliuti* addresses the caribou as *kumarjuait*, big lice, and refers to the small gifts that open the hunting season.

The second *irinaliuti* was acquired from Inutuk.

Magic words to bring luck when hunting caribou.
qugjugʃuaq, qugjugʃuaq,
Great swan, great swan,
paŋnerʃuaq, paŋnerʃuaq,
Great caribou bull, great caribou bull,
siʷunera man·a
The land that lies before me here,
kisimilo neqiɡikpɔq
Let it alone yield abundant meat
nunaɡikpɔq

Be rich in vegetation,
näkʃo·ʃa·gʃatit Y
our moss-food
quiaɡaluɡit ma·uŋa qai
You shall look forward to and come hither
atuŋauʃa·gʃatit quiaɡaluɡit
And the sole-like plants you eat, you shall look forward to
ma·uŋa qai, ma·uŋa qai!
Come here come here!
a·verʃuartit erparta·rʟuɡit
Your bones you must move out and in,
man·iviuŋ·a·
To me you must give yourself! (Rasmussen 1931: 280–81)

In this *irinaliuti,* the caribou are addressed as great swans. The hunter tries to lure them to his land, and the resemblance between the plants they eat and the soles they receive is invoked.

A third *irinaliuti* was acquired from Nakasuk, who was an important Nattilik informant for Rasmussen.

Magic words to help when out hunting caribou.
acai, acai siʷunera man·a kisime
The land before me here, it alone
neqiɡikpɔq
Abounds with food,
quara·rikpɔq
Abounds with reindeer moss –
siʷunivnut man·a
On the land before me here
tukla·rasuktutit
You will want to set your footprints
quak·a tikitluɡit
My reiŋdeer moss you must come to! (Rasmussen 1931: 286)

The use of *irinaliutiit* was not without risk. Nuliajuk related: 'I have been taught two *irinaliutiit.* I have not used either of them and I don't want to use them. I was taught to use one if I was hungry and there were no caribou. The other one was about using an *avataq,* a float. I have also heard that they can be dangerous. I have not used either of them' (quoted in Oosten and Laugrand 2002: 104). Angutinngurniq was told that people were advised not to use *irinaliutiit* when they were young (Oosten and Laugrand 2002: 37). The use of shamanic practices was often connected to shortening one's life span (see e.g. Oosten and Laugrand 2002: 34, 35, 57) and this was probably also the case with the use of *irinaliutiit.*

Elders related that some missionaries seemed to procure animals in much the same way as Inuit did with *irinaliutiit*. Pisuk from Kangiq&-iniq related,

> I was told by my father that there was a priest named Father Thibert who was present when there was a famine around Qamanittuaq. Father Thibert told people not to constantly pray for animals. He said that just praying once would be enough. There is a place called Sattiumanittuaq. Father Thibert was waiting there to see if we got any caribou, and prayed for my father. He said that he hoped he would get enough. He said that when my father shot his rifle, none of the caribou would flee. It seemed as though it was the priest who was doing the *manilirijjuti*. During this time of hunger Iqqukti was camped at Nuvugusiq. We camped there although we were supposed to leave the next day to go caribou hunting. My father had started walking inland and came upon eighteen caribou that were gathered together grazing. They were in an area that was partly hidden from us. He thought that if he shot one, the others would flee. When he shot his rifle, they all looked up and moved slightly, but none of them fled. It seemed like the priest had made the *manilirijjuti* for him.
>
> My uncle also taught me that if I were even in a situation where I thought I was going to starve to death or I would no longer be able to use this *manilirijjuti*, I was to give it to a person younger than myself. The only thing I heard from my father about this was about the time the priest said that *manilirijjuti* for him. My father died still being amazed over this incident. (quoted in Oosten and Laugrand 2002: 109–10)

Missionaries were well aware of the impact of what they were doing. Father van der Velde (1956: 8): observed: 'I think that to the Eskimo mentality there is a very close link between their conception of the sorcerer and the priest ... and that the acceptation of the priest in place of the sorcerer is usually easily accomplished, either consciously or unconsciously.' The use of prayer as a form or *irinaliutiit* was rapidly adopted by Inuit. Ollie Itinnuaq from Kangiq&iniq emphatically stated: 'Prayer is a form of *irinaliutiit*' (quoted in Laugrand and Oosten 2002: 106).

## Caribou Hunting

Caribou were hunted throughout the summer, but especially in the spring and the fall, during their great migrations. In the Kivalliq the signs of caribou hunting could be seen in many places. Rasmussen (1930: 39) described the area around Hikoligjuaq:

From a hill close to the camp we could see for long distances, and everywhere we found stone erections, and caribou fences with hiding places
for bowmen, and many small cairns, often with a sod on the top, to represent a human head; these were all relics of the days when the caribou
was hunted without white men's weapons and was chased down to the
crossing places, where the kayak men lay in hiding to attack the herd
with their lances as soon as the animals swam out into the lake.

The *angakkuq* Igjugârjuk provided Rasmussen with an account of
the old ways of caribou hunting.[13] The hunters might drive the caribou
between cairns with sods on top so they looked like human beings. In
the beginning of the trap the distance between the cairns was quite
wide so the caribou did not suspect anything. The hunters hid themselves behind a rampart of stones and shot the animals with bows and
arrows as they were driven between the cairns. 'This method of hunting caribou is called pihin·iartut; the cry with which the leading man
at a village calls his fellows to go out hunting with him is: *pihin·iarta.* ...
Another way of hunting was called '*tuktuŋ·niarta:* literally: let us go
after caribou. It was said by the hunters when the chase proceeded
by means of *aularqazigſät:* that by means of which one makes something move' (Rasmussen 1930: 40). Sticks with bird wings, gull skins or
pieces of skin were inserted into the ground. The caribou took them for
wolves and were driven between the sticks to a crossing place. Swimming caribou were an easy prey for the hunters concealed in their kayaks. They could easily overtake the caribou with their kayaks and kill
them with caribou spears.

A third way of hunting was called *qaχzitaq,* the name of a deep pitfall
that was dug in the snow. 'It is covered over with a thin crust of snow,
above which are scattered reindeer moss and the frozen urine of dog
or wolf. A lucky hunter can get as many as three caribou at once in a
pitfall of this kind.' If the snow was not deep enough, a narrow path
was made in the snow, and along this path moss and urine were scattered; caribou would follow such a path, which led to a small pitfall
into which the caribou would tumble. It should be small so the caribou could not turn round and get out of it. Such a pitfall was called
an erχit·aq. A variant of this hunting method was *inukjugaq.* A pitfall
would be dug close to a hummock of snow. The urine of a dog or a wolf
was deposited beside it and the caribou would always come to it as
they can scent it at long distances (Rasmussen 1930: 40–41).

Murjungniq from Arviat recalled how hunters used to kill caribou
by hiding in trees and spearing the caribou when they passed by. Kappianaq (quoted in Oosten and Laugrand 2001: 91) also recalled some
of the old ways of hunting:

They would place heather and *paurngaqutit,* crowberry bushes, on the top of the *inuksuit,* so they would blow in the wind. That was when they only hunted them with bows and arrows. They would hide behind these and use them as blinds. As the caribou went by, they would shoot them with arrows. They would not kill the first one that went by, because they did not want to startle them. They would kill the ones that came after.

Barnabas Peryouar from Qamanittuaq also related that hunters 'would wait until the first caribou leaders have passed before they start shooting so they can make sure the leaders don't turn back or go a different route, or the herd doesn't stampede' (quoted in Mannik 1998: 171). The need not to disturb the herd was also emphasized by Paulosie Ataguta-alukuttuq (IE 230):

All you have to do is keep out of sight so that they do not see you, when you shoot your first caribou you aim it so that you do not kill it so that it falls, you shoot to wound so that it will jerk with the wound but soon it will appear as if it was sniffing the ground, the rest of the herd will be alarmed at first but soon they will get used to it. You also must not shoot successively otherwise the rest of the caribous are going to get scared and flee away. So what you do is you give a shot away and wait for a little while before you give another shot away. If you are not in a hurry you can take your time to shoot, but shoot to wound in the midsection so that they do not fall down. What it will do is to start sniffing the ground and soon it is going to get down to the ground. If you feel that there is one caribou in the herd that can take the rest of the caribou away, usually a bull, you must shoot it first, once it is wounded the rest will not leave him behind, so this gives you the opportunity to shoot the rest of the caribous in the herd.[14]

However, the injunction to not shoot the first caribou in the herd so as not to startle the entire herd did not always apply. For example, Naikak Hakongak (1998) from Cambridge Bay related,

If you ignore the first caribou you see and you do not shoot it, then you are not going to have good luck after that. You should not be choosy when you are caribou hunting.... You are not supposed to just bypass the first caribou that you see, hoping to see a bigger or better one. I just bypassed that one caribou and I said we might see more today. Sure enough, we did not see any more caribou all day long. (quoted in Thorpe 2001: 77)

Thus, if you only saw one caribou, you should shoot that caribou, and not assume that something bigger or better would come your way. This would show respect to the caribou that you did encounter.

Caribou were often killed in multitudes at the *nablut,* the crossing places of the caribou (see figures 8.3 and 8.4). A favourite method was to attack the caribou in *qajait* at the *nablut* and to stab as many as possible with spears. George Tataniq from Qamanittuaq described this technique:

> When the herds start coming from across the river the men would be in their qajaqs, waiting for the time to attack, sitting very still, and when

**Figure 8.3.** Hunting caribou at the *nablut. Source:* Anglican Church of Canada/ General Synod Archives/Peck Papers, M56-1, series XXXIII, 4–6, 8–13.

**Figure 8.4.** Caribou killed from a boat in Nunavik. Photo: Robert Fréchette/Avataq Cultural Institute.

the caribou notice that they are too close to the men and start turning back, the men in qajaqs move forward around the caribou to turn them back and try to get them together. The men would be around the caribou, side by side, or across from one another and there would be other qajaqs behind the swimming caribou to keep them from going back, and the men would start to spear the caribou and most of the time the men's faces would be splattered with caribou blood. … We didn't start spearing the caribou until they were close to the shore or land, so the men in qajaqs waited until the herd was close to the land and then they'd start spearing them, looking and choosing which caribou they would kill and never minding skinnier caribou, because when the caribou with no fat go to other small or large lakes they will get more fat on them after they have shed. We would pull the killed caribou to land with a rope tied to the qajaq. (quoted in Mannik 1998: 225–26)

According to Silas Kalluk, hunters were taught 'to place the front point of the *qajaq* on top of the caribou, and which ever way the caribou turns, it will be easy to spear' (quoted in Mannik 1998: 80; see also Mannik 1998: 15 for a similar statement by Silas Putumiraqtuq).

Kappianaq (IE 329) explained how a hunter used to hunt the caribou swimming behind their leader: 'He would get in the middle of swimming caribou and place his paddle on the back of a swimming caribou on both sides so now he can be towed by the two caribou, that was the way they used to hunt swimming caribou, particularly more agile [hunters] that can handle the qajaq with efficiency.' He also related another technique of caribou hunting that he had practised himself:

> When the caribou were feeding on flat areas the hunter could stalk them by crawling, I know that from personal experience. When one is crawling, when the caribou does not have eye contact, then one can crawl at it with confidence; that is, as long as the caribou will not hear you. When the eyes can be seen, then one would stop crawling. One must try to keep your butt section elevated and your head down at all times. As long as the caribou does not notice any movement you can get really close to it. … The caribou would be feeding alone. When there is more than one caribou, when you are not too good you will find it difficult to get close to the caribou. … One must not hurry when you are stalking a caribou. You must have patience when stalking it. Whenever the eyes are going to become visible, then you must stop crawling. This way you can get close enough to shoot it, even with a .22-calibre rifle. (Kappianaq, IE 329)

He also recalled the old technique of *maliruaq*, which had been practised by his grandfather Ujarak. The men would approach the caribou slowly, so the caribou would get used to their presence. 'As the hunters *maliruaq* the caribou, the caribou would stand up after being curled, then eat. When the hunters start to pass close to the caribou when they are curled, then the men would kick a small piece of snow towards the caribou.' When the caribou were no longer alarmed by the presence of the hunters, even when they were almost among the caribou, the hunters would return home and tell the people that the caribou were now ready to be killed so that there would be meat for food (Kappianaq, IE 329).

Rasmussen (1931: 174–75) presents the hunting scores of a good summer at Malerualik: 'Eqaluk: 80 caribou; Qaqortingneq 76; Ni£nuaq 70; Tarrƒjuk 61; Inutuk 55; Alorneq 53; Itqilik 29; a score of twenty to thirty in the actual season, i.e. in the period when the skin was serviceable for garments, was the most common.' He concludes that even these numbers did not completely meet the needs of the hunters. Job Murjungniq from Arviat confirmed, 'The ones who were good at spearing were able to catch between sixty and eighty caribou' (quoted in Oosten and Laugrand 2010: 134).

Indeed, caribou were often killed in great quantities. George Tataniq related, 'The reason our ancestors tried to kill a lot of caribou is because they didn't think only of themselves. They also thought about people somewhere else who might be hungry, so they caught more than they needed in order to help others' (quoted in Mannik 1998: 224–25).

Inuit were aware that caribou sometimes became scarce, but they did not attribute that to an overkill of caribou. Alain Ijiraq (IE 121; see also IE 231) related how the caribou disappeared after his father used powerful words and the owner of the caribou appeared to him in a dream. When his father was preparing to camp away from the main camp, he heard rumbling sounds coming from a group of rocks. The sound become louder until it was deafening, and it appeared to be coming from under the ground.

> At this time the sound was starting to sound more like a voice that he would understand. He had with him an amulet against evil spirits (*tu-urngait*). There were three words that came with the amulet, which Pin-guaq had taught him in case my father would have to resort to them as a last recourse. As my father had no other alternative but to resort to this amulet, so he said the three words. Soon afterwards, the sound started to disappear. At this time his ears rang from the deafening sound. He tried to sleep later but he kept thinking about the experience he had just had so he could not get to sleep. He felt that he was having a dream, when someone spoke to him 'look this way'. So he did to find a huge woman standing near him. She wore an Uqurmiutaq *atigi*. She told him to look in another direction. When he did so, he saw the whole surface of the earth. As it was dark he saw some sparks flying around in succession. He was asked if he could see them, and of course he answered 'yes'. Then he was told 'keep your eyes open and see what is going to happen'. The big woman started to wave her hand above the surface of the earth and at the same time the sparks started to fly all over the place as if there was a campfire burning. As this was going on, the sparks started to get into her clothing. As this continued, most of the sparks got into her except for a few of them that were flying far apart. Then she stopped and she said to my father that from this moment on the caribous were going to get scarce, there would be only a few around. She added that it was going to be difficult to obtain enough skins for clothing. She said that it was to continue until he was old or died of old age before the caribous would start to return in quantities. The caribou population would only return if the bones and the antlers are buried beneath the soil. Some of it will still show a little bit when the caribous start to return. After that experience the caribou started to disappear.... In our time the caribou were really scarce, sometimes there would be only a few. Now we can see the old bones sticking out from the ground, this is about 1970 when the caribou started to return. We have heard that there is someone who controls them that is usually referred to as 'someone powerful'. It is believed that she is the one who controls all living animals. Perhaps she still controls them.

The sounds of the stones and the sparks suggest the presence of *apsait*, non-human beings who cause the earth to shake.[15] Thus, periodical scarcity as well as abundance of the caribou were attributed to the *inua* of the caribou, not to an overkill of the caribou.

## Rules of Sharing

Meat was shared. It was usually shared within the camp, but if need be it could be shared with other camps. In the Kivalliq, many elders remember periods of starvation. Margareth Uyauperk Aniksak recalled a case of starvation in another camp where many relatives were living:

> Thinking [relatives] to be dead, people at the dance, including the Ahi-armiut, began to weep ... The Ahiarmiut who came to our camp were on their way to Churchill to trade. But they aborted their plan and turned back to go look for the starving people and bring them to us.
>
> When they got there sure enough there was not a single person up and dressed. Each and everyone was lying under skin covers. When food was brought in, their joy turned to tears as they saw food. The rescuers prepared small portions of food, just a single bite at first and fed them. They also cooked small portions of food for them to eat.
>
> Ihumatarjuaq, my father, Piglimi'juaq Atuk's father, Tabbataa'naaq and Qasli along with my husband's brother all went out to bring he starving people to out camp. We had many dogs and a stash of unskinned caribou carcasses up on the hill. (Bennett and Rowley 2004: 91)

Elders were taken care of. Etuangat Aksaayuk recalled, 'Young couples or the hunters would give their parents or older people the delicacies of caribou or other animals caught. This was practised then and before I can remember. It was not embarrassing to provide delicacies to the elders in those days' (Bennett and Rowley 2004: 87).

Caribou hunting among the Nattilingmiut was determined by specific rules of sharing. Rasmussen (1931: 172) relates,

> If two hunters have been after a caribou, the one who killed it gets the forequarters, the other the hindquarters. As in sealing, the hunter himself always gets the smaller share of the meat. Nevertheless the stomach with its vegetable contents (nErub/kAq) – a favourite delicacy – is always part of the hunter's share. Otherwise the sharing of the meat is to some extent dependent upon whether there is a general shortage or not, just as in the case of seal meat. If there is sufficient the rules are not always observed to the letter; but it is always considered to be good form for the one who brings down a caribou to give his fellow villagers a feast and not cache all the meat for himself. The share of the beaters, un/c/-rtut, who drive the animals to the crossing place, is also dependent to some extent upon present needs. Thus it might happen in the height of the autumn

season, especially if they belonged to the same household as the hunters, that they received no meat at all; otherwise the hindquarters with the legs were shared among them, and if a large number of animals were brought down, the beaters received one out of every five.

Furthermore, Rasmussen reports (1931: 173), 'The custom is that the one who first spears a caribou gets the skin, even though another may actually kill the animal; and one can never have too many skins.'

Michel Kanajuq from Qamanittuaq reports that the one who killed the caribou would not be in charge of the meat:

> In those days when someone caught a caribou, the person who caught it was not in charge of the meat; the person who did not catch the caribou would be the first one to take what meat he wanted.... They called this qaluhiqtuq, meaning that even if he did not catch the animal he had the right to take all of the meat and the skin. That is what our ancestors did. They used the term qaluhiqpunga so that people would know that he was not the one who caught it. No one was selfish in those days. The person who killed the animal would not touch the animal, not even a little bit, and the one who hadn't killed it would have the whole animal. When a person wanted to catch a caribou, they would let another person kill it, so the one who wanted the caribou would have it. When people went by qajaq, if a person did not want the meat, then he would be the one to catch it. (quoted in Laugrand and Oosten 2009: 79–80)

According to Kanajuq this applied not only to caribou, but also to all game.

## Rules of Respect

### *Killing and Slaughtering Caribou*

Hunters always slaughtered caribou on the spot and then took home the skins and the meat. Rasmussen (1930: 50) relates,

> Caribou Eskimos, who only have the caribou to live upon and clothe themselves in, must exercise the greatest caution in handling the killed animal. When a caribou has been killed, everything that is not taken home must be covered up. This applies especially to entrails, paunch and blood. In these there is a great part of the strongest life of the caribou, and Pinga must not see that this is treated with disrespect. Finally, Pinga does not want too many animals killed; some, certainly, but no extermination.

The following rules pertained specifically to caribou in the Iglulik area (Rasmussen 1929: 190–94; see also Rasmussen 1931: 503):

When a caribou is cut up, a small piece of skin must always be left on round the eyes and genitals, for the caribou souls do not like women to touch those parts of their bodies. ....[16]

During the time when caribou are hunted with bow and arrows, the dogs are not allowed to gnaw the bones of the legs or any other bones. This would hurt the souls of the caribou, and the caribou themselves would disappear.

During the same period, men are not allowed to work on iron; if arrow heads have to be sharpened, the women must do it for them.

The eyes and genitals as well as the bones appear to be sensitive areas, not to be touched by women and dogs. The prohibition to work on iron also applied after the killing of a sea mammal, but there is an important difference. Whereas for the sea mammals the rules usually pertain to a few days after the killing of an individual animal, in the case of the caribou the rules refer much more to the hunting season as a whole. Time is a very important factor in the organization of these rules. Rasmussen (1931: 181) reports,

On sea ice, marrow bones or skulls of newly-shot animals must not be broken before the month that is called avun-ivik, or the month when seals miscarry (March). The same taboo applies even to animals that have been cached since the summer and autumn hunts. The soul of the caribou is very touchy about its marrow bones, which all Netsilingmiut consider to be the best of all delicacies. They must not be broken at all until all the caribou have left the country.

Thus, the rules pertaining to the caribou not only organized relations between human beings and caribou, but also between men and women and between human beings and dogs, specifying what they could or could not touch.

Special rules applied to caribou that were caught in the traditional way, with bows and arrows:

In the case of animals killed with the bow, no bones, marrow bones or skull had to be broken before the skin had been dried. Since the introduction of firearms this rule now only applies to caribou brought down with the gun of one who is now dead. And this taboo sticks to the gun for all time, even if it changes owners. (Rasmussen 1929: 194)

The idea that a gun maintains its connection to a deceased owner and this affects how a caribou killed with such a gun can be slaughtered suggests a connection between caribou and the deceased. Such a connection is marked in other ways as well.

Samson Quinangnaq from Qamanittuaq relates, 'Mamnguqsualuk was my father, and when he died we weren't allowed to break any bones of the caribou that were caught' (quoted in Mannik 1998: 118). And he added, 'When Innakatsik's father died he wasn't allowed to break any bones for a whole winter and a whole summer until the day of his father's death anniversary' (quoted in Mannik 1998: 119).

Special rules applied to a widower when he caught his first caribou after the death of his wife: 'The first three caribou he kills must also be specially treated: he may only take the skin and lean meat, the skeleton must be covered up with stones. In the case of walrus there is no special taboo' (Rasmussen 1929: 201).

A connection to the dead was also marked in rules pertaining to the igloo. Leah Arnaujaq, who lived in many places along Hudson Bay, recalled,

> Another tradition was that caribou meat could only be brought through the back of the iglu and not through the front door. At the back of the iglu there was a little door which was kept covered against the snow, and this is what they used. They could bring seal through the front door but not cached caribou meat. (*Recollections of Inuit Elders* 1986: 12)[17]

This could be connected to the tradition in which a human corpse is brought out of the igloo through a hole in the back of the wall. A human corpse also used to be wrapped in a caribou skin. Uyarasuk (quoted in Oosten and Laugrand 1999b: 153) related, 'In the days before there were coffins, and because we did not have fabric, the bodies were wrapped in caribou skin. The caribou skin was either an *alliniq* or a *qipik*.'[18] Peck (quoted in Laugrand et al. 2006: 320) related, 'Deer skins intended for clothing must be put outside before the person dies, for if they are in the house when death takes place, they must in no wise be used for clothing. And the dead person's property of various kinds such as deer skins which he got, these must also be thrown away for they are not to be used.'

Kappianaq reported that people should not hit a caribou head or heart with a stone;[19] nor should they hit or break a caribou bone. 'Whenever people knock on a caribou bone, when they are breaking bones or something, then you would hear *apsait* later on.... *Apsait* are very loud' (quoted in Oosten and Laugrand 2007: 168). Incorrect treatment of the heart might also evoke the *apsait*. Itinnuaq from Rankin Inlet stated that if one chopped the frozen heart of a caribou the *apsait*, beings that were said to have only heads and legs, would come right away (quoted in Oosten and Laugrand 2002: 182). Ijiraq (IE 232) explained that *apsait* would often reside in lakes and make banging noises, and 'if you pound on the frozen heart of a caribou you are likely to experience them'.[20] Thus, *apsait* as well as caribou are associated with the sound of thunder.

The bones of the caribou had to be treated with respect. Aupilaarjuk (quoted in Oosten et al. 1999: 35) stated, 'We were told that if we are from the land we would not enjoy being in the water. ... That is why we were told not to throw caribou bones in the water. They were collected and left on the land.' Even though caribou bones should not be deposited in the water, there were exceptions. Rasmussen (1931: 67) reports, 'If a caribou head is brought to a fishing place it must, as soon as the flesh is picked off, be carefully sunk in an adjoining brook where no fish are caught.'

The head had to be handled carefully. Particular effort had to be made when flaying the head of the caribou. Rasmussen (1931: 180) reports, 'When flaying caribou killed in migrating time, care had to be taken never to cut the ears off by the root; otherwise the soul of the animal would turn into an evil spirit and kill the hunter when winter came.'

Rasmussen (1929: 181) reports that when departing from a hunting area the heads of the caribou must always face in the direction in which the party is setting out. The souls of the animals slain will then follow the same course, and good hunting will result. Thus, the heads always remain in the area where the animal was killed. The modern tradition of placing caribou heads on top of the houses may be connected to this old custom. Since the Inuit no longer live a nomadic life, the permanent resting place of the caribou head has become the house of the hunter.

### Nablut

The *nablut*, the spots where the caribou crossed the rivers, were particularly marked by rules. Rasmussen (1931: 179–80) relates,

The ancient taboo rules were, as has also been stated, especially strict in the days when the bow was the only hunting weapon. Particularly strict observance was necessary at all crossing places where there were house ruins or tent rings after the Tunrit. These nab/lut were considered to be sacred places and were called tErin/nArtut, because the taboo was so inexorable in its demands. Certain customs were connected with certain localities, as for instance with the well-known crossing place of Kingaq, close to Netsilik Lake. For every caribou killed there the following parts had to be left at the spot where it was brought down:

The whole of the brisket, forelegs and hind legs with unbroken marrow, the two outermost ribs, called ituai, the diaphragm, throat, head

and neck, more particularly described as niugs/ra; all these pieces had
to be covered with stones together with the animal's blood, which was
poured into the two inner stomachs alrArusia and pisigsita; neither the
blood nor any of these parts could be taken away for a long time after the
animal had been killed. Nor could the skin be taken into a tent, but had
to be laid in the separate caches that were made for caribou skins and
called ujArqɔt saunive-t.

Caribou killed at Talorssuit and Taluarssuit, near to Kingaq, were under the same taboo. It was considered to be most dangerous to break the
taboo at all these places; one ran the risk of famine or sickness.

Among the Utkuhigjalingmiut, 'The strictest taboo is laid over the
caribou that are caught with the kayak at the crossing places. Of those
so caught no bone must be broken, no marrow bone must be eaten, no
bone must be gnawed by dogs, as long as the hunter sojourns at the
crossing place. Only when camp was broken is it allowed to split marrow bones and eat the marrow' (Rasmussen 1931: 503). In addition, no
work should be done on materials derived from sea mammals. 'Dangerous things to have near a crossing place are, in particular, the skin
of the bearded seal and the walrus, and walrus tusks. If people work in
that kind of material they die, because tuktut naʀutɔ·rjuit: the caribou
are very fastidious and easily offended' (Rasmussen 1930: 48).

**Figure 8.5.** Peter Suvaksiuq from Arviat with his catch. Photo: Frédéric Laugrand,
2011.

A hunting place was called 'saunive-t – the place where the bones were left (of the caribou that where caught) ... great care had to be observed as regards the bones of the animals that had been eaten, these often having to be protected by caching against wild beasts' (Rasmussen 1931: 110).

Especially women had to take care at these places. Rasmussen (1931: 182) relates, 'At caribou crossing places women must never make any other kind of footwear than the waterproof, unhaired seal-skin kamiks that are called ipErA-rutit.' Elsewhere, Rasmussen (1929: 56–57) states that at the crossing places, 'No woman was allowed to work there, no bone of any animal might be broken, no brain or marrow eaten. To do so would be an insult to the souls of the caribou and was punished by death or disaster.' Rasmussen (1929: 56–58) adds the story of the woman who boiled fat from caribou bones at a crossing place and was swallowed up by the earth for having offended the souls of the caribou. He concludes, 'So the woman perished because she had done what was forbidden at the sacred places. The powerful souls of the caribou had killed her.'

### Cooking and Eating Caribou

The cooking and eating of caribou meat was restricted by many rules. Rasmussen (1931: 181) relates, concerning the Nattilingmiut,

> Unlike seal meat, caribou meat may not be cooked over any kind of fuel, for instance never driftwood or animal bones. This would give pain to the soul of the animal, even if the bones were very old. The soul of the caribou is much more sensitive than that of the seal; seal meat may be cooked over seal bones if only they are old and sun-bleached.
>
> Nor must hay be used for kindling a fire over which caribou meat is to be cooked. For caribou live on grass, and it would shock the soul if the fire over which its flesh was to be cooked were to be lighted with something that is the caribou's own food.

Rasmussen (1931: 181) adds that among the Nattilingmiut a strict separation of caribou meat and seal meat was required for caribou that were killed in the traditional way with bows and arrows.

> Caribou killed with the bow and arrow had never to be eaten on the same day when seal meat was eaten. Nor was it allowed to sleep with seal meat in either house or tent.
>
> If travellers came on a visit to people who lived on seal meat, and the visitors had eaten caribou meat the same day and therefore were not allowed to start eating seal meat, great care had to be observed that the

caribou meat they took into the house was laid on the floor and eaten from there, and was not mixed with seal meat. This taboo, however, only applied to caribou killed with the bow and arrow.

Monique Vézinet (1980: 47) reports that many rules applying to eating caribou were similar to those to be followed for sea mammals in Nunavik. Some parts of the caribou were only given to men (such as the *taqtuq,* the kidney), whereas other parts were only given to women, such as the *uumati,* the heart, or the stomach and the intestines. Elder men and women, young ladies and children all received specific parts.

According to Rasmussen (1931: 503), the Utkuhigjalingmiut attached great importance to the separation of caribou meat and newly caught fish:

> Caribou meat of newly shot animals or from a cache must never be put together with newly caught trout on the side platform. If they must be in the house together, care must always be taken that there is a space between the meat and the fish. This does not apply to salmon that has been cached, which may be mixed with caribou meat with impunity. Caribou and salmon must not be eaten the same day.

According to Rasmussen (1929: 195), a caribou is no longer edible if an animal has eaten from it: 'Human beings must never eat of a caribou if any part of it has been eaten by fox or wolf. But it may be given to the dogs. A human being eating such meat will never again be able to satisfy his hunger.'

Specific rules of respect pertained to various parts of the body. Notably, the head, the forelegs, especially the marrow, and the heart were considered very sensitive parts. Young women were not supposed to eat those parts. According to Rasmussen (1929: 177), 'Young women must never eat tongue, head or marrow of caribou, and little girls must not eat those of seals. Women who have ceased to bear children are exempt. A woman with young children must not eat any caribou meat save the flesh of the hind legs.' Julie Hanguhaaq Tuluqtuq from Qamanittuaq remembers that her mother was not allowed to eat the tip of the caribou tongue before missionaries came (quoted in Mannik 1998: 205). Rasmussen (1929: 196) states, 'Caribou tongue must never be eaten while any one of the family is out on a journey.' According to Rasmussen (1929: 196–97), 'Marrowbones must never be thawed over a woman's drying frame.'

An analogy between the body parts of the human body and that of the caribou is often evoked: thus, if a man has a pain in the upper arm, he must not eat the upper foreleg of a caribou (Rasmussen 1929:

197).[21] 'Boys and young men must never eat fat or suet from the upper part of a caribou breast; if they do, they will get out of breath when running'; 'Boys must never eat marrow from the forelegs of a caribou; to do so would render them slow in running' (Rasmussen 1929: 177). The forelegs of the caribou are considered to be very strong. In a story called 'The Bear That Thought It Was Stronger Than a Caribou', related by the Aivilik storyteller Ivaluardjuk, the caribou defeats the bear in an arm-pulling contest.

Rasmussen (1931: 67) relates with respect to the Nattilingmiut, 'Some of the most severe of these rules are, for instance, that no marrow bone must be broken, and people with a "sweet tooth" must never regale themselves with fresh caribou brains.' If people wished to eat caribou marrow, they should proceed carefully. Betty Inukpaaluk Peryouar from Qamanittuaq reports,

> We weren't allowed to break the leg bones of caribou with any metal tool and we weren't allowed to use any small metal thing to scoop out marrow. During the summer when our men started to catch more caribou they always used to bring back caribou legs, but we could only use either bones or rib bones to scoop out marrow from the end of the leg bones. … When my mother was going to fold and pile the dry skins and put them in a stretched bull skin, she would cut the legs, but not all the way. She wasn't allowed to do so, so I would finish cutting them for her. (quoted in Mannik 1998: 156)

The heart of the caribou also had to be handled with care. Pisuk from Rankin Inlet related how he was saved by an *angakkuq*.

> Qaviajak said, 'If you want to die, you can eat caribou heart. If you want to die, you can eat caribou liver.' People eat both of these, but to this day I have never eaten a whole caribou liver or heart. She said if somebody served me caribou heart, then I was only to take a bite of it. I did not really understand this, but fear made me not eat it. I believe this to be a *tirigusungniq*. I was almost sixteen years old when I started this, and I follow this to this day. (quoted in Oosten and Laugrand 2002: 67)

Tungilik (quoted in Oosten and Laugrand 1999b: 95) recalled,

> The heart was not to be eaten. My grandchild has Tungilik as a surname. … We named him after Pakak who was to have been my son-in-law but he shot himself. After the baby arrived I took a caribou heart from the freezer and thawed it out. Although it was boneless I could not swallow a bite. I tried to eat it but was unable to do so. Then my wife told me the baby has stopped breathing. It had died. The baby's lips were totally pale. My wife took the baby outside and then it started breathing again. I

called Ullatitaq, Pakak's mother, and I told her that the baby had stopped
breathing for a time because I ate a heart. She said it was because when
Pakak committed suicide he shot himself through his heart. Even though
I was not to *tirigusuk*, I was to wait a year before eating heart again. She
told me that. Now when I eat heart, I'm fine.

Among the Nattilingmiut, 'No woman may eat of caribou that has
been shot in the heart or "the little caribou stomach", called alrArusEq'
(Rasmussen 1931: 181), and among the Utkuhigjalingmiut, 'Animals
hit in the heart must not be eaten of by women who have infants in their
back pouch' (Rasmussen 1931: 503).

Betty Inukpaaluk Peryouar from Qamanittuaq reports how an old
lady made her eat caribou heart, although she was prohibited from
eating it:

> When we cook caribou heart, we split them into five pieces, and there
> was a cooked heart inside of the packs. She [the old lady] took off one
> piece and gave it to me. I wasn't allowed to eat any heart, cooked or raw,
> so I couldn't just eat it, so I took it home and gave it to my mother. My
> mother told me to eat the cooked heart, since it was given to me by an old
> lady. I ate it, and from that time on I've been eating the hearts of animals,
> it was a joyous time for me. (quoted in Mannik 1998: 157)

Clearly the old lady had the power to terminate the prohibition. Betty
Inukpaaluk Peryouar adds that the same old woman 'made my brother
Akilak with words, but I don't remember exactly what she said to him,
I didn't hear about it' (quoted in Mannik 1998: 157). She also gave him
her seal skin belt with dead bees in a piece of caribou hide sewn onto
the belt. Children often were given amulets to wear and specific restrictions to observe until they became adolescents.

Eating caribou kidneys could be helpful. Naqi from Iqaluit (quoted in
Briggs 2000: 34) related, 'If you eat caribou kidneys, you will have beautiful babies. This applies to both men and women. There are certain
things we can eat if we want our children to have a particular feature.'

Michel Kanajuq from Qamanittuaq relates that special rules regarding the eating of caribou applied to shamanic initiation:

> Also, they were not allowed to eat some foods such as *patiq*, the marrow;
> or intestines, or *kiksauti* which is the fat around the second stomach,
> or tongue. The one who desired a *tuurngaq* wouldn't eat these until the
> prescribed number of months was up. (quoted in Laugrand and Oosten
> 2009: 75)

Although some rules applied to everyone, most rules applied to specific categories of society such as boys, girls, young men, young women,

*angakkuit* in training, etc. The rules might apply to specific periods or contexts (e.g. when a family member is out on a journey). Some rules even applied only to specific individuals and often only for a limited period. The rules of consuming the caribou divided society in significant categories in terms of the body of the caribou. In particular, the consumption of caribou heart, tongue and marrow was subject to many restrictions and could be a matter of life and death.

## Preparing and Sewing Caribou Skins

In the fall, caribou hunting was particularly important, as their furs were then in optimal condition for preparing clothes (see also Rasmussen 1931: 502 on the Utkuhigjalingmiut).

Women dried the caribou skins and prepared the precious sinew thread. Only caribou sinew, *ivalu*, should be used for sewing. Boas (1907: 501; see also Rasmussen 1929: 186) reports a tradition from the west coast of Hudson Bay: 'A woman who had no caribou-sinew used the sinew of a seal instead. This made the seal's soul feel ashamed, because seal-sinews are so much shorter than those of the caribou. Therefore the seal caused the woman to become sick and die.'[22]

The curing of the skins was done by the men (Rasmussen 1931: 173). Rasmussen (1931: 174) discusses the preparation of caribou skins:

> At night, when man and wife lay down to rest, they each laid a raw skin over their naked body, with the fleshy side next to their skin. Their own body heat warmed the hard leather so that it was now easy to stretch and fold it by means of a blunt scraper of bone (sErLejaut). This done, the skin was moistened slightly on the fleshy side, rolled up and put aside for a day or two. This part of the process was called sErLe-jainEq, and it was vital to the quality of the skin as a material for garments.

Along the coast, the transition of the caribou season to the winter seal hunting season was strongly marked by rules regarding the preparing and sewing of caribou skins. Rasmussen (1929: 191) relates,

> From the moment the party leaves the coast and moves off up country, the women are not allowed to do any needlework, except small repairs, and even these must not be done in the tents, but always out in the hills, far away from the camp. This prohibition of needlework holds good throughout the whole of the autumn, and is not removed until the hunting is over and the party have again moved into snow huts. Women are not allowed to sew during that time, it is said, because amuklaiʃiʃu-ᵂaɳmata tɔ·ʳɳʳa·rmik: 'they would draw an evil spirit to the place with

their thread'. This taboo against needlework is removed during the time when new clothes are being made in the first snow huts of autumn, and then all sewing is once more taboo as far as caribou skins are concerned, throughout the time when the party are living out on the sea ice, and when only sealskins may be used.

The rules varied by season as well as by location and were lifted in the new hunting season, when people moved into igloos. According to Rasmussen, all the various rules associated with caribou and women's work are outlined in the following, as formulated by Orulo (Rasmussen 1929: 191–92):

No new garments may be made as long as the party are living in tents; not until they have moved into snow huts. If it should be absolutely necessary for a man to have a new garment before there is snow enough to make a proper snow hut, but some snow and ice have appeared on the lakes, then a little temporary snow hut is built, large enough for the woman who is to do the sewing, and in this she does the work. But the skin must not be softened in the usual way with a sakut, or scraper; it must be wetted on the inner side with water and softened with the feet, being stretched at the same time.

When the caribou have shed their old coats and the new ones have come, material of sealskin and used for footwear must no longer be used. If there are men who must absolutely have new soles to their boots, then the sole leather must be laid on the floor to be trodden on, so that it is no longer new, but soiled, and old kamiks may then be soled, but the work must be done out of doors, not in the tent.

No one is allowed to make new garments of caribou skin as long as the animals still have the 'velvet' on their antlers.

If the snow is late in coming, i.e. before there is material available to build snow huts, and there is great need of new garments, then instead of snow huts, ice huts may be built, and this is done in the form of qArmAq: i.e. with ice blocks for the walls and the tent placed over as a roof. The hairy side of the tent must be turned inward, in contrast to the usual custom when using skins for tents. Not until all items of caribou skin, clothing, outer furs, sleeping places, inner garments, footwear, sleeping bags etc. are finished may the party move down to the coast and out on the sea ice to commence hunting the creatures of the sea.

The organization of these rules connects the rhythm of the physical changes of the caribou (the shedding of the fur, the velvet on the antlers) with the seasonal hunting patterns (organized by location, tents versus igloos and mode of hunting, caribou versus seal). Rasmussen (1931: 181–82) reports that among the Nattilingmiut,

The rigorous prohibition against stitching caribou skin in hunting camps on the ice was slackened when the sun was high in the heavens, i.e. in

April and May. But it was always an inviolable rule that no work was ever to be done in caribou skin in a hunting camp where the first seal cub of the year had been caught.

Having moved from sea ice to land, there must be no sewing of seal skin until all the snow has melted from the ground and the caribou have received their new coat.[23]

Boas (1907: 520) relates a story of the consequences of transgressing these rules, when women continued to work on caribou skin after a bearded seal had been killed and were attacked by a *nanorluk*, a giant bear. Rasmussen (1929: 71) relates how a family was punished by the sea woman for not observing these rules and the whole family drowned in a storm.

In South Baffin the transition from caribou hunting to seal hunting was also safeguarded by many rules. Peck (quoted in Laugrand et al. 2006: 324) related, 'And the Eskimo do not dress deer skin before the ice forms, for this is said to be a custom to be observed. When a large seal has been recently captured, they must not dress deer skins. For if they dress such skins, they think that there will be quite a number of deaths amongst the people, and that they will also not be able to capture animals for food. … And (also) when a walrus is captured, they do not work at deer skins. For if they work at such, they will die.' Boas (1888: 595) stated with respect to caribou skins,

No skins of this kind obtained in summer may be prepared before the ice has formed and the first seal is caught with the harpoon. Later, as soon as the first walrus is caught, the work must stop again until the next fall. For this reason all families are eager to finish the work on deerskins as quickly as possible, as the walrusing season is not commenced until that is done.

Thus, in Cumberland Sound not the contrast between caribou and seals but that between caribou and walrus is emphasized.

There were many strict rules regarding the skins of caribou for women who were menstruating or had just had a miscarriage. Among the Iglulingmiut, 'Women menstruating, or having a miscarriage, or in childbirth, may not prepare the skins from the legs of caribou; the skin of caribou legs is altogether regarded with quite particular respect. There are some hunters, for instance, whose own wives are not allowed to prepare the skins of caribou legs from animals killed by their husbands, this work having to be done by other women' (Rasmussen 1929: 179).[24] Marion Tulluq Angohalluq from Qamanittuaq remembers a traditional practice 'that you could not take a certain person's things. One of Nataaq's sons was one of those people whose things could not be taken. The caribou skins that belonged to his wife couldn't be spread open on the ground, and they weren't allowed to be touched or taken, especially when she was having her menstruation' (quoted in Mannik 1998: 48). In this case, the prohibition was probably connected to the husband. In most cases, the rules of sewing affected the women most. It was their task to prepare caribou winter clothing for the family before the start of the sealing season. Even though the rules were strict, there were also rules for exceptions in case of need. The transition from caribou hunting to seal hunting was much more marked by rules than the transition from seal hunting to caribou hunting.

## The Uses of Caribou Skins and Hair

The skins of the caribou were used for a wide range of purposes. They were the preferred material for clothing, providing the people with a second skin, that of the caribou. By taking the skins from the animals they killed and making them into human clothes, a symmetry between human beings and animals was created. Issenman and Rankin (1988: 104) emphasize this symmetry between animal skins and human clothing: 'The Inuit incorporated the features of animals in their clothing. The skins protect the human body in the same way they covered the animal: the skin of the head becomes the hood; the supple shoulders and back fur cover the human shoulders and back; the rump fur is used to make trousers; the tough leg skins become boots and mitts.'

Clothes were made of the skins of beings who were once alive, and even as clothes they could come to life again: old clothes should be torn into pieces before they are thrown away. Otherwise, their owner will have to wear them in the land of the dead (Rasmussen 1929: 182).

Many books and papers have already been devoted to the excellent quality of Inuit clothing and the great skills of the Inuit seamstresses. We cannot discuss the wide range of Inuit clothing here, and we refer the reader to the work of Isenman, Oakes Buijs and others for more details.[25]

Some clothes had important significance in a ritual context. Concerning the Inuit in the west of Hudson Bay, Boas (1907: 509) relates,

> A man who desired to become an angakok hung his coat down the face of a precipice, so that it was near a hawk's nest. On the fifth day, when he went up to look at it, the coat had come to life and was climbing up the face of the precipice. He became frightened, and killed it by throwing stones at it. If he had not done so, but had put on the jacket, he would have become a powerful angakok, able to walk up and down the faces of cliffs.[26]

Similarly, the clothes of a shaman might come alive during shamanic séances and fly round the house above the heads of singers sitting with closed eyes (Rasmussen 1929: 125).

Angutinngurniq (quoted in Oosten and Laugrand 2007: 209) related, 'My father-in-law, who was my uncle Iksivalitaq, was initiated because they wanted him to become an *angakkuq* shortly after he was born. If the egg of a peregrine falcon dropped on a caribou *qulittaq* without breaking, this would be his *aarnguaq* to help him become an *angakkuq*. If it had broken, he would not have become one.'

In a story told by Aava about his father Qingailisaq, an *angakkuq* had a coat made as a representation of his encounter with *ijirait*:

> My father, who was a great shaman, went home and had a dress made like that of the *ijeraq*, but with a picture of the hands in front, on the chest, to show how the *ijeraq* had attacked him. It took several women to make that garment, and many caribou skins were used. There were a number of white patterns in the dress, and it became a famous dress, which was bought by him who was called: *angakoq* (the well-known whaler and collector for the American Museum of Natural History, Capt. George Comer) and my father was paid a high price for the garment, which is the only *ijeraq* tunic ever made by human hands. (Rasmussen 1929: 206)

Caribou coats might also be used in a shamanic séance, as Nuliajuk from Gjoa Haven related:

> I have watched an *angakkuq* healing a sick person. When this person became sick the *tarniq*, the soul, did not want to remain with this person. The term that the *angakkuq* that I saw used for this was *tarniritaqtuq*. He took the outer layer of a parka outdoors with him. It was only the *angakkuq* that went outside. He tied a rope around the middle of the parka. When he came back into the tent, he was pulling on the rope which was very taut. I saw this with my own eyes. There were a number of us who were pulling on this rope together. It was very difficult to pull. The rope was being pulled very hard but there was nobody out there. When we finally pulled the parka inside, it was very light. (quoted in Oosten and Laugrand 2002: 23)

Kupak used a caribou coat in a demonstration of *qilaniq* in Kuugaar-ruk in 2004. He covered a snow beater with the coat and the combination represented a human person. Thus, as mentioned above, clothes come to life in a shamanic context.

Especially the shamanic belt, *angaluk* or *tapsi*, is marked in this respect. Helen Paungaq related with respect to the death of her grandfather, who was a shaman: 'One night, before he passed away, while I was lying in my sleeping bag near my grandmother I looked towards the wall above my feet and saw his belt. As I was looking, it started to move. I said, "Grandpa, grandpa's belt is moving." She asked me, "Are you sure you saw it move?" I answered, yes. So she told me that there must be something wrong with grandpa and this was his way of telling us.' (Recollections of Helen Paungat 1988: 3)

A *tapsi* was usually made out of *pukiq*, the white skin of the belly of the caribou.[27] According to Tungilik, 'When people found out that I was an *angakkuq*, the belt was made for me out of white caribou skin. I would be given little things, for that was what the *tuurngaq* wanted. I would tie these little things onto the fringe. There would be a little string attached to tie them to the fringe. It was called a *qalugiujaq*. They looked like little toys and were tied to the fringe. These were called *qalugiujait*' (quoted in Oosten and Laugrand 1999b: 90; see also Rasmussen 1929: 275). *Pukiq* was also supposed to bring luck in sealing (Rasmussen 1929: 270) and was part of the *kiversautit* offering to the sea woman. Rasmussen (1929: 194) relates,

> If a white caribou is brought down – a so called pukEq – then the hunter is subject to the same taboo as a man who has lost his sister. The meat must not be eaten, and the skin must be dried and then placed unused in the sErluAq. At Taserssuaq, a lake near Tununeq, no women are allowed; caribou killed here require the same taboo as is imposed upon a man who has lost his sister. Women must not look about in this neighbourhood, for if they should look out over the lake they would soon have bad eyes, a sort of snowblindness; the eyes water continually and they cannot see anything.

The first rule refers to a specific kind of caribou and the second to a specific place. In both cases rules applying to the loss of a sister are involved. In the third case women acquire a feature of the caribou, bad eyesight. In all these cases a metaphorical relationship between caribou and women is suggested. Thus, a person who kills a *pukiq* relates to it as a dead sister, and a hunter who kills a *silaaq* relates to it as a brother (see Rasmussen 1929: 203). In such cases a close kinship relationship is metaphorically created by the killing of such an exceptional animal.

Caribou skins were not only used as clothing, but also as menstruation pads (see Rasmussen 1929: 129), napkins and shrouds. Uyarasuk (quoted in Oosten and Laugrand 1999b: 38) related with respect to the newborn baby, 'It had clothing made out of the skin of a caribou foetus. They were made out of caribou *illauq*, after it had fur. The fur of newborn calves was also kept for the baby.' In the traditions concerning Sila, a newborn's napkin had cosmic significance:

Later on that infant went up to the sky and became Sila. The wickedness of mankind turned him into a to-nrAq who in time came to rule over wind and weather, rain and snow. He is wrapped up in the piece of caribou skin that was his napkin, and when he loosens the thongs that hold the skin together it begins to blow and rain. (Rasmussen 1931: 230)

Nuliajuk from Gjoa Haven related that an *angakkuq* would lace his clothing up (quoted in Oosten and Laugrand 2002: 94). Restoring his clothes implied restoring the cosmic order.

Even caribou hair is powerful material. Rasmussen (1929: 270) reports, 'Caribou hair which in the mouth of a shaman has been turned into a piece of caribou fat, worn sewn into the coat: makes the wearer clever at shamanizing.' Caribou hair protects and separates. 'Anyone dressing a corpse for burial must stop up his or her nostrils with caribou hair' (Rasmussen 1929: 197). 'If a man is compelled to go hunting at a time when any of his neighbours are holding the death taboo, he must stuff caribou hair into his nostrils' (Rasmussen 1931: 265). Rasmussen (1929: 181) also reports a custom that causes a disjunction between game and the new owners of an igloo:

When a family leaves a snow hut and does not wish others using it after them to have good hunting, one of the party leaving must sweep all the caribou hairs which are always left behind on the sleeping platform, in towards the inner side. All game will then leave the immediate neighbourhood of that hut, and the new people will hunt in vain. This method of making a snow hut unlucky is called piusErluinEq.

Nutaraaluk (quoted in Oosten et al. 1999: 188–90) related, 'Sedna's ears would become full of caribou hair when a *pittailiniq* was broken. Those who stole meat or broke other *pittailiniq* would cause caribou hair to fall in the water and it would collect in her ears. It was only after removing this hair and by shouting in her ear that she could hear and the *angakkuq* could tell her that he had come to get animals.'[28]

In this case, the caribou hair also causes a disjunction between people and caribou. Thus, not only caribou clothing but also napkins and hair were significant in the context of ritual.

## Ijirait

Rasmussen (1929: 113; see also Boas 1888: 232; 1901: 213–14) observed with respect to the Iglulingmiut that the *ijirait*, or mountain spirits, were among the most powerful helping spirits of the *angakkuit*.

Rasmussen (1929: 204) glossed the meaning of the word as 'those who have something about the eyes', explaining that their eyes and their mouths were not set transversely in their faces, but lengthwise so that they 'blink sideways'. They have excellent eyesight. They live inside the hills, which they have fitted up like great stone houses, much resembling those inhabited by white men. They are not visible to human beings but only to shamans. One should never show any fright when one hears them, for they only attack the timid and cowardly.

According to George Tataniq from Qamanittuaq, *ijirait* were known to visit human beings and to take one back with them by giving a drink to their victim:

> Those who lived before us would also talk about *ijirait*. The *ijirait* would not often come among people. When they did come among people, they would want to take a human with them. When they were in human form, they looked different than us, because their mouths, rather than having a sideways slit, had a slit vertically, up and down. As they were very fast, they were able to grab caribou as they were running along side of them. The *ijiqqat* lived at Uvingajuttuaq in the ground. Those that saw them know that they were numerous, that they were large, and that they were very fast. Whenever they come upon humans, they like to take them away with them. Some humans would be returned but others would be kept. When the *ijiqqat* wanted to take someone, they would have them drink something. I don't know what it was. It wasn't a very large amount, it was around a teaspoonful. Those that came upon *ijirait* and were not given anything to drink would be able to return.
>
> There are a number of us who have seen where the *ijirait* live. Even Amit'naaq's wife saw this dwelling with us. They do not live in *igluit* and they do not live in tents. They live in the ground. We saw this at Nauhaat. We would hear from the people that came before us that *ijirait* lived in the ground. They do not have tents and they do not have *igluit*. They live in the ground. We said to each other, 'Maybe this had been an *ijiraq* dwelling.' It was too dark to really see inside. We couldn't really see how deep it was because it was dark. We have not yet seen how deep it is. There is a cave at Nauhaat. It is still there. This is situated just beyond Uqpiktujuq, which is where the Hudson Bay Company first had a trading post. (quoted in Laugrand and Oosten 2009: 77–78)

Iqallijuq (IE 91) associated the *ijirait* with *inurajait* and recalled how her husband used to live with them:

> *Ijirait* will not be visible at encounter; first they will be heard, usually they will make sounds like birds or other animals, then they will be seen running like a caribou. Amarualik, my late first husband, was approached by them and immediately surrounded by them. Once he was surrounded, they got closer to him and at that moment he was asked if

he was dangerous. He replied that since he had never seen them before, he would not intimidate them. At that moment he was asked to join them, so he started to flee from them since he had no intention of joining them. However, he soon was overtaken and held making it virtually not possible to break free from the grasp. He again was asked to join them, but he continually told them he had no desire to be amongst them. As he was a shaman, he called upon his helping spirits to assist him, so they let him go. So he left them, and they disappeared at the same time. Then later he had another encounter with them, but this time he did not flee from their presence but he was stoned until he lost consciousness. He was now living amongst them. Two females were now after him so he submitted to one of them. He started to live with her. She decided that he would surely be missed by his own people, so she suggested that he return to his people as she would be able to see him now on a frequent basis. So he went back to his people. Before he joined his people, he had planned to tell about his encounter but he completely forgot about them including the time he was stoned.... After the passage of winter, when summer arrived he was planning to go inland to hunt for caribou but for some reason he was hesitant at first but he started to hear noises that sounded like a rattling of pebbles and the sound of birds. He recognized the female that he had submitted to. They were getting closer and closer so he got concerned that they might get discovered by his people, so he left. He was the only one who could hear them. He had left sometimes in June but it was so that he would not be back until the autumn. By the time he returned his mother was mourning him as she thought that he would not return. When spring arrived he made a trip to Naujaan to seek for a woman for his wife. He found me and brought me to Igloolik.... We were living at Qupiruqtuuq ... as he and I started to walk inland, I started to hear them. They sounded like birds so I was getting scared but he kept telling me there was nothing to be afraid of. When we made camp each night, they would take him away while I slept. But each time he wanted to get back, so he would get back in the mornings, and he and I would be together during our waking hours. I had not suspected anything all along. One morning I woke up to hear him carrying a conversation with someone. When I started to hear him, I opened my eyes and looked at the sleeping bag. I saw a nozzle of a caribou sticking out beneath the sleeping bag, I glimpsed at the movement of the mouth speaking in garbled noises. At that moment it disappeared. Afterwards he woke me up. So I asked him. 'What was that?' 'That was nothing, perhaps you were dreaming. When one is dreaming sometimes you hear sounds', he answered. He told me not to think about it as he took advantage of my innocence. During that day I completely forgot about it.

People who met *ijirait* tended to forget about them. Itinnuaq from Rankin Inlet related that he killed a bull that was probably an *ijiraq*, but he forgot about it. Taparti observed, 'I have heard that *ijirait* make you forget' (quoted in Oosten and Laugrand 2002: 132–34). In Iglulik,

Quassa (IE 156) heard about a person who had encountered *ijirait:* 'When he was putting on his seal skin pants, the pants started to move on their own so he did remember about his encounter with them. What you have seen. You only recall it afterwards.'

The notion that *ijirait* capture people is also a recurrent feature of *ijirait* stories. Pujuat Taparti from Rankin Inlet refers to a human whistling sound as the indication of *ijirait* being near (quoted in Oosten and Laugrand 2002: 132). Ordinary people are afraid of them as soon as they hear their whistling in the air.

*Ijirait* are fast runners and can overtake caribou easily. When they capture human beings, they make them into fast runners by having the flesh from their shinbones or toes eaten away by worms in the earth or tiny creatures in the lakes (Rasmussen 1929: 205). This method of transforming a human being into an *ijiraq* evokes techniques of shamanic initiations involving having the flesh of arms or hands eaten by insects or worms.

*Ijirait* look like humans and live like humans, but they can take on the shape of caribou. Their faces look like the muzzles of caribou, they use caribou skins as clothes and they dislike everything originating from the sea. Rasmussen (1929: 205) reports, 'The men are dressed in human fashion, only the women's garments are otherwise, their breeches consisting of the white skin from the belly of the caribou; white belly skins all cut up into strips.' Thus, the women are dressed with the *pukiq* that is used in many ritual contexts.

'They are as strong as wolves; when they have killed a caribou, they run home with it, slinging it over their shoulders just as a wolf does with its prey. They have always a great store of all manner of delicacies in the way of food, especially fat and suet from the caribou, which they boil down and leave to set in great skin bags made from the hides of bull caribou' (Rasmussen 1929: 205). In an account of a meeting with *ijirait,* the *angakkuq* Oqamineq related, 'They had a small pocket in their tunics, in which they kept two small stones. They were mighty runners, and could outrun the caribou; when they came up quite close, they killed them with the stones in their pockets' (Rasmussen 1929: 206).

Rasmussen reported, 'Shamans have found among them strange implements very much like the mirrors used by whitemen. This implement is at once a mirror and a spyglass. It glitters like mica, and when one looks down into it, all that is passing far away among the dwellings of men is reflected in this mirror; therefore the ijerqat know all about mankind' (Rasmussen 1929: 204–5). Thus the *ijirait* are visually marked by their eyes and their implements. They see everything.

The *ijirait* dislike anything connected to childbirth. 'If a woman becomes insane it is either because she has committed some serious breach of taboo, or because she has once seen some ijerqat and thereafter visited a woman in childbirth. The ijerqat will not endure this; they feel such dread of women in childbirth that they deprive any woman who has done this of her wits' (Rasmussen 1929: 197). Rasmussen (1929: 197) adds, 'If a man loses his wits, it is because unclean women have secretly eaten of his catch or prepared skins from the legs of caribou which he has killed; the insane person is called pulamitɔq: i.e. one who falls down flat on his face.'

Deceased people may join the *ijirait* (see Saladin d'Anglure 1983). Nutaraaluk from Iqaluit suggested, 'Maybe they are the deceased's people's *tarniit* that remain on the land' (quoted in Saladin d'Anglure 2001: 54). And Aupilaarjuk from Rankin Inlet stated, 'Dead people turn into *ijirait*. That is what I have heard. I have not seen this personally, but I believe it … *ijirait* are said to be deceased people that turn into caribou' (quoted in Saladin d'Anglure 2001: 56, 60). Nutaraaluk suggested that *ijirait* live forever: 'Some of those who roam the earth are said to never leave it' (quoted in Saladin d'Anglure 2001: 55). Aupilaarjuk related, 'They can go to the store, but no matter how many times they shop, the stock never depletes. Over time they can buy snowmobiles just like we do. When we had dog teams, they had dog teams. When we no longer used dog teams and we used snowmobiles, they used snowmobiles' (quoted in Saladin d'Anglure 2001: 55). Thus, their development is correlated to that of ordinary human beings.

*Ijirait* are also known in Nunavik (see Weetaluktuk and Bryant 2008: 207) as well as in the Kivalliq.[29] Suvaksiuq from Arviat observed, 'In our area there is a place called Ijiralik. I have never seen an *ijiraq*. They say that they do exist around Arviat. Others have seen them. They look like caribou, but they also have a human form. People say that those who go there often lose things like pocketknives, etc.' (quoted in Oosten and Laugrand 2002: 132). Mark Ijjangiaq (IE 184) reports that *ijirait* – as he experienced them in the past – make you *taurhittut*, 'that is, when a person or persons when travelling or walking cannot seem to reach their destination even as they walk'. Illuituq from Kugaaruk once met a caribou that appeared to come out of the ground and decided that it was an *ijiraq*. Therefore, he did not shoot it. 'I wanted to eat it, but my wife told me not to. If we had eaten it, I wonder what would have happened to us' (quoted in Oosten and Laugrand 2002: 133).

Angutinngurniq from Kugaaruk related, 'Because my mother was named Ijiraq, I often thought that maybe it was because of her that I saw *ijirait*. I have seen them more than once. Even though they are close by, and there isn't anywhere for them to hide, they tend to disappear' (quoted in Oosten and Laugrand 2007: 167). John Makitgaq from Qamanittuaq remembered he had seen one and 'its legs were like the kamiks that women make from caribou leg skins'. He also noticed the caribou did not look at him the way most caribou would as it moved its head towards its side. He shot it and when he came to pick it up, he noticed that its body had become different, turning brownish, and that it was no longer a bull caribou but a caribou with female antlers (quoted in Mannik 1998: 139).

Aupilaarjuk commented that although *ijirait* can easily retaliate if one of them is killed, Inuit who had a tattoo between the eyes, a *kigjugaq*, were usually protected from their attacks. The marking provided protection (quoted in Saladin d'Anglure 2001: 60, 62).

Kappianaq gave an extensive account of an encounter with *ijirait*:

> I don't think *ijirait* are ever going to die out. The ones closer to shore are as big as humans. The ones that live more inland are larger. If you haven't heard about them and you encounter them, they can be very scary. I have heard that they have a snout like a caribou. ... If there was an *ijiraq* close by, I would not be able to feel the ground much. My feelings would be numbed because I was in fear. They are not evil, and therefore they are able to help. They could be scary, or they could be helpful. *Qajaaksaqtuq*, is when the ice is thin and the waves make the ice ripple. An *ijiraq* is able to make the land ripple. ...
>
> I saw three of them as they were playing on the rocks. Another time I saw those same three in the form of caribou. They were three different sizes. I wanted to catch them, but they would move further away. I got lost for three days because of them. I was lost for three days and three nights. It was very scary, even though I did not see them in their true form. I had left my dogs behind even though I wanted to get home. ... They didn't make any sound at all. You could see them in between the ropes of the tent. I think it was because they didn't attempt to scare me that I was not scared. I just watched them, and I talked to my wife about them. The *ijirait* stayed close by. I think those three had been childhood playmates of my wife. My wife knew them and had been taken inland by them. If it had been only me, I would have ended up without a wife, but because my father was there this didn't happen. The old woman Qaataniq told me that her father had taken my wife back from the *ijirait* ... they had actually taken her home. She had large bruises on her thighs and on her upper arms. ... The bruises appeared as two thumb and eight finger prints. The *ijirait* can hold you down as though you were a child. Even if I was screaming and kicking, I could be held as though I were a child. ...
>
> My wife was not able to talk about what happened to her for a long time. She could not remember. It was only about three years later that

she was finally able to talk about this. Whether male or female, the *ijirait* can make a person forget what has happened to them. It can be very scary if you don't know anything about them. ... There are times when I feel the need to talk about this. Not often, but the need comes upon me to talk about it because I experienced it. Therefore I know that there are *ijirait* even though I am Christian. If I said they didn't exist, I know that I would be lying. (quoted in Oosten and Laugrand 2001: 71–74)

Rasmussen (1929: 205–6) related an encounter of the *angakkuq* Qingailisaq or Oqaminiq, the father of the *angakkuq* Aava, Rasmussen's main informant, with the *ijirait*. One *ijiraq* tried to throw him down, but the *angakkuq* withstood the attack. They separated on friendly terms, and the *angakkuq* had a coat made with ornamentations that depicted the encounter.[30] Rasmussen also presents stories about two women who were kidnapped by the *ijirait* and two old men who joined the *ijirait* (see also the story of the woman called Javaranaaq, who had relatives among the *ijirait*). The stories refer to two recurrent features of the *ijirait:* they kidnap people, and the shades of the deceased join them.

> Once two Inuit women were out gathering fuel. They fell in with some ijerqät, who seized them and took them home with them. The women did everything they could to escape, but they were guarded so well that finally they became content to stay there.
> One day they were out running, all the people from the ijerqät village. The two Inuit women, however, could not keep up. So the ijerqät took them and softened their legs in water, and when they were swollen right up they cut something out — that which on ordinary people is in the front of the leg between the skin and the shin bone; it is not bone, nor is it gristle, but is called igligtɔrqät. This they loosened and took out through the big toe. As soon as this was done the women could run just as quickly as the ijerqät and, like them, could catch up with caribou. (Rasmussen 1931: 244)[31]

The *ijirait* thus appear as caribou people, sharing features of caribou and also hunting them, and human beings can join them after death. The contrast between *ijirait* and animals is marked by eyesight: whereas caribou see very badly, *ijirait* have excellent eyesight.

Whereas the relations between human beings and caribou seem straightforward, as hunters and prey, this relation is complicated by the *ijirait*, who appear to identify both as caribou, in their capacity to transform into caribou, and as deceased human beings, in the fact that deceased as well as living human beings can join them. When they transform into caribou, they should not be killed, and they are very capable caribou hunters themselves.

## Discussion

Caribou were hunted everywhere in northeast Canada. Most Inuit hunted for sea mammals and caribou, but there were some small groupings in the Kivalliq who did not hunt sea mammals and survived mainly on caribou and fish. One might expect that among these groups ideas, rules and practices with respect to the caribou were further developed than among the other groups, but the ethnographic data do not support this. On the contrary, many elaborate ritual structures seem to be confined to the coast. The information on feasts relating to the caribou comes mainly from Labrador and Baffin Island. The emphasis on the contrast between caribou and sea mammals is much more marked on Baffin Island than in the Kivalliq.

There is some discussion about the relationship between the mother of the caribou and the mother of the sea mammals. Are they the same person? In the Kivalliq this is not an important issue. Pukimna remains a rather vague figure and she is not the focus of stories or rituals. The members of the Fifth Thule Expedition postulated that the inland groups were the ancestors of those living along the coast (see Csonka 1995). This assumption is no longer accepted. Even though the body of ritual rules, practices and stories among the inland Inuit is less developed, many of the same basic tenets can be found.

The connection between the caribou and the land is always strong, and *ijirait* seem to be present everywhere. The *ijirait* are connected to the land, the caribou and the deceased. They carry connotations of caribou as well as of caribou hunters and may to some extent represent the owners of the caribou. But Pukimna or Pinga may also have been an owner of the caribou. Moreover, the deceased also figure as owners of the caribou in the account of Kanajuq, when they send the caribou to the hunters to be killed. A fixed model of ownership did not exist, and more than one agent could represent the owner(s) of the caribou.[32]

Not only the *ijirait* but the caribou themselves may also have been connected with the deceased. According to one of the origin myths they came out of the earth, which receives the dead bodies of human beings after death, and their bodies were brought in through the back of the igloo, just as the corpses of people, wrapped in a caribou skin, were brought out. The human faces of the caribou described by Kanajuq would also fit into such a pattern. The caribou may have represented anonymous deceased ancestors.

The symbolism of the caribou remains very complex. A strong connection existed between human beings and caribou, shaped by the *pukiq*, the white belly skin of the caribou, which took a central place in shamanism and various rituals. If a *pukiq,* a white caribou, was killed, mourning rituals evoked a kinship relationship with the deceased animal, in this context connected to a deceased sister. When a *silaaq* was killed, relations with a deceased brother were evoked by the mourning rules that had to be observed. Thus, in the context of death these exceptional animals were viewed as close kin.

Caribou provided human beings with a second skin that allowed them to survive in the Arctic climate. The caribou clothes could come to life in the context of shamanism and provided the *angakkuit* with tools for communication or other purposes. The belt, made of *pukiq,* and the coat are especially marked in this respect.

Hunting caribou was considered the only way to preserve them, and Inuit hunters very much dislike the way biologists pursue and capture caribou with helicopters and nets to study their behaviour. The size of caribou herds has been an issue of debate for a long time, and Inuit hunters and *qallunaat* often disagree with biologists on the estimates.[33] In the Inuit's view, the caribou and their lifestyle have to be respected, and attempts to introduce herding in the northeast have completely failed. Inuit looked with some amazement at the Saami who were brought in from Norway by the Hudson's Bay Company in the early 1920s, but were never inclined to take over the herds from them.[34]

Caribou were closely associated with the land, referred to as the big lice of the earth. As the *qupirruit* are considered masters of life and death, this may also apply to caribou, who always return in great numbers despite the recurrent cycles of increase and decrease that characterize the great herds in the north. They are often defined as a multitude and the sound of the herds is associated with thunder. Thunder is also connected with the *apsait,* and that connection should be explored further.

In the past complex feasts connecting successful hunting with the fertility of women were celebrated. Ritual injunctions ensured that caribou and sea game were separated. Women, especially menstruating and pregnant women, were subject to all kinds of restrictions with respect to the caribou, and these applied particularly to the *nablut,* the crossing places of the caribou, where they used to be killed in multitudes.

Today, many of these practices have disappeared, but caribou remain a major prey for Inuit, who still expect the big herds to arrive each summer.[35]

## Notes

1. An extensive vocabulary existed, distinguishing caribou by gender and age. *Illauq:* Foetus. *Nurralaaq:* At birth, the fur is blackish and called

*qirnirujuk. Aupallattuq:* When it turns kind of brown. *Qakuallaliqtuq* or *qujjurujuk:* When the fur is getting ready for winter. *Nurraq:* A first-year calf. *Nukatugaq:* About one year old. *Angusallukuluk:* A male, about two years old. *Arnarlukuluk:* A female, about two years old. *Nurralik:* A female with a calf. *Nurraqanngittuq:* A female without a calf. *Panniq:* An adult male (Paniaq, quoted in Oosten and Laugrand 1999a: 130).

2.  Naikak Hakongak reported in 1998 that even the unborn foetus received a drink of water: 'I can remember one time my mom saying when you catch a pregnant cow in the spring you are supposed to take the foetus out and put snow in its mouth as water for the afterlife. Give it snow.... Supposed to give you good hunting luck too' (quoted in Thorpe 2001: 78).

3.  For the connection between the thunder and caribou, see Thorpe (2001).

4.  See also Boas (1901: 150): 'To kill an albino caribou would bring sickness and death to the hunter. It is said that an Eskimo a few years ago shot a white caribou, and, although he was warned not to do so, he pursued it in his kayak, and killed it. A few months later he was covered with boils, and died. The Eskimo say that if he had eaten out of a dish by himself, and had refrained from eating certain parts of the caribou-meat, he might have escaped death; but since he did nothing by way of repentance, Nuliayoq caused his death' (see also Boas 1901: 493).

5.  Rasmussen (1929: 69–70) records another version by Orulo. In this account great attention is paid to the direction of the hair. Her accounts testify to the expert knowledge of Inuit women of caribou skins, which were a preferred material for making clothing.

6.  It is not easy to assess the nature of Pinga, 'the one up there', the most important spirit among the Inuit inland. Rasmussen (1930: 49–50) discusses the relations between Hila (Sila), Pinga and Nuliajuk: 'Even such an outstandingly clever shaman as Igjugârjuk had difficulty in defining the spirit Hila, declaring time after time that Hila was the same as Pinga, and that Pinga corresponded to the Nuliajuk of the coast dwellers. But as soon as we went further into the various functions of these spirits, it was found that Pinga did not quite coincide with Nuliajuk; Pinga had the special care of the caribou, whereas Hila, as among the coast dwellers, represented everything one feared in the air.'

7.  The brow-band, of the white belly skin of a caribou and decorated in front with beads, is a sign of his dignity as a shaman. See the photograph of Nigtajok, the son of Orpingalik from Pelly Bay 2 in Rasmussen (1931: 44)

8.  L. Turner ([1894] 1979: 197–98) provides a detailed description of the paraphernalia.

9.  Boas (1888: 609)) reports that according to Turner a similar feast was celebrated in Ungava Bay.

10.  Similarly, the eider duck becomes a walrus on the level of the dwarves (Rasmussen 1931: 259).

11.  For the association between the gull and vitality, see the magic song about a gull provided by Rasmussen (1931: 285).

12.  The same was the case with a piece of a caribou humerus used as an *armiutaq*, which is the special term for a humerus amulet, according to Rasmussen (1931: 179; see also Rasmussen 1931: 43).

13. Many of these techniques are well documented by archaeologists, show-
    ing that they have been used for a long time. See Brink (2005) for the
    study of two caribou communal kill sites on Victoria Island, Nunavut. See
    Saladin d'Anglure and Vézinet (1977) and Vézinet (1980) for a description
    of caribou collective hunts in Nunavik.

14. See also Kappianaq (IE 097): 'As for the caribou when there were a herd,
    one should not shoot to make the kill but one should aim at the hind sec-
    tion just before the rump on the midsection, the wounded animal will not
    stir suspicion with the rest of the herd but will walk a little backwards,
    in this manner of wounding the caribou a hunter was able to get all of
    the caribou that were in the pack. Once most of the animals had been
    wounded then it was only a matter of finishing them off. Should a caribou
    be shot a fatal wound then the caribou would have panicked and start to
    run around spooking the rest of the herd thereby the herd would have fled
    away.'

15. According to Aupilaarjuk, an *apsaq* was 'a being that only has a head and
    legs. They usually travel in family groups and become noisier as they get
    closer. They are said to live in the rocks that oil lamps are placed on in
    an *iglu*, if the rocks are not thrown out of the *iglu* when it is permanently
    vacated. They are considered dangerous as they can create fires in *igluit*'
    (Saladin d'Anglure 2001: 65, summarized in Kublu 2004). See also Kappi-
    anaq (IE 233) on *apsait*.

16. See also Boas (1907: 489): 'The skin near to the eyes of a killed caribou is
    left on the skull.'

17. Rasmussen (1929: 46) relates that the transport of caribou skins through
    the house entrance was prohibited. He specifies, 'A childless couple may
    bring the skins for their sleeping place into a new snow hut through the
    entrance in the ordinary way. But those with children must cut a special
    hole in the wall above the sleeping place through which the caribou skins
    are drawn' (Rasmussen 1929: 182). According to Rasmussen (1931: 181),
    this rule did not apply to the Nattilingmiut, 'There was no objection to
    bringing skin and meat of caribou from the big autumn hunts into a snow
    hut through the entrance passage, even if the house was built on sea ice.'

18. Rasmussen (1929: 94) reports, 'The body is tied up in the caribou skin
    which was used by the sick person to sleep on, and is set up in a crouch-
    ing position.' And according to Rasmussen (1930: 63), 'The dead, who as
    stated is tied up in a caribou skin, is carried on another caribou skin to the
    place where he or she is to be buried.'

19. A close connection between caribou and people is suggested by Rasmus-
    sen (1929: 196): 'Caribou skulls must never be cracked with hammer or
    stone. If this were done, the people of the village would have pains in the
    head.'

20. See also Kappianaq (IE 167).

21. See also the illustration of W. Noah showing the interior of a shaman and
    caribou's body.

22. The same story is reported by Boas (1888: 501).

23. Rasmussen (1931: 502–3) reports with respect to the Utkuhigjalingmiut,
    'Whereas the making of clothing is permitted after the autumn hunts, no

skin may be prepared or sewn into garments until the autumn trek is over and people can move into snow huts. If the snow is late in coming, it is permitted to sew in an ice hut.... Caribou killed in winter after migrating time require no special taboo. The same is the case with caribou meat that has been cached; marrow bones of it may be broken, and the dogs may gnaw the head and all bones.'

24. See Rasmussen (1931: 181) for similar rules among the Nattilingmiut.

25. See Issenman and Rankin (1988), Issenman (1997), Oakes (1988), Oakes and Riewe (1991), Buijs and Oosten (1997) and Buijs (2004).

26. Pisuk from Rankin Inlet presented an interesting variant of this story (quoted in Oosten and Laugrand 2007: 239–40), connecting a peregrine falcon and an *atigi* to a shamanic initiation.

27. According to Kublu (2004), the word *pukiq* refers to the white part of a caribou skin when it is used as trim on a garment as well as to a giant female albino caribou (smaller than a *silaaq*).

28. In this account, caribou hair has a function that is often attributed to *pujuq*, the vapour emanating from menstruating women or women who have just delivered a child.

29. See also Kalluak (2010: 47–60), Rasmussen (1930: 104–5; 1931: 244), Oosten and Laugrand (2002: 132–36) and Evic-Twerdin (1991: 17).

30. See also Boas (1907: 509–10), Saladin d'Anglure (1983) and Oosten (1995).

31. Aqatsiaq (IE 079) related a story of two brothers who lived with the *ijirait* for some time. The elder brother only recalled his experiences after his younger brother Qattalik had died. 'When he heard that Qattalik had passed away, he is known to have said that perhaps if he could have related the story about their experience with Iyiqqat earlier, perhaps he [Qattalik] would have not died.'

32. The notion of more than one owner can also be found among the neighbouring Innu. Among the Innu, Papakashtshishk is the master of the caribou (Clément 2012: 414). He is himself protected by another entity, Atshen, who makes sure that hunters do not mistreat the caribou. The caribou is used in divination, and scapulimancy has been documented extensively.

33. See the case of the Beverly caribou herds in the 1970s. The herds ranged from northern Saskatchewan and the eastern Northwest Territories into the Kivalliq region. In 1994 their population was estimated at 496,000 animals. About 16,000 people in 22 communities depend on the herds (Inuit as well as Metis, Cree, Dene). See Bell (2008b), George (2009a) and Zarate (2008, 2010). See also Collings (1997) on the debates in Holman Island after the decline of the caribou herds in 1992–93.

34. On caribou hunting and reindeer herding, see Burch (1972) and Anderson (2000). More specifically on herding, see Anderson and Berglund (2003), Anderson and Nutall (2004) and Vitebsky (2005).

35. For a detailed description of a caribou hunt in Iglulik, see Randa (1996). On the problem of codifying knowledge about caribou, see Thorpe (2004).

# CHAPTER 9

# The Seal, the Offspring
# of the Sea Woman

Seals were hunted extensively along the coast, especially the ringed seal, *nattiq*, and the bearded seal, *ukjuk*. In summer they were hunted at the floe edge, when they were basking in the sun and in the open water. In winter they were hunted at the breathing holes in the sea ice. Seals constituted the most important prey in winter in many areas along the coast. The Nattilingmiut, 'the people of the seal place', derive their name from the seal. Seal meat was eaten and sealskin was used for many purposes depending on the quality of the skin and the type of seal.[1]

The origin myths of seals related that ringed seals and bearded seals originated from the fingers of the sea woman, and they were considered to be very close to the sea woman. Rasmussen (1931: 226) relates, 'Whenever people have been indifferent towards her by not observing taboo, she hides all the animals; the seals she shuts up in her iṇ·aut: a drip-basin that she has under her lamp. As long as they are inside it, there are no animals to hunt in the sea, and mankind has to starve; the shamans then have to summon their helping spirits and conjure her to be kind again.' The *angakkuq* has to calm down the sea woman so she will release the sea game to be caught by the hunters. In this chapter we will explore the rituals connected to seal hunting, the making of a seal hunter and the hunting practices. We pay particular attention to seal hunting at the breathing holes and the symbolism associated with this custom. We examine the rules of respect and rules of sharing pertaining to the seal. Finally, we discuss various forms of transformation of the seal and the *tuutaliit*, non-human beings that appear to be masters of the seal.

## Initiating the Hunting Season

Sealing was only allowed after the preparation of caribou skins had been completed. Often a winter feast was celebrated that served to prepare for the winter season, when seal was the main source of food. Boas provided an extensive description of an Inuit winter feast ([1888] 1964: 195) he witnessed in Qiqirtat (Kekerten Island), Cumberland Sound, on 10 November 1883. The feast was celebrated late in the fall. The *tupilait*, the spirits of the dead who had not arrived at their final destination in the land of the dead, attacked the community, people as well as dogs. These evil spirits brought sickness, death and bad weather. The *angakkuit* performed their practices extensively inside the houses to protect the people from the *tupilait*. On the eve of the feast the ritual of harpooning Sedna, the sea woman, was conducted by the *angakkuit* in a large hut. Boas (1964 [1888]: 195) relates,

> The hardest task, that of driving away Sedna, is reserved for the most powerful angakoq. A rope is coiled on the floor of a large hut in such a manner as to leave a small opening at the top, which represents the breathing hole of a seal. Two angakut stand by the side of it, one of them holding the seal spear in his left hand, as if he were watching at the seal hole in the winter, the other holding the harpoon line. Another angakoq, whose office it is to lure Sedna up with a magic song, sits at the back of the hut. At last she comes up through the hard rocks and the wizard hears her heavy breathing; now she emerges from the ground and meets the angakoq waiting at the hole. She is harpooned and sinks away in angry haste, drawing after her the harpoon, to which the two men hold with all their strength. Only by a desperate effort does she tear herself away from it and return to her dwelling in Adlivun. Nothing is left with the two men but the blood sprinkled harpoon, which they proudly show to the Inuit.

The harpooning of the sea woman was clearly modelled on the harpooning of a seal at its breathing hole, and the sea woman was treated as if she were a seal.[2]

Elsewhere, Boas (1901: 131) relates that Sedna is first harpooned and then stabbed with a knife. The blood on the harpoon, the knife and the floor predicted the success of the hunt in the winter season. He observes that the Inuit compared the harpooning to the gift of a drink of water.[3] In an Iglulik story the harpooning of a seal is compared to a drop of water falling on its head (Rasmussen 1929: 57). Traditionally, seals received a drink of fresh water once they were killed (see Rasmussen 1931: 242–43). Pelly (2001: 60) reports, 'In the northwest corner of Hudson Bay, 7-year-old Mikitok remembers seeing and following this practice: "When we got the *nattiq* back to the iglu, never out where it was caught, we took some snow, dipped it in melted water, and put it in the seal's mouth".' In the central Arctic, another respected elder, Analok, related, 'Before you cut up a seal, you would get some melt water from your mouth and pour it into the seal's snout. First you melt fresh snow in your mouth, then you pour it into the seal's mouth.' George Kappianaq (IE 155; see also IE 174) recalled,

> When a seal or a walrus was caught, I used to see a small amount of water poured into the mouth of the animal. That was for every catch. When an animal was caught it would be brought back to camp where it would be taken indoors and placed on the floor. The wife would pour some water to the mouth of the animal. This practice was called *immitaujuq* before the people were made to *siqqitiq*. I used to watch my mother *immitaujuq* with the seals caught by my father or my older brother. Why this was practised stems from the fact that it is said that when the animals are caught they get thirsty.[4]

The day after the harpooning of the sea woman, many games and festivities were organized. Boas ([1888] 1964: 195–98) relates,

> The men assemble early in the morning in the middle of the settlement. As soon as they have all got together they run screaming and jumping around the houses, following the course of the sun (nunajisartung or kaivitijung). A few, dressed in women's jackets, run in the opposite direction. These are those who were born in abnormal presentations. The circuit made, they visit every hut, and the woman of the house must always be in waiting for them. When she hears the noise of the band she comes out and throws a dish containing little gifts of meat, ivory trinkets, and articles of sealskin into the yelling crowd, of which each one helps himself to what he can get. No hut is omitted in this round (irqatatung).
>
> The crowd next divides itself into two parties, the ptarmigans (axigirn), those who were born in the winter, and the ducks (aggirn), the children of the summer. A large rope of sealskin is stretched out. One party takes one end of it and tries with all its might to drag the opposite party over to its side. The others hold fast to the rope and try as hard to make ground for themselves. If the ptarmigans give way the summer has won the game and fine weather may be expected to prevail through the winter (nussueraqtung).
>
> The contest of the seasons having been decided, the women bring out of a hut a large kettle of water and each person takes his drinking cup. They all stand as near to the kettle as possible, while the oldest man among them steps out first. He dips a cup of water from the vessel, sprinkles a few drops on the ground, turns his face toward the home of his youth, and tells his name and the place of his birth (oxsoaxsavepunga – me, I was born in). He is followed by an aged woman, who announces

her name and home, and then all the others do the same, down to the young children, who are represented by their mothers. Only the parents of children born during the last year are forbidden to partake in this ceremony. As the words of the old are listened to respectfully, so those of the distinguished hunters are received with demonstrative applause and those of the others with varying degrees of attention, in some cases even with joking and raillery (imitijung).

Now arises a cry of surprise and all eyes are turned toward a hut out of which stalk two gigantic figures. They wear heavy boots; their legs are swelled out to a wonderful thickness with several pairs of breeches; the shoulders of each are covered by a woman's overjacket and the faces by tattooed masks of sealskins. In the right hand each carries the seal spear, on the back of each is an inflated buoy of sealskin, and in the left hand the scraper. Silently, with long strides, the qailertetang (fig. 146) approach the assembly, who, screaming, press back from them. The pair solemnly leads the men to a suitable spot and set them in a row, and the women in another opposite them. They match the men and women in pairs and these pairs run, pursued by the qailertetang, to the hut of the woman, where they are for the following day and night man and wife (nulianititijung). Having performed this duty, the qailertetang stride down to the shore and invoke the good north wind, which brings fair weather, while they warn off the unfavourable south wind.

As soon as the incantation is over, all the men attack the qailertetang with great noise. They act as if they had weapons in their hands and would kill both spirits. One pretends to probe them with a spear, another to stab them with a knife, one to cut off their arms and legs, another to beat them unmercifully on the head. The buoys which they carry on their backs are ripped open and collapse and soon they both lie as if dead beside their broken weapons (pilekting). The Eskimo leave them to get their drinking cups and the qailertetang awake to new life. Each man fills his sealskin with water, passes a cup to them and inquires about the future, about the fortunes of the hunt and the events of life. The qailertetang answer in murmurs which the questioner must interpret for himself. The evening is spent in playing ball, which is whipped all around the settlement (ajuktaqtung).

The feast was celebrated to prepare the land for the winter hunting. It did not exclusively concern seals, but as seals were the most important prey in winter, seal hunting symbolism played a central part in the feast. The harpooning of the sea woman as well as the identification of the *qailertetang* as seal hunters (Boas 1901: 140) carrying seal spears indicates the significance of seal hunting in the feast.

As in the caribou feasts described in the preceding chapter, the festivities preceded the hunting season itself. Many features of the symbolism of the caribou feasts can also be found in the winter feasts, such as the importance of play and competitions, the representations of human beings as birds, the killing or shooting prefiguring the killing of the prey and the ritual intercourse between men and women.

In the course of the feast, the success of the coming hunt was determined in various divinatory games, such as the tug-of-war between the ptarmigans and the ducks and the killing of the *qailertetang*. Leah Arnaujaq, who lived in the Hudson Bay region, recalled,

> In the spring it was a tradition that all the people would get together for a big celebration. Everybody got very excited and happy. People from Pelly Bay would come to Repulse Bay to join in the festivities. We would play games: one particular game was one in which the men picked a challenger from the other settlement. They both then took off their shirts and hit their opponent on the shoulders with their hands. There was another game where a ball, made out of caribou, was kicked around like in soccer. There were two teams, the one that was closest to the shore called *aagiarjuit*, which means pin-tailed duck, and the one further inland was called *aqiggiit*, which means ptarmigan. These two names are also used when babies are born. The ones born in the summer are called *aagiarjuit* and the ones in winter are called *aqiggiit*. Another game was played with partners, one of whom was blindfolded. Old men played a game with walrus bones, which was always accompanied by a great deal of laughter. The men would also try to spin around as fast as they could. We always had a lot of fun playing these games. (*Recollections of Inuit Elders* 1986: 13)

In the winter feast, human beings represented ptarmigans and ducks. The ptarmigan and the hare were the only prey that was available at the beginning of time, when animals were still scarce (Rasmussen 1929: 153); the duck and the fox represented the primordial clothing in this same period (Rasmussen 1929: 67). Dividing the society into two groups representing these birds suggests a return to the original poverty at the beginning of the hunting season, when people were in need of meat and skins.[5]

The connection to the deceased played an important part in the feast. It started with the anonymous spirits of the dead (*tupilait*) attacking the camp. When each person pronounced his name and his place of birth, the relationship with the deceased namesake was acknowledged and we may infer that by this procedure the anonymous *tupilait* were transformed into named ancestors who would no longer attack people but instead would support their namesakes. A similar procedure was followed in the shamanic séances described by Rasmussen (1929: 125), where the participants named the deceased who were heard making the sounds of the game animals during the séance. At the end of the feast people even appear to have represented the deceased by playing the game of the *ullurmiut*. Thus, care was taken that before the start of the hunting season correct relationships with the deceased ancestors were established.

Relations between the genders also played a central part in the feasts. Whereas in the caribou feasts the sexual symbolism often remained implicit, in the winter feasts it came openly to the fore and was a matter of great concern for the missionaries.

The exchange of women was at the core of the feast. Bilby (1923: 213) observes that pregnant women and the elderly were not included in the feast: 'These women are *Kooveayootiksatyonerktoot*, i.e., "no-longer-the material-for-a-rejoicing".' The pairing was organized by *angakkuit* acting as representatives of Sedna, who made fun of the pairs; the pairs had to restrain from laughter. Bilby refers to the temporary husbands as 'Sedna mates' and to the children of such unions as the 'offspring of Sedna', suggesting that the women involved in the exchange represented the sea woman.

In the North Baffin variants of the feast, the *tivajuut*, a connection to only the sea game is suggested. In this area the sea woman played no part in the feast and it focused mainly on the masked dancers and the exchange of women. It was celebrated in a feast house. The platform was removed and two men would dress up, one in female and the other in masculine attire. Both dancers, called *tivajuut*, wore masks of skin. According to Rasmussen (1929: 241–43),

> The woman's dress would be drawn in tight wherever it should ordinarily be loose and full, as for instance the large baggy kamiks, the big hood and the broad shoulder pieces; the dress in itself should also be too small. The same principle was observed in the case of the man's costume, which was barely large enough for him to get it on at all. The man dressed as a woman should have an anautAq, or snowbeating stick, in his hand, that is, a stick used for beating or brushing snow from one's garments; the male figure should carry a te·ᵍarut, or short dog whip. Finally, the 'man' should have fastened in the crutch a huge penis, grotesque in its effect, fashioned either of wood or of stuffed intestines.

Two blocks of snow were placed in the feast house – the jumping block, half the height of a man, and the lamp block, the same height as a man. Then,

> All the men and women assemble in the qagge, and now the two masked dancers, who are called tivajuut, come bounding in. They are dumb performers, and may only endeavour to make themselves understood by signs, and only puff out breath between the lips and ejaculate 'pust, pust' exactly as if they were trying to blow something out. They come bound-

ing in, taking great leaps through the entrance hole, and must jump over the aterartarwik, this also to be done whenever they re-enter after an exit. The first thing the tivajuut now do is to chase out all the men with blows, the woman striking with her anautaq, the man with his te·ᵍarut, the women of the audience being suffered to remain behind. They then caper about, with light, adroit movements, among the women, peering everywhere to see if any man has concealed himself in their ranks.

Should a man be so discovered, he is recklessly and mercilessly thrashed out of the house. As soon as the tivajuut are sure all the men have gone, they themselves must dash out of the qagge, to where the men are assembled in a group outside. One of these men then steps up to the tivajuut, and with his face close to the mask, whispers with a smile the name of the woman inside the qagge, with whom he wishes to lie the coming night. The two tivajuut then at once rush back, gaily into the qagge, go up to the woman whose name has been whispered to them outside, and touch the soles of her feet with anautAq and te·ᵍarut respectively. This is called ikufifut: the ones who hack out something for themselves with an axe or a big, sharp knife. Great rejoicing is now apparent among all the women, and the one woman chosen: ikut·aujəq, goes out and comes in again with the man who has asked for her. Both are expected to look very serious; all the women in the qagge however, must be quite the reverse, laughing and joking and making fun, and trying all they can to make the couple laugh; should they succeed, however, it means a short life for the pair.

The women in the feast house chanted a song while the *tivajuut* performed all kinds of grotesque sexual acts, striking at the artificial penis of the man and imitating coitus. The game continued until all men and women had been paired, and then the men returned home with the women they had chosen.

Saladin d'Anglure (1989: 165n29) points out that the word for the distribution of women by the two masked *angakkuit* was the same as the word for the distribution of frozen meat, *ikujijut*. The woman was referred to as an *ikuktaq*, a part separated from a whole by a violent act. The term evokes the origin myth of the sea woman; according to the myth, sea mammals originated from the finger joints cut off of the sea woman's hands (see chapter 2), suggesting a homology between the women and the sea mammals in the context of the ritual.

As in the caribou feasts, the fun, jokes, happiness and joy connected to the pairing of men and women in the rituals may have served to seduce the game. The sexual relation itself may have prefigured the killing of the game, as the harpooning of the seal was often thought to be homologous to sexual intercourse. Tungilik from Naujaat related that he never had any luck in *mauliqpuq* hunting until his stepfather revealed to him how it should be done.

We would be hunting at the seal hole that was covered with snow. He
would just tell me that if I saw that the seal was coming, then I was to
stab at it. Then the floater would start moving. He would just tell me
these things. So whenever I thought that there was a seal, I would stab
at it. I would never be successful because I was not being shown. I was
not being taught. The other people were catching seals, and I would be
envious of them, but I was unable to do it. I'll tell of his words. It might
be embarrassing, shameful. When he finally started telling me about how
to hunt, he said that if there was a woman that I had already had sex
with, I was to recall the time that I first had sex, and to remember what
my breathing was like. I was to remember my breathing. He said that's
the kind of breathing that the seal would have. I had never had had sex
with a woman at the time, so I didn't know anything about the kind of
breathing I was to have. Then one day, I am not sure what I was thinking, but the *qiviutaq*, the piece of down that would be placed, moved.
You should just wet the very tip, not the rest of it, because if it was made
completely wet, it would not be able to move. I was told that this piece
of down was used so you would know that there was a seal. When it was
moving, I started watching my breath. When the feather started going
up, it fluttered a bit, and I was finally aware of my breathing. I was shaking because I knew there was a seal there. Before this time I never knew
about this. I never thought about how it was going to be. My breathing
was shaking. When it moved up it was shaking, when it was going down
again, it was fluttering. I started using my breathing. I thought maybe
the seal is coming up, and I thought maybe its time for me to stab. I went
to stab and the seal was very close. This is how I learned to get seals. I
was observing my breathing. My knee joints seemed very low because I
was shaking so much. That's the way it was. I understood how this piece
of bird down was used. It was because of the movement of the water that
it started moving. Then it seemed to stop, and then it started moving
again. When it went down a bit, that's when the seal was coming up and
it was time to harpoon it. I found this out by myself. In a way it seemed
as if I taught this to myself, and it helped me. (Oosten and Laugrand
1999b: 67–68)

The recollections of Tungilik emphasize the sexual dimension of the
act of killing. The hunter should feign sexual excitement and breathe
like he would in copulation. But this behaviour should remain symbolic.[6] Men should not have intercourse with game, but kill it so that
its meat can be shared. Women should be shared within the community in ritual contexts, ensuring that the game becomes abundant.

Although the winter feast prepared for the winter hunting season,
specific rituals were still required to make seal hunting possible. Traditionally, the hunting season began with small gifts made to the owners of the game. Captain Comer reported (quoted in Boas 1901: 148–
49),

Before going out sealing for the first time in the season, the natives gather some dried seaweed or kelp, set fire to it in the snow house, and hold their clothes and their harpoons over the smoke, saying, 'Mammak-poq!' This is believed to drive away the odor of caribou-skin, which seals dislike. Then the key-block of the snow house is cut with a knife in all directions. This is believed to bring good luck and to drive away sickness.

Soon after the sealing begins, a piece of white caribou-skin and a bit of thread are carried out and deposited on the ice.

Elsewhere he provides more information on this ritual. Comer (quoted in Boas 1907: 502) reports,

After the new caribou-skin clothing has been made for the winter, and when the men are ready to go sealing for the first time, the whole of their clothing and hunting-implements are hung over a smudge made of dry seaweed. The Netchillik use nests of small birds for making the smudge. It is supposed that the smoke takes away the smell of the caribou, which would offend the sea-mammals.

When the men go sealing for the first time, they take along a little moss, a small piece of caribou-skin, and sinew-thread, which are left on the ice as an offering to Nuliayoq. It is believed this will induce her to send a plentiful supply of seal. The women, before cutting up the meat of the first seal for cooking, wash their hands with a piece of dry skin wetted by their sons. It is believed that this takes away the smell of caribou from their hands.

In Comer's description the emphasis is on the removal of the caribou smell from the hands before seal hunting can be started. In a description by Rasmussen (1929: 193), the emphasis is on the small gifts to the sea woman,

On first setting out for walrus or seal hunting after having hunted summer or autumn caribou up inland, a fire must be lighted in the snow hut, with fuel of dried seaweed, and over this are held clothing, mittens of caribou skins, harpoon with line and head, and the words 'namarmik-mamarmik', meaning 'give us something nice' are uttered. Then, in leaving the hut to set out on the hunt, one must step across the fire.

As soon as sealing begins after the close of the caribou season, a small narrow strip of pukeq (white skin from the belly of a caribou) is set out, and a piece of sinew thread from the short end (sinew thread is made from the back sinews of the caribou, and that part lying nearest the spine gives the longest threads, the outermost being quite short). This is a sacrifice to Takánalûk, and is called kiversautit: 'that wherewith something is lowered down' meaning presumably that offences are thus lowered down in the deep.

Prior to first hunting sea game, clothes of caribou skin or a piece of caribou skin were brought into contact with the domain of the sea game, and this was thought to effect good hunting. Inversely, a small offering of sealskin was made to the owner of the caribou.[7] Thus, in these rituals a connection between the domains of land game and sea game was required. These small gifts opened the hunting season and induced the owners of the game to provide the animals the Inuit needed to survive.

## The Making of a Seal Hunter

In Inuit traditions Akkolookjo and Omerneetoo were the first human beings. They came from the earth and instituted the rules of respect. According to Boas (1901: 143–44),

> Akkolookjo said, 'When a child is born, the mother shall not eat of the seal's intestines, else she will die.'
> She also said, 'A woman who has a new-born child, and who is not yet clean, shall not touch the meat of seal killed by any one except her husband, unless it be caught by a boy or by an old man. If she eats of a seal caught by a person not her husband, it may cause the death of one of her relatives.
> 'If a woman who has a child less than one year old eats the intestines of seals, she will waste away without feeling sick. A year after the birth of a child, when the moon is in the same phase as at the time of birth the mother will go to every door of the village in which she is living, and may visit a few huts. After that she is at liberty to partake of any part of the seal or of any other animal.'

Boas (1907: 484) provides various rules for the mother and the infant boy that will help to make him a successful hunter in Cumberland Sound:

> A pregnant woman, or a woman who has a young child, must not eat any animal that has been shot through the intestines. She must not eat of a seal which has been harpooned, and dies without coming up to breathe.
> The mother will take her infant boy on her knees, and let him throw the fork into the dish from which she is eating. Afterwards she will place him on the bed, and let him go through the movements of paddling and harpooning in the kayak, and of shooting with bow and arrows, in order to make him a successful hunter when he is grown up.
> The mother cooks the sweet-breads of a seal, and places a small piece on the soles of the feet of her infant boy. This enables him to walk safely on thin ice. The boy must sprinkle some water in the direction of the new moon the first time he sees her. Then he will become a successful sealer.

Boas (1901: 159) also relates that a pregnant woman should not eat from a seal 'that died under water without having come up once to breathe.... Therefore the natives make it a point not to kill seals out-right, but to let them blow once before despatching them.'

Boas (1901: 160) reports that on the west coast of Hudson Bay,

> For three months after the child is born, the mother must stay in her house. During this time she is not allowed sexual intercourse. A woman who has an infant boy keeps a kettle full of snow, which she melts over the lamp. She holds him in her lap while eating. She puts a small piece of meat to the child's mouth, and then places it in a bag. When the bag is full, the contents are thrown away, and it is filled again in the same way. This is believed to please the child's guardian spirit (tornaq). At night a piece of meat is placed in a dish near the child. If the child's guardian spirit should visit it at night, he would look for food, and, if he should not find any, would eat first the mother's vital organs, then the father's, and finally those of the other natives. To have anything left after eating would bring hunger to the child when it became a man. The angakok's power to remove sickness from the child will be impaired. After she has finished eating, she pulls gently, first on the right leg and left arm, and then on the left leg and right arm, of the child. Then the child is placed in a sitting position, and it is put through the motions of paddling a kayak. Then the mother darts her fork into the dish out of which she has been eating. This represents harpooning a seal. Next the child's hands are put through the motions of pulling a bow and shooting an arrow. This cere-mony is repeated after each meal. All this is believed to make the child a successful hunter.[8]

Rasmussen (1929: 173–74) also gives a description of this ritual, which he calls minulErtErivoq, among the Iglulingmiut. He specifies that the skin bag for the food of the child should hang beside the lamp. The rit-ual 'protects the child against hunger, and renders it skilful in hunting later on, bringing abundance of game'. He does not connect this ritual to a *tuurngaq*, but explains that some think that the ritual is performed so the 'child's namesake soul may have something to eat'. He adds,

> The ceremony comes to an end when the stay in the kinErvik is over, and the woman then takes the skin bag, filled with tiny fragments of meat, and carries it to the blowhole of a seal. Into this she throws all the scraps of meat, the first meat which has touched the boy's lips, and in a way served as his first flesh food. They are thus thrown back into the sea whence they came, and some people believe that by minulErtErinEq the separate pieces receive souls and become seals once more, which can be caught again by the boy when he grows up. If the child is a girl, the scraps of meat are merely thrown out on the edge of the beach at the expiration of the kinErvik period. The empty skin bag is flung out on the ice.
>
> While a woman remains in the kinErvik she must always have the skin from the head of a seal spread over her lap while eating. This is

called her aklEra, or apron. When the kinErvik period is over, the aklEra is also laid out beside a seal's blowhole, if the child is a boy.

According to Rasmussen (1931: 261), the Nattilingmiut did not observe the minulErtErinEq custom:

> Nor do they stretch a child's body after a meal, first taking the child by the ring finger of the left hand and the corresponding toe of the right foot, blowing on the fingers and smacking the tongue, and then doing the same thing with the other hand and foot. But they do exactly the same with all seal foetuses, in order that the soul of the little foetus may grow up quickly and become a big seal that will be worthwhile killing.

Thus, the baby seal and the human baby are treated in a similar way.

Children were prepared to become seal hunters in many ways. Concerning the Iglulingmiut, Rasmussen (1929: 177) relates,

> A woman with a baby must always have water in her water vessel, which must always be placed on the left of her lamp, on the spot which is called kit*iane. This is in order that all who are thirsty may come in and obtain water. The seal thus learns that no one in the vicinity of this boy need ever be thirsty, and many seals will afterwards come to the boy and let him capture them. Thirst is the worst thing seals can suffer from.

Boas (1901: 160–61; see also Rasmussen 1929: 75–76) relates that when boys were a little bit older,

> In winter, at the appearance of the new moon, boys must run out of the snow house, take a handful of snow, and put it into the kettle. It is believed that this helps the hunter to capture the seal and to bring it home. The boys are told by their parents that this act pleases the man in the moon, who is watching them; that when they grow older and go sealing, the seals will come to them to be caught, for it is understood that seals do not like to be caught by lazy people. This practice is kept up throughout the winter.

Moreover, boys should not play cat's cradle. Mark Ijjangiaq (IE 184) recalled, 'The boys were discouraged from playing with the string games, the reason given was that when they harpooned a bearded seal they could get their hands tangled which they could lose a finger from.'[9] Ijjangiaq (IE 184) also explained that boys should not watch the girls play while leaning with their hands on the drying rack. If this rule was not observed it might happen that 'as an adult he would appear to be pulling a seal when he actually was not, this was called *igjuksukpuq*'.

Lisa Koperqualuk (2011) collected an interesting belief from Peter Itukallak from Puvirnituq: 'A cord, a regular cord, is very important in the catch of animals, or in its use with dogs. We used to be told to not cut for example the intestine of the seal (after cleaning out the intestines of seals, these are cooked and eaten and are some of the favourite parts to eat). We used to be told that, this was so that the cord we were using to catch the animal would not be cut.'

Rasmussen (1929: 172) reports, 'When a boy is out visiting, he must not remain too long in one house. If he does so, the seals he is to hunt will remain long under water, i.e. he will find it difficult to catch them.'

Mothers might wear *aarnguat* amulets on behalf of their sons. Rasmussen (1931: 275) relates that Nâlungiaq had the head and feet of a red-throated diver and an eider duck as well as the tailbones of a seal fastened to her amulet belt so her son would be lucky when sealing. Another Nattilik woman, Quvli'q, wore for her son 'seal claws, sewn on at the armholes: strength; katjuaq (the sinew of a seal's fore flipper), sewn to the upper arm of the inner coat: strong arms; seal snouts, sewn in a line round her waist: luck in breathing-hole hunting; nigvik (the inner part of a seal gut), sewn on the stomach outside her own intestine: a healthy and strong stomach; … seal lower jaws, all from her husband's kill, hanging by her lamp: give him luck when sealing' (Rasmussen 1931: 275).

Boys might be given *aarnguat* to wear as well. Aupilaarjuk from Rankin Inlet recalled, 'My grandfather Qimirluk, who was also called Uyarasuk, who I never knew, was a good seal hunter. I had his *uqsiut*, a thong used for dragging seal, as an *aarnguaq* placed on my hood. My father threw it away when we became Christian. He said we did not need those things any more. If then was now, I would have kept it' (quoted in Oosten et al. 1999: 133). Itinnuaq from Rankin Inlet remembered having to wear a sealskin as an *aarnguaq:* 'I was also given the skin of a seal that had died in the winter. The outer claws had been tied together. I was told it would protect me and that I would not be struck whenever there was lightning' (quoted in Oosten and Laugrand 2002: 124).

Rasmussen (1931: 272) lists many amulets intended to make a boy a good seal hunter among the Nattilingmiut: 'two drag lines for seals (ɔrʃiutit), belonged to his father and his elder brother, worn sewn to the hood: luck when sealing' (1931: 271), 'sewn into the left sleeve seven seal snouts: luck when sealing' and 'seal claw from the fore flipper: strength in the arm' (Rasmussen 1931: 272).

Amulets served a variety of purposes. 'An old harpoon head placed on the piece of skin (tuteriAq) that the hunter stands on at the breathing hole: makes the seals tame' (Rasmussen 1931: 269). '[F]ringing of white caribou skin: brings luck when sealing. A seal's snout and a harpoon head: bring lucky sealing' (Rasmussen 1931: 270). 'A strip of the skin of a bearded seal to which hang seven bear teeth, worn as a scarf: health and strength' (Rasmussen 1931: 272). The skin of a stillborn seal was used as an amulet to drive away thunder. It was made into a jacket, which must be taken off when thunder was heard, and which was then struck against the ground (Boas 1907: 505).

Boas (1901: 152) related that throwing a stone held by a seal would bring luck to the hunter.

> It is believed that some seals, when coming up to their hole to breathe, break away the young ice that may have formed over the hole with a stone held in one of their flippers. If a hunter strikes such a seal, and seizes the stone with his hand before the seal can drop it, he must not look at it, but must throw it over his shoulder. Then, after having killed the seal and landed it on the ice, he may pick up the stone. This insures good luck in sealing. The stone turns into pyrites when thrown over the shoulder.

Magic words might also be used to become successful in seal hunting. Boas (1901: 153) relates,

> It is believed that success in hunting may be obtained by means of magic formulas. One man who is very successful in catching salmon stated that his grandmother had taught him what to sing when fishing. This song for salmon is also effective for seal; but for ground-seal he must sing another one, and still others for musk-oxen and for caribou. He had not taught these songs to his children, but intended to do so before he died.

Rasmussen (1931: 288) provides an example of such magic words intended to bring meat to the house:

> Great giant bear
> The great giant bears that belong to you, it is said, come
> As a gift of welcome you must bring something, that will make soup
> A seal it must be
> Come hither and see
> puh – puh!
> puh – puh!

Another example is provided by Hawkes (1916: 162) for Labrador:

> Today I am hunting for seals in the kayak.
> Come over here, all of you.

(I am very cold.)
You are not unwelcome, we are glad to see strangers.
Where are you going?
(I am very tired; I have walked from far.)
What is that like deer far away?
Today it rains again.

In 2013 Myna Ishulutaq from Pangniqtuuq produced a beautiful film showing how in the Cumberland region Inuit hunters would sing to the seals. They would sing *avaala*, songs or Christian hymns (*pisiit*) to make the seals fall asleep. Approaching the animal, the hunter would then whistle to wake the seal up and shoot it. According to the various stories recorded by Mynah, hunters performed *avaala* until the mid-1960s. Other elders, such as Ikpelee, recalled, 'Seals basking in the sun were also caught by confusing them, circling them on all sides and making as much noise as possible, then harpooning them as soon as they were in range. Sometimes a lone hunter would attract a seal's curiosity by singing,[10] then the seal would not go down; this was true of only some seals' (quoted in Bennett and Rowley 2004: 56).

## First Catches

First catch rituals ensured that a good relation was built between the hunter and his prey. Boas (1901: 161) describes a first catch of a seal on the west coast of Hudson Bay:

> As soon as the other men see that he has harpooned a seal, his jacket and shirt are taken off, and the seal, even before it is dead, is dragged across the boy's back. Then it is cut up, and each man takes a piece. The boy's father takes the head. When they come home, the meat is cooked and eaten. Then the boy's mother gathers all the bones and throws them into a seal-hole. It is believed that these bones will become seals which the boy is to catch in later life.
>
> In one particular case a boy's grandfather gave the instructions for this ceremony before the boy went out on his first seal-hunt, and also directed that some caribou meat should be cooked with the seal-meat, because that would make the boy successful in caribou-hunting.

Boas (1907: 484–85) provides a similar account for Cumberland Sound, but here '[t]he skin of the head is given to an old woman to make a bag out of. The bones of the head are kept for a year. Then they are put into the grave of a relative. The first joints of the flippers are kept, and disposed of in the same way.'

Rasmussen (1929: 178–79) reports,

When a firstborn son gets his first seal, an old woman makes a bag out of
the skin of the animal's head, and in this bag she must afterwards keep
the moss which serves as wick for her lamp. This bag is called mAr*un:
moss wick ('bag' is understood), and must remain in the old woman's
possession as long as she lives and be buried with her when she dies.
This gives the seals which the boy catches good blubber for lamp oil. ...

The extreme joints of the flippers of the first seal caught by a firstborn
son are kept for a year and then placed in a grave. Then, when the young
man later on becomes a great hunter, and some shaman or other grows
envious, and endeavours to take away his catch by magic, i.e. steal the
souls of the animals he gets, the attempt will prove fruitless. The shaman's helping spirits will be afraid of the outer part of the flippers placed
in the grave, and will then protect the boy's catch against all evil.

When a boy get his first seal, he must take off his outer and inner
jackets, lay them on the ice and throw himself down flat on them, and
before the seal is yet dead, his father must drag it across his back; this
will prevent the seals from being afraid of him. The first seal is cut up in
the house, and eaten by the parents and as many others as they can. It is
distributed among the houses and eaten as quickly as possible. The head
may only be eaten by the father or mother. When the skin has been taken
off, it must be shared out among as many men as possible for slippers,
but all the bones of this first caught seal must be gathered together and
dropped through a blowhole. When this is done, the soul returns to the
bones, and the young man may keep on catching the same seal.

A young man must never eat the flesh of the first animal of any species
he kills.

When a young man comes home after killing his first seal, he must not
beat the snow from his clothes with the snow beater; for to do so would
frighten away the seals he would otherwise catch later on.

Rasmussen (1929: 179) adds, 'Sometimes the first seal a boy kills is cut
up by women alone; but there must be many women present in such
case, and the mother must hold the seal by a line fastened round its
head, pulling at the line occasionally and raising the head a little, for
the head is to be her share.'

In Boas's and Rasmussen's accounts the seal is dragged over the
body of the young hunter. However, the *angakkuq* Aava related to Rasmussen that his first seal was dragged over the body of his father: 'At
last I was big enough to go out with the grown up men to the blowholes
after seal. The day I harpooned my first seal, my father had to lie down
on the ice with the upper part of his body naked, and the seal I had
caught was dragged across his back while it was still alive. Only men
were allowed to eat of my first catch, and nothing must be left. The
skin and the head were set out on the ice, in order that I might be able
later on to catch the same seal again. For three days and nights, none

of the men who had eaten of it might go out hunting or do any kind of work' (Rasmussen 1929: 117). Rasmussen does not explain why the father took the place of his son. The normal pattern seems to have been that the seal was dragged over the young hunter.

Lucassie Kattuk, born 1928, from Sanikiluaq, related,

> I have heard what they used to do when a boy caught a seal for the first time. They pulled the seal over the chest of the person who caught the seal, as he was lying on the ice. He lay on his back, and sometimes he took his parka off so his skin was exposed. The seal was pulled across the boy's chest, still attached to the naulak. Then he would give the seal to his sanariarruk, the one who had dressed him when he was born. (quoted in Pelly 2001: 55)

Thus, in this account the midwife was entitled to the first seal.

Usually the young hunter was not allowed to eat anything of his first catch. Imaruittuq from Iglulik related, 'Up in our area, the meat would be given to the elders, first making sure that no elder was left out. In order for another seal to be caught soon after, every bit of the meat would have to be consumed. If it was the first ring seal, the whole seal needed to be consumed' (quoted in Oosten et al. 1999: 133).

## Seal Hunting

Traditionally, a variety of techniques for seal hunting existed (see figure 9.1). The most important modes of hunting were hunting seals in open water, hunting seals when they bask on the ice in spring and early summer, and hunting seals at their breathing holes. Seal hunting in open water used to be done in kayaks and then in motorized boats. In the past a harpoon was used to kill the seal. Later rifles were used, but many seals that were killed sank before they could be towed in.

Hunting seals basking in the sun was done in spring and early summer. Rasmussen (1931: 160) describes the technique:

> The hunt itself, which is called ArnEq, proceeds in the usual manner; the hunter crawls over the ice but stops every time the seal he is stalking wakens and looks at him. As long as his prey is observing him he has to roll about in the snow exactly like another wet seal that has just come up out of the water. The o-t-c/q, which is very suspicious at first, at last believes it is another seal that like itself has come up to bask in the sun, and by and by takes no more notice of the hunter, who at last gets so near that he can jump up and harpoon it. Usually it takes an hour to crawl up to a seal, and of course the method necessitates great knowledge of the habits and movements of the seal and the noises it utters.

**Figure 9.1.** A hunter hides behind a snow wall to hunt a seal. *Source:* Anglican Church of Canada/General Synod Archives/Peck Papers, M56-1, series XXXIII, 4–6, 8–13.

This *uutuq* technique requires the hunter to imitate the seal. If the deception is successful, the seal will be killed. The technique is a good example of the themes of deception and seduction that play an important part in Inuit hunting.

A variety of other techniques existed. Rasmussen (1931: 162) pro-vides a description of a special technique for hunting the bearded seal:

> The bearded seal is especially hunted out in Ukjulik, as they never come in through Simpson Strait but keep to Queen Maud's Sea. There, too, they know the special method of catching these seals, called qc/qErtulEr-inEq; this means 'to bewilder the game', or 'stupefy it with noise'. It can of course only be used for bearded seals that appear as o-t-ut. A number of hunters crawl towards it in the usual manner until about a hundred meters away; then all jump to their feet at once and shout and scream all together while they run towards the seal. The sudden commotion makes it wild with fear; so great is its bewilderment that it practically becomes unconscious and lies motionless until it is harpooned.

## Mauliqpuq *Hunting and the Symbolism of the* Aglu

A famous hunting technique, called *mauliqpuq,* essential to survival in winter, is hunting at the seal breathing holes. An *aglu,* a seal breathing hole, is an opening two to three centimetres wide in the ice. In the past hunters used the dogs to find the *agluit* by smell. They still do this, but often they also look for them themselves, inspecting the cracks on fresh ice. Once an *aglu* has been located, the hunter positions himself near the hole. He takes the direction of the wind into account and takes care that no shadow is cast over the breathing hole. He then stands with straight legs, bent at the waist so he is ready to harpoon his prey. Once the seal appears, the hunter harpoons it, makes the hole wide enough for the seal and hauls it onto the ice (see figures 9.2 and 9.3). He then immediately skins it.

This waiting required much endurance. Shaimaiyuk recalled,

> In the wintertime when hunters are hunting seals, they would wait by the hole all night, without any source of warmth. What I am explain-ing is how it was when I was raised. The hunter would tie his legs up, and be unable to move. They would be tied at the thigh. I would have a caribou-skin covering on a snow seat and a snow shelter by the breathing hole, so that I could hear when the seal was breathing, when it is windy in the middle of the night. When people hunted like this it was called *unnuijuq.* ... I did this before, I didn't catch a seal, and I spent all night trying. No seal came to the hole, so I didn't catch a seal. This is part of my experience and the way of our ancestors. They would wait all day and all night and feel discouraged when they couldn't get an animal to feed their children. (quoted in Bennett and Rowley 2004: 53)

*Mauliqpuq* hunting was usually most successful if it was a collective effort. A group of hunters out on the sea ice first located the breathing

**Figure 9.2.** At the *aglu*, the seal comes to the hunter. *Source:* Anglican Church of Canada/General Synod Archives/Peck Papers, M56-1, series XXXIII, 4–6, 8–13.

holes of the seals in an area. Each hunter took his position at one of the breathing holes, and the more hunters who participated, the greater the chance of a kill. The breathing hole was opened wider and carefully explored so the hunter would know the correct angle for his harpoon. Then a floater was inserted that would indicate the presence of the seal and the hunter would then wait until a seal approached the breathing

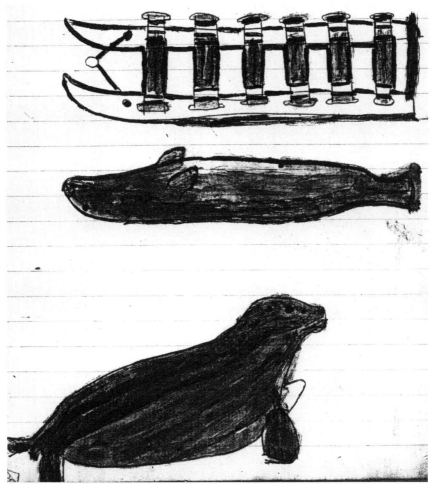

**Figure 9.3.** Seals and a sled. *Source:* Anglican Church of Canada/General Synod Archives/Peck Papers, M56-1, series XXXIII, 4–6, 8–13.

hole. It was important that he made no noise that might frighten the seal.

Imaruittuq (IE 101) explained the various types of seal breathing that could be distinguished by the hunter:

> As one waits for a seal to come up to the breathing hole, one can hear a ruffling sound of the water. This is the indicating factor that there is a seal breathing through this *aglu*. So one can hear a short burst of breathing and at the same time there is a sound of ruffle from the disturbance of the water. This indicates that the seal immediately dove back into the

water with only one burst of breath. When this happens, it is called *atau-siattattuq*, that means to breathe only once. When that happens, it is not wise to give out a shot, as the seal will have dove back into the water before one even gives a shot away. This is the case when the thickness of the ice is still thin. When a seal gives out a long breath when they get into the breathing hole, that means it will be in that breathing hole for some time breathing through it without a burst of breath. This is the good time to give a shot away. Some seals are called *pullaittut*. This is for the seals that do not make sounds when they are breathing through the breathing holes. If a seal comes to the breathing hole, you will hear the ruffling of the water but soon there will no longer be any sign of the presence of the seal. So if you watch the water inside the *aglu*, it will make small disturbances. That means the seal is breathing, and the breath makes the water ruffle, so a hunter can tell that the seal is right in the *aglu* breathing; yet one cannot hear the seal breathing.

Imaruittuq explained that *pulaittut* are usually fully matured seals or seals that have been hunted before. He emphasized that the hunter should never feel superior to the seals he hunted.

Bearded seals have been caught with a harpoon even though the hunter may fear their strength, but that was the way they had been hunted; but one must never feel superior to them, as they are known to have maimed fingers. The bearded seals have massive strengths, especially to these who breathe with a whistling sound, and the younger ones are stronger then the fully matured bearded seals. So one must always be prepared when one is going to harpoon a bearded seal. At one time my adoptive grandfather was pulled through an *aglu* by a seal for he had thought he was much better than a seal. When he was pulled through, he grabbed hold of the edge of the *aglu* and hung on to the harpoon thong for he did not want to loose his harpoon. He held on hoping that the seal would be so desperate for air that it would weaken, so he hung on until he was able to pull himself out of the breathing hole when the seal weakened. No wonder other hunters that were around got concerned and alarmed. I once almost got pulled to the *aglu* myself. When the seals have been basking on the ice, the snow surrounding the breathing holes becomes very slippery so they can prove to be dangerous. One time I harpooned a seal but I slipped and my legs were tangled so I tried in vain to scratch a surface so I could get my grip, but I succeeded and was able to hang on. It was scary. (Imaruittuq, IE 102)

The breathing hole of the seal is marked as a place where different levels of reality can connect. It is the place where the seal comes up to breathe and can be killed. In a description of a shamanic séance by Rasmussen (1929: 130), the passage of the *tarniq* of the *angakkuq* is compared to the breathing hole of a seal: 'An opening has been formed for the soul of the shaman, an opening like the blowhole of a seal, and through it the soul flies up to heaven, aided by all those stars which were once human beings.' Rasmussen (1931: 238) also relates how a man hunting at the breathing hole travelled to the land of the moon:

> There was once a man who was standing at a breathing hole waiting for a seal. Suddenly he had a feeling as if he were being lifted up from the ice, and, on looking round, caught sight of the moon spirit who was standing close by, waving. The man went to the moon spirit who simply pointed to his sledge. The man sat on it, and the moon spirit said: 'Close your eyes.'

The moon man took him up to the land of the moon and there he met Aujuk, the eater of entrails. She offered him food, but he refused, fearing he would not be able to return if he ate it. Finally he fled from her:

> He ran on as hard as he could and descended from the sky, coming down just at the breathing hole where he had been hunting. It was not difficult to find his way back to the same place, because his hunting companion shouted now and then: 'qo-qo!' just as people do when they cannot find each other.
>    Just after the man had come down on to the ice his companion caught a seal. But as he went over and ate with him without first having told that he had been up at the moon spirit's, his jaws clashed together and he could never open them again.[11]

Thus, the breathing hole is not only a privileged point of connection between this world and the world below us, but also between this world and the upper world.

It was also a place where one might communicate with non-human agents. Takornaq related (quoted in Rasmussen 1929: 23–24) how her father went to a breathing hole to assess her fate:

> Some time after I was born, there came a season of scarcity, and all were in want of food. My father had gone out to a hole in the ice, and here, it is said, he spoke as follows: 'If my daughter is to live, you will remain as you are. If my daughter is to die, you will close over, and keep away all the seal. Now give me this sign.' The hole in the ice did not change, there was no movement in the water, and my father began to catch seals, and he knew that I was not to die.

Aipilik Inuksuk recalled the conversion to Christianity of one of his relatives after an experience at a breathing hole.

> Ivalu was talking about Christianity. As he was hunting bearded seal, he was over there and he said to himself if there is a God, I am going

to catch that bearded seal. As he was still coming closer to that bearded seal, the bearded seal went through the hole into the water. He started throwing his mitts and all that stuff and he said to himself: I think there is God, I think there is Jesus. As he was saying that, the bearded seal came back up to the ice and he just shot it. He understood that there was God and Jesus now. I just heard of it. My father probably did *siqqitiq* after that. (quoted in Laugrand 2002: 448)

Thus, the decision to convert was made at the breathing hole. Then his father went through the ritual of *siqqitiq*, a ritual of eating the prohibited parts of sea mammals to effect the transition to the new religion. Benjamin Arreak related the conversion of his grandfather at the breathing hole:

My grandfather asked his wife: 'Why the others are gone, they were probably running out of food?' So he said: 'if I can catch a seal, I will go through *siqqitiq*'. As he went out hunting, he saw three human beings who then disappeared. Then he saw the seal. As he saw two black marks, he harpooned the seal and he got it. Then he went through *siqqitiq*. This happened before 1927, all my relatives were Christians at that time. (quoted in Laugrand 2002: 448)

We find more reports of conversions to Christianity at breathing holes. Pitseolak related,

Simigak was out hunting one night, sitting by the seal hole waiting for a seal to come up. All of a sudden he saw Jesus coming down to watch him. He thought it was Jesus but he was mistaken; it was Satan. When he returned home he told the people he had seen Jesus. Then Simigak said, 'We must get together, everybody must get together', and they all went to a place near Cape Dorset called Tooneen. There they built a giant igloo for a church. It had no roof so they could see the Heavens. (quoted in Pitseolak and Eber 1993: 40)

Thus, the aglu, the breathing hole, was a central point for the communication and interaction between human beings and non-human agents.

## Rules of Respect

Many ritual rules referred to the seal. We have organized them in four categories pertaining to (1) the *tarniq*, (2) work, (3) food and (4) birth and death. This distinction is somewhat artificial, as often several categories come into play; for example, Rasmussen (1929: 185) relates,

When a seal is caught in Tasiujaq, the great lake at Pingerqalik, near Iglulik, the same sacrifice must be made as in the case of a man who has lost his brother. The severity here is due to the fact that it is a fresh-water lake, and the seal is thus not in its proper element. Perhaps the soul of the seal regards the lake as a sanctuary, and this has therefore to be specially considered. The rule to be observed is that the hunter concerned must not sanäʃ·arpɔq: work with hunting implements, fashion hunting implements and the like. He must also cook all his food in a special pot until a year has elapsed from the time of the capture. There was once a man who caught a seal in this lake without observing the prescribed taboo. He fell down dead shortly after, without any previous illness.

There is also much local variation, as special rules applied to particular places. Here we will confine ourselves to some of the main patterns.

### The Tarniq

Women took care of seals inside the house, the body as well as the *tarniq*.[12] 'Men may cut up their catch on the ice-edge if food is to be eaten out there, but a seal brought home must not be cut up except by the women' (Rasmussen 1929: 185). Rasmussen (1929: 186) adds, 'Meat of seal or walrus must never be brought into a house immediately after the animal is killed, but not until the day after. Otherwise, the neighbourhood will suffer from a scarcity of game.' Once the seal was brought into the house, women had to be especially careful. 'When the seal has been cut up and lies in pieces on the floor, a lump of fresh snow is laid on the spot where its head was. The sea spirit does not like women to tread on the spot, where the seal's head has lain' (Rasmussen 1929: 185; see also Boas 1907: 489). According to Boas (1901: 147–48),

> When a seal is brought into the snow house, a piece of snow is dipped into the kettle and held over its mouth, allowing the melting snow to drip into it. This signifies giving a drink to the seal, and is intended to please Nuliayoq. After the seal has been cut up and put away, a handful of snow is put down in the place where the seal was carved. The snow is then stamped down in this place.

Rasmussen (1929: 185–86) reports, 'If a seal or bearded seal is captured, all the women of the village must touch the meat of it with their first fingers. Before the seal is cut up, the woman's husband must sprinkle water on its face.'

Particularly important was respect for the *tarniq* of the animal. It should accept the separation of its body and its ensuing fate. Boas (1907: 500; see also Rasmussen 1929: 185) reports,

A captured seal must be treated with great consideration. In addition to the customs described before, the harpoon must be taken into the hut and placed near the lamp. This is supposed to please the soul of the seal, which is believed to hover around the harpoon. If the harpoon should be left outside, the soul would become cold; and, if it should report this to Nuliayoq, she would be displeased. It is said that long ago, when a harpoon had been left outside, the seal's soul begged a woman to take it in. The woman did not comply with the request, and the seal's soul entered her, and later on was born as her child.

At dawn, the seal's *tarniq* was expected to move from the wife's lamp to the lamp of the *inua* of the sea. She would make sure that the *tarniq* would reincarnate and return to the same hunter.

When the hunters left the camp to move on to another area, a final ritual assured that the seals would always follow the hunter. Rasmussen (1929: 181) relates,

> Finally, before setting out, all gnawed skulls of seals caught from the site to be abandoned must be set out on the ice some little way from the house. The same is done with caribou recently shot. The heads must always face in the direction in which the party is setting out. The souls of the animals slain will then follow the same course, and good hunting will result.

### Work

Boas (1888: 595) relates that when the seal was brought into the house, all work had to be stopped until the seal was cut up.

> When a seal is brought into the hut the women must stop working until it is cut up. After the capture of a ground seal, walrus, or whale they must rest for three days. Not all kinds of work, however, are forbidden, for they are allowed to mend articles made of sealskin, but they must not make anything new. For instance, an old tent cover may be enlarged in order to build a larger hut, but it is not permitted to make a new one. Working on new deerskins is strictly forbidden.

Captain Comer reported for the west coast of Hudson Bay (quoted in Boas 1901: 147):

> No work must be done for three days after a bear or ground-seal has been killed. The women must not comb their hair. The bedding must not be disturbed until late on the day when a ground-seal has been caught.
> Frost must not be removed from the window until after the head of a newly-captured seal has been cooked. The family must not move camp until after the whole seal has been cooked.

Comer adds, 'No work on skins of seals caught in winter during the walrus-hunting season must be done until the seals have pups (in March)' (quoted in Boas 1901: 148). Furthermore, 'No work on seal-skins must be done during the caribou hunting season. Seal-meat and caribou-meat must not be eaten on the same day. Comer also states that no work on iron must be done until the seals have their pups. If work of this kind is unavoidable, it must be done by a woman' (Boas 1901: 149). Thus, as we saw with the caribou, the restrictions not only refer to the three days after the kill of the seal, but are also determined by the seasons.

Rasmussen describes some of the most important rules regarding work in the Iglulik area. When a whale, a bearded seal or a bear is killed, no man's work must be done for three days. It is also strictly forbidden during these three days to cut turf or gather fuel from the earth (Rasmussen 1929: 184). Rasmussen (1929: 184) provides a detailed list of rules that apply after the killing of a seal:

> When a seal is brought into a house no woman in the house may sew or do any other work until the seal has been cut up. This applies, however only to winter hunting, in snow huts, not in tents during summer.
>
> As long as a newly captured seal has not been cut up, the following things are taboo:
>
> Rime must not be wiped from the window pane.
>
> Skins from the sleeping place must not be shaken out over the floor.
>
> The mats of plaited willow twigs must not be straightened or rearranged.
>
> No oil must be spilled from the lamp.
>
> No work must be done with stone or iron.
>
> Women must not comb their hair, wash their faces or dry any footwear.
>
> When a bearded seal has been captured, no scraping of hair from skins must be done for three days.
>
> When seals are caught, it is not allowed to shift camp the next day, but not until two days after the first catch; this is because the seals would be offended if the hunters were not grateful for the catch they got.
>
> When a seal is brought into a snow hut, a lump of snow is dipped into the water bucket, and allowed to drip into the seal's mouth; it is the soul of the seal that drinks. In summer it does not require water.
>
> Persons hunting seal from a snow hut on sea ice may not work with soapstone.

Many rules that applied to the killing of a seal were also observed after a human being died. Thus, the deceased seal is respected as if it were a deceased human being.

### Food

Special measures had to be taken to keep the meat of the sea game and
the land game separated. According to Boas (1888: 595),

> The laws prohibiting contact with deer and sea animals at the same time
> are very strict. It is not permitted that both sorts of meat lie on the floor
> of the hut or behind the lamps at the same time. If a man who has eaten
> venison in the morning happens to enter a hut in which seal meat is
> being cooked he is allowed to eat venison on the bed, but it must be
> wrapped up before being carried into the hut and he must take care to
> keep clear of the floor. Before changing from one food to the other the
> Eskimo must wash themselves.

Sometimes, however, different kinds of sea game such as seal and
walrus also had to be kept separated. Boas (1901: 122–24) reports,

> The natives always change their clothing or strip naked before eating
> seal during the walrus season. Among the Nugumiut of Frobisher Bay,
> seal may be eaten during the walrus-hunting season on the same day
> with walrus-meat only after one has changed one's clothing. Salmon may
> not be eaten on the same day as walrus is eaten.
>
> Seal, caribou, and salmon may be eaten on the same day. Walrus and
> caribou may be eaten on the same day. A person who eats walrus and
> caribou on the same day is called 'nokoeyewyourlow'.
>
> If a person has been eating or hunting walrus, he must change his
> clothing before eating seal and before going caribou hunting, else these
> transgressions will become fastened to the walrus's soul. When the cari-
> bou-hunting season begins, the winter clothing and winter tents are bur-
> ied under stones, and new clothing is put on, and new tents are made.
> The old ones have become 'shongeyew', that is, tabooed. Caribou meat
> and salmon and walrus-meat must not be put into the same boat. When
> there is any caribou-meat or caribou antlers in a boat which goes wal-
> rus-hunting, the boat is liable to be broken by the walrus.

Change of clothing, therefore, helps to keep different types of meat
separated. However, Boas (1907: 489) reports, 'To cook caribou-meat
and seal-meat together in the same kettle creates friendship between
the souls of the caribou and the seal.' Land game and sea game should
be separated in eating, but not necessarily in cooking.

### Birth and Death

Boas (1901: 120; see also Boas 1901: 144) explained that sea mammals
can actually see the transgressions of human beings.

The souls of the sea-animals are endowed with greater powers than those of ordinary beings. They can see the effect of the contact with a corpse, which causes objects touched by it to appear dark in color; and they can see the effect of flowing human blood from which a vapor arises that surrounds the bleeding person and is communicated to every one and everything that comes in contact with such a person. The vapor and the dark color of death are exceedingly unpleasant to the souls of sea-animals that will not come near a hunter thus affected. The hunter must therefore avoid contact with people who have touched a body, or with those who are bleeding, more particularly with menstruating women or with those who have recently given birth. The hands of menstruating women appear red to sea-animals. If any one who has touched a body or who is bleeding should allow others to come into contact with him, he would cause them to be distasteful to seals, and therefore to Sedna as well. For this reason custom demands that every person must at once announce if he has touched a body, and that women must make known when they have had a miscarriage. If they do not do so they will bring ill luck to all the hunters.

These rules concern the relationship between the hunter and his wife and specify when contact has to be avoided. They also affect the consumption of seal meat. Boas (1901: 125) reports,

A woman who has a new-born child, and who has not quite recovered, must eat only of seals caught by her husband, by a boy, or by an aged man; else the vapor arising from her body would become attached to the souls of other seals, which would take the transgression down to Sedna, thus making her hands sore.

The vapour is usually thought to attach itself to the hair of the sea woman, who would then keep the seals with her. Then the *angakkuq* would have to descend to the abode of the sea woman and clean and comb her hair so she would set the seals free again.

Rasmussen (1929: 174) also specifies that the mother in the *kinirvik* should only eat seals caught by her husband. He also adds a few more rules: 'Women in the kinErvik may not eat the meat of animals killed suddenly; seals for their eating must after being wounded have life enough left to come up at least once to the surface and breathe, i.e. they must not eat sa·muŋa·rtɔq or one that dies immediately after sinking. The mother should not eat raw meat for a year after the birth' (Rasmussen 1929: 175). It is unclear whether the lack of vitality in a seal that dies immediately after being wounded is supposed to affect the mother or the unborn baby. Boas (1888: 611) relates that after the death of an infant, 'For a whole year, when outside the hut, the mother must have her head covered with a cap, or at least with a piece of skin. If a ground seal is caught she must throw away the old cap and have a new one made.'

According to Captain Comer (quoted in Boas 1901: 147–49), on the west coast of Hudson Bay women who have lost a relative must not work on fresh skins, although work on dry skins is permitted. They must not cut the hair off of sealskins, except from seals caught before the ice formed in the fall. They must not mention the names of any animals.[13] Rasmussen (1929: 200) relates, 'If there is seal meat in a house of death, the meat may be eaten, but the skins of these seals must not be used, dried, or in any way made into clothing.' Thus, death appears to affect the use of the skins more than the consumption of the meat, whereas in the rules pertaining to birth there is more emphasis on the avoidance of raw seal meat by the young mother.

In the South Baffin area we find similar rules. Boas (1900: 628) relates, 'All the clothing of a dead person, more particularly the tent in which he died, must be discarded; for if a hunter should wear clothing made of skins that had been in contact with the deceased, these would appear dark and the seal would avoid him.'

After a death, the resumption of hunting is a gradual process. Boas (1907: 487) reports,

> After the fourth night after death, the relatives of a deceased person may go sealing. If one of them succeeds in killing a seal, he must not cut it, but must take it home whole. There he must cut it without witnesses being present. The entrails must be thrown into the sea. The relatives of the deceased must not eat meat of the first sea-mammal killed after the death has occurred.

An analogy between a human being and a seal is suggested by the rules applying to a widower. According to Rasmussen (1929: 201),

> The first time a man who has lost his wife goes out hunting and gets a seal, he must nacevoq it for three days, that is to say, he must observe a kind of taboo, as he is considered unclean in relation to game; in cutting up the carcase, he takes the meat, but leaves the bones whole without cutting them out (tanErlugo); entrails, skin and blubber are likewise left untouched. It is this to which he must pay sacred attention for three days, wrapping the skin and blubber round the skeleton, after which it is placed out on the ice, as a sacrifice to the soul of his dead wife. In the case of the two next seals he catches, he is not required to nacevoq, but they must be cut up in the same fashion, skin, blubber and bones being laid out on the ice, care being taken also to see that the backbone is not

broken. No stranger may eat of the meat of these three seals, only the man himself. Not until the fourth capture is normal procedure resumed, and only then is the death taboo removed from the seals he gets.

The first bearded seal he catches must be dealt with in a similar manner. In cutting it up, care must be taken not to break the spine; the meat is cut away from the bones, and skin and blubber flayed off, only the skeleton is sunk. Here also the catch is subject to some taboo; the meat may be eaten by others, but only by men, and in their own house, and no portion of blubber or skin may be given away; the hair must not be removed from the skin, but if the hide is required for thongs or sole leather, it must be left until the hair rots off (utiq). This applies only to his first bearded seal.

After the killing of his first seal after the death of his wife, the widower observes *nasivuq* for three days.[14] Then he places the remains of the seal 'as a sacrifice to the soul of his dead wife'. If his wife had still been alive, the hunter would have brought it to the house and given it to his wife, who would have taken care of the butchering of the seal. The ritual acknowledges the connection between the deceased wife and the seal, but also serves to disconnect the relation so the husband can resume his normal life as a hunter.

## Sharing of the Seal

Once a seal was killed, the liver was shared by the hunters, a practice that can still be observed today, though some Inuit now also share the heart. This is consistent with the *siqqitiq* ritual that marked the transition to Christianity.[15]

With respect to the liver, Rasmussen (1931: 159) reported,

Inutuk and I had just decided to abandon the hunt at this hole and to try to find another one, when we caught sight of a man who had got his harpoon firmly into a seal. As soon as the happy hunter had got his catch hauled up on to the ice we ran over to him for the purpose of partaking of the feast, which always assumes the character of a ceremony on account of the gravity with which it is eaten. All knelt down, the man who had made the catch on the right side, the others on the left side of the seal. The hunter cut a tiny hole in the belly, through which he took the liver and a piece of blubber. This done, the hole was closed up again with wound pins so that no blood would run out and go to waste. The liver and blubber were cut up into small squares and eaten in the same kneeling position. Whenever I took part in one of these meals I felt something fine and affecting in the manner in which they knelt to 'the daily meat'.

Tungilik from Naujaat (quoted in Oosten and Laugrand 1999b: 166) related,

> Once you had harpooned the seal and pulled up on the ice, all the other hunters would come over to the person who had pulled up a seal. When I pulled up a seal, it would be cut up. The liver would be removed. The blubber and the kidneys would be removed. These would be put on the ground. We never cut off a piece ourselves. They would be cut into small pieces by one person. The liver and the kidneys, the blubber and the spleen would all be cut into tiny pieces. We would have a *kapurauti*.[16] Those that did not want to use the *kapurauti* would use their fingers. Every time that a seal was caught, we would all eat like this. Even when it was deep winter and when things would freeze right away, somebody would take a piece of ice. The piece of ice would be put into the sled and it would stick there and it wasn't going to come off. And there was a slit placed where they went after the liver, and this stayed there until it had thawed out enough to come off. It would only be removed when we got home. That's what we used to do. We would eat on the ice like this and we would bring seal meat home like this. When it got warmer, there would be a *tuputaq* made of polar bear shin. It was about four or five inches long and you would use it to close the slit. You didn't want the insides or the blood to come out.

The liver is closely associated with the *tarniq* of the animal and therefore its ability to reincarnate again. The blood on the harpoon head is not removed, and the wife of the hunter will take care of it so the *tarniq* can move on. Eating the liver marks the special relationship between the hunters and the prey at the place of the kill.

In the sharing of the liver the unity of the hunters is ritually shaped through the consumption of a part of the animal closely associated with the *tarniq*. Consumption of the most dangerous part of the animal may make it accessible to the community at large. Potential violence between hunters and game as well as between hunters themselves is controlled by and subordinated to the ritual itself. Hunting is governed by positive prescriptions from the beginning to the end, consistently structuring contexts of potential violent disorder into ordered social relationships.

Boas (1888: 582) relates, 'When the seal is brought to the huts everybody is entitled to a share of the meat and blubber, which is distributed by the hunter himself or carried to the individual huts by his wife. This custom is only practiced when food is scarce. In time of plenty only the housemates receive a share of the animal.' Elsewhere he adds,

> While it is customary for a successful hunter to invite all the men of the village to eat of the seal that he has caught, they must not take any of the

seal-meat out of the hut, because it might come in contact with persons who are under taboo, and thus the hunter might incur the displeasure of the seal and of Sedna. This is particularly strictly forbidden in the case of the first seal of the season. (Boas 1901: 125–26)

The first seal of the season as well as the first seal caught by a boy are shared as well, but in different ways. Boas (1901 489) relates, 'The first seal caught at a breathing-hole in the fall is divided among the hunters, except its skin. The first seal caught by a boy at the breathing-hole is divided among the hunters, including the skin.'
Michel Kanajuq from Qamanittuaq reports,

> If a person caught a seal, then he would be allowed to take only the head. The rest of the seal was to be shared by others. That is why people who went seal hunting did not really want to be the one to shoot the seal, because the person who caught the seal was left only with the head. The rest of the camp would take the rest of it. When there were many men there with the person who caught it, and they gathered around, one man would cut the seal on the back or on the flippers, or in the middle part, and the men knew how it would be distributed without anyone saying anything. They would know who it belonged to. They respected that. That is how they hunted seals. (quoted in Laugrand and Oosten 2009: 80)

In 1956 Van de Velde published a study on the sharing of seals caught in *mauliqpuq* hunting among the Nattilingmiut. The hunters addressed each other with the name of the particular part of meat they were entitled to when the meat was shared. A hunter, A, who received a shoulder from another hunter, B, if he caught a seal, would call him his *aksatkoliga*, 'my shoulder'. Hunter B would also receive a shoulder if hunter A was successful, so the address, *aksatkoliga*, was reciprocal. Van de Velde provides fourteen reciprocal terms referring to the different parts of a seal: *niakroga*, my head, *tunnerdjuga*, my kidney, *sennerara*, my side, and so forth. The partnerships between the hunters were therefore organized in terms of the parts of the body of the seal. The body of the seal thus encompassed the system of social relationships organizing *mauliqpuq* hunting. The partners were usually selected by parents for their children. If one of the partners died, a new partner might be selected, such as brother of the deceased or a namesake. The system also applied to the sharing of the blubber of the seal. Thus, part of the blubber of the belly went to the *okpat*, the one entitled to the rump of the animal, another part of the blubber went to the *niakrok*, and so forth. Thus, the system did not just connect two partners in a binary relationship, but involved all the partners in the sharing of meat as well as blubber. Even the dog of the owner received part of the blubber and thus participated in the system. The seal was divided in the igloo of the one who had killed the seal. The women of the seal partners came in to cut the part of the meat and the blubber they were entitled to. First the skin was removed; then the blubber and finally the meat was divided. Van de Velde describes the sequence of the various parts that were taken. All the people in the camp, even if they were not seal partners, could fetch some of the blubber (Van de Velde 1956: 5–14). This example shows clearly how the social relationships were shaped through the body of the seal, which had made itself an object of sharing by allowing itself to be killed by the hunters. In most camps, however, the rules were less strict than those described by Van de Velde.

Imaruittuq from Iglulik (quoted in Oosten et al. 1999: 134) related, 'Bearded seal, walrus, and polar bear had an order for distribution. For ring seal, you did not have that system. And again, don't forget that each camp had a different method of distribution.' And Nutaraaluk from Iqaluit observed (quoted in Oosten et al. 1999: 135), 'Around the Kinngait area where I was born, they didn't really distribute ring seal meat except for those caught by harpoon in the winter time. That's when they used to distribute the meat. Around the Kinngait area we used to get a lot of meat so we had plenty of meat for the dogs.'

The customs varied locally, but seal meat was always shared in times of need. Inuit are still very much aware of the role of the seal in constituting and preserving social relationships.

## Reincarnation and Transformation

When seals were killed by the Inuit, their *tarniit* were supposed to return to the sea woman, who would reincarnate them. Rasmussen (1931: 217) collected a version of the famous story of 'ᴀrnäktᴀrtɔq: The Soul That Let Itself Be Born Again in All the Animals of the Earth'. It relates that a great *angakkuq* let himself be reborn in all kinds of animals.

> Then he became a fjord seal, and he relates that the seals were always in the humour for playing. They are ever full of merry jests, and they leap about among the waves, frolicsome and agile, till the sea begins to move; their high spirits set the sea in motion.
>     There was not much difference between humans and seals, for the seals could suddenly turn themselves into human shape; when in that form they were skilful with the bow and amused themselves by setting up targets to shoot at, targets of snow, just as men make them.

An Iglulik version of the story provided by Rasmussen (1929: 59) relates,

> At one time it was a fjord seal. It lived down under the ice, and had its blowhole like the other seals. The seals were not afraid of death, and therefore had no fear of man, but would agree among themselves which hunter they would allow to capture them. And then they would lie there under the blowholes waiting till a little thing like a drop of water should fall down on them. It pricked their bodies, and often hurt.

The narrative compares the blow of the harpoon to a drop of water. The stories evoke an Alaskan variant of the narrative studied by Fienup-Riordan (1994, 2007) emphasizing the importance of the correct moral behaviour of the hunter.

Transformation into a sea mammal, however, was sometimes considered a punishment by the sea woman for a transgression (Rasmussen 1929: 100):

> Inugpasugjuk also stated that Nuliajuk, which was his name for the Sea Spirit, would sometimes carry off human beings, either because they had themselves committed some breach of taboo, or because some near relative of the victim had done so. She did not always punish the one actually guilty, and that was the cruel part of it; for when anyone had done anything wrong, there was no knowing which of his dear ones might suffer for it. Instances were known where Nuliajuk, having carried off a human being, did not kill, but turned the victim into some creature of the sea, so that the man or woman in question would have to live on as a seal or walrus or one of the animals that belonged to her.

In an account by the *angakkuq* Aava of the descent of the shaman to the home of the sea woman, a connection between seals and the deceased also comes to the fore. Rasmussen (1929: 125) relates,

> Meanwhile, the members of the household pass the time by singing spirit songs in chorus, and here it may happen that the clothes which the shaman has discarded come alive and fly about round the house, above the heads of the singers, who are sitting with closed eyes. And one may hear deep sighs and the breathing of persons long since dead; these are the souls of the shaman's namesakes, who have come to help. But as soon as one calls them by name, the sighs cease, and all is silent in the house until another dead person begins to sigh. In the darkened house one hears only sighing and groaning from the dead who lived many generations earlier. This sighing and puffing sounds as if the spirits were down under water, in the sea, as marine animals, and in between all the noises one hears the blowing and splashing of creatures coming up to breathe.

The anonymous dead appear as sea mammals in the séance and are released by the participants in the séance, who name them. Thus, the boundary between human beings and animals is preserved by the knowledge and use of the names of the deceased.

Inversely, seals might adopt a human appearance, a theme preserved in a story recorded by Lisa Koperqualuk from Qupirrualuk, originally from Puvirnituq. A hunter saw a house and a human being standing next to it.

> As he gets closer and closer he notices that the human has very short legs and arms. And as he approaches closer, there it is standing in front of the entrance of the shelter. At once he realizes that it is a seal turned into a human, and the *inuruursimajuq* speaks to him, 'Come inside, for there is a birth taking place and help is needed.' The hunter only glances very quickly and is unable to look at the *inuruursimajuq* out of fear, who repeats his request for him to come inside so as to help the woman giving birth inside, and gestures for him to enter. But the hunter ignores him and passes by. As the hunter keeps walking and does not even look behind him toward the *inuruursimajuq*, the *inuruursimajuq* shouts after him, 'From this day forward you may never catch seals again!' The hunter never caught another seal in his life. (Koperqualuk 2011)

Some seals had to be left alone, notably *silaat*, white seals. According to Boas (1888: 640), white seals, like white caribou, came from earth eggs: 'It is said that albinos of seals and deer spring from an egg of about half a foot in length, which forms itself in the earth. The seal digs an underground passage to the sea, the deer a similar one to a distant part of the country, and there they rise. The albinos are said to be very quick.'[17] Today, Inuit still acknowledge the existence of these beings. Kappianaq (IE 359) related,

> There are albino bearded seals. It is said that if you saw one you should not hunt them down. They are known as *silaat*, their hair is all white. At their back is a diamond shaped dark skin part.... It is also said that if you catch it your life might be cut short. This was what was said by the people before us. We were discouraged from hunting those types of bearded seals. It is said that this type of bearded seal is huge, it might be about the size of a beluga whale because it is a *silaat*.[18]

The semantics of the seal are quite complex. Hunters always had to take care when they encountered a seal, and they needed to be able to distinguish between seals that could be killed and eaten and non-human beings that were not really ordinary seals.

## *Tuutaliit*

A special category of non-human beings are the *tutaliit*. According to Rasmussen (1931: 247),

> The totalet, people say, are some spirits that resemble both humans and seals. In fact people call them the seal-men. Where they come from nobody knows, but some people believe that their first father was the totalik who avenged his father's death. In the story of Kivioq it is related how the mother drew the skin of a newly-born seal cub over her own newly-born child and taught it to swim. Afterwards, when the boy grew up, he became just as clever at living in the sea as a seal, and in that manner he enticed all the murderers in their kayaks out to sea so that they were lost in a storm. It is thought that this totalik was the first seal-man. (see also Rasmussen 1931: 365–66)

The *tuutaliit* are thought to be great seal hunters. Nakasuk (quoted in Rasmussen 1931: 248–49) related,

> Once upon a time some totalet were out hunting at the breathing holes. There a seal escaped, and one of them thought the best thing to do was to go down into the sea through the breathing hole to look for it. And he did so. He let himself slide down into the sea and, when he had caught the seal, he shouted up through the breathing hole that he had made his catch. The others peeped down and, true enough, found him stuck fast in the opening of the hole together with the seal he had caught.
> No hunting is impossible to people who can catch seals in that way.

The *tuutaliit*, therefore, have features of human beings as well as seals. They appear to constitute an intermediate category between humans and seals. On this level, transformation of human beings into seals and vice versa seems possible. *Tuutaliit* eat seals, but never human beings.

Kappianaq (IE 100) related that his mother used to tell him about a powerful creature in the waters that could do anything. It had a fluke like a whale and the upper body of a human being with a head. It could penetrate the earth and was known as a *tuutalik*. He heard that one was caught around Kinngait, and people buried it like a human being because people feared that it might take revenge. He related,

> We call them *tuutaliit*. I have never experienced one or seen one. I have heard that the top part of their bodies has a human form, and the bottom part is the flipper of a whale.... When they come up, they use their right hand, and when they submerge they use their left hand. They have the proportions of a human. My younger brother saw one when he was

young. What he saw must have been an adult, because it was quite large.
... I think it was a big male. The chest was quite wide. Those who have
seen one say their flesh is quite dark. They have hair similar to a seal because they are sea mammals. ... I have heard that when a *taliillajuuq* was
trying to help a person, it could come up on land. If an *angakkuq* calls on
a *taliillajuuq*, it is able to come right away through the earth. ...

My grandfather Tulugaarjuk had a *taliillajuuq*, a *tuutalik*, as a *tuurngaq*. It helped him physically. If my grandfather was in need of his helper,
the moment he thought of it, it would appear right away. (quoted in
Oosten and Laugrand 2001: 76–77)

Sometimes the categories of *tuutaliit* and *talliilaajut*, beings who are
usually considered to have the upper parts of a human being and the
lower parts of a fish, merge.[19] Kappianaq described *tuutaliit* as beings
with flukes but an upper body like a human being. He relates that they
would come to your help immediately if you appealed to them:

This practice is known as *qingnaaq*, this is to cry out in desperation just
out the empty space. You would tilt your head up and cry out numerous
times, this is known as *qingnaaq*. It is said that a *tuutalik* will immediately, right at the instance will come to your aid. This may be an animal,
but it can come at an instance, even if it does not surface it can assist the
person to get back on the land from the water. It is said that they have a
soft touch. ... When it dives in, it will raise its arms just to let you know
what it is, and, usually the left arm. That is to show the person that it is
that thing, so upon diving it will raise its right arm. ... It is said that if it
was a fully grown animal it would be huge, possibly about the same size
as a beluga whale. The reason why they are referred to as *taliillajuuq* is
because it tends to raise its arm (*taliq*). (Kappianaq, IE 359)

Peck (quoted in Laugrand et al. 2006: 422) describes a *tuutalik* (no.
13) in his list of helping spirits: 'Like a human being but naked. One
who hands over something like a line. It is said that the above spirit
used to come up to the kiyaker and say, I am totalik, *aksheganga*, stab
me and then disappear quickly below.' Thus, in this instance the *tuutalik* tricks the hunter into believing that he is dealing with prey.

## Discussion

In the past, seals were hunted in open water, on the ice edge and at
breathing holes. Their meat was thought to be highly nutritious. Tipuula
Qaapik Atagutsiaq, a healer from Arctic Bay, stated, 'Seal oil is still
used today. Amongst all the animals, the seal is the most useful. ... It is
the most abundant. It is easier to catch than many other animals. Its

blubber is used for food, and for heat. Seal oil is used to waterproof *kamiik* and of course for healing' (quoted in Therrien and Laugrand 2001: 51).[20] Borré (1994) showed how Inuit appreciate the healing properties of seal blood, which warms up the body of a person and strengthens his identity. Sealskins were used for many purposes: clothing, kayaks, tents and so forth. Almost every part of the seal was used. In winter, the seal was often the main source of survival. The *aglu*, the breathing hole, where the seals were caught, acquired great symbolic value. Here the killing of the seal was modelled on sexual intercourse. It was the place where the decision to convert to Christianity could be made. It was a point of transition between different worlds, separating the seals and the *tuutaliit* from human beings. Here the liver of the seal, associated with the *tarniq,* was eaten by the hunters as soon as the seal was caught. The *tarniq* would enter the harpoon point and would then descend to the sea woman. The symbolism of the *aglu* was also central to the winter feast, where it was represented by a coiled rope that Sedna was supposed to ascend, and her harpooning was modelled on that of a seal.

The opening of the winter season, focusing on *mauliqpuq* hunting and seals as the main source of food, required complex rituals. The winter feasts prepared the land and restored relationships with the deceased. As in the caribou feasts, various contests took place, and a general exchange of women was a central feature of the feasts. The sexual intercourse between the pairs formed by the messengers of Sedna or other transcendental agents prefigured the hunt. The killing of the game evoked the sexual intercourse between human beings, as came to the fore in the account of Tungilik.

Seals originated from the fingers of a woman who did not want to marry a human husband and took animal husbands instead. She became the sea woman. Like the seals, she lives in the sea, and when people do not respect the seals or other sea mammals, she will keep the seals with her. Seals should not be brought into contact with women who are menstruating or have just delivered a child, deceased people, or caribou. Whereas caribou are always slaughtered outside the house by men, seals are always butchered inside the house by women. Moreover, women have to take care of the *tarniq* of the seal, which after the kill still resides in the harpoon head, and keep it close to their lamp. Doing so would please the seal's *tarniq,* and the sea woman would then ensure that the seal was reincarnated and allowed itself to be hunted again by the same hunter.[21] Therefore, especially women have to be very careful with seals. When women were menstruating or had just delivered a child, they should avoid contact with the game and avoid eating fresh meat. Similar rules applied to people who had been in contact with death, suggesting that a separation of the cycles of life and death of human beings and the cycles of life and death of animals was crucial to the maintenance of the flow of life. Sexual intercourse with animals, any form of bestiality (*sunarlluk*), was strictly prohibited.

Just as the relations between caribou and human beings are mediated by the *ijirait*, the relations between seals and human beings are mediated by the *tuutaliit*. In both cases the non-human beings appear to have features of the prey, but at the same time they are hunters of that prey, encompassing the relation between the hunters and the prey. Thus, *ijirait* appear to be masters of the caribou and *tuutaliit* masters of the seals. But they constitute a contrast, as the *ijirait* are well dressed, whereas the *tuutaliit* are naked. They do not live on the land, like human beings, but in the water, a domain where human beings cannot survive. Distinctions between *tuutaliit* and other beings such as *talliillaajuut* are not always clear. We do not find the notion that the deceased join the *tuutaliit;* instead, *tuutaliit* appear to prevent this by saving people from drowning. The seals themselves can be associated with the deceased, as in the shamanic séance described above, in which seals appear to represent the anonymous deceased.

In the rules pertaining to the seal, the emphasis is on the killing of an individual seal, whereas in the case of the killing of caribou, little emphasis is placed on the individual animal. Thus, the two animals constituting the most important prey of the Inuit contrast in many respects.

Today, Inuit have to fight to preserve their seal hunting traditions. Animal activists often depict Inuit as 'natural ecologists' or as 'corrupted by modern civilization', such as the fur trade and the use of new technologies such as guns and snowmobiles (Wenzel 1991: 163, 175). Wenzel points out that 'the opening of markets for *natsiq* pelts provided Inuit with a culturally coherent means of retaining control over the local economies of their settlements'. In other words, seals allow Inuit to participate not only in what is called the 'traditional economy' but also in the cash economy. Today, Inuit are still fighting against deep ecology and its influence, especially in Europe, hoping to be fully recognized as hunters of the seal. Fynn Lynge (1992), a *kalaallisuk*, a Greenlander, argues that the so-called animal rights movement has put whales and seals above humans.[22] In November 2010, Nunavut's minister of environment blasted an American proposal to list bearded and ringed seals under America's Endangered Species Act, considering such a proposal a 'senseless', 'unwelcome and misguided initiative'.[23]

Complex systems of sharing often organize relations between the hunters in terms of the body of the seal, as shown for the Nattilingmiut in a paper by Van de Velde (1956) and for Clyde River by the *ningiqtuq* system, as described by Wenzel (1995). In 1998 four Inuit students presented a paper at the ninth Inuit conference in Copenhagen entitled 'Natsiq, the Seal; an Integral Part of Our Culture'. The students state in their paper: 'Our ancestors (*sivullit*) believed that the seal made itself available to the hunter so that he could catch it. From the time that the seal gave itself the hunter had an obligation. His obligation was to share the seal with the people of the camp. If he failed to honour his obligation, the seal would not give itself to the hunter again'. Thus, the notion that society is constituted by sharing is still very much alive. The same authors (Peter et al. 2002: 167) explain,

> With the advancement of modern technology and the media, our way of life and our dependency on the seal for our subsistence has come increasingly under scrutiny. Much has been said, and some have gone on to say, that because we do not hunt the seal in the traditional way, we are no longer true Inuit and do not solely rely on the seal for our subsistence. It is true that we could probably live in today's world without the seal, as long as we would have money to go to the local Northern store where we could buy many things, except for the seal and the caribou. The seal, however, provides us with more than just food and clothes. It provides us with our identity. It is through sharing and having a seal communion[24] that we regain our strength, physically and mentally.

## Notes

1. For an extensive discussion on the importance of sea mammals and seals in particular in Inuit ecology and economy, notably in Baffin Island, see Sabo and Sabo (1985) and Wenzel (1986, 1989, 1991, 1995).
2. Rasmussen (1931: 226) relates that there are some *angakkuit* 'who draw Nuliajuk [the sea woman] herself up to the surface of the land. They do it in this way: they make a hook fast to the end of a long seal thong and throw it out of the entrance passage; the spirits set the hook fast in her, and the shaman hauls her up into the passage. ... Only when she has promised the shaman to release all the seals into the sea again does he take her off the hook and allow her to go down into the depths again.'
3. According to Fienup-Riordan, the gift of fresh water to the recently killed seal by the Yup'ik produced the possibility of receiving that same seal in the future (see Fienup-Riordan 1990: 171; 1994: 49). Another interpretation would be to connect the gift of fresh water with the same gesture in the context of the *kangiliriyaraq*, the naming ritual feast, or the feast of the dead (see Fienup-Riordan 2000: 189), where this is done in order to recall the person. In the naming ritual, she describes how the person naming the child drops water at the four corners of the child's head to say that 'the one whose name the child was receiving had come'.

4. The topic of thirst also plays an important part in the myth of the sun and the moon. When the brother and sister arrive at the camp of the *kukilin-giattiat*, non-human beings with claws like seals, the brother asks his sister to fetch him some water from the *kukilingiattiat*. However, instead of giving her water they sexually assault her with their claws. Her brother then kills all of them. The *kukilingiattiat* seem to be associated with seals and the story suggests a reversal of roles, where human beings ask for water and a refusal results in the death of those who should have given.

5. Pisuk from Rankin Inlet observes that the caribou 'were also called *aqiggit*. They would say things like, "By such and such a lake", because all lakes have names, "there are some *aqiggit*", meaning there were caribou there' (quoted in Oosten and Laugrand 2002: 148).

6. In Inuit culture we find an elaborate discourse on bestiality as an act to be avoided at all costs (see Rasmussen 1931: 197).

7. 'People hunting caribou in kayaks on a river or lake must, while hunting, lay out a piece of sealskin under stone as a sacrifice to Tugtut Igfianut, the Mother of the Caribou' (Rasmussen 1929: 195).

8. Rasmussen (1929: 176) also describes this ritual of making the little boy go through the movements of an adult hunter: 'When a boy's limbs have been stretched, he is taken on the lap, set upon the apron (the piece of skin from the head of a seal which a woman after childbirth wears over her lap in order not to spill on her clothes), which is folded, and a piece of meat is then placed on the pugutaq, or meat tray; the meat fork is then placed in the child's hands, and the hands guided so that the child harpoons the meat; at the same time, motions must be made as if the child were rowing in a kayak: parting'uarlugo: he is made to go through the same movements as a man paddling in his kayak.'

9. This rule was already reported by Boas (1901: 160): 'Boys must not play cat's-cradle, because in later life their fingers might become entangled in the harpoon-line. They are allowed to play this game when they became adults. Two cases were told of hunters who lost their fingers, in which the cause was believed to be their having played cat's-cradle when young. Such youths are thought to be particularly liable to lose their fingers in hunting ground-seal.' Rasmussen (1929: 172) adds that offenders may get entangled in the harpoon line and be dragged out to the sea.

10. Innu hunters also used to sing to the seals. Among them, the seal is known for its healing powers and is said to be owned by a master that is half-human, half-seal (Clément 2012: 103).

11. See Rasmussen (1929: 82–83) for another version of this story.

12. Lea Arnaujaq, who lived in various areas west of Hudson Bay, reported that women were not supposed to step on the floor while their men were out seal hunting. They could work on the oil lamps by putting blubber on them with a curved piece of antler or bone (*Recollections of Inuit Elders* 1986: 12).

13. See also Rasmussen (1929: 200): 'Women whose relatives or nearest neighbours have died within the year must not prepare raw skins, but only work on dried ones. Nor may they mention the animals by name, but only refer to them in the shaman language.... If there is seal meat in a house of

death, the meat may be eaten, but the skins of these seals must not be used, dried, or in any way made into clothing.'

14. A similar tradition can be found among the Nattilingmiut. Rasmussen (1931: 265) reports, 'If there is a shortage of food at a village and a man has to go sealing while the death taboo is being held over his wife, the seal he catches must not be eaten until nagtenɛq is over. The first seal he gets after the end of nagtenɛq must lie a whole day without being touched. The same rules apply if it is a caribou that is killed under similar circumstances.'

15. Eating the seal heart is a recent practice. Thus, the governor general of Canada, Michelle Jean, participated in the eating of a seal heart to support Inuit hunters on 26 May 2009 (Panetta 2009).

16. An implement that can be used as a fork.

17. See also Boas (1907: 493): 'Albino caribou and seals are believed to originate from white eggs as large as those of geese. They are found in the ground, generally partly protruding. Other albino animals are also believed to originate from such eggs, which are called sila.'

18. See also Kappianaq (IE 097): 'It is said that when a bearded seal is albino you while be able to see a diamond-shaped mark on the back between the shoulders of the bearded seals. Should one come across this type of bearded seal, no matter how close it may get, especially when it appears as if it is not afraid and would splash dive, it is advised that this animal should be left alone. It is also said that in the event that one is caught, Sila can make her grieving known in a powerful way.'

19. *Tuutaliit* and *taliillajuut* are often represented by Inuit artists. See Laugrand and Oosten (2008).

20. Seal oil plays a key role in Inuit traditions, and its qualities are strongly emphasized in different contexts.

21. Fienup-Riordan (1994: 88) relates that among the Yup'ik the animals are treated as honoured guests. Among the Inuit, the seals appear much more to be treated as honoured deceased, as the rules that apply to them are quite similar to those pertaining to deceased human beings.

22. On the seal controversy, see Wenzel (1991).

23. See *Nunatsiaq News,* 9 December 2010.

24. On the role of the seal as a substitute for communion, see Borré (1994) and Kleivan (1978).

# CHAPTER 10

# The Whale, Representing the Whole

Whaling is an old tradition in Inuit culture.[1] Archaeological evidence shows that whaling already had an important place in Dorset and Thule culture. Large-scale Euro-American whaling in the eighteenth and nineteenth century was responsible for the decline of Inuit whaling in the Arctic seas. In the final stages of the heydays of whaling in the second half of the nineteenth century, whalers began to establish whaling stations and employ Inuit hunters to catch whales for them (see figure 10.1). This employment was profitable for both parties until whaling collapsed at the end of the nineteenth century.[2] The whalers brought many changes, introducing Western clothes, materials, music and Christianity. Nineteenth-century sources such as Warmow, Kumlien, Peck and Bilby point out that many old Inuit traditions such as the Sedna feast rapidly declined. Today, the number of rules and stories relating to whales is relatively small compared to those pertaining to animals such as caribou and seals, the most important prey in the twentieth century. Inuit still attach great importance to whaling, however, and now that whales are again numerous in Arctic waters, the revitalization of whaling has become an important issue in the revival of Inuit culture.

Inuit used whales for many purposes. In the past, whalebones were used for making houses, and many archaeological sites still contain well-preserved structures showing the importance of whalebones for large constructions.

Whale oil was used for the *qulliq*, the lamp of the house. Ilisapi Ootoova from Baffin Island related, 'When it was used for the lamp, the flame tended to be higher and it really heated up our dwelling. It really brightened it up. After we used up the whale oil, we would use seal oil. It would be a lot darker and the flame was really red. Our dwelling would not be as warm' (quoted in Therrien and Laugrand 2001: 12).

**Figure 10.1.** Whalers and a whale. *Source:* Anglican Church of Canada/General Synod Archives/Peck Papers, M56-1, series XXXIII, 4–6, 8–13.

To what extent whale oil had healing properties remains unclear. Kumlien (1879: 27) reports that in cases of scurvy Inuit would use the stomach of a freshly killed reindeer, with its vegetable contents. He adds that if the scurvy patient was very bad, and if a whale was available at such a time, 'the patient is sometimes bodily shoved into the carcass, or the lower extremities only are sunken into the flesh'. Ootoova did not recommend the use of whale oil, indicating that it is too strong for the human body: 'They tried not to use whale oil. We children did not know why but our mothers did. When a whale was freshly caught, it would be cut up and we would eat. If we got a cut while eating it, the cut tended to swell up and get itchy. I think that whale oil is quite strong so it was never used for earaches. We did not use it on our faces as it had a powerful stench' (quoted in Therrien and Laugrand 2001: 12).

Whales were used for a variety of other purposes. Whalebones and jawbones were also extensively used to make hunting tools, harpoons, knives, pots, containers, cups and pails, blades, and also tent poles, sled runners, kayak frames and toboggans (Boas 1888: 529–30; 1907: 474). Boas also (1888: 510–11) reports the use of whalebone to hunt wolves: 'Another method is to roll a strip of whalebone about two feet long, in a coil, which is tied up with sinews. At each end a small metal edge is attached to the whalebone. This strip, wrapped in a piece of blubber or meat, is gulped down by the hungry wolf. As it is digested the sinews are dissolved and the elastic strap is opened and tears the stomach of the animal.'

## The Significance of the Whale

Whale symbolism is extensively documented in the western Arctic. After the pioneering study of Margaret Lantis (1938), Froelich Rainey (1947) provided a rich and detailed ethnographical study of whaling in Tigara. These studies revealed the importance of the symbolic dimensions of the whaling complex in that area. In his study of whaling in Tikigaq, Tom Lowenstein (1993) concluded that the symbolic harpooning or stabbing of the whaling captain's wife[3] performed before the real hunt could be interpreted as an equivalence between the whale and the woman's body. Edith Turner (1990), who worked with the Inupiat of Point Hope and commented on Lowenstein, equates the whale not only with the woman but also with the shaman.[4] In an important study on the symbolism of the whale in the eastern Arctic, Bernard Saladin d'Anglure (1992, 1999) emphasized the phallic connotations of the whale, for instance in the story of the giant who took his penis for a whale. These discussions illustrate the complexity of whale symbolism, which cannot be reduced to one particular relationship.

Many studies of the whale explored its socio-economic aspects. Thus, several researchers studied the transformation of whaling practices with the coming of the Euro-American whalers (Ross 1975, 1977, 1984, 1985; Bockstoce 1986; Eber 1989; Stevenson 1997). Others focussed on the importance of whales as food and sustainable resources (Krupnik

1981; Caufield 1993, 1997; Marquardt and Caufield 1996; McDonald et al. 1997). In recent studies the values of respect and reciprocity at play in sharing the whale have been emphasized (Bodenhorn 1988, 1990, 2000) and have resulted in descriptions of whaling as a 'sacred' practice (Freeman et al. 1992, 1998; Freeman 2005: 67; McCarney 1995). Everywhere in the Arctic whaling activities give space to the expression of strong indigenous ethical views, suggesting that the capture of a whale is always connected to cosmological issues (Black 1987; Victor 1987a, 1987b; Saladin d'Anglure 1999: 116; Sakakibara 2009).

In this chapter, we will examine the beliefs and customs relating to whales and whale hunting in the eastern Arctic by relying largely on ethnographic data collected between 1880 and 1930, the period of classic ethnography extending from Boas until Rasmussen, as well as on ethnographic data available in various contemporary reports, notably documents released by Nunavut and federal institutions such as the Bowhead Report. We will first discuss the origin of whales, explore the connection between the whale and shamanism, and discuss contemporary whale hunting rules and practices. Finally, we will focus on the sharing practices connected to the whale hunt and show how the reintroduction of whale hunts can not only be seen as an empowerment of Inuit but also as a means of valorizing hunting and sharing practices as core elements of Inuit traditions.

## Recollections of Whaling in Nunavut

Mittimatalik, Pangniqtuuq and Wager Bay were well-known centres of whaling in the Canadian Arctic. Boas (1888: 499–501) described the old whaling practice:

> Formerly whaling was one of the favorite hunts of the Central Eskimo and in some places it is even continued to this day…. The whale is pursued by a great number of kayaks and every boatman endeavors to drive his harpoon into the animal, which, by the loss of blood and the resistance of the niutang and floats, is tired out and killed with lances. More frequently it is pursued in skin boats, which for the purpose are propelled by means of paddles (angun). In this case the crew consists entirely of men, although on other occasions the rowing falls to the women's share; a skillful boatman steers the boat and the harpooner stands in the bow watching his opportunity to strike the whale.

Today elders recall how their ancestors used to hunt whales, but the ritual complex associated with it has largely faded from memory.

In the 1960s Father Mary-Rousselière interviewed several elders in Mittimatalik who still recalled the time when whaling was important in that area. Qiliqti (quoted in Laugrand and Oosten 2009: 253–54) from Mittimatalik recalled,

> They used to hunt bowhead whales a long time ago. They used to get bowhead whales in just *qajait*. There would be numerous *qajait* out there and when someone would harpoon one, they would kill it only using their paddles. This is what I have heard. I have heard more than one elder talking about killing bowhead whales. A *qajaq* would be on either side of the bowhead. They would attack the bowhead from both sides. Also, a person in just one *qajaq* would be able to kill it and tow it to land. I would also hear they would attach floats to it. Sometimes the float would only be a small seal. It wouldn't be very large. Normally there would be five floats attached to one bowhead whale.... They say there were a lot of bowhead whales back in the days when they just used *qajait*. They also say that the wife of the man who killed the bowhead had to remain in bed while the whale was being butchered.

Many South Baffin elders recalled the happiness of the people when a whale was caught. Etuangat from Pangniqtuuq related how he used to hunt for the whalers: 'Everything was well organized. The qallunaat (white people) would take the skins and the blubber and the meat would be given to the women for food' (*Recollections of Inuit Elders* 1986: 32). Markosie Pisualak from Pangniqtuuq related how they used to work for the whalers, and gives vivid accounts of the catch of a sperm whale (*Stories from Pangnirtung* 1976: 18–25). He recalled the reactions of the people when a whale was caught: 'There were always men waiting for us on land. When they saw that we pulled a whale behind us, they were so happy that they fired guns into the air and came over to help pull it in. As soon as we landed the whale we started to work on it. The women helped with the work. They were happy because it was fun' (*Stories from Pangnirtung* 1976: 22–24). Even though Inuit enjoyed the hunt, Pitsualak thought they did not get a fair reward. 'We didn't get any money even though we worked so hard on the whales. We got what the whalers gave us. The person who had shot the whale would get a boat and a rifle. We, the whalers, didn't get what we deserved to get. Now that I think about it, we were all fooled. For working so hard we got a new pair of pants, shirt, smoking pipe, and tobacco' (*Stories from Pangnirtung* 1976: 24–25).

In the 1990s the Nunavut Wildlife Management Board (NWMB) carried out an Inuit knowledge study of the bowhead that was published in 2000 (Hay et al. 2000, referred to as the Bowhead Report). In the report Joanasie Kakka recalled, 'When it was time to harpoon the whale, it was believed that the bowhead could be very selective regarding the hunter who was chosen. The bowheads would manifest their preferences regarding the hunter designated to harpoon them. Their wishes had to be respected' (Hay et al. 2000: 59).

Today, whales are not only hunted less; according to elders, they also come less to the coast. In the 1920s Rasmussen already recorded a tradition among the Aivilingmiut explaining that whales do not come as close to the coast as they used to because a whale had been harpooned by a woman (Rasmussen 1929: 187). Women should leave the harpooning to their husbands. Piugaattuq from Iglulik related that whales became more difficult to hunt after a hunter was pushed into the water and kept there until he died while they were cutting up a bowhead whale (Hay et al. 2000: 61).[5]

Nutaraq from Mittimatalik explained the scarcity of whales in terms of the noise people make today with snowmobiles:

> Nowadays … the floe edge is never without people anymore. When people started hunting there constantly, the whales stopped going under the ice. It is much later in the spring now before they make it to the cracks in the ice. It is because there are so many people down to the floe edge now that it takes the whales longer to come towards land.[6] (quoted in Oosten and Laugrand 2001: 134)

Elders are aware that much knowledge has been lost. In the Bowhead Report, Jaco Evic from Pangniqtuuq observed, 'It is unfortunate that this workshop is only starting now … [because] Inuit who are knowledgeable in whaling are no longer with us – they could have relayed information on what is needed and what needs to be done when actually harvesting a bowhead whale' (Hay et al. 2000: 58).

The Bowhead Report provides much information on whaling and related rules and beliefs. Philip Kripanik explained that hunters should never approach or attempt to hunt a bowhead asleep at the surface because it could be very dangerous (Hay et al. 2000: 45). Pisuk explained that great care had to be taken when a whale has a calf:

> When they (hunters) accidentally killed a calf, when the mother is feeding off somewhere else, the mother would keep coming back to the same location the next year, at the date when the young was killed; the Inuit said that it was mourning its young, with cries, which the Inuit would be able to hear from under water very loud, that is what I heard, and my late uncle confirmed that; he said that it is very sad to watch them mourning; and the traditional law was that you were not supposed to kill the calves of the bowhead whale. (Hay et al. 2000: 46)[7]

Martha Kutiutikku from Pelly Bay explained, '[If her calf is killed] the mother will always know what area and what kayak has killed the calf. I think it is because they have souls, too, that they would know which kayak had killed their calf' (Hay et al. 2000: 46). Thus, the elders view whales as sentient beings endowed with a conscience and awareness whose feelings have to be respected. Sometimes whales would punish wrong behaviour. Pisuk from Rankin Inlet relates how the *angakkuq* Paumiarjuk, who killed a lot of people, was disciplined: 'He was out bowhead whale hunting when his penis was castrated by a bowhead whale and he became a female. He was such a powerful *angakkuq* that he was even able to give birth' (quoted in Kolb and Law 2001: 38). The story confirms the close association between the penis and the whale established by Saladin d'Anglure (1999).

Today, elders still remember some of the rules that pertained to whales. Jaikku Pitsiulaq stated, 'Boys would be told to carry babies on their backs so they could catch a whale easily when they became older. Preparing boys to become whale hunters is an old tradition' (Therrien and Laugrand 2001: 177). Boas (1901: 363) related, 'The carving of a whale is put into the mouth of a new-born male infant in order to make him a good hunter.'

Good hunters used to transmit their ability to catch whales. Comer (1910: 89–90) gives the example of a whale hunter called Cumercowyer who could see the whale under water: 'When he died he requested that his body should be placed on the ice so that later it would drop into the sea. At the same time he charged his people that when they went off on the ice or in their kayaks for whales, they must throw a piece of meat into the water and call on his spirit to aid them. He promised that he would hear their call and come to their assistance' (quoted in Hay et al. 2000: 45).

Pitsiulaq related, 'Men were advised not to wipe themselves with rocks after defecating. This was so their catches wouldn't sink under-water if the animal was too lean and didn't have enough fat to stay afloat' (quoted in Therrien and Laugrand 2001: 177). This advice may be related to a hunting technique described by Boas (1888: 501) of hunting whales in a shallow bay: 'If a shoal of them has entered such a bay, the Eskimo take to their boats and kayaks, and by throwing stones frighten them into the shallowest part, where they are easily harpooned.'[8]

Happiness or joy should not be expressed during the hunt until the whale is dead and landed; otherwise, the whale could be lost (Participant /ws, HB231; P. Kripanik/ws, HB243 in Hay et al. 2000: 59). Showing too much happiness before the whale is dead could result in a *pelurqtuuq* or *pilluktuk* (Participant/ws, HB221; A. Tagornak, HB178 in Hay et al. 2000: 59), 'a transformation of one species into another'. In the past Inuit believed that bowhead whales could sometimes turn into narwhals when they were harpooned (Hay et al. 2000: 59). Thus, joy and happiness should be shown after the catch was made and was also expressed in the scramble for the meat (*parlaniq*) and the feast that followed.

## The Origin of Whales

In the Canadian eastern Arctic, Inuit myths provide many details about the origin of whales. Like seals and bearded seals, whales were created out of the fingers of the sea woman. Whales, seals and bearded seals are therefore closely associated with the sea woman, who now lives on the bottom of the sea.[9]

In contrast to bowhead whales, the beluga and the narwhal were not considered to be under the sway of the sea woman. They did not originate from her fingers. The sharks were associated with Sedna, however, as they were thought to come from her urine pot.

The narwhal is considered a transformation of the mother of the moon spirit. He was a blind young man who was mistreated by his mother. After he regained his sight he decided to kill her. He and his sister went beluga hunting. Boas (1888: 626) relates,

When he went to hunt white whales he used to wind the harpoon line round his body and, taking a firm footing, hold the animal until it was dead. Sometimes his sister accompanied him and helped him to hold the line.

One day he told his mother to go with him and hold his line. When they came to the beach he tied the rope round her body and asked her to keep a firm footing. She was rather anxious, as she had never done this before, and told him to harpoon a small dolphin, else she might not be able to resist the strong pull. After a short time a young animal came up to breathe and the mother shouted, 'Kill it, I can hold it'; but the boy answered, 'No, it is too large.' Again a small dolphin came near and the mother shouted to him to spear it; but he said, 'No, it is too large.' At last a huge animal rose quite near. Immediately he threw his harpoon, taking care not to kill it, and tossing his mother forward into the water cried out, 'That is because you maltreated me; that is because you abused me.'

The white whale dragged the mother into the sea, and whenever she rose to the surface she cried, 'Louk! Louk!' and gradually she became transformed into a narwhal.

*Aarluk*, the killer whale or orca, also constitutes a separate category, but it is considered a predator. Whereas the shark is connected to the raven, the killer whale is connected to the wolf. Papatsie from Pangniqtuuq explained, 'Ravens go following polar bears. If a polar bear catches a seal, they will leave something behind. The same happens with sharks; they follow some predators that leave something behind. They are ravens of the sea and the killer whales are the wolves of the sea' (quoted in Idrobo 2008: 52). Today, it is interesting to observe that Inuit hunters do not bother much about sharks and ravens but express concern about wolves and killer whales as competing predators. Thus, Inuit hunters worry about the fact that killer whales are now more common in Arctic waters, as if they have expanded their range to the north and west of Baffin Island. Well-known for their cunning hunting practices and hearty appetites, killer whales are feared because they may ravage seal, beluga, bowhead and narwhal populations (George 2009c).[10]

Ethnographic sources testify to the power of whales to retaliate. A story collected by Dorothy Eber (1989: 125–26; see also 1989: 36–37) from John Atuat illustrates how the sea woman could retaliate through sea animals, and particularly through whales, if one did not follow the rules, especially those related to human bones. According to Atuat, *qallunaat* whalers were no exception. Thus, Captain George Cleveland, known as Suquortaronik, was once severely punished for removing and collecting Inuit skulls from different places. Atuat recalls,

> His Inuit helpers knew the boat was carrying a load of Inuit skulls, but they didn't know why, or what the skulls were to be used for. Probably he just had them along and meant to put them away with his collection when he got to the shore. But he had an accident. While he was following the whale, his boat got hit by the whale's tail and turned over. He had been warned by Uvinik and Tugaak, expert whalers and members of his whaling crew. He really had no choice but to follow their advice because they knew more about whaling than he did. The whale was harpooned and wounded and surfacing here and there. 'You better stay away from that whale', one of them said. 'He is going to whip you with the tail or with the flipper when he surfaces and the boat is going to capsize.' But Suquortaronik paid no attention and that is exactly what happened. He didn't drown because Uvinik and Tugaak were nearby in their boat to rescue him. But he lost all his bones.

In another story collected by Boas (1907: 478), the sea woman punished the famous whaling captain Comer by delaying the recovery of a whale:

One day a large whale to which we were fast went under a body of ice; and after it had taken five hundred fathoms of line, we had to let go, and lost the whale. That night, after we had gone ashore, my natives wanted to go to the tent of a woman who was reputed to be a great angakok. The woman, in her trance, said that I had offended the goddess in the sea by cutting up caribou-meat on the sea-ice, and by breaking the bones there. She also said that her guardian spirit would hold the whale by a turn of the line around his wrist. Two days later the whale was found. In hauling in the line, it was seen that it had a turn around a rock in the bottom, and required the united efforts of two boats' crews to haul it clear.

Captain Comer, however, was prepared to respect Inuit customs:

This morning the natives told me that the anticok (the shaman) was told by the deities who look after the whales that we had worked on the musk-ox skins at a season when we had not ought to, or perhaps we worked on them on the vessel and that being on the water was wrong. Also we had an owl skin which we had saved and we had done wrong again in picking the feathers off the ducks. We had done wrong. We should have skinned them. I was told to throw up my hands several times as though throwing things away. After I had done that (which I did) they told me I was all right now and would have good success in the future. (quoted in Eber 1989: 112–13)

Euro-American whalers were well aware of many Inuit rules pertaining to whaling. They introduced new technologies and styles of hunting, however, and this may have contributed to the decline of many rules pertaining to older forms of Inuit whaling. Captain Comer was nicknamed the *angakkuq* because he took photographs (Eber 1989: 111–12). The nickname may have agreed well with his position as a whaling captain. According to Ipeelee of Cape Dorset, the shamans knew where to find the whales: 'A shaman wouldn't tell people about his powers, but on a hunt, if a shaman wanted to go in a certain direction, that is where the people would go. The shaman would say, "That's where the whales are"' (quoted in Eber 1989: 37).

## Whale Hunting and Shamanism

The Anglican missionary Peck presents a text by Qoojessie from South Baffin that connects the origin of shamanism to whale hunting. It consists of an Inuktitut text and a verbatim translation dating from the early 1900s. It relates that a woman was the first one to acquire the art of shamanism by lying down on a mattress. She descended to a land

below. Her father made her reappear, and she became a shaman. Peck
(quoted in Laugrand et al. 2006: 392) relates,

> *Angakotahanarevohtauk ningeookoulehtomik*
> She also likewise acquired a conjuration (became a conjuror), one who
> was getting an oldish woman
>
> *sakhonut sakkotahakpuktok agvekoyelerîgame*
> with the hunting implements, [so] she was the one who generally ac-
> quired hunting implements as often as she commanded whales to be got
>
> *asswela sakhotahaliktidlugo agverhtahanukpat*
> this is so while she had hunting implements, whales were got by the
> Eskimo
>
> *qaumayuâlonarame sakkotahaglune*
> because she was altogether a fountain of light having acquired imple-
> ments
>
> *perhattakoyerame agverngmik agverktoharîngmut*
> because she often commanded a getting of whales, as often as a whale
> was got
>
> *innugalakrangmut tussûgeyouvulehpok*
> by the whole community, now she was quite desired
>
> *kisseane peyoutitsingmut nerkiksannik*
> she alone, because she caused an acquisition of food.

The text connects the origin of shamanism to the acquisition of hunting implements that enabled Inuit to successfully hunt whales.[11]

The fact that the woman in Qoojessie's account is described as 'a
source of light' and 'able to command the whales' suggests a close relationship between shamanism, women and whaling. Rasmussen (1929:
188) notes that in the Aivilik area, 'During a whale hunt, the women
were obliged to wear a head ornament consisting of a white quartz-
stone, fastened to a strap round the forehead. This was done to show
a light for the soul of the whale.' Thus, the women guided the whale
to the land.

The act of lying down on the mattress that initiates the whole process immediately evokes the practice in which the wives of the hunters
had to lie down on their beds while their husbands were whale hunting, and emphasizes the importance of their role in the whale hunts.[12]
Rasmussen (1929: 187) relates,

When a whale has been harpooned, all the women must lie down on
the sleeping place with limbs relaxed, and loosen all tight fastenings in
their clothes, laces of kamiks, waistband: teqiʃ·iut. Unless this is done,
the whales will run the boat far out to sea, dragging it by the line that
is made fast to the harpoon head. All this applies to young women and
wives. Old women on the other hand may look on freely at the whaling.

Lying down on a mattress during the whale hunt places the woman
in the position of an *angakkuq*. The shaman was traditionally bound
during the séance and freed himself of his ties, whereas the other participants had to loosen their belts, laces, fastenings and so forth, just
as the wives of the hunters in the whale hunt had to do. A metaphorical relation is suggested between the shamanic séance and the whale
hunt. Piugaattuq from Iglulik recalled a tradition about a strong man,
Tapatai, who went out to harvest a bowhead whale and then brought it
back while on his bed, in his sleep:

> [Tapatai] was away for quite sometime and by the time he arrived back
> at the camp it was quite windy.... When he arrives he goes to bed and
> stayed in bed for most of the day – the wind was blowing strongly from
> the open sea.... As the afternoon falls, he started saying 'avataqjuk qin-
> niktauqataklii taimma tiktaunajaktuq tammaunga' ('Look for the float,
> it should be floating this way'). As it turns out, the float (made from
> young ringed seal) was attached to a dead bowhead whale. Meanwhile
> he remained in bed as he was quite tired and by the time he started to
> get better, people sighted the float. When the float was sighted he got
> up and beached the bowhead whale and cut it up. (quoted in Hay et al.
> 2000: 59–60)

Tapatai played a double role in this story, that of a hunter, going out to
harpoon the whale, and that of a woman, lying down on a mattress so
the whale would come to the shore. Once the float (and therefore the
whale) came into sight, he could get up.

Whales could also be brought in through shamanic objects. Pisuk
from Kangir&liniq relates that his uncle told him that the shaman
Taliriktuq once put his *qalugiujait* behind a ship and got a bowhead
whale (quoted in Kolb and Law 2001: 120–21):

> He said that Taliriktuq wore a *qalugiujaq*. They were at a place called
> Qikiqtait. They went to a whaling boat. It was on a Saturday. He left his
> *qalugiujait* behind when he went on board the ship. This person on the
> ship had given him metal for a harpoon because he said he had heard
> that he was an *angakkuq* and that he wanted to get an *arviq*, a bowhead
> whale, during the summer. He asked him to make it possible for him to
> catch a whale. Taliriktuq said he had left his *qalugiujait* behind and he

asked if someone could go and get it for him. They heard rattling. His *qalugiujait* were rattling on their own. The whaler, who had given him the metal, heard this. Taliriktuq told the whaler he would get a whale after the ice left. The whaler wanted to get a whale so badly that he started to disclose his wrongdoings just like an Inuk. The *angakkuq* had told the man who wanted to kill the whale that he would get the one he wanted with ease. It had been very easy to kill, but it had been very difficult to tow, so he went to ask the *angakkuq* why this had happened. Taliriktuq told him that he wanted them to be able to kill the whale quickly, but take a long time to land it. Although the water was calm and although there was another boat helping them, it took them three days to tow it to shore.

Some *tuurngait* were thought to provide whales. Peck reports that the helping spirit Angmaniq looks like a man, with his eyes, nose and mouth always open. He is very large and gives 'whales in answer to the conjuror's invocations' (quoted in Laugrand et al. 2006: 607). The helping spirit Qilialik looks like a bear. He is 'said to hide the souls of whales, and if whales and other creatures are so treated, they are said to be easily caught by the Eskimo as they cannot hear or see well neither are they frightened'; he hides the souls of whales so they can be easily killed (quoted in Laugrand et al. 2006: 615). Qakkoktînak is described as appearing like a man, with white clothing but with black hands and face and shining eyes. He is a good spirit who always comes swiftly to *angakkuq* and who has a whale that draws him about. Poo-eyak is described as a grampus, a good spirit, and said to bite with his large teeth whales, white whales, seals and so forth and thus kill their souls. Finally, Amouyak is the only *tuurngaq* described as appearing '[l]ike a whale. Like a hump backed creature. Good spirit. Gives food freely.' Whales are not very prominent as helping spirits. Killer whales are not very prominent either, although one of the *tuurngait* of the Nattilik *angakkuq* Iksivalitaq is described as a killer whale, white and very big (see Balikci 1970: 204).

In the shamanic language, the whale, known as *arviq* in the ordinary language, is called *taakslaingiq*, 'the one that should not be mentioned' (Rasmussen 1930: 70). As in the case of the sea woman, often called 'the one down there' (Rasmussen 1929: 106), one should not name the whale out of fear and respect.

Another interesting feature of whales is that they connect different scales. For instance, Randa (1994: 236) observes that *taakslaingiq* not only designates a whale but also a *kanajuq*, a sea scorpion. According to Rasmussen (1930: 79), 'the sea scorpions are said to be degenerated whales', or whales as they are perceived by giants (Rasmussen 1929: 214). This capacity to operate at different scales plays an important part in Inuit cosmology (see Saladin d'Anglure 1999). Sizes always depend on the context, and in the world of spirits, small beings can be very powerful ones, such as the bumblebee of the sea (Laugrand and Oosten 2012b). The *angakkuit* were especially equipped to deal with changes of scale, as their most effective weapons, the *qalugiujait*, miniature objects, operated on the level of the *tarniq*, the miniature image of a being.

Whales are not very marked in dreams, but a few stories indicate that in the past dreaming of a whale might mean death (see, e.g., Law and Kolb 2001: 211, interview no. 9). Itinnuaq from Rankin Inlet related that he had seen a whale in a dream predicting the death of many people from sickness in Igluligaarjuk:

> There was one sickness in Igluligaarjuk where many people were dying. One night there were three who died. During the week there would be one or two who died each night. In our area we also have an area we call Umingmattuq. Before this started, Nagjuk was there and he said, 'There is going to be a lot of death in Igluligaarjuk.' We had an iglu on flat land. There were hills around. I said to my father, 'I think I just saw a whale.' My father did not see this but he could tell that something was going to happen. (quoted in Oosten and Laugrand 2002: 46)

The appearance of the whale portended a disaster that affected the whole community. The *angakkuq* Nagjuk ended the epidemic by choosing to die so the sickness would stop.

## Attracting the Whale

Boas (1907: 499) reports that according to Captain Comer, 'When a whale was seen, it was customary to point at it with the third finger of the right hand.' He does not specify who did the pointing. Rasmussen (1929: 187–88) relates that in Naujaat (Repulse Bay), 'If a woman sees a whale, she must point to it with her middle finger.' This custom evokes an old Aivilik tradition recorded by Rasmussen, as told by Ivaluardjuk: 'It is said that in the days when the earth was dark, the only creatures men had to hunt were ptarmigan and hare, and these were hunted by wetting the forefinger and holding it out in the air; the finger then became luminous and it was possible to see the animal hunted.' Nutaraaluk from Iqaluit related how the deceased 'used their forefinger as an *angmaaq*, a flint to light fires' (quoted in Oosten et al. 1999: 30).

The power of the middle finger was referred to by Pisuk from Rankin Inlet when he explained how his grandmother taught him to use it as a protection in an *aqtuqsinniq*, a paralyzing dream. When he was attacked in a dream, he made his opponent disappear by pointing at him (quoted in Kolb and Law 2001: 192):

> I told you about the time when there was a man who was about my age wearing caribou clothing. He was wearing a very thin sinew belt. He was not wearing his kamiik. He was wearing mitts made out of caribou foreleg. I thought maybe he had been sent to me. I was lying in bed and his face became uglier and uglier and he seemed to be getting closer and closer. He seemed to move. I went to push my middle finger at him and when it touched him, he disappeared.

Rasmussen (1929: 173) relates how the power of this finger was used by a mother who has just delivered a son:

> Every morning she has to melt ice or snow for drinking water. Every time she drinks, she must put a drop of water into the child's mouth with her middle finger. This must be done immediately after the child is born, and repeated every time the mother drinks. The finger in question is supposed to possess a peculiar power in regard to infants, so that the water thus dripping into the mouth will prevent the child from ever suffering from thirst.

Is the pointing connected to the providing of a drink to the whale? According to Boas (1901: 139), the harpooning of Sedna was compared to the offering of a drink of water. 'As to the reason why Sedna must be cut, the people say that it is an old custom, and that it makes her feel better that it is the same as giving a thirsty person drink.' The relation between harpooning and providing a drink of fresh water was emphasized by Nutaraaluk from Iqaluit in the story of a hunter who met a walrus that said to him, 'I'm so thirsty. Please harpoon me' (quoted in Oosten and Laugrand 1999a: 197). In a variant of the story of the man who travelled to the land of the birds (Rasmussen 1929: 267), the bird the man married tries to escape from him all the time. Finally he 'wetted his first finger with spittle and touched her with it before sitting down. Then she stayed where she was and did not fly away from him again.' Thus, he was able to fix the bird and connect her to him. The pointing of the middle finger appears to be connected to the providing of a drink and the harpooning of an animal. The woman's pointing appears to prefigure the harpooning of the whale by her husband. After the whale is killed, it receives a drink of fresh water. The gift or water has a central place in the cycle of life and death. When a deceased person appears to a pregnant woman in her dream and asks for a drink of water, this is usually interpreted as a request of the deceased that his or her name will be passed on to the baby that is about to be born.[13]

In the western Arctic the drum is used to attract whales. Ernie Frankson Sr., an Inupiaq whaling captain from Point Hope and leader of a group of dancers in Tikigaq, stated, 'The drum is the whale and the whale is the drum' (Frankson 2005, quoted in Sakakibara 2009: 291). In the Canadian eastern Arctic there are also references to this relationship. Pauta Saila from Cape Dorset related, 'In the old days when they caught big whales by kayak, they would drum to attract the animal – to make it easy catching' (quoted in Eber 1989: 35). Boas (1888: 601) reports the use of the fin of a whale when making a drum: 'The drum is made from the skin of the deer [or seal], which is stretched over a hoop made of wood, or of bone from the fin of a whale, by the use of a strong, braided cord of sinew passed around a groove on the outside.' Today, northern communities often organize music or drumming festivals before they start whale hunting.

Music and songs facilitate the connection between humans and animals. If animals are pleased, they will give themselves to the hunter. Abe Okpik recalls,

> Some people would see an animal in the sea, like a bowhead whale for instance. They would get some old man or old woman who knew their language and they would chant and the whale would come closer. That's when they would get it. They called that *atulluk* which means that through your song you hypnotize the mammal to come near. It is like when you go hunting seals, if you have a guitar, piano, accordion or something, and you make noise, they will come right over. (McComber 2005: 63)

Pauta Saila related, 'When a hunter on a kayak speared a whale, other kayakers would be nearby. They'd begin to chant – so the whale would not try to get away from the hunter. People would chant in order that the whale would stay in one place – to make it easier to kill – and while they chanted, they took out the laces from their kamiit. They would take out the laces so the muscles of the whale would be loose' (quoted in Eber 1989: 36). Music is thus a means to attract animals, especially seals and whales. This may also explain why Inuit were fascinated by foreign musical instruments and traditions brought by the Euro-American whalers (see Lutz 1978).

## Rules of Respect

A close connection between whale hunting and shamanism appears in the old hunting techniques Inuit used before they were introduced to the Euro-American mode of hunting. These techniques most probably continued into the twentieth century, but they gradually declined, especially when whale hunting was prohibited by the Canadian authorities. The practice of whaling involved the whole community, not only the *angakkuit* and/or the hunters. Women, children and old people were all involved in making the hunt successful.

Rasmussen (1929: 187) relates,

> As soon as a whale is harpooned, the boys must be tied up together, in pairs, one's left leg to the other's right, and thus bound, they must hobble off inland until out of sight of the sea. If the boys are an odd number, so that one is left over, then it is his business to push the bound pairs and make them tumble over; for the more they do so, the better. It is supposed that the difficulty experienced by the boys in their progress is communicated to the whale, so that after being harpooned, it finds it hard to swim away. Old women may also be lashed together, but not in the same way. All that is done is to tie their legs together a little above the instep, and in this manner they must also hobble off inland, often falling, rolling about at the small declivities; the harder they find it to advance, and the more they roll about, the slower will be the progress of the whale dragging the boat out with it, and it will not move far from the spot where it was harpooned.

Thus, not only the wives of the hunters, but also the boys and the old women have their part to play so the whale will be towed in without problems. The community as a whole supports the hunters wherever possible.

> When it has been observed from on shore that a whale is harpooned, no one is allowed to fetch water. When out whaling, a boat must never be baled out. No one on board is allowed to make water or spit over the side; if spitting is absolutely necessary, one must spit on one's own person. As soon as the whaleboat with the whale in tow is about to land, all young mothers must try to be first down to it, running right out into the water, sometimes up to the waist, and then leap on board with water for their husbands; this will make their sons good hunters. (Rasmussen 1929: 187–88)

The prohibition disallowing any water to go out of the boat may be related to the symbolic association of harpooning with offering a drink to the prey. The provision of water should be through the harpooning of the animal. Rasmussen (1929: 188) adds, 'In the olden days, when whales were hunted in kayaks, the boys had to do as the young mothers do nowadays, come down and pour water over the fore end of the kayaks as soon as they came towing in to shore. This would make them good whalers.'[14] Thus, the water seems to be intended for the prow of the kayak, linguistically marked as the penis of the boat. The actions of the women and the boys connect the killing of the whale to the reproduction and regeneration of human society.[15]

Rasmussen (1929: 188) continues,

> Women with infants, or women who have had a miscarriage, may not boil walrus meat until the backbone of the whale has been broken. When the boat is within a stone's throw of the shore, maktak is cut up into strips, and the boys and girls divide into separate groups, and the maktak is thrown to them to scramble for. Older persons may also take part. The pieces obtained by women with infants or women who have their menses, or women who have had a miscarriage, are given to old women. The pieces thrown to the boys must be cut with a dice pattern along the strips, those thrown to the girls are marked crosswise.... The more one could smear oneself over with blood and blubber when a whale was being cut up, the better, for this would please the Mother of the Sea Beasts.

A scramble was expected for the *maktaaq* as an appreciation of the catch. Women who had just delivered children or were menstruating were restricted in their participation and their shares were passed on to the older women.

Rules also dictated what could or could not be done in the days following a whale hunt:

> For three days after the capture of a whale, no work was allowed to be done by men or women. In a village where a whale had been captured, no cooking was allowed to be done with fuel obtained from the ground, but only over fires made of bones and blubber, or over the lamp. Clothing which had been worn at a whale hunt must never be taken inland in the spring for the caribou hunting. (Rasmussen 1929: 188)

Rasmussen's descriptions are very close to the information provided by Boas (1907: 499–500) and derived from Captain Comer. Comer connects the custom to pour fresh water over the prow of the kayak specifically to the kayak of the hunter who first struck the whale. He also relates the use of old clothing during the celebration of the catch: 'In cutting up the whale, the people did not avoid getting covered with grease and blood, in order to show to Nuliayoq that they were well pleased with the gift of the whale. For this reason the oldest clothing was worn during this time.' With respect to the South Baffin area, Boas (1888: 603) reports, 'After a successful whaling-season, all clothing is discarded near the shore, so that in the deer-hunting season the deer may not be offended.'

Freeman (1968: 26–28) mentions that the return of the whale hunt was marked with singing and thanking acts performed by the hunters and their women:

> When a hunter returns with game, teenage girls stand one behind another in line and give vocalized appreciation for the good fortune of the hunt. The sound made partly voiced, partly in the throat. Women and girls standing on the beach may make this same vocal response when watching men tow a whale to shore.... One 39-year-old man recounted how men towing large whales back to shore in Cumberland Sound would sing when in sight of land, 'Of course they were very happy, they might have rowed three or four days without sleeping. The women and the other people on land would start singing as soon as the men's' singing was heard. When the men reached shore, some would roll on the beach; this general happiness and excitement evoked *qujaliniq* responses including songs. The informant had heard of this from his father, being too young to know of whaling activities first hand.

According to Freeman, the notion of *qujaliniq* is now used for a Thanksgiving prayer in the morning and evening services by Anglican Inuit (see the Book of Common Prayer 1960), suggesting that Christian prayers and hymns now play a part in contemporary whaling.[16]

## The Whale as a Whole

In the past, the whale was a catch that concerned the community as a whole. Boas (1888: 582) states emphatically, 'A whale belongs to the whole settlement and its capture is celebrated by a feast.' The notion of a whole may also play a part in the connection between the whale and the house. Comer (1910: 87) and Boas (1888: 550) relate that Inuit often used old houses with walls made of whale ribs as *qarmat*. These old houses could be found everywhere on the land, and Inuit today still talk about these houses. Nataq discussed the use of whale jawbones for the construction of houses in a workshop in Rankin Inlet in 2010. According to Boas (1901: 165), the sea woman lives in a house built of stone and whale ribs. The notion of the house suggests a whole that often encompassed several families. Boas (1888: 603) quotes Captain Parry relating that after a successful whale catch the whale was dragged into a stone enclosure:

> It appears that the whole whale or a principal part of it is dragged into the enclosure, where some of the men are employed in cutting it up and throwing the pieces over the wall to the rest, who stand ready to receive them outside; while within the women range themselves in a circle

around the whale and continue singing during the operation. Each of these structures was the distinct property of a particular individual; and had probably, in its turn, been the seat of feasting and merriment either to the present owner, or those from whom he had inherited it.

Captain Parry's description suggests that the whaling rituals provided a framework to build individual prestige. Whereas in the western Arctic an *umialik,* the owner of a whaling boat, was a recognized leader or 'chieftain' and given an 'unrestricted authority' over its crew (see Rasmussen 1927: 312), the owner of such a construction may have had a similar position in the Canadian Arctic (see Stevenson 1997).[17]

Boas reports (1907: 493) on a whaling feast in which the *angakkuit* danced within a circle of stones:

> When the whale-meat was cooked, the people sat down in a half-circle of stones, to which all the food was brought. There they had a feast, accompanied by games. It is said that the whale skin and meat where piled up in the centre, and that each angakok in turn would dance around this pile, while the people sat around the circle of stones. Women sang songs, accompanying the dance. Evidently the half-circle of stones here mentioned is the same as the structure described by Parry. Captain Comer states that he has seen several of these half-circles in various parts of the country.

Rasmussen (1929: 188) provides a description of such a feast organized in a stone enclosure, emphasizing the role of the older women, who would feast with the men and eat from the cooking pot, whereas the younger women and children would not be allowed to take part in this meal.

The meaning of the stone enclosure is unclear. It may evoke the shape of the house or that of the drum. Other sea mammals such as the seal were taken into the house of the hunter to be butchered by his wife. In the case of the whale this was not feasible, and the stone enclosure may have provided a 'house' for the whale, contrasting with the houses of human beings, which were made of whalebones and sod.

Although these feasts disappeared when the whale hunts were no longer performed, in some regions old whaling traditions have been retained or renewed.

## Bowhead Hunting Today

In the 1960s and 1970s a few whales were caught (see Saladin d'Anglure 1999: 89), but after that no whales were caught until 1994, when Noah Piugaattuq announced on the radio that he wished to taste once more whale *maktaaq* before dying. His relatives heeded his wish and killed a whale. The catch was followed by a feast.

Since 1994, especially after the NWMB showed that bowhead whales were more numerous in the eastern Arctic than once thought, a dozen legal bowhead hunts have been organized in Nunavut and two in Nunavik. The first approved bowhead hunt took place in Naujaat in 1996 and was filmed by CBC and IBC. A whale was shot, but it sank and only rose to the surface two days later. Its *maktak* was lost. The hunt was described as a fiasco by the local and international press. Inuit whale hunters explained that they didn't use the harpoon gun they were instructed to use and that they would now purchase a proper harpoon and elect a hunt captain (Bourgeois 1998).[18] During the second whale hunt, hunters were trained and Jaco Eevik was named captain of the hunt. The whale hunt took place in 1998 in Pangniqtuuq, and after the kill of a whale its meat and *maktak* were distributed throughout Nunavut so that all residents could participate in the feast (see George 2008c). Since 1998, legal whale hunts then took place every two years, in Coral Harbour in 2000 and Iglulik/Hall Beach in 2002 (see Bell 2005). Today a bowhead hunt is allowed one a year in each of the three regions of Nunavut. Communities take turns and the selected community in charge of the legal hunt shares meat and *maktak* with the other communities.

In August 2005, a crew of hunters led by Marcel Mapsalak caught a 54-foot-long bowhead whale in Naujaat (Bell 2005). Mapsalak stated that the fact that the Naujaat community keeps tradition alive explains why the 2005 hunt went more smoothly than the one in 1996, which attracted hunters who didn't know one another from around Nunavut. Journalist Folger (2005) quoted Mapsalak:

> 'This time the crew is from Repulse. We picked some younger guys, and some older guys', Mapsalak said before the hunt. 'We have teenagers because we want them to learn more about bowheads. The younger guys are going to help a lot because they've learned a lot from their parents.' Laimikki Malikki is one of the parents passing on traditions to his children – and he takes pride in it, showing off the skull of a two-tusked narwhal his son Jason caught a few weeks before the bowhead hunt. ... Malikki helps strengthen the community in other ways, too. During games at the grand opening of the new hamlet offices, he was first in for the rock-throwing contest, showing an enthusiasm that rubbed off on everyone.

Malikki was selected to chair the Naujaat Arviq (Bowhead) organizing committee (Folger 2005). The whale hunt has rapidly become a sign of

cultural vitality in Naujaat and a key element in the transfer of knowledge between elders and youth in that community.

In 2008, more bowhead hunts took place in Kugaaruk, Hall Beach
and Cape Dorset. In Cape Dorset the hunt was very successful, but the
towing of the whale took many hours. The *Nunatsiaq News* reported,

> The hunt crew, led by Captain Qimmiataq Nungutsuituq, killed the whale
> only 45 minutes after sighting it about 40 km east of Cape Dorset. But it
> took the crew about seven hours to tow it back to their community. The
> whale was well over 50 feet in length. Crew member Egeevadluk Suvigak
> is credited with the catch because it was he who first wounded the ani-
> mal. The lead harpooner was Daniel Taukie, who handled the penthrite
> grenade device. (*Nunatsiaq News* 2009a)

In Nunavik, two bowhead whale hunts were also organized in 2008
and 2009. The first hunt took place near Kangiqsujuaq (see figures 10.2
and 10.3). Journalist Noble (2008b) reported,

> Noah Annahatak thrust a harpoon into a bowhead whale August 10,
> making the first bowhead kill on Nunavik's Hudson Strait in more than
> a century. The animal measured 15-metres and weighing in at 49 tonnes.
> 'This is so special for us', Pirlurtuut said, practically speechless with joy.
> 'It makes us proud; we're back with our ancestors.' Annahatak and 50
> other hunters had been out on the water near Kangiqsujuaq, search-
> ing for a bowhead since Aug. 1. They failed to snag a whale in time for
> the Bowhead Whale Music Festival, organized in honour of the hunt.
> But around 6 p.m. last Saturday, hunters finally spotted a 15-metre-long
> whale. Annahatak threw his harpoon, designed to plunge a grenade filled
> with water and inert gas deep inside the whale. Other hunters flung tra-
> ditional harpoons and fired rifles. Some recalled how a bowhead whale
> was lanced in the 1960s and how it was lashed to a boat and slices of
> maktak were even severed from its tail fluke. But somehow that whale
> wriggled free and escaped. Shortly before 8 p.m., whaling captain Aquu-
> jaq Qisiiq pulled alongside the bowhead whale. Annahatak fired the sec-
> ond and final grenade-loaded harpoon. Three minutes later the whale
> was dead. The bowhead whale reached Akulivik, a cove near town, at 6
> a.m. Sunday. The 49-tonne whale was moored to three orange buoys on
> the edge of the bay where it bobbed, with a long knife stuck in its top,
> until early afternoon, when the tide lowered. Canoes ferried onlookers to
> the site and the slicing of maktak began. Slabs were shorn off, hooked,
> pulled ashore and then passed around. Maktak was laid atop plywood
> strips, Tupperware tops and bare rock, then diced with ulus and pocket-
> knives. Naalak Nappaaluk, who at age 80 is one of the few Nunavimmiut
> to remember tales of bowhead hunts that once took place, sat on a rock
> with a pad of maktak nearby. 'Today, I've seen people standing on the
> bowhead for the first time', Nappaaluk said. 'It's overwhelming.' ... As

for the maktak, it will be shipped to communities around Nunavik, so everyone can have a taste.

In this hunt as well as in those held in Nunavut, the whale clearly provides a lot of joy to the hunters as well as to the community. The hunt reconnects the hunters to the traditions of their ancestors, giving strength to Inuit cultural traditions. Freeman et al. (1998: 19) quotes Johny Mike from Pangniqtuuq:

> The reason I exist today as an Inuk is because of my ancestors really tried and survived on wildlife and whales.... When I go whale hunting ... there's lot of things that go through my mind ... about the world where we were before, where my ancestors were coming from. Yeah, you can almost hear echoes [from the past] when you are whale hunting.

Elsewhere, Noble (2008a) reported,

> The bowhead whale hunt began with a prayer on the beach. Aqujaq Qisiiq, the whaling captain, and Vincent Cormier, from the Federal Department of Fisheries and Oceans, signed a licence authorizing the take of one bowhead before a cheering crowd. Within hours the first hunters were off.... The next day, Sunday, the hunters sighted another bowhead. 'The whale was huge', said a young hunter. 'When it blows you can see

**Figure 10.2.** The hunters about to harpoon a whale in Kangiqsujuaq, Nunavik, in 2008. Photo: Robert Fréchette/Avataq Cultural Institute.

**Figure 10.3.** The whale has been dragged onto the shore to be butchered. Photo: Robert Fréchette/Avataq Cultural Institute.

it from miles away.' But no one hunts on Sundays, so this whale also went free. Instead, hunters came ashore for a music festival – called the Bowhead Whale Music Festival – in honour of the hunt. 'We were hoping to have a whale by the festival', said Mary Pilurtuut, the mayor of Kangiqsujuaq.

The festival included a bevy of local drummers and a family band from Nunavut.

As of Nunatsiaq News press time, hunters in Kangiqsujuaq had yet to catch their whale. But Nappaaluk was confident they would get it though, remembering what elders once told him. 'If a bowhead doesn't want to be hunted the skin will tense up and it's impossible to hunt him. When he doesn't mind being hunted you can go at him and cut him up easily. That's how they are', he said. (Noble 2008a; see also George 2008c)

The second Nunavik bowhead hunt conducted in 2009 resulted in mixed feelings due to various difficulties met by the hunters. Journalist Sarah Rogers (2009a) reported,

Nunavik hunters brought in a 56-foot-long bowhead whale, second catch in two years. The hunt leader Aloupa Kulula had a team of about 20 hunters from across Nunavik in a number of canoes and speedboats setting out from Kangiqsujuaq. The bowhead whale was harpooned, an adult female whale, but the explosive device in the harpoon did not detonate and so the hunters continued to pursue the whale into the evening. The hunters used rifles until a lance finally killed the whale early on Sunday. That was an unfortunate incident but the rest went well. The bowhead whale, seven feet longer than the one caught the year before in 2008, was towed to a site not too far from the kill site on the same day to be butchered. The community welcomed the hunters and their catch to a cove near Kangiqsujuaq. The meat was then distributed free to families across the region and whale meat shipped out to other communities in Nunavik on Monday. No music festival was organized in Kangiqsujuaq this year in honour of the hunt, but the community is expected to gather and celebrate the return of the whaling crew.

In her second report, Rogers (2009b) related,

> A 60- to 70-pound calf was removed from the bowhead whale during the butchering process, Pilurtuut said. It was already dead. 'That day was full of mixed emotion, for sure', Pilurtuut said. 'We didn't know if it was a female or male while it was in the water.' Before deciding to follow and then to kill this bowhead whale, hunters had previously followed another bowhead whale – that is, until they realized the whale was a female and travelling with a young calf. Federal department of fisheries regulations say hunters shouldn't kill a juvenile bowhead whale or an adult that is accompanied by its offspring. But hunters say there was no way to tell if this bowhead whale was pregnant.

The hunt involved the participation of many people and most communities in Nunavik.

> Once the 56-foot long (17 metres) bowhead whale was towed on to shore at Qitik, a campsite 20 kilometres southeast of Kangiqsujuaq, about 50 people helped butcher the whale – a five-hour long feat that Pilurtuut described as 'very well organized'.... To avoid the meat from spoiling, as some portions did last year, the butchering was done as close to the hunting site as possible....
>
> Twelve of the 14 communities in Nunavik – all except Salluit and Kuujjuaraapik – joined in the hunt. These communities will receive a portion of the bowhead whale meat and muktuk in return [see figure 10.4]. 'If we were to hunt again next year, I would love it to be in another community', Pilurtuut said. 'Just to give them the experience.' (Rogers 2009b)

In 2009, a bowhead whale hunt took place in Rankin Inlet and a 56 feet-long whale was caught. The Nunavut's Inuit land claims organization, Nunavut Tunngavik Inc., has fought hard to open up the harvest and managed to convince the NWMB to recommend raising

**Figure 10.4.** Butchering the whale is done immediately so the *maktaaq* can be shared by the hunters and the surrounding communities. Photo: Robert Fréchette/ Avataq Cultural Institute.

the annual quota from two to three whales a year, a decision that was approved by the federal minister of fisheries and oceans, Gail Shea, in 2009. In 2010, three communities – Kugaaruk, Naujaat and Mittimatalik – were awarded licences to hunt bowhead whales, but only the latter two were successful. In 2011, Iqaluit hosted one of the three prized bowhead whale hunts. In coming years, more bowhead whale hunts will probably be organized, since it is now clear that the number of whales has greatly increased in the past decades. The Department of Fisheries and Oceans (DFO) recently conceded that Inuit hunters were right in assessing an increase of whales in Arctic waters. In 2008, the DFO acknowledged that the eastern Arctic bowhead whale population was in fact fifteen times greater than they thought eight years before. Journalist Jane George (2008b) reported:

> DFO scientist Pierre Richard says Inuit traditional knowledge was right all along, but the problem was that there were no 'numbers' to back it up.... Since 1996, DFO scientists' old figure of 345 bowhead whales was used to determine an Inuit bowhead whale quota in Nunavut of about one every two years. But the scientists' new, much higher bowhead whale estimate – showing a population that could run as high as 43,105 – supports an annual hunt of between 18 and 90.... It took more than seven

years for the DFO's science to catch up. The DFO's estimates of the bowhead population jumped from 345 in 2000 to about 3,000 in 2003, then
to 7,309 in 2007, and now to 14,400. The DFO's most recent stock assessment from February says this latest number of 14,400 is only a 'partial
estimate' and that there could actually be as many as 43,105 bowhead
whales in the Eastern Arctic. The DFO also concedes that there aren't
two populations of bowhead whales in the Eastern Arctic, but one.

These last estimates are quite surprising, as they may imply that bowhead whales are more numerous now than they were before the era of
commercial whaling, when the population probably stood at around
twelve thousand. Taking into account this increased abundance of
whales, the Committee on the Status of Endangered Wildlife in Canada (COSEWIC) changed the status of bowhead whales in the eastern
Arctic from 'threatened with extinction' to 'special concern' (*Nunatsiaq
News* 2009b).[19]

Elders such as Aupilaarjuk from Kangir&iniq have argued for a long
time that Inuit never hunted the whales to extinction, and that this was
due to commercial whaling. He argues that Inuit should thus be the
ones in charge of contemporary whaling activities:

> I am not a whale hunter, but I have been against the bowhead whale hunt
> since it became commercial. In the old days, we just hunted whale for
> the meat. We also didn't try to hunt them to extinction. Inuit were not
> able to hunt bowhead for a long time. We feel that it wasn't the Inuit that
> made the bowhead an endangered animal, it was the whalers.... Inuit
> should be in charge of how the bowhead are hunted. Inuit should be in
> charge of their land because we do not try to hunt animals until they are
> extinct. We have always tried to be careful with our hunting.

However, modern whale hunts are very different from those of the
past. The technology hunters use today is entirely up-to-date. A harpoon with a grenade is shot into the animal to avoid a long drawn-out
death. It is expected that after about five to six seconds the grenade
explodes. To be successful, hunters need to be well trained, since the
harpooner must aim at the brain, the heart or the lungs. Benn Ell, an
elder from Iqaluit, emphasized that nowadays training should be required to go hunting for bowhead whales.

> We are not bowhead hunters, although we were born in the time of bow-
> head hunting, but when one is a child at that time it is hard to know
> about them too much, we only know about what we have heard.... I do
> not think the Inuit should say that they are professional bowhead whale
> hunters, the bowhead whale is such a large mammal and they are not
> easy to kill when you do not know them, so that is why I would like to

see some kind of training before we can actually go out and hunt one for the first time, perhaps getting people from different communities to hunt for the bowhead. (quoted in Hay et al. 2000: 58–59)

## Sharing *Maktaaq*, Valorizing Hunting

The sharing of *maktak* is a key element in contemporary whale hunting activities. The *maktak*, which can be eaten in great quantities, was and still is a most appreciated part of the whale. This appetite for *maktak* is nothing new and was already observed by Kumlien (1879: 20) at the end of the nineteenth century:

> The 'black skin' of the whale, called by them muktuk, is esteemed the greatest delicacy. When they first procure a supply of this food, they almost invariably eat themselves sick, especially the children. We found this black skin not unpleasant tasting when boiled and then pickled in strong vinegar and eaten cold; but the first attempts at masticating it will remind one of chewing Indian rubber. When eaten to excess, especially when raw, it acts as a powerful laxative. It is generally eaten with about half an inch of blubber adhering.

The taste of whale is an issue of great interest to the elders: 'What the elders stated was very true; the first time you bite the whale skin, it will have a strong taste to it. The second time you eat it, it will be all right. The third time you eat it, the true taste will finally come out, it will be delicious' (Hay et al. 2000: 57–58). Elders remember the taste of *maktak* from eating it in their youth and can develop a craving for it: 'The older people consider the bowhead whale meat as a delicacy, and they crave for the bowhead whale meat. After the older people have eaten something they have not eaten for a long time, their spirits seem to lift up; and they seem to be more alive' (Hay et al. 2000: 52). Lypa Pisiulak from Pangnirtuuq declared, 'The Inuit at Ummangjuaq were "thirsty" when it came to the bowhead whales.... Those Inuit were hungry for bowhead mattak.... I think it is essential that we learn about the bowhead whale, how it tastes and its other uses' (quoted in Freeman et al. 1998: 29).

Adina Duffy from Coral Harbour related,

> I recall as a young child visiting my grandparents' house.... One conversation is still alive in my memory. My grandparents and many relatives were gathered and eating *mataaq* [beluga mattak] when my grandfather sighed and said in himself ... 'just one more time before I die'. I did not understand what this meant; then I understood, for my grand-

mother turned to him and said, 'One day we will eat, one day there will be bowhead meat for us.' I've heard many conversations similar to the one between my grandparents, but none in all my fifteen years were as memorable and sad. ... Many elders have passed on without tasting their beloved *mataaq* [bowhead mattak] one more time. (quoted in Freeman et al. 1998: 37)

In 1994 Iglulik hunters killed a bowhead whale because a very re-spected Inuit elder, Piugaattuq, had expressed the wish to taste *maktak* again before he died. Inuit elders generally supported honouring such a request. John Kaunak stated,

The elders of today are living and always longing to eat what they were raised with. For example, we had a grandmother who was very old and she used to repeat saying 'I wish a bowhead whale could be harvested while I am still alive' and this was because she missed the maktak of bowhead whale, but she died before a bowhead whale was ever har-vested. And my feeling has always been that if she was able to eat maktak of the bowhead whale I am sure that she would have lived longer. Elders must be respected and provided with food that they had grown up with. (quoted in Hay et al. 2000: 56–57)

Nauja Tassugat agreed, emphasizing the need to resume bowhead hunting:

I'm sure that they [the elders] are craving for it [bowhead] since they grew up on it, and I'm sure that they love to eat it again while they are still alive, so, we Inuit think that they should try and harvest one as soon as possible. Especially the elders think like that, the elders who are left would like to have bowhead whale meat again before they die, they should be given their wishes. (quoted in Hay et al. 2000: 56–57)

Freeman's interviews conducted with elders in 1995 shed much light on the great significance of the whale. Elders stated that beyond the meat and *maktak,* the whale hunts were also very important for the feasts and gatherings that accompanied them. Oolletoa Temela from Kimmirut stated, 'These gatherings and sharings are as much a part of our culture as our language' (quoted in Freeman et al. 1998: 33). Tina Netser, also from Coral Harbour, stressed the importance of the whale for the body: 'Once we don't have the whales' nutrients in our bodies, it's like part of our bodies is missing' (quoted in Freeman et al. 1998: 39).

The sharing of whale meat is also very important. Charlie Novalinga from Sanikiluaq stated, 'When a whale is caught it's shared with the whole community. Whales provide a lot of food. There is lots to go around. Some families do not get whales so other families will share their whale with them. This tradition always will be around in our community' (quoted in Freeman et al. 1998: 34). Freeman (2005: 66) quotes an anonymous student hunter: 'When a hunter kills a whale, the meat is never wasted. Everyone gets a piece of the whale for the family. God put them for a reason, and the people use it wisely … if people do have too much, they give the leftovers to the people who need it.'

Many elders assume that there is a need to take up bowhead hunting again to keep these animals from disappearing. Sabina Issigaitoq from Hall Beach stated, 'The bowhead whale too, if it is not hunted anymore will become less and less. With regards to the one that was recently killed [at Iglulik in 1994], people are saying some of the maktak was very rough and it didn't seem to be very healthy. People say that the animals have to be hunted continuously' (quoted in Hay et al. 2000: 59). Thus, even the taste of whale is thought to decline when it is no longer hunted.

Today, after being banned or restricted for so many years, whale hunting has become a sign of political empowerment, a question of respecting cultural traditions and a way to valorize hunting in Inuit cultures.

## Discussion

Whale hunting has been an integral part of Inuit culture for a very long time. The whale hunt involved the whole community. Hunters, women, old people and children all contributed to the success of the hunt. It provided opportunities to build individual prestige, and the owner of the whalebone construction was probably also the host of the whale feast in the eastern Arctic. Just like a house built with the bones of the whale, the stone constructions of the whale feast encompassed all participants.

Traditional whaling was firmly embedded in a cosmological framework, as shown by the myth of origin connecting whaling to shamanism, as recorded by Peck, and the ritual rules organizing the whale hunt. The collaboration of husband and wife was essential to the success of the hunt. In the context of whaling, most acts of so-called imitation are in fact 'prefiguring', as in the case of the pointed finger. The acts of human beings, notably women, enticed and seduced the whale to imitate the behaviour of the human beings. Women tried to trick and manipulate the whale. For example, the woman lying down invited the whale to become passive and immobile so it was more easily dragged towards the land by the hunters. Thus, the whale was made to imitate the human beings and not vice versa. Music also played a part in attracting the whale.

When the whalers came, Inuit adapted to the new technologies and collaborated closely with the whalers. Many ritual rules were still observed in the nineteenth and the beginning of the twentieth century, and even the Euro-American whaler captains took them into account. The overkill of whales by Euro-American whalers in the Arctic waters meant the end of a long tradition of whaling in most Inuit communities. Many elders still remember the whaling of the past, and in their testimonies the great value attached to whaling comes to the fore. Even though many Inuit desired to resume whaling, the hunt was prohibited to ensure the survival of the whale in Arctic waters. The famous whale hunt organized to provide Noah Piugaattuq from Iglulik with a taste of *maktak* before he died played an important part in triggering the revival of whaling in the eastern Arctic. Most Inuit approved of the hunt and advocated a resumption of whaling. The DFO revised its estimate of the number of whales and conceded that Inuit hunters were better aware of the resurgence of whales in Arctic waters.

After 1994 the Inuit resumed whaling with great energy and enthusiasm, and the revived whaling traditions show many features that were characteristic of the traditional whaling complex. Today whaling not only involves the whole community, but also the whole area, as meat is shared between the communities. Whaling is still firmly embedded in a ritual context, although this has changed from a traditional context to a Christian one. Thus, a whale cannot be caught on a Sunday, and any whale hunting has to be prepared for carefully with prayer and religious services. A few years ago, when 629 belugas were trapped in the ice, Inuit from Mittimatalik connected this providential hunt to a gift from God. Today, most hunters believe that whales, like other animals, belong to God, who is now their real owner.

The connection between whale hunting and Christianity is also very strong in the western Arctic. Thus, Eben Hopson, founder of the Inuit Circumpolar Conference (ICC) and the Alaska Eskimo Whaling Commission, is not afraid to compare the whaling traditions with Christian feasts: 'We are the People of the Whale. The taking and sharing of the whale is our Eucharist and Passover. The whaling festival is our Easter and Christmas, the Arctic celebrations of the mysteries of life' (1979, quoted in Freeman et al. 1998: 55; 2005: 70).[20]

Hunters in the eastern Arctic emphasize that whaling connects Inuit to the past. In 2008, when Kangiqsujuaq in Nunavik got its first bowhead in a century, local elder Pirlurtuut emphasized this feeling of reconnecting with his own tradition when he declared to the *Nunatsiaq*

*News* journalist, "'This is so special for us", Pirlurtuut said, practically speechless with joy. "It makes us proud; we're back with our ancestors'" (Noble 2008a).

The whale constitutes a whole, encompassing the community in the past as well as the present,[21] and connecting the communities in Nunavut in the hunt and the sharing of its meat.

## Notes

1. On the old Arctic whale cults and the uses of the whale in the Canadian Arctic, see Taylor (1985, 1988). On whale hunting and its importance among the Siberian Inuit, see Chichlo (2000). On prehistoric whaling, see Krupnik (1993).
2. See Ross (1975, 1977, 1984 and 1985), Dorothy Eber (1989) for more detailed information on the whalers and Ludger Müller-Wille and Bernd Gieseking (2011).
3. According to Bodenhorn (1990), whales take notice of the behaviour of the wives of the Inupiat hunters and give themselves to those hunters whose wives share their game generously.
4. She observes that in Tikigaq, many masks of a woman's face are still carved with the whale's tail emerging from her mouth, and that other Alaskan stories, notably among the Yup'ik, identify the whale with the woman's child, as if whales were children of the sea woman.
5. A similar version of this story is provided by Nathan Qamaniq (IE 380).
6. Lee and Wenzel (2004) report with respect to the narwhal hunt in Pond Inlet that 'strict rules on human behaviour while at the floe-edge' are still utilized in order to minimize noise disturbance. Hunters have to remain silent and avoid any unnecessary movement. Elders mention that 'the contemporary snowmobile noise along the floe-edge had drastically changed narwhal migration behaviour along the floe-edge'. Narwhal hunting has also been studied in Greenland (see Sejersen 2001). Alayco et al. (2007) relate that in Nunavik beluga hunting is still a major component of Inuit culture and diet. Elders express their fear that noise pollution caused by snowmobiles, motors and so forth is depleting the beluga in some areas.
7. See also Philip Kripannik and Joseph Oqallak on the same issue (quoted in Hay et al. 2000: 46).
8. With respect to beluga hunting, Alayco et al. (2007) report that Nunavik elders stress that belugas are very sensitive and can hear everything. They describe an interesting technique that consisted of throwing rocks in the water and making noise with the paddle of the *qajaq* in order to create a kind of passage to guide the beluga to the shore or to a suitable hunting spot. For additional information on beluga hunting, see Kishigami (2005) for Nunavik and Kilabuck (1998) for Nunavut.
9. A connection between seals, whales, fish and shellfish appears in another story collected by Boas, entitled the 'Great Flood' (1888: 637–38): 'A long

time ago the ocean suddenly began to rise, until it covered the whole land. The water even rose to the top of the mountains and the ice drifted over them. When the flood had subsided, the ice stranded and ever since forms an ice cap on the top of the mountains. Many shellfish, fish, seal, and whales were left high and dry and their shells and bones may be seen to this day. A great number of Inuit died during this period, but many others, who had taken to their kayaks when the water commenced to rise, were saved.'

10. Nutaraq from Mittimatalik (quoted in Oosten and Laugrand 2001: 130) attributed a positive role to the killer whale: 'When the seals would come close to shore because they were fleeing from a killer whale I was able to get numerous seals.'

11. Hunting implements for whaling had a special status in the western Arctic. Rasmussen (1927: 312) refers to the destruction of the hunting implements at the end of the whaling season: 'Whaling implements were only allowed to be used for one season; this applies to the skins of the boats, and all gear and equipment. In earlier times, all the harpoons were burned with the other implements in a great bonfire during the festivals held at the conclusion of the season; later, it became the custom simply to hang up the harpoon heads on a frame, where they were left until the chieftain died, when they were placed with him in his grave.'

12. Similar practices existed in the western Arctic. Rasmussen (1927: 313) relates, 'Thus, for instance, a chief's wife, on learning that her husband's crew has harpooned a whale must at once take off one boot and remain quietly in her house. This preliminary step towards undressing was supposed to affect the soul of the whale and draw it towards the house. When then the boat neared the land, she must fill her water-vessel with fresh water and go down to the dead whale in order to refresh its thirsting soul with cool water.'

13. For a discussion of the drinking of water in relation to naming, see Laugrand and Oosten (2009b: 128)).

14. See also the account by Leah Arnaujaq in *Recollections of Inuit Elders* (1986: 11).

15. See also the demand of the deceased to be given a drink of water in a dream, interpreted as a request for their name to be given to a new baby.

16. Saladin d'Anglure (1999: 94) observed that when the whale was killed in Iglulik at the request of Piugaattuq, a feast was organized, and the old man started singing, mixing traditional songs with Christian hymns.

17. See also Rasmussen (1927: 312–15) for the Nalukataq whaling feast in the western Arctic.

18. See Saladin d'Anglure (1999: 96–100) for a description of the ill-fated whale hunt at Repulse Bay in 1996.

19. See also George (2009d). A similar debate with respect to beluga hunting developed in Nunavik. Inuit hunters even proposed to film the beluga, because they were becoming quite numerous; see George (2007; 2009a) and Kishigami (2005). On the debates between Inuit and Canadian wildlife officers regarding beluga whales, see Tyrrell (2007).

20. For additional similar comments, see Freeman et al. (1998: 57).

21. See also Dahl (2000) and Nuttall (1992) for the relation between whale hunting and the community at large in Greenland. Dahl (1990, 2000: 67) describes the same passionate atmosphere, a real fever, when beluga hunting is open and qualifies it as a community-wide activity expressing the collectivity of this small community: 'The days of beluga hunting are days of nerve-racking and intense waiting and watching. Young and old are on the lookout. As soon as the cry *qilalukkat* (belugas) is heard, each and every hunter rushes to his boat. The beluga is on everybody's mind. Women, children, hunters, and old people talk about it, longing for the hunt to be plentiful.'

# Comparisons and Conclusions

## The Predicament of the Hunter

Tivi Etok, from Kangiqsualujjuaq, Nunavik, related a story that expresses the predicament of the Inuit hunter very well:

> The next day the hunter set out to hunt the walrus by qajaq. As he paddled toward the island, a suckling walrus came to greet him. 'Harpoon me, as I would like a drink of water', the suckling walrus said to the great hunter. The man saw how tiny the walrus's tusks were, and did not reply. 'Harpoon me as I would like a drink of water', repeated the walrus. To which the man replied, 'I do not want you, for you have tiny tusks.'
>
> Rebuffed, the suckling walrus turned and fled toward the walrus herd. It shouted to the herd, 'He does not want us! He does not want us!' Hearing this, the herd of walrus began to tumble off the island, and those already in the water swam away. The whole herd fled on hearing such offence.
>
> The caribou also heard the walrus' words, and fled the area. The suckling walrus kept repeating, 'He does not want us!' Whenever it surfaced for air. All kinds of animals heard, and abandoned the area. For many years after, no game ever came to that area. All kinds of seals, walruses, the caribou … even the birds had left. Only the land and water remained.
>
> The entire area was devoid of game and the great hunter's band had lived in a cave on the hill. When they perished, the cave collapsed over their corpses. So they were buried in their own home. When I was a youth, if any stones or ground were disturbed at that site, there was always a strong stench of decay.
>
> When the suckling walrus said, 'Harpoon me, as I would like a drink of water', it is said that it meant, 'Accept me, that there may be plenty of game.' All creatures ever created should be accepted. It has also been said that the animals will return to that area when Inuit begin to act more respectfully toward them. Nowadays, the area is not entirely devoid of game, but there is not an abundance. That is the legend of Alluriliik. (quoted in Weetaluktuk and Bryant 2008: 187–88)

The story relates that the animal requests a drink of water. This refers to the custom that the animal receives a drink of water after it has been killed. It also evokes the fact that the harpooning itself is described as the gift of a drink of water in the Sedna feast. Moreover, it evokes the tradition that a deceased person appears to a pregnant woman in a dream with a request for a drink of water. Such a dream is generally interpreted as a request by the deceased person that the unborn child should receive his/her name. Whereas for a deceased person it means that his name will come to life again and there will be a namesake he/she can support, for the animal it means certain death. But the catch will also enter human society, as its meat will be shared, its skin will be transformed into clothing and all parts of its body will be used. Thus, the animal will become part of society, while its *tarniq* will descend to the sea woman to be reincarnated.

The pregnant woman and the hunter have no choice but to agree to the request. When a game animal approaches the hunter, he must accept the invitation. He knows that each killing entails great risks. As Ivalu-ardjuk explained, the *tarniit* of animals must be propitiated, 'lest they should revenge themselves on us for taking away their bodies'. Thus, the rules of respect have to be observed, and if a transgression is made, things can go awfully wrong. But nothing compares to refusing the request. Then the game will disappear, human beings will starve and ultimately nothing is left but stench, as in the story related by Tivi Etok.

Killing game is not only a necessity to survive, it is also an obligation placed upon the hunter by the animals themselves. Hunting is not a matter of choice, but a moral obligation one cannot escape. Only by hunting can Inuit as well as animals prosper. The hardships and sufferings entailed in hunting and the risks involved in killing the animals must all be accepted. Human society itself is made possible by consuming and sharing the game animals.

Inuit are well aware that other people exist who do not hunt or hunt in other ways. To what extent these people are human, however, is not immediately obvious.

## What Are Human Beings?

The modern worldview teaches us that human beings resemble animals. The shamanic perspective informs us that animals resemble human beings. Like human beings, they have a *tarniq*, a miniature image or shade, and sometimes they can appear as human beings, because they have an *inua*, its human person or owner. Yet, they all resemble human beings in different ways, and in this book we have explored some of the variations in this respect.

The distinction between animals and human beings is by no means straightforward. What does it mean to be human in Inuit culture? Inuit traditionally do not classify all human beings in an encompassing universal category. The concept 'Inuit' applies specifically to the Inuit themselves. White people are *qallunaat,* and Indians are *itqilît* or *allait.* They are different from Inuit, as they are not owners and inhabitants of the land. They have different customs and traditions. They do not follow the same rules of respect as the Inuit do. In a mythical past white people and Indians were supposed to be descended from the union between a dog and an Inuk woman. *Allait* were sometimes thought to behave like dogs. Thus, one might suspect that in an Inuit perspective these non-Inuit were in some respects closer to animals than they were themselves. However, in an Inuit perspective there is little sense in looking for a fundamental distinction between Inuit, *allait* and *qallunaat* on one side and animals on the other.

In Inuit culture we find many traditions about beings that might look like human beings but were not real humans, *inuunngittut,* such as dwarves, giants and *ijirait.* It was useful to know how they behave so one could deal with them when one encountered them, and one should be aware that they were not real Inuit. Just as in the case of a meeting with an animal in human appearance an *angakkuq* would perceive the true nature of such beings. One might have sexual relationships with them, but usually such relations were not supposed to last.

Thus, Inuit did not have a universal notion of humanity, but a differentiated one that allowed for other beings that might look like Inuit, but were not really Inuit. Stories warned people to be cautious in becoming too close to these non-Inuit beings.

## Humanity as a Moral Condition

According to Descola, the common ground of all the entities populating the world is not the humans as a particular species, but humanity as a condition (2005: 30). As we have seen, Inuit are hunters, with all the moral implications this condition implies. In contrast to many other Amazonian groups (see Hugh-Jones 1996), they never feel uncomfortable with killing and eating animals when they need them. They look for game and start their exchanges as soon as the animal has been killed. Their ethics remain that of a hunting society. This morality is complex and not without contradictions. To some extent it could be summarized by the injunction, 'Kill only what you need and share it with others.' The game that offers itself, however, should not be refused, and that may sometimes result in killing more animals than are actually needed. Descriptions of massive killings can be found in historical sources. But once the game is killed, the spoils should be shared. A stingy hunter is not really behaving like a human being. The animals are not afraid of being killed, but of being treated in a disrespectful way.

Inuit are aware that the social nature of human beings cannot be taken for granted. Their survival depends on the observation of social and moral rules. Cannibalism is a case in point. It may happen that in extreme conditions people have to take recourse to the eating of human flesh, as in the case of Attagutaaluk, the wife of the famous Iglulik leader Ittuksarjuaq. Everyone pitied her, and she went through certain rituals to be able to resume ordinary life as a human being. Nowadays, her descendants praise her for surviving such an ordeal, and the primary school in Iglulik is named after her. But Inuit also believe that someone who eats human flesh can acquire a taste for it and will crave it so much that he cannot stop eating it. He becomes a cannibal. Such persons lose their social nature and can no longer be considered part of society. They have to be killed.

Only by observing the rules and rituals of their ancestors can people preserve their human and social nature. A person is not a human being by nature, but by being a moral and social person in terms of the ideas and values of his society. The human moral condition is defined in relation to the parties that sanction the existence of human beings, notably the animals, non-human beings such as the as sea woman and the ancestors. The ancestors are primarily the deceased namesakes. Rasmussen (1929: 58–59) reports,

> Everyone on receiving a name receives with it the strength and skill of the deceased namesake, but since all persons bearing the same name have the same source of life, spiritual and physical qualities are also inherited from those who in the far distant past once bore the same name. The shamans say that sometimes, on their spirit flights, they can see, behind each human being, as it were a mighty procession of spirits aiding and guiding, as long as the rules of life are duly observed; but when this is not done, or if a man is tempted to some act unwelcome to the dead, then all the invisible guardians turn against him as enemies, and he is lost beyond hope.

Whereas the deceased namesakes will support the hunter who derives his skills and abilities from them, the punishments for transgressions usually come from the animals and their owners, not the deceased. In particular, the animals will no longer offer themselves to be killed.

The discussion on the distinctions between humans and animals tends to focus on concepts that are perceived to transcend cultural differences such as soul, subject and person. Viveiros de Castro (1998: 476) states that it is the soul that makes a being into a subject:

> To say then, that animals and spirits are people is to say that they are persons and to attribute to non-humans the capacities of conscious intentionality and agency which define the position of the subject. Such capacities are objectified as the soul or the spirit with which these non-humans are endowed. Whatever possesses a soul is a subject, and whatever has a soul is capable of having a point of view.

The meaning of Western concepts such as soul, spirit, subject and consciousness are by no means clear and central topics in academic debates. They are very hard to translate into Inuit concepts. Viveiros de Castro points out that in many societies animals and human beings were originally the same, and he postulates: 'Any being which vicariously occupies the point of reference, being in the position of the subject, sees itself as a member of the human species' (1998: 477). This perspective does not apply to Inuit. We have no evidence in Inuit stories or other testimonies that animals consider themselves human beings.

Viveiros de Castro's theory of perspectivism is based on his valorization of the subject. He argues, 'It is not that animals are subjects because they are humans in disguise, but rather that they are human because they are potential subjects. This is to say Culture is the Subject's nature, it is the form in which every subject experiences its own nature' (1998: 477). Instead of considering culture as the nature of the subject, as proposed by Viveiros de Castro, we prefer to view the person as well as the subject as social constructs that vary for each particular society.

It is quite clear that Inuit attribute awareness, intelligence and feelings to animals. Inuit assume animals have their own communities where they live in human appearance and follow their own rules. Rasmussen (1929: 269) presents a story called 'The Owls That Talked and Lived Like Human Beings'; he also relates the story of a shaman who visited the foxes in human appearance. When he returned later he only found a foxhole with foxes in it. The story concludes, 'the foxes live just like human beings and have their shamans just like all others' (Rasmussen 1931: 306–7). Another story relates how Kiviuq, on a quest for one of his non-human wives, entered into a hole in which the animals had a songfest and competed with each other via their songs. Thus, animals are social in their own terms, but their sociality is irrelevant in human society. Here they do not acquire a social status, and they remain anonymous beings to be killed by the hunter. Hunters should kill animals, and animals prosper when they are killed by hunters. But there is no such thing as a social contract between social parties. The hunters may bring small offerings to the deceased or to the owners of the game or even to the animals themselves, but success in hunting is never ensured.

According to Willerslev (2007: 106), hunters undergo a process of corporeal dehumanization in order to be reshaped in the image of their prey. By mimicking an animal's bodily behaviour, senses and sensibilities empathetically the hunter can really assume the quality of the other's perspective. Inuit hunters sometimes adopt the image and the actions of the animals (see, e.g., the technique of *uutuq* hunting, approaching the seal on the ice), but they are very well aware that they are not seals and adopt this technique to trick the seal. Shamans are often able to transform into an animal, but they should retain the awareness that they are not really animals so they can transform into human beings again whenever they want to.

Willerslev (2007: 108) also observes, 'Mimetic empathy registers not only similarity, but also difference', since '[f]eelings of empathy arise precisely because the other's experiences are not mine, because we are different beings that, in the face of our dissimilarity, possess similar access to basic bodily and sensory experiences'. Inuit always value the recognition of differences. Humans and animals share the same world and nature, but not the same level or degree of humanity. Human beings have to remain hunters and not become prey, and animals are expected to remain prey and not become hunters of human beings.

Willerslev (2007: 127) argues, 'During hunting, the boundary between self and other, human and nonhuman, is somehow dissolved, and the hunter comes to experience himself ambiguously as both hunter and animal'; 'killing the animal, then, is for him rather like killing a fellow person, although it is not the same as killing someone identical to himself'. This brings us to the notion of the person that plays a central part in the debates on hunting societies.

## Non-human Persons

Already in the early 1990s Ann Fienup-Riordan qualified animals as non-human persons, implying that even though animals are not humans, they are persons. She emphasizes that the mutual respect between humans and animals has to be 'understood in both positive and negative terms, including love and fear'. She explains that among the Yup'ik, the most commonly used term is *takar-*, which means 'to be shy of, respectful toward' and/or 'intimidated by'. She observes that this notion is used by juniors in reference to their relationship with elders as well as by humans in reference to their relationship with certain animals, and may also refer to the weather (Fienup-Riordan 1990: 169).[1] But respect does not mean that humans and animals are equivalent. According to Fienup-Riordan, animals can reveal themselves in human form once they have been skinned (see Fienup-Riordan 1990: 169–70), but this visual aspect does not imply that they are human beings. On the contrary, as stated by Fienup-Riordan (1990: 170), these tales '[d]epict animals appearing as humans and describe their social interaction, [but] they also serve to underline the differences between them and their contrasting perceptions'.

Fienup-Riordan (1994: 159, 188) argues that humans and animals are conceived as incomplete without the other, and '[t]he relationship between men and women and the relationship between humans and animals are represented as analogous in some contexts'. She emphasizes reciprocity: 'The seal's thirst for water motivated its gifts of meat and oil to human hunters, while human hunger required careful attention to the seals' needs.' According to Fienup-Riordan (1994: 48–49),

> The differentiation of persons into humans and nonhumans was for Eskimo peoples at the foundation of social life.... The essential relationship in the Arctic is between humans (male or female) and animals.... The ritual process creates the passages between worlds as cultural rules set the boundaries between them. Food sharing and gift giving constitute the core of Yup'ik social life. During the annual cycle of ceremonies, dead humans and animals were gradually drawn into living society, feasted and hosted, and finally sent away again.

Fienup-Riordan states that Yup'ik differentiate between persons who are human beings and those who are non-human beings. Thus, the notion of person becomes an encompassing concept. But what is meant by the term 'person'? The original meaning of the word is 'mask': it is an identity someone can adopt.[2] A mask may hide someone by providing him with a new identity, but it may also represent someone's true identity. Thus, the mask can reveal what the face hides, and it can hide what the face reveals. The use of masks in play, ritual and so on usually provides an insight into the relations between different perspectives of human identity. R. Nelson (1983: 394) states that among the Inuit of the Bering Strait, 'It is also believed that in early days all animate beings had a dual existence, becoming at will either like men or the animal forms they now wear; if an animal wished to assume its human form, the forearm, wing or other limb was raised and pushed up the muzzle or beak as if it were a mask and the creature became manlike in form and features.'

Thus, the distinction between humans and animals did not exist in the mythical past in the way it does now. Yet, the masks preserved the ancient unity of humans and animals. In the context of ritual the wearer of the mask represented the animal, and when he opened the mask, his face represented the *inua* of the animal. Thus, the ritual use of masks enabled the Inuit to encompass contrasts between different modes of being.

The human appearance of the animal is a mask that hides its lack of a social identity, as the animal is not named and cannot be identified with a particular person. An Inuk story related how the true nature of a bear in human appearance visiting human beings was revealed. When asked what his name was, he could only answer 'Bear'.

Animals can be killed and eaten, because they are not human and do not have a social identity. They remain anonymous. We may find traditions (as in the story of Arnaqtaaqtuq) that human beings can be reborn as animals, but if this happens, they do not acquire a social identity. It can only be recovered when they are born again as human beings and receive a name. The *atiq*, name, connects one to a deceased namesake and firmly positions one in a social network. The importance of the name also comes to the fore in the old tradition that a newborn could no longer be killed once it was named. Human beings die and they do not return to life. Their *tarniit* are supposed to travel to the land of the deceased under the sea or in the sky. Only when something goes terribly wrong, usually through the transgressions of people, will they turn into evil spirits, known as *tupilait*, that roam the earth. Their names are passed on to their namesakes, who will be supported by their deceased predecessors, and in this way the continuity of society is ensured. However, animals will return time and again to the same hunter who killed them and treated them with respect. They are not connected to their ancestors, but to the hunter who kills them.

In Inuit societies, animals have consciousness and awareness, but they are different from human beings in that they lack names that connect them to their ancestors. It is this relationship that provides human beings with a social identity and the lack of this relationship makes it impossible for animals to be part of human society. They are anonymous beings who can only participate in human society by allowing themselves to be killed. Through death they become part of society, as their meat is shared and eaten and their skins are transformed into the furs that enable human beings to survive. The killing of game makes the existence of society possible, as the animal becomes an object of social exchange through sharing. As the example of the seal shows, the patterns of sharing and the community itself are shaped by the seal that is killed. The seal can only become part of society by being killed, and the society can only take shape through the seal that allows itself to be killed on the condition that it is shared, thus creating society.

## Transformations

Transformation from human beings into animals and animals into human beings is a recurrent theme in Inuit mythology and art. Mythology relates how originally human beings could become animals, and an animal could become a human being. Transformation of a human being into a non-human being usually implied loss of humanity and desocialization. Inversely, transformation of an animal into a human being did not imply that the animal became a social being.

The origin stories of animals and their owners often relate how someone through his own faults or those of others was turned into an animal or a non-human being who no longer participated in human society. The story of the origin of the ptarmigan as told by Ivaluardjuk (quoted in Rasmussen 1929: 164–65) is a good example of this pattern. It relates that an old woman frightened her child so much by a story that it changed into a snow bunting. The old woman wept so much that she herself changed into a ptarmigan.

The pattern is also very clear in the myth of the origin of the sea woman, which not only explains her origin, but also those of the animals that originated from her finger joints after they were cut off by her father. The sea woman herself sank to the bottom of the sea, and there she still lives, immortal, disabled and transformed into an awesome being the shamans have to face when they wish to make the sea mammals accessible to human beings. The non-social nature of the animals and their owners is marked in these stories and constitutes an essential feature of their nature.

In Inuit traditions, an animal can adopt a human appearance that may fool ordinary people. *Angakkuit*, shamans, however, are able to perceive the true nature of such an appearance and recognize the animal behind it. In the Kiviuq narratives, the hero meets a wide range of animals who all turn out to be unsuitable as spouses. Some, like the big bee and a female black bear, try to eat him; others actually offer themselves to him as wife, but the relation cannot last, and sooner or later those animals usually resume human shape. In the Nattilik version of the story, Kiviuq ends up as a rich man with many lives in the land of the white men, but without a wife. Most stories of temporary alliances between animal and human spouses exhibit this pattern. Eventually, an animal in human appearance will resume its animal shape.

Inuit cannot switch from one mode of being to another, unlike in the mythological past. As opposed to spirits, they can only be in one place at one time. Animals and spirits lack this temporal feature, and transformation is essential to their nature. They can still change their appearance, whereas for human beings this applies only to the shaman. It is a risky business, however, as the shaman may lose his human nature by crossing the boundaries between human and non-human and mixing with non-human beings.

Transformations from one animal into another were also possible. In the past, Inuit believed that bowhead whales could sometimes turn into narwhals when they were harpooned. Isa Koperqualuk from Puvirnituq related, 'One should not attack a polar bear by surprise, the bear may transform into a fox, or even worse, a ptarmigan' (quoted in Avataq Cultural Institute 1984: 165). He related that in the same fashion a bearded seal should also be warned before one was going to kill it. This need to prevent the transformation of the animal into a much less desirable species may explain whistling to a seal before shooting it.[3]

On the level of the *tarniq*, transformation plays a central part. The story of Arnaqtaaqtuq relates how a human being transformed into many animals before finally being reborn as a human being and receiving its own name again. The sea woman was able to reincarnate the *tarniq* of human beings in animals, and in the descriptions of shamanic séances the *tarniit* of the deceased appear as anonymous animals. On this level the distinction between human beings and animals can easily collapse. The distinction is maintained by names, as illustrated by the séance described by Rasmussen (1929: 125) in which the deceased namesakes of the *angakkuq* can be heard puffing and sighing like marine animals until the participants in the séance address them by their names. Names are the prerogative of human beings and they are only shared with dogs, the animal companions of human beings in society. But whereas the names of human beings connect them to their deceased namesakes, the names of dogs only connect them to their owners and not to ancestors.

## Keeping the Correct Distance and the Problem of the Gift

The non-social nature of animals requires that human beings keep their distance from animals and not become too close to them. In the Iglulik Oral Traditions Project database we find an extensive discourse on bestiality as a relation that has to be avoided. We also find various stories relating the disastrous consequences of a too-intimate relationship, as in the story of a woman who nursed a larva. Thus, human beings should not become too intimate with animals. The dog is the animal that comes closest to human beings, as a hunting companion that only survives in human society. But Inuit always maintain their distance to dogs and traditionally never allowed them in their living space. Sometimes other animals, such as bears, could be adopted and kept in the igloo for some time. Inuit were aware that such a relation could not last, and when the animal grew too big, it was set free again (see figure 11.1). But such animals were not considered suited for consumption. The failed introduction of herding caribou in the 1920s is a case in point. It required that the Inuit accompany and supervise the herds of caribou, and this did not appeal to the Inuit. Pauloosie Kilabuk, one of the Inuit herders, related that human beings and caribou would become too close and that it would not be good if human beings saw the caribou mating.

**Figure 11.1.** Inuk holding a lemming and a falcon in Nunavik, where these birds are sometimes kept for a short period before being released in the tundra. Photo: Robert Fréchette/Avataq Cultural Institute.

If the correct distance between hunters and animals is maintained, animals will offer themselves to be killed and human beings will be able to survive by killing their prey. It is tempting to interpret this in terms of a gift, in accordance with the magnificent scheme developed by Mauss (1989) in his study of the gift. The notion of the gift is certainly important in Inuit hunting. In the past the owners of the game such as the sea woman and the moon man might act as givers of game. In the South Baffin area, many *tuurngait* were marked as givers of game. The ancestors were also usually considered givers of game. After the adoption of Christianity, God became the true owner of the game and it was believed that God had created the animals to be hunted by humanity. The model of the gift operated within a religious context and required a notion of ownership of game. The owners of the game will give up the animals if human beings observe the necessary moral and religious rules of respect towards the animals and their owners. Animals itself were usually considered as object, not as subject, of the gift, but sometimes the animal itself is referred to as a giver. In chapter 2 we quoted Simionie Akpalialuk from Pangnirtung stating, 'A whale gives of itself: it's an animal that you feel fully about, it's something that gives itself up to you and that's an important thing in our beliefs, that's still very strong' (quoted in Freeman et al. 1998: 42). It should also be emphasized that even in this case the gift of the animal only implied that it made itself available. The hunter still had to capture it and take its life.

The notion of the gift does not exclude an awareness of the violence that is done to an animal in killing it. Even though Inuit always tried to make a clean kill that would not cause unnecessary suffering, violence could not be avoided. The killing and preparation of the meat as well as the preparation and sewing of skins were complex operations fraught with danger. The rules of respect were intended to safeguard these processes. Mauss was fascinated by the notion of the gift and the idea of a counter-gift, postulating that each gift required a counter-gift. This may apply to relations within society where human beings are by definition social beings, but it is rather doubtful whether it can apply to beings who lack a social nature. Animals and their owners have to be induced to make the game available by observing ritual injunctions, making small offerings or tempting and seducing their prey. If all this fails, human beings have to force these beings to supply human beings with the food they need and coerce them into continuing to allow animals to be killed. This is the key to the shamanic performances where the *angakkuit* struggle with the sea woman in times of starvation so she will finally succumb and set the game free again. The violence involved in the relation between hunters and their prey also applies to the relation between hunters and the owners of the prey. The killing of the prey remains the key moment in the hunting process, bringing great enjoyment to the hunter as well as all who depend on him for their survival.

Regardless of the small gifts that may be given to the owners of the game at the beginning of the hunting season, an asymmetrical relationship continues to exist between the owners of the game (the sea woman, the *tuurngait*, God) and human beings. Human beings cannot reciprocate with a gift of equal value to the prey. They remain indebted to these transcendental agents. By giving animals, these owners not only enable human beings to survive but also enable them to become social beings by sharing the catch. In Inuit society there is an obligation to share the meat with others. The owners of the animals and the animals themselves observe whether the prey is handled correctly by the hunter and his wife, whether it is shared in the camp and how it is celebrated in the feasts. The sharing of meat results in more game. The sharing of goods also contributes to the abundance of game. In his brief description of the Inuit winter feast, Hall notes, 'Finally presents of various articles are thrown from one to another, with the idea that each will receive of Sidne[4] good things in proportion to the liberality here shown' (1864: 2:323). In the maintenance of the flow of life the Inuit give to each other and their generosity maintains the flow of life. We should not underestimate the significance of the small gifts to the owners of the game and the spirits of the dead; they open the path for the game. But in those domains people cannot gain status as a giver of meat or goods. The abundance of game depends on the generosity of the owners. In relations with the owners of the game, the Inuit respect the game and observe the rules; in relations with each other, they share so that the flow of game continues.

## Trickery and Seduction

The analogy between hunting and seduction appears in many contexts. According to Therrien (1987a: 64), the term *qiniqpuq* means 'to look for a proper game' and 'a woman who agrees'. Chaussonnet (1988) explored this topic in Alaska, analyzing the beauty of the hunter's woman as if the hunter would have to seduce the animal through the beauty of his wife. The relation of the hunter to the game is often perceived in terms of the male-female relationship, the hunter being the man and the prey the female. The killing is modelled on sexual intercourse. In dreams the prey often appears as a woman, and in both cases an element of seduction may be implied. Many hunting techniques imply an element of trickery (e.g., the use of traps, the *uutuq* technique of seal hunting) and/or seduction (e.g., the singing to the animals, the imitation of the animal behaviour) (see figure 11.2).

**Figure 11.2.** Imitating the seal, *uutuq* hunting. *Source:* Anglican Church of Canada/ General Synod Archives/Peck Papers, M56-1, series XXXIII, 4–6, 8–13.

The feasts celebrated before the beginning of the caribou hunting season convey a seductive image of society to the prey. They show the men and women in their finery and at their best. The men show themselves to be hunters, and in the rituals described by Kumlien and Boas, the shamans play the roles of the game, showing the animals their part in the hunt. The women show themselves to be sexually attractive, seductive beings. Men and women show their enjoyment in the games. This seductive image of society is conveyed to the animals, and it is not supposed to be contaminated by any dimension of human existence that might spoil this image: menstruation, birth and death. Moreover, in these rituals men and women often identify with birds. The women move like gulls, and the men identify with the bird whose skin was used when they were wiped clean after birth. Thus, in the context of ritual the distinction between human beings and animals can to some extent be lifted.

Stories do deal with actual marriages between human beings and animals (such as the Kiviuq stories). But these marriages usually do not last. They illustrate that the differences between Inuit and animals do not allow for permanent spousal relationships. Thus, the marriage remains an illusion that can never become reality.

Exchange of women was a widespread phenomenon in Inuit culture. It seems everywhere to have been a basic shamanic practice. Boas (1901: 158) reports that each shamanic séance was followed by an exchange of wives and that the partners should not be close relatives. Ethnographic sources indicate that sexual intercourse with a shaman was often part of a healing practice[5] and the missionaries always associated shamanic practices with an exchange of women. Exchange of women often was obligatory and could not be refused (see the discussion of the bumblebee in chapter 5).

In the ritual feasts preparing for the hunting season, sexual intercourse often takes place between partners who are not married. Usually a contest or a test is involved. The winner of an archery contest has the first choice of a woman in the caribou ritual in Labrador, men may express their preference in the selection of a woman in the Sedna feast in South Baffin, men and woman should not smile in the Tivajuut in the North Baffin area and so on. Prowess and dexterity of men as well as women appear to play an important part in the preparation for sexual intercourse with the partner. In showing their skills they make themselves attractive. The sexual intercourse itself appears to prefigure the killing of an animal, an act that is already modelled on sexual intercourse, just as killing with the spear or harpoon is often a metaphor for the act of sexual intercourse. Sexual intercourse may take place between unmarried partners representing animals or transcendental agents, but never between the hunter and the prey itself. Seduction may be an effective means to lure the animals to the hunter, but in the final act the sexual intercourse should remain a metaphor as the animal falls prey to the hunter.

This act of prefiguring is to some extent a form of non-verbal communication par excellence that allows Inuit and animals to build the correct relationship of hunter and prey between them. The game comes to the hunter and offers itself. That offer should not be ignored or slighted, but it is not a simple gift. Once the hunting starts, the animal will try to escape the hunter, and the hunter will need all his skills and resourcefulness to make the kill. And he may also fail. There is no such thing as a free gift.

## Animals and Humans in Context

Animals as well as significant places such as the crossing places of caribou or lakes have an *inua*, a person, inhabitant or owner, who has to be respected. All these owners are different. Thus, the owners of lakes and other significant places do not have camps where they live together as some animals do. But they may require certain offerings and observance of specific rules of respect. Instead of generalizing about a shared human nature of all animals and places, we have to take the variations of different animals and places into account.

For example, insects can also appear as human beings. Stories tell that they are masters of life and death because they operate on the level of the *tarniq*. Often they have the nature of predators, attacking animals as well as human beings, and if they come too close, entering the human body, they can be lethal.

In the case of the whale the notion of the *inua* is less emphasized and it seems more often to be a metaphorical relationship with encompassing categories such as the house and the camp. Today, the whale allows Inuit to encompass the past and the present and to connect communities. Whale hunting has acquired great significance, connecting people to God as well as to their ancestors. Some animals are often placed in a metaphorical relationship to human beings such as the bear, a fellow hunter, or the raven who like human beings has *isuma*. When a metonymical relation comes into play the bear and the raven may become eaters of men. Other animals are usually placed in a metonymical relationship with human beings. This may also apply to some extent to ravens, who as scavengers tend to live close to human beings.

Prey animals such as seals and caribou are also in a metonymical relationship with human beings, as their meat is eaten and their skins are used for clothing and other purposes. The metaphorical relationship with human beings is less emphasized, and instead their humanity is to some extent transferred to non-human beings such as *ijirait* and *tuutaliit*. Moreover, they may become associated with the ancestors. In the case of the *ijirait* the deceased may join them, and in the case of the seals, they appear to represent the anonymous ancestors in the context of a shamanic séance.

Perceptions of animals depend on contexts. In the case of birth or death, hunting or shamanic séances, perceptions may vary. And Inuit are well aware of the significance of these contexts. Contexts of birth and death have to be strictly separated from those of hunting, and many rules pertain to that[6]. In the context of shamanism, many things are possible that cannot happen in other contexts: shamans may transform into animals, they may travel to the land of the deceased and so on. In many respects shamanism constitutes an encompassing context, as it adds a new level to the experiences of everyday life. Thus, the connection between ancestors and seals does not play a significant part in the practice of hunting, only in the context of the séance. However, we should be cautious. There is no strict distinction between shamans and non-shamans and the use of *irinaliutiit* or specific ritual acts may create a shamanic context regardless of whether a shaman is participating or not. Many hunters can give accounts of encounters with non-human beings, and people have to be prepared all the time for a shift from ordinary life to a shamanic context. Inuit are very much aware of differences in context, and are very cautious in their generalizations about the distinctions between animals and human beings.

## The Debate on the Protection of Animals

After the adoption of Christianity the old owners of the game disappeared and God became the sole owner of the game, but this change of role did not change the view that the game was intended to be killed by the hunters. Even today many hunters believe that the game will disappear if it is not appropriately hunted. The modern debate on quotas and the abundance of game is closely related to this view.

Biologists try to protect the game by asking for quotas to reduce hunting. Many Inuit feel that only if the game is hunted and feels appreciated by human beings can animals prosper and multiply. The debate is exacerbated by the fact that Inuit hunters often completely disagree with the estimates biologists make of the availability of game, and in recent years Inuit hunters have often been proven to give better assessments than biologists (as in the case of the bowhead whales discussed in chapter 10).

Even though the old rules have largely disappeared, the notion of respect is still very much alive in the debate on the relations between hunters and prey. Piugaattuq and Imaruittuq emphasized one should not quarrel about game, as that would negatively affect the hunt. Hunters also state that people should not quarrel among themselves if they wish to be successful as hunters. Thus, the hunting life implies a moral discourse where relations between human beings and relations between animals and human beings determine the prosperity and well-being of society. Obviously this has an impact on Inuit perceptions of attempts by *qallunaat* to stop or reduce hunting by introducing quotas on hunting and boycotting furs of seals and other prey. These measures can easily be perceived as a means to destroy the hunting life and culture of the Inuit. The result is a growing distrust, leading to prohibitions on filming Inuit hunting activities such as the narwhal hunt in Clyde River. The debates on whaling also prove this point.

During the early fall of 2008 about 629 narwhals were trapped by the winter freeze-up of the sea ice (*Northern News Services* 2008)[7]. Normally, narwhals would have migrated to their wintering area in Baffin Bay, but for unknown reasons they became trapped and were doomed to starve or drown when their last breathing holes disappeared. With the authorization of the DFO, the NWMB and local elders, the Mittimatalik Hunters and Trappers Organization (HTO) spent two weeks killing the narwhals, pulling them out of the water to harvest the meat. This massive catch gave the hunters an occasion to teach the younger generations how to kill and harvest whales and it soon became the largest bounty in decades.

The Evangelical movements acknowledged the significance of the catch. Thus, Roger Armbruster, the director of the Canada Awakening Ministries, quotes an Inuk from Mittimatalik on his blog:

> The people of Pond Inlet are doing everything they can to help out with the harvesting of the whales so that nothing goes to waste. Inuit have great respect for the animals that they hunt.... 'We thank the Creator for giving us the animals as we thank Him every time we harvest something. ... We hope you learn that Inuit respect the animals, and nothing will go to waste. We are so thankful to our Creator for giving us all the meat we can use, and thank you for the people who supported us!!!'

This successful catch resulted in a bitter debate between Inuit leaders and an environmentalist group, the Sea Shepherd Conservation Society, which called on the government to send an icebreaker to save the narwhals. The society's leader, Paul Watson, called the killings a war crime that could have been prevented by the Canadian government, and subsequently two federal ministers demanded the resignation of Watson as leader of the Sea Shepherd Conservation Society (see Zarate 2008). Watson described the killings as a 'bloody massacre' where 'Inuit killers roared and laughed barbarously as they inflicted torturous death upon these gentle creatures'. In a reaction to Terry Audla, the executive director of the Qikiqtani Inuit Association, Watson stated,

> Don't give me that mealy mouthed tripe about respect. What the men with the rifles did to those intelligent and gentle sentient creatures was NOT respect by any stretch of the imagination ... it was a savage display of human arrogance.

This statement implies a complete inversion of Inuit values. Arrogance is substituted for respect. A fruitful dialogue between environmentalist groups and Inuit can only develop if environmentalist groups learn to better understand Inuit perspectives and grasp that animals can be respected and protected in many ways and that for Inuit, hunting is a way of respecting animals.[8] Through hunting, human society can take shape, and the well-being of animals as well as human beings depends on it. This awareness that animals depend on human beings and human beings depend on animals is what makes an Inuk. Being an Inuk is not just an identity constructed by people; it is also provided by the animals themselves.

## Notes

1. Regarding the Dene, Sharp (2001: 67–68) writes that animal abuse is not about predation, but about '[w]hy an animal is killed, the wastage of an animal that has been killed, the means by which the animal is killed, or the exposure of its remains to pollution'.
2. In Greek and Roman theatre the use of masks allowed an actor to adopt the identity of the person he wished to represent.
3. The transformation of a boy into a girl before birth may be connected to this (see Dufour 1988).
4. Sedna, the sea woman, the *inua* of the sea.
5. See Oosten (1986) for a discussion of this practice.
6. People connected with birth or death should not be seen by game animals, and all contact with game should be avoided. These processes are thought

to give rise to a vapour, *pujartuq*, emanating from the human body that can be observed by the animals.

7. On this issue, see also Bird (2008c) and CBC news (2008).

8. A few years later, in 2010, a new scientific study raised the total estimate of narwhals in the High Arctic from 30, 000 to 60, 000 (see Boswell 2010). DFO was obliged to revise its count, showing that Inuit hunters were quite right.

# Inuit Elders

Most elders presented in the following list are identified by their place of residence when they were participating in our courses or workshops or when they were interviewed. However, the relation between an elder and a community is not always straightforward. Some elders may have grown up in another community, they may identify more with a specific category (e.g., Nattilingmiut) than with a specific community and so forth. We also list major Inuit informants of Peck, Rasmussen and Mary-Rousselière, including some renowned *angakkuit*.

| | |
|---|---|
| **Aava** (also spelled **Aua** or **Ava**) | Aivilingmiutaq *angakkuq;* informant of Rasmussen |
| **Akpalialuk** | elder from Pangniqtuuq |
| **Akpik, Simeonie** | elder from Kimmirut |
| **Aksaajuq, Etuangat** | elder from Pangniqtuuq |
| **Alaralak, Felix** | elder from Iglulik |
| **Alogut, Peter** | elder from Coral Harbour |
| **Amarualik, Eugene** | elder from Iglulik |
| **Analok** | elder from the central Arctic |
| **Anarqaq** | informant of Rasmussen (Nattilingmiut) |
| **Anautalik, Luke** | elder from Arviat |
| **Anautalik, Mary** | elder from Arviat |
| **Angmaalik, Pauloosie** | elder from Pangniqtuuq |
| **Angohalluq, Marion T.** | elder from Qamanittuaq |
| **Angutinngurniq, Jose** | elder from Kugaaruk |
| **Annahatak, Noah** | elder from Kangirsujuaq |

| | |
|---|---|
| **Aqatsiaq** or **Aqattiaq** | elder from Iglulik |
| **Aqiaruaq, Zacharias** | elder from North Baffin |
| **Arnatsiaq, Peter** | elder from Iglulik |
| **Arnaujaq, Leah** | elder from Hudson Bay |
| **Arngnasungaaq, Barnabas** | elder from Qamanittuuq |
| **Arreak, Benjamin** | elder from Mittimatalik |
| **Ataguttiaq, Tipuula Qaapik** | elder from Ikpiarjuk |
| **Aua** | See **Aava** |
| **Aupilaarjuk, Mariano** | elder from Kangiq&iniq |
| **Ell, Benn** | elder from Iqaluit |
| **Etok, Tivi** | elder from Nunavik |
| **Evik, Jaco** | elder from Pangniqtuuq |
| **Gibbons, Angela** | elder from Coral Harbour |
| **Hakongak, Naikak** | elder from Cambridge Bay |
| **Haqpi, Annie** | elder from Qamanittuuq |
| **Idlout, Mosesie** | elder from Resolute Bay |
| **Igjugârjuk** or **Igjugaarjuk** | famous *angakkuq* from the Kivalliq; informant of Rasmussen |
| **Ijiraq, Alain** | elder from Iglulik |
| **Ijjangiaq, Marc** | elder from Iglulik |
| **Ijjangiaq, Teresi** | elder from Iglulik |
| **Iksivalitaq** | famous *angakkuq* from Kugaaruk; informant of Rasmussen |
| **Iluittuq, Levi** | elder from Kugaaruk |
| **Imaruittuq, Emile** | elder from Iglulik |
| **Innakatsik, Olive M.** | elder from Qamanittuuq |
| **Innuksuk, Aipilik** | elder from Iglulik |
| **Inugpasugjuk** | from Nattilik; informant of Rasmussen |
| **Inuksaq** | elder from Arviat |
| **Ipeelee, Osuitok** | elder from Kinngait |
| **Iqallijuq, Rose** | elder from Iglulik |
| **Iqijjuk, Celestine** | elder from the Kivalliq |
| **Issigaitok, Sabine** | elder from Sanirajak |
| **Itinnuaq, Lizzie** | elder from Kangiq&iniq |
| **Itinnuaq, Ollie** | elder from Kangiq&iniq |

| | |
|---|---|
| **Itqiliq** | elder informant of Rasmussen |
| **Itukallak, Peter** | elder from Puvirnituq |
| **Ivaluardjuk** | Aivilingmiutaq informant of Rasmussen |
| **Joamie, Aalasi** | elder from Iqaluit |
| **Joamie, Akisu** | elder from Iqaluit |
| **Kakka, Joanasie** | elder from South Baffin |
| **Kalluk, Silas** | elder from Qamanittuaq |
| **Kanajuq, Michel** | elder from Qamanittuaq; informant of Mary-Rousselière |
| **Kappianaq, George Agiaq** | elder from Iglulik |
| **Katsak, Rhoda K.** | elder from Mittimatalik |
| **Kattuk, Lucasie** | elder from Sanikiluaq |
| **Kaunak, John** | elder from Naujaat |
| **Kilabuck, Annie** | elder from South Baffin |
| **Kripanik, Philip** | elder from Naujaat |
| **Kunuk, Paul** | elder from Iglulik |
| **Kupaaq, Michel** | elder from Iglulik |
| **Kupak, Felix** | elder from Naujaat |
| **Kutiutikku, Martha** | elder from Kugaaruk |
| **Makitgaq, John** | elder from Qamanittuaq |
| **Malikki, Laimikki** | elder from Naujaat |
| **Manelaq** | Nattilik elder; informant of Rasmussen |
| **Mapsalak, Marcel** | elder from Naujaat |
| **Mike, Johnny** | elder from Pangniqtuuq |
| **Mitiarjuk Nappaaluk, Salome** | elder from Kangiqsujuaq (Nunavik) |
| **Muqyunniq, Eva** | elder from Arviat |
| **Muqyunniq, Job** | elder from Arviat |
| **Nagjuk** | *angakkuq* from the Kivalliq |
| **Nakasuk** | Nattilik informant of Rasmussen |
| **Nakasuk, Saullu** | elder from Pangniqtuuq |
| **Nalungiaq** | Nattilik informant of Rasmussen |
| **Nappaalk, Naalak** | elder from Kangirsujuaq |
| **Nasook, Martha** | elder from Iglulik |
| **Natak, Johny** | elder from Kangir&iniq |

| | |
|---|---|
| **Netser, Tina** | elder from Coral Harbour |
| **Netsit** | Umingmaktormiut informant of Rasmussen |
| **Novalinga, Charlie** | elder from Sanikiluaq |
| **Nuliajuk, Luke** | elder from Uqsuqtuuq |
| **Nutaraaluk, Lucassie** | elder from Iqaluit |
| **Nutaraq, Cornelius** | elder from Mittimatalik |
| **Okpik, Abe** | elder living in Iqaluit |
| **Okpik, Peter** | elder from Uqsuqtuuq |
| **Oosutapik** | elder from Cumberland Sound; informant of Peck |
| **Ootoova, Elisapee** | elder from Mittimatalik |
| **Ootoova, Regilee** | elder from Mittimatalik |
| **Orpingalik** | Nattilik informant of Rasmussen |
| **Orulo** | Iglulik informant of Rasmussen |
| **Paniaq, Herve** | elder from Iglulik |
| **Paniaq, Martha** | elder from Kugaaruk |
| **Panikpakuttuk** | elder from Iglulik |
| **Peryouar, Barnabas** | elder from Qamanittuaq |
| **Peryouar, Betty** | elder from Qamanittuaq |
| **Pirlurtuut** | elder from Kangiqsujuaq |
| **Pisiulak, Lypa** | elder from Pangniqtuuq |
| **Pisiulak, Markosie** | elder from Pangniqtuuq |
| **Pisuk, Felix** | elder from Kangiq&iniq |
| **Pitseolak, Peter** | elder from Kinngait |
| **Pitsiulaaq, Jaiku** | elder from Iqaluit |
| **Piugaattuq, Noah** | elder from Iglulik |
| **Putumiraqtuq, Silas** | elder from Qamanittuaq |
| **Putumiraqtuq, Winnie T.** | elder from Qamanittuaq |
| **Qaggutaq** | elder from Iglulik |
| **Qajuina** | elder; informant of Métayer |
| **Qalasiq, Salome** | elder from Kangiq&iniq |
| **Qamaniq, Nathan** | elder from Iglulik |
| **Qavviaktok** | elder; informant of Métayer |
| **Qiliqti** | elder from Mittimatalik; informant of Mary-Rousselière |

| | |
|---|---|
| **Qimuksiraaq** | famous Nattilik *angakkuq* from Igluligaarjuk |
| **Qipanniq, Philip** | elder from Iglulik |
| **Qojessie** | South Baffin informant of Peck |
| **Quassa, François** | elder from Iglulik |
| **Quinangnaq, Samson** | elder from Qamanittuaq |
| **Saila, Pauta** | elder from Kinngait |
| **Sikkuark, Nick** | elder from Kangir&iniq |
| **Suvaksiuq, Peter** | elder from Arviat |
| **Tagoona, Armand** | Inuit Christian leader from the Kivalliq |
| **Taipanaaq** | elder from Qamanittuaq |
| **Takornaq** | Iglulik informant of Mathiassen |
| **Taliriktuq** | famous *angakkuq* from Igluligaarjuk |
| **Tapaqti, Pujuat** | elder from Kangir&iniq |
| **Tarkik, Kaudjak** | elder from Salluit |
| **Tassugat, Nauja** | elder from Kangirtugaapik |
| **Tataniq, George** | elder from Qamanittuaq; informant of Mary-Rousselière |
| **Temela, Oolletea** | elder from Kimmirut |
| **Tookoome, Simon** | elder from Qamanittuaq |
| **Tullaugak, Josie T.** | elder from Nunavik |
| **Tuluqtuq, Julie H.** | elder from Qamanittuaq |
| **Tungilik, Victor** | elder from Naujaat |
| **Ujaraq** | elder from Iglulik |
| **Ukkumaaluk** | elder from Iglulik; informant of Mary-Rousselière |
| **Uninnak, Marc** | elder from Aupaluk |
| **Uqalik** | elder from Iglulik |
| **Uqsuralik** | elder from South Baffin |
| **Uuttuvak, Ilisapi** | See **Ootoova** |
| **Uyarasuk, Rachel** | elder from Iglulik |
| **Weetaluktuk** | elder from Inukjuak |

# Glossary of Inuktitut Words

The glossary is intended to facilitate reading. The spelling is not always consistent, as words in the glossary stem from different areas. Moreover, different styles of transcription were used by different authors. For a more elaborate and detailed glossary that gives valuable information on local variations, we refer the reader to Kublu (2004).

| | |
|---|---|
| **aagiarjuit** | Pin-tailed duck |
| **Aakulugjuusi** (also **Akkolookjo**) | First ancestor of the Inuit |
| **aarluk** | Killer whale, orca |
| **aarnguaq**, pl. **aarnguat** | Amulet |
| **aasivak** | Spider |
| *agliruruti* | Tattoo accros the jaw |
| **aglu** | Breathing hole of a seal |
| **airujjait,** sing. *airujaq* | Fairy shrimps |
| **Aivilingmio,** pl. **Aivilingmiut** (also **Aivilingmiutaq**) | Inhabitants of Aivilik |
| **aivingnguujaq** | Pretending to be a walrus |
| **aja** | Aunt. Term also used by bears to designate humans |
| **akkak** | Father's brother |
| **akkiviujuq** | Causing someone to die an unnatural death |
| **aklaq** | Land bear |
| **Akudnirmiut** (also **Akudnermio**) | People living near Baffin Bay |
| **alianait** | Expression of gladness |

**allaq,** pl. **allait** (also **itqiliq,**
  pl. **itqilît)**      Indian, First Nations person
**alliniq**      Mattress
**allituq**      Taboo. To refrain from doing
  something
**amauti** (also **amaut)**      Hood
**anaana**      Mother
**ananngiq**      Dung fly, house fly
**angajuqqausiqpuq**      Person or dog trying to abuse its
  power
**angakkua**      See **qaumaniq**
**angakkuq,** pl. **angakkuit**
  (also **angatquq)**      Shaman
**angakkuuniq**      Shamanism
**angaluk**      Shamanic belt. See also **tapsi**
**angiaq**      Undisclosed stillborn child
**angiraaliniq**      The return of an animal once it has
  served humankind
**angmaaq**      A flint to light fires
**angujjuaq**      Full-grown male polar bear
**angusallukuluk**      A male caribou, about two years old
**Anirnialuk**      God (Christian)
**anirniq**      Breath
**anu**      Dog harness
**apitiq**      Shelter of the bear, den
**apsait,** sing. **apsaq**      Non-human beings who cause the
  earth to shake
**aqiggiq**      Ptarmigan
**aqsaqniit**      Northern lights, non-human beings
**aqtuqsinniq**      A paralyzing dream
**armiutaq**      Humerus of a caribou used as an
  amulet
**Arnakäpˢha·luk**      Sea woman
**arnaliaq**      Midwife. See also **sanaji**
**arnaq**      Woman, female polar bear
**arnaquti**      Midwife of a male child

| | |
|---|---|
| **Arviligjuarmiut** | People from Pelly Bay |
| **arviq** | Whale |
| **ataata** | Father |
| **atausiattattuq** | When a seal breathes only once at a breathing hole |
| **atigi** | Inner caribou parka |
| **atiq,** pl. **atiit** | Name, namesake |
| **atirpuq** | The travelling of a bear |
| **atirtalaalik** | A she-bear with nearly newborn cubs |
| **atirtalik** | A she-bear with cubs |
| **atittaittuq** | Female polar bear without a cub |
| **atittaq,** or **atirtaq** | Polar bear cub |
| **atulluk** | Singing to an animal |
| **avaala** | Songs or Christian hymns to make the seals fall asleep |
| **avalaqsiut** | An *irinaliuti* to surround a bear or a person |
| **avataq** | Sealskin float |
| *avigiin* | Share partners |
| **avinnaajjuk** | Small polar bear cubs |
| **avutijuq** | Small polar bear cub separated from the mother |
| **avvait** (also **avvariik**) | Namesakes. See also **illuriik** |
| **Guuti** | God |
| **Harvaqtôrmiut** | An Inuit people in the Kivalliq |
| **igjuksukpuq** | He pulls out a seal when in fact there is not |
| **iglu,** pl. **igluit** | Igloo, snow house |
| **Iglulingmiutaq** (also **Iglulingmio**), pl. **Iglulingmiut** | Inhabitant of Iglulik |
| **igunaq** | Fermented walrus meat |
| **iguptaq** | Bumblebee of the land or the sea |
| **ijiralik** | A place where *ijirait* live |
| **ijiraq,** pl. **ijirait** (also **ijiqqat**) | Invisible non-human beings that can appear as caribou |

| | |
|---|---|
| **ikuꭍiꭍut** | The one who hacks out something with an axe or knife. See also **ikujijut** |
| **ikujijut** | Part of frozen meat |
| **ikuktaq** | Part separated from a whole by a violent act |
| **illauq** | Caribou foetus |
| **illuriik** | Exchange partners, song partners, cross-cousins |
| **immitaujuq** | He pours some water into the mouth of the animal |
| **inaluat** | Guts |
| **inua** | Its person, inhabitant, owner |
| **Inuk**, pl. **Inuit** | Person, owner, inhabitant |
| **inuksuk** (also **inuksugaq**), pl. **inuksuit** | Stone marker in the shape of a human being |
| **inummariit** | True Inuit |
| **inurajaq**, pl. **inurajait** | Invisible being that has footprints |
| **inuruursimajuq** | He adopts a human appearance |
| **inusia** (also **inusiq**) | Appearance as a human being, identified with the *tarniq* by Rasmussen |
| **inutuinnaq** | a 'genuine Inuk' |
| **inuunngittut** | Non-human beings |
| **iqalugait** | Fish |
| **iqiannguruittuq** | Refers to a brave person or dog |
| **iquliniq** | Dog fur around the anus area |
| **iqurniit** | Dogs that are good at finding seal holes |
| **irinaliuti**, pl. **irinaliutiit** (also **irinaliut**) | Powerful word, shamanic formula, incantation |
| **irniq** | Son |
| **isuma** | Reason, thought |
| **isumalialuk** | The one who thinks much |
| **isumataq** | Camp leader |
| **itaapuq** | Pilfering person or dog |
| **itiq** | Sea urchin |

| | |
|---|---|
| **Itqiliq**, pl. **Itqilît** | Indians. See **Allaq** |
| **ivalu** | Caribou sinew |
| **iviutaq** | Down indicator used in hunting seals at breathing holes |
| **Kajagsuk** | Name of a mistreated orphan boy in a famous story |
| **kakiniit** | Tattoos |
| **kalaallisuk** | A Greenlander |
| **kamik,** pair **kamiik,** pl. **kamiit** | Boot |
| **kanajuk** | Sea scorpion |
| **kapurauti** | Implement used in the same way as a fork |
| **kigluraq** (also **kigjugaq**) | A little tattoo between the eyebrows |
| **kiksauti** | Fat of the caribou round the second stomach |
| **kikturiaq** (pl. **kikturiat**) | Mosquito |
| **kilinngajunnirtuq** | Taboo |
| **kinguk** | Sea louse, shrimp |
| **kinirvik** | Special birth hut |
| **kisiaq** | Bone from the shoulder of a caribou |
| **kiversautit** | Ritual consisting of small offerings to the sea woman |
| **Kiviuq** (also **Kivioq**) | Inuit traveller |
| **kujapik** | Lower part of the backbone of a walrus |
| **kukilingiattiat** | Non-human beings, people with claws |
| **kumak** | Louse, larva living under the skin of the caribou |
| **kumarjuait** | Big lice. Caribou are called ' Big lice [of the earth]' in the shamanic language |
| **maktaaq** or **mattaaq** | Whale blubber |
| **maligaq** | Rule to be followed, Canadian law |
| **maliruaq** | Technique of caribou hunting |
| **manilirijjuti** | Formula to procure game such as caribou |
| **mauliqpuq** | Seal hunting at a breathing hole |

| | |
|---|---|
| **milugiaq** | Black fly |
| **minnguq** | Beetle |
| **na·ce·vəq** (also **nasivuq**) | Period when men and women have to abstain from working, hunting, cutting meat, etc. See **nasivik** |
| **nablut** | Crossing places in the rivers used by caribou |
| **nakujjaksaijut** | Training dogs to be aggressive |
| **nanukuluk** | A polar bear cub |
| **nanuq** | Polar bear |
| **nanurluit** | Giant polar bears |
| **Narssuk** (also **Nartsuk**, **Narshuk**, **Nârssuk**) | Spirit of the wind, child of a giant, often identified with *sila*, the (owner of) the sky |
| **nasivik** | Period of observing rules especially after a death or funeral |
| **Nattilingmiutaq,** pl. **Nattilingmiut** (also **Netsilingmio**, pl. **Netsilingmiut**) | Inhabitant of Nattilik |
| **nattiq** | Ringed seal |
| **nattiujaq** | Pretending to be a seal |
| **naujaa** | Seagull |
| **niaqutait** | Hillocks, tufts of moss |
| **ningiqtuq** | Sharing system |
| **ningirniq** | Sharing |
| *niqituinnaq* | Real or country food |
| **niriujaaqtuq** (also **niriujaarniq**) | Dreaming of something good |
| **niviuvaq** | Dung fly |
| **Nugumiut** | People living in the South Baffin area |
| **nukatugaq** | About one year old caribou |
| **nukauq** | A male polar bear that is not yet mature |
| **Nuliajuk** (also **Nuliayok**) | Sea woman. See **Sedna** |
| **nuna** | Land |

**nunagiqsaqtuq**,
  (pl. **nunagiqsaqtut**)
  (also **nunagisaktut,
  noonagekshown,
  nunajisartung** (Boas) or
  **noonagêksaktuq** (Peck)          *Angakkuq* preparing the land for
                                     hunting

**Nunaliurti**                       God

**nunaqqatigiit**                    Those who share the land

**Nunavut**                          Our land

**nungutautuq**                      Devoured

**Nuqumiut**                         See **Nugumiut**

**nurraq**                           A first-year caribou calf

**nurraqanngittuq**                  A female caribou without a calf

**okjuk** (also **ukjuk**)           Bearded seal

**Oqomiut**                          See **Uqqumiut**

**Padlirmiutaq**,
pl. **Padlirmiut**
  (also **Pallirmiut**)              A member of a people in the Kivalliq

**pamilulik**                        Water insect

**panniq**                           Adult male caribou

**parlaniq**                         Scramble

**patiq**                            Marrow

**paurngaqutit**                     Crowberry bushes

**pihiniartut**                      Hunting caribou with bows and
                                     arrows

**pihuqahtaq**                       The one who walks, a bear

**pijaqsaijuq**                      Giving a boy the skills to be a good
                                     hunter

**pilluktuk** (also
  **perlurqtuuq**)                   A transformation of one species into
                                     another

**piqujaq**, pl. **piqujait**        Rule, something that must be done

**pisiliit**                         Hymns

**pisuqsauti**                       Something that enables you to do
                                     something

| | |
|---|---|
| **pitailiniq**, pl. **pitailiniit** (also **pittailiniq**, pl. **pittailiniit**) | Rule, refraining from doing something |
| *piusiq* | Custom |
| **puijiit** | Sea mammals |
| **pujartuq** | Vapour emanating from the human body |
| **pujuq** | Vapour women were thought to emanate during menstruation |
| **Pukimna** (also **Pukimma**) | Owner of the caribou |
| **pukiq** (also **pukeq**) | White part of a caribou skin |
| **pullaittut** | Seal breathing without making noise |
| **pullalik** (also **pullaalik**) | He still has air |
| **pullaq** | Bubble of air containing the *tarniq* |
| **putjuuti** | Crab, sea spider |
| **Qaenermio** (also **Qainirmiutuaq**) | Member of a people in the Kivalliq |
| **qailertetang** | See **qiluktelãk** |
| **qajaaksaqtuq** | When the ice is thin and the waves make the ice ripple |
| **qakuallaliqtuq** or **qujjurujuk** | When the fur of a caribou is getting ready for winter |
| **qallunaat** | White people |
| **qallupalik** (pl. **qallupilluit**) | Non-human beings in the sea |
| **qalugiujaq** (pl. **qalugiujait**) | Miniature objects attached to a shamanic belt |
| **qamutiik** (also **komitik**) | Dogsled |
| **qaqsauq** | The red-throated loon |
| **qarmaq** | House covered with skins |
| **qau** | Light |
| **qaujimajatuqangit** | Knowledge that is still useful today |
| **qaumaniq** (also **angakkua**) | Shamanic light and vision |
| **qayaq** (also **qajaq**, pl. **qajait**) | Kayak, canoe |
| **qilaniq** | Head lifting, a technique of divination |
| **qiluriaqsiuqtuq.** | To create folds in the land |
| **qiminitseq** | Hanging a dog |

| | |
|---|---|
| **qimmiq,** pl. **qimmiit** | Dog |
| **qimuksiit** | The collective action of dogs and humans when they are pulling the sledge together |
| **qiniqpuq** | To look for a proper game; a woman who agrees |
| **qinngaq** (also **qingnaaq**) | Praying by shouting words |
| **qipaluk** | Corner of the eye |
| **qipik** | Blanket |
| **qitirulliq** | Maggots |
| **qiturngaq** | Child |
| **qiviutaq** (also **kiviutaq**) | Piece of feather used while hunting at a seal breathing hole. See **kiviutaq** |
| **qujaliniq** | Thanksgiving prayer |
| **qulittaq** | Caribou parka |
| **qulliq** | Seal oil lamp |
| **qupirruit** | Insects and other small life forms |
| **sakkuujaq** | Toy harpoon |
| **Sanah** (also **Sanna**) | See **Sedna** |
| **sanaji** | Midwife. See also *arnaliaq* and *arnaquti* |
| **saqusiniq** | Putting your hand on the abdomen after a first catch |
| **saunivet** | Place were the caribou bones were left |
| **savik** | Knife |
| **Sedna** (also **Nuliajuk, Nuliayok, Sanah, Sanna, Takanakapsaluk, Takannaaluk, Uinigumasuittuq**) | The one down there, the sea woman |
| **sila** (also **hila** in the Kivalliq) | Reason, weather, sky |
| **silaq,** pl. **silaat** | Earth eggs |
| **silaqqatigiit** | Those who share a piece of Sila (i.e., a piece of air, wind, weather) |
| **silaup inua** | The person, owner, of Sila, the weather spirit |

**siqqitiq** (also **siqqitirniq**)     Conversion ritual involving the eating of forbidden meat

**sivullit**     Ancestors, those who go in front

**sunarlluk**     When a man engages in sexual conduct with non-human beings (bestiality)

**taakslaingiq**     The one that should not be mentioned

**tagiut**     Worm infesting nostrils of caribou

**Takanakapsaluk** (also **Takannaaluk** and **Takaanaaluk Kapsaluk**)     See **Sedna**

**taliillajuuq**, pl. **taliillajuut**     Non-human beings in the water, usually with the tail of a fish

**taliq**     Arm of a person

**talluruti**     Tattoo on the chin

**tapsi**, pl. **tapsiit**     Shamanic belt. See also **angaluk**

**taqtuq**     Caribou kidneys

**tariuq**     Sea

**tarniq**, pl. **tarniit** (also **tarneq, tarninga, inusia**)     Miniature image of a being contained in a bubble of air, 'soul'

**tarniritaqtuq**     When the tarniq of a person no longer wants to remain with them

**tarralikitaq**, pl. **tarralikitaq**     Butterfly

**tiglikti**     Thief

**tigliktituinnaruluk**     It is only a bad thief

**tiguaq**     Adopted (for humans and bears)

**Tikkitserktok**     South Baffin name of the owner of the caribou

**tiqittuajjuit**     Bigger cubs

**tirigusungniq**     The fact that you have to refrain from something

**tirigusuusiq**, pl. **tirigusuusiit**     Rule, refraining from something that is forbidden

**tiringnaqtuq**     When a person has to follow certain rules, especially relating to clothing and food

| | |
|---|---|
| **tirlisi** | Using an *irinaliuti* so an animal would not be aware of the presence of the hunter |
| **tivajuut** | Inuit winter feast (North Baffin) |
| **tonraq hiqloriqtuq** | An evil spirit |
| **Tugtut Igfianut or Pakitsumanga** | Name of the mother of the caribou |
| **tuktuujaaq** (or **tukturjuk**) | Long-legged, long-winged water fly |
| **tulu** | To hit |
| **tulugaarruluit** | Young ravens |
| **tulugaq** | Raven |
| **tulugarjuaq** | Big raven |
| **tulugarnaq** | Diving beetle |
| **tulurialik** | The one with a fang, the bear |
| **tuluriaq** | Canine tooth |
| **tulurpuq** | he/it gives him a blow of his tusk or a bite of his teeth; to hit an obstacle |
| **tunillainiq** (also **tunillai**) | Offering |
| **tuniq,** pl. **tuniit** (also **tunrit**) | People preceding the Inuit as inhabitants of the land |
| **tupilaq,** pl. **tupilait** (also **tupelat)** | Evil spirit |
| **tuputaq** | A peg used to pin the cut made in a seal while still out hunting |
| **tutiriaq** | Sealskin disguise worn by hunter at a seal's breathing hole in the ice |
| **tuurngaq** (also **torngaq, torngak**), pl. **tuurngait** | Helping spirit. See also **ikajuqti** |
| **tuurnginngujuq** | Being spooked by a *tuurngaq* |
| **tuutalik,** pl. **tuutaliit** | Non-human beings in the sea |
| **Udleqdun** (also **Udleqdjun** or **Ullaaktut**) | A bear pursued by dogs and men, Orion's belt |
| **udlormiut** (also **ullormiut**) | Deceased people in the land of the day. See also **ullurmiut** |
| **ugjuk** | Bearded seal |
| **ugpikjuaq** | Big owl |

| | |
|---|---|
| **Uinigumasuittuq** | She who did not want a husband, the sea woman (North Baffin) |
| **Ukjulingmiut** | Inuit from the Back River area |
| **ukpigjuaq** | A big owl |
| **ulikapaaq** (or **ulikappaalik**) | Kind of shrimp |
| **ullurmiut** | Deceased people in the land of the day |
| **ulrunnapiat** | Word used by polar bears for human beings, meaning 'those who are shaky on their legs when they walk' |
| **ulu** | Woman's knife |
| **umialik** | Owner of a whaling boat, leader |
| **umiaq** | Woman's boat |
| **umingmak** | Musk ox, but also bison |
| **Umingmaktormiut** | A people in the Qitirmiut area |
| **unaaq** | Harpoon for seal |
| **unikkaaqtuat** | Stories referring to a distant past |
| **unngiqtaq** | Women's pants |
| **unnuiijuq** | Hunting in the middle of the night |
| **Uqqumiut** | A people in South Baffin |
| **uqsiut** | Thong for dragging seal |
| **uqsuralik** | The one with fat, the bear |
| **uqumiut** | A type of shrimp, yellow and long |
| **Utkuhigjalingmiut** | A people in the Qitirmiut area |
| **Uumaarniittuq** (also **Omerneeto**) | First ancestor of the Inuit |
| **uumajuit** | 'Those who live', Animals |
| **uumati** | Heart |
| **uunarsiqunagu** | The earth getting hot |
| **uutuq** | Hunting technique, approaching the seal on the ice by imitating its movements |
| **uviluit** | Mussels |

# References

Alayco, Salamonie, Mathieu Bergeron and Marco D. Michaud, with the participation of Anguvigaq (HFTA, Nunavik), mayors and elders from Umiujaq, Inukjuak, Salluit, Kangiqsujuaq and Kangirsuk. 2007. *Inuit Elders and Their Traditional Knowledge: Beluga Hunting and Sustainable Practices.* Report published by DFO, Avataq Cultural Institute.

Anderson, David G. 2000. *Identity and Ecology in Arctic Siberia: The Number One Reindeer Brigade.* Oxford: Oxford University Press.

Anderson, David G., and E. Berglund. 2003. *Ethnographies of Conservation: Environmentalism and the Distribution of Privilege.* New York: Berghahn Books.

Anderson, David G., and Mark Nutall. 2004. *Cultivating Arctic Landscapes: Knowing and Managing Animals in the Circumpolar North.* Oxford: Berghahn Books.

Anglican Church of Canada/General Synod Archives/Peck Papers, M56-1, series XXXIII, 4–6, 8–13.

Anonymous. 1985. 'Mosquitoes', *Inuktitut* (59): 50–52.

Anonymous. 2005. *Regarding the Slaughtering of Nunavik 'Qimmiit' (Inuit Dogs) from the mid-1950s to the late 1960s.* Report submitted to Makivik Corporation.

Armitage, Derek. 2005. 'Community-Based Narwhal Management in Nunavut, Canada: Change, Uncertainty, and Adaptation', *Society and Natural Resources* 18: 715–31.

Armitage, Peter. 1992. 'Religious Ideology among the Innu of Eastern Quebec and Labrador', *Religiologiques* (Fall): 1–51.

Arnakak, Jaypete. 2002. 'Incorporation of *Inuit Qaujimanituqangit*, or Inuit Traditional Knowledge, into the Government of Nunavut', *The Journal of Aboriginal Economic Development* 3(1): 33–39.

Avataq Cultural Institute. 1984, *Northern Quebec Inuit Elders Conference. Kangiqsujuaq, Quebec, August 30 - September 6, 1983.* Inukjuak, Avataq Cultural Institute.

Balikci, Asen. 1970. *The Netsilik Eskimo.* New York: Garden City.

Bell, Jim. 2005. 'It's a Good Bowhead Hunt for Repulse Bay', *Nunatsiaq News,* 26 August.

———. 2007. 'Scientists Are Wrong on Polar Bears, NTI Says', *Nunatsiaq News,* 9 March.

———. 2008a. 'GN Plan to Tag 300 Bears Angers Hunters', *Nunatsiaq News*, 9 May.

———. 2008b. 'Measures Aren't Effective. Survey: Beverly Caribou Herd in Big Decline', *Nunatsiaq News*, 4 December.

Bennett, John, and Susan Rowley (eds). 2004. *Uqalurait: An Oral History of Nunavut*. Montreal and Kingston: McGill University Press.

Berkes, F. 2008. *Sacred Ecology*, 2nd ed. New York: Taylor and Francis.

Bilby, Julian W. 1923. *Among Unknown Eskimos: An Account of Twelve Years Intimate Relations with the Primitive Eskimo of Ice Bound Baffin Land, with a Description of Their Ways of Living, Hunting Customs and Beliefs*. London: Seeley Service.

———. 1926. *Nanook of the North: The Story of an Eskimo Family*, 2nd ed. New York: Dodd, Mead.

Bird, John. 2008a. 'Baffin Bay Bear Quota Raises Southern Ire', *Nunatsiaq News*, 14 November.

———. 2008b. 'Europe Bans Bear Imports from Two Regions', *Nunatsiaq News*, 12 December.

———. 2008c. 'Hundreds Trapped by Ice: Narwhal Tragedy Yields "Harvest" for Community', *Nunatsiaq News*, 28 November.

———. 2009. 'Inuit Would Suffer Even if Exempted from Ban: Peter', *Nunatsiaq News*, 8 January.

Bird-David, Nurid. 1990. 'The Giving Environment: Another Perspective on the Economic System of Gather-hunters', *Current Anthropology* 31: 189–96.

———. 1991. 'Animism Revisited: Personhood, Environment, and Relational Epistemology', *Current Anthropology* 40: 67–91.

———. 2006. 'Animistic Epistemology: Why Do Some Hunter-Gatherers Not Depict Animals?', *Ethnos* 71(1): 33–50.

Birket-Smith, Kaj. 1924. 'Ethnography of the Egedesminde District, with Aspects of the General Culture of West Greenland, Copenhagen', *Meddelelser om Gronland* 66: 3–476.

———. 1929. *The Caribou Eskimos: Material and Social Life and Their Cultural Position*, vol. 5 (pts 1–2) of *Report of the Fifth Thule Expedition 1921–24*. Copenhagen: Gyldendalske Boghandel.

Black, Lydia T. (trans. and ed.). 1977. 'The Konyag (the Inhabitants of the Island of Kodiak) by Iosaf [Bolotov] (1794–1799) and by Gideon (1804–1807)', *Arctic Anthropology* 14(2): 79–107.

———. 1983. 'Eskimo Motifs in Aleut Art and Folklore', *Études Inuit Studies* 7(1): 3–23.

———. 1987. 'Whaling in the Aleutians', *Études Inuit Studies* 11(2): 7–50.

Blaisel, Xavier. 1993. 'La chair et l'os: Espace cérémoniel et temps universel chez les Inuit du Nunavut (Canada), les valeurs coutumières inuit et les rapports rituels entre humains, gibiers, esprits et forces de l'univers', PhD dissertation. Paris: École des hautes études en sciences sociales.

Blaisel, Xavier, and Jay Arnakak. 1993. 'Trajet rituel: Du harponnage à la naissance dans le mythe d'Arnaqtaaqtuq', *Études Inuit Studies* 17: 15–46.

Blaisel, Xavier, Frédéric Laugrand and Jarich Oosten. 1999. 'Shamans and Leaders: Parousial Movements among the Inuit of Northeast Canada', *Numen* 46: 370–411.

Boas, Franz. 1888. 'The Central Eskimo', in *6th Annual Report of the Bureau of American Ethnology for the Years 1884–1885.* Washington DC: Government Printing Office, pp. 399–669.

———. (1888) 1964. *The Central Eskimo.* Lincoln: University of Nebraska Press.

———. 1900. 'Religious Beliefs of the Central Eskimo', *Popular Science Monthly* 57: 624–31.

———. 1901. 'The Eskimo of Baffin Land and Hudson Bay: From Notes Collected by Capt. George Comer, Capt. James S. Mutch, and Rev. E.J. Peck', *Bulletin of the American Museum of Natural History* 15(1): 1–370.

———. 1907. 'Second Report on the Eskimo of Baffin Land and Hudson Bay: From Notes Collected by Captain George Comer, Captain James S. Mutch, and Rev. E.J. Peck', *Bulletin of the American Museum of Natural History* 15(2): 371–570.

Bockstoce, John R. 1986. *Whales, Ice, and Menu: The History of Whaling in the Western Arctic.* Seattle and London: University of Washington Press.

Bodenhorn, Barbara. 1988. 'Whales, Souls, Children, and Other Things that are "Good to share": Core Metaphors in a Contemporary Whaling Society', *Cambridge Anthropology* 13(1): 1–19.

———. 1989. 'The Animals Come to Me, They Know I Share: Inupiaq Kinship, Changing Economic Relations and Enduring World Views on Alaska's North Slope', PhD dissertation. Cambridge: Cambridge University.

———. 1990. 'I'm not the Great Hunter, My Wife Is', *Études Inuit Studies* 14: 55–74.

———. 2000. '"He Used to Be My Relative": Exploring the Bases of Relatedness among Inupiat of Northern Alaska', in J. Carsten (ed.), *Cultures of Relatedness: New Approaches to the Study of Kinship.* Cambridge: Cambridge University Press, pp. 128–48.

Bogoras, William. 1904. *The Chukchee.* Leiden: E. J. Brill.

———. 1913. 'The Jesup North Pacific Expedition, Part I: Chukchee Mythology'. *Memoirs of the American Museum of Natural History* 12.

Bordin, Guy. 2003. *Lexique analytique de l'anatomie humaine.* Collection Arctique 6. Paris: Peeters, Selaf.

Borré, Kristen. 1994. 'The Healing Power of the Seal: The Meaning of Inuit Health Practice and Belief', *Arctic Anthropology* 31(1): 1–15.

Boswell, Randy. 2010. 'DFO Doubles Arctic Narwhal Population Estimate: North Baffin Number Rises from 30,000 to 60,000', *Nunatsiaq News,* 8 April.

Bourgeois, Annette. 1998. 'QWB Planners Work Out Details of Bowhead Hunt', *Nunatsiaq News,* 14 May.

Brandson, Lorraine. 1994. *Carved from the Land: The Eskimo Museum Collection.* Altona, Manitoba: Friesen Printers.

Briggs, Jean L. (ed.). 2000. *Childrearing Practices.* Interviewing Inuit Elders 3. Iqaluit: Nunavut Arctic College.

Brightman, Marc, V. E. Grotti and O. Ulturgasheva (eds). 2012. *Animism in Rainforest and Tundra: Personhood, Animals, Plants and Things in Contemporary Amazonia and Siberia.* Oxford and New York: Berghahn Books.

Brightman, Robert. 1993. *Grateful Prey: Rock Cree Human-Animal Relationships.* Berkeley: University of California Press.

Brink, Jack W. 2005. 'Inukshuk: Caribou Drive Lanes on Southern Victoria Island, Nunavut, Canada', *Arctic Anthropology* 42(1): 1–28.

Brody, Hugh. 1976. 'Land Occupancy: Inuit Perceptions', in M. Freeman (ed.), *Inuit Land Use and Occupancy Project*. Ottawa: Department of Indian Affairs and Northern Development, pp. 185–242.

———. 1979. 'Inummariit: The Real Eskimo', in M. R. Freeman (ed.), *Inuit Land Use and Occupancy Project*, vol. 2. Ottawa: Department of Indian Affairs and Northern Development, pp. 223–26.

———. 1987. *Living Arctic: Hunters of the Canadian North*. London: Faber and Faber.

Buijs, Cunera. 2004. Furs and Fabrics. *Transformations, Clothing and Identity in East Greenland*. Leiden: CNWS Publications.

Buijs, Cunera, and Jarich Oosten (eds). 1997. *Braving the Cold: Continuity and Change in Arctic Clothing*. Leiden: Centre of Non-Western Studies.

Burch, Ernest. 1972. 'The Caribou/Wild Reindeer as a Human Resource', *American Antiquity* 37: 339–68.

Caufield, R. A. 1993. 'Aboriginal Subsistence Whaling in Greenland: The Case of Qeqertarsuaq Municipality in West Greenland', *Arctic* 46(2): 144–55.

———. 1997. *Greenlanders, Whales, and Whaling: Sustainability and Self-determination in the Arctic*. London: University Press of New England.

CBC News. 2008. 'Killing Pond Inlet Narwhals "Humane Harvest": DFO', 24 November.

———. 2011. '"Exotic" Species Come North to Nunavut', 11 July. Retrieved 26 December 2011 from http://www.cbc.ca/news/canada/north/story/2011/07/11/nunavut-arctic-species.html.

Césard, Nicolas, Jérémy Deturche and Philippe Erikson. 2003. 'L'utilisation des insectes dans les pratiques médicales et rituelles d'Amazonie indigene', in Élisabeth Motte-Florac and Jacqueline M. C. Thomas (eds), *Les insectes dans la tradition orale*. Paris: Peeters, pp. 395–406.

Charrin, A.-V. 1983. *Le Petit monde du Grand Corbeau, récits du Grand Nord sibérien*. Paris: Presses Universitaires de France.

Chaussonnet, Valérie. 1988. 'Needles and Animals: Women's Magic', in W. W. Fitzhugh and A. Crowell (eds), *Crossroads of Continents: Cultures of Siberia and Alaska*. Washington DC: Smithsonian Institution Press, pp. 209–26.

Chichlo, Boris. 2000. 'Sous le toit de la qaygi: Folklore et pratique rituelle chez les Yuit de la Tchoukotka', *Études Inuit Studies* 24(2): 7–31.

Clark, Douglas, Martina Tyrrell, Martha Dowsley, A. Lee Foote, Milton Freeman and Susan G. Clark. 2008. 'Polar Bears, Climate Change, and Human Dignity: Disentangling Symbolic Politics and Seeking Integrative Conservation Policies', *Meridian* (Fall/Winter): 1–6.

Clammer, J., S. Poirier and E. Schwimmer. 2004. *Figured Worlds: Ontological Obstacles in Intercultural Relations*. Toronto: University of Toronto Press.

Clément, Daniel. 1995. *La zoologie des Montagnais*. Paris: Peters.

———. 2012. *Le bestiaire innu: Les quadrupèdes*. Quebec City: PUL.

Collings, Peter. 1997. 'Subsistence Hunting and Wildlife Management in the Central Canadian Arctic', *Arctic Anthropology* 34: 41–56.

Comer, George. 1910. 'A Geographical Description of Southampton Island and Notes upon the Eskimo', *Bulletin of the American Geographical Society* 42(1): 84–90.

———. 1921. 'Notes on the Natives of the Northwestern Shores of Hudson Bay', *American Anthropologist* 23(2): 243–44.

Community of Kugaaruk. 2005. *Unikkaaqatigiit: Putting the Human Face on Climate Change: Perspectives from Kugaaruk, Nunavut.* Ottawa: joint publication of Inuit Tapiriit Kanatami, Nasivik Centre for Inuit Health and Changing Environments at Université Laval and Ajunnginiq Centre at the National Aboriginal Health Organization.

Community of Naujaat. 2005. *Unikkaaqatigiit: Putting the Human Face on Climate Change: Perspectives from Kugaaruk, Nunavut.* Ottawa: joint publication of Inuit Tapiriit Kanatami, Nasivik Centre for Inuit Health and Changing Environments at Université Laval and Ajunnginiq Centre at the National Aboriginal Health Organization.

Condon, R. G., P. Collings and G. Wenzel. 1995. 'The Best Part of Life: Subsistence Hunting, Ethnicity, and Economic Adaptation Among Young Adult Inuit males', *Arctic* 48(1): 31–46.

Crantz, David. 1767. *The History of Greenland*, 2 vols. London: Brethren's Society.

Cruikshank, Julie. 2004. 'Uses and Abuses of Traditional Knowledge: Perspectives from the Yukon Territory', in D. Anderson and M. Nutall (eds), *Cultivating Arctic Landscapes: Knowing and Managing Animals in the Circumpolar North.* Oxford: Berghahn Books, pp. 17–32.

Csonka, Yvon. 1995. *Les Ahiarmiut: A l'écart des Inuit Caribous.* Neuchâtel, Switzerland: Victor Attinger.

Cummins, B. D. 2002. *First Nations, First Dog.* Calgary: Detselig Enterprises.

Dahl, J. 1990. 'Beluga Hunting in Saqqaq', *North Atlantic Studies* 2(1–2): 166–70.

———. 2000. *Saqqaq: An Inuit Hunting Community in the Modern World.* Toronto: University of Toronto Press.

Danks, Hugh V. 2004. 'Seasonal Adaptations in Arctic Insects', *Integrative and Comparative Biology* 44(2): 85–94.

D'Argencourt, L. 1977. 'Atuat's Tattoos', *Inuit Today* 6(4): 56–61.

Delaby, Laurence. 1993. 'Le chien du maître de la montagne: Chez les Ghiliaks de Sibérie extrême-orientale', *Études mongoles et sibériennes* 24: 53–65.

Delâge, Denys. 2005. 'Vos chiens ont plus d'esprit que les nôtres: Histoire des chiens dans la rencontre des Français et des Amérindiens', *Les Cahiers des Dix* 59: 179–215.

Delalande, Lucien. 1958. *Sous le soleil de minuit.* Montreal: Rayonnement.

Descola, Philippe. 1986. *La nature domestique.* Paris: MSH.

———. 2005. *Par-delà nature culture.* Paris: Gallimard.

———. 2007. 'Le commerce des âmes: L'ontologie animique dans les Amériques', in F. Laugrand and J. Oosten (eds), *La nature des esprits dans les cosmologies autochtones.* Quebec City: PUL, pp. 3–44.

Désveaux, Emmanuel. 1995. 'Les Indiens sont-ils par nature respectueux de la nature?', *Anthropos* 90: 435–44.

Donaldson, Judith L. 1994. 'The Economic Ecology of Hunting: A Case Study of the Canadian Inuit', PhD dissertation. Cambridge, MA: Harvard University.

Dorais, Louis-Jacques. 1984. 'Sémantique des noms d'animaux en groenlandais de l'est', *Amerindia* 9: 7–23.

———. 1997. *Quaqtaq: Modernity and Identity in an Inuit Community*. Toronto: University of Toronto Press.

Dowsley, Martha. 2007. 'Inuit Perspectives on Polar Bears (*Ursus maritimus*) and Climate Change in Baffin Bay, Nunavut, Canada', *Research and Practice in Social Science* 2(2): 53–74.

———. 2010. 'The Value of a Polar Bear: Evaluating the Role of a Multiple-use Resource in the Nunavut Mixed Economy', *Arctic Anthropology* 47(1): 39–56.

Driscoll, Bernadette. 1982. *Inuit Myths, Legends and Songs*. Winnipeg: Winnipeg Art Gallery.

———. 1985. *Uumajut: Animal Imagery in Inuit Art*. Winnipeg: Winnipeg Art Gallery.

Driscoll-Engelstad, Bernadette. 2005. 'Dance of the Loon: Symbolism and Continuity in Copper Inuit Ceremonial Clothing', *Arctic Anthropology* 42(1): 33–47.

Dufour, Rose. 1988. *Femme et enfantement: Sagesse dans la culture inuit*. Quebec City: Éditions papyrus.

Eber, Dorothy Harley. 1989. *When the Whalers Were Up North: Inuit Memories from the Eastern Arctic*. Montreal and Kingston: McGill-Queen's University Press.

Egede, Hans. 1729. Det gamle Grønlands nye Perlustration. Copenhagen.

———. 1818. *A Description of Greenland*. London: T. and J. Allman.

———. 1925. 'Relationer fra Gronland 1721–36 & Det gamle Gronlands nyPerlustration 1741', ed. L. Bobé, *Meddelser om Gronland* 54.

Egede, Poul, with Niels Egede. 1929. 'Continuation af Hans Egedes Relationer fra Gronland', ed. H. Ostermann, *Meddelser om Gronland* 120.

Ekblaw, W. E. 1928. 'The Material Response of the Polar Eskimo to Their Far Arctic Environment', *Annals of the Association of the American Geographers* 18(1): 1–24.

Evic-Twerdin, Leena. 1991. *Traditional Inuit Beliefs in Stories and Legends*. Iqaluit: Nortext/Baffin Divisional Board of Education.

Fausto, Carlos. 2007. 'Feasting on People: Eating Animals and Humans in Amazonia', *Current Anthropology* 48(4): 497–530.

Feit, Harvey A. 2000. 'Les animaux comme partenaires de chasse: Réciprocité chez les Cris de la baie James', *Terrain* 34: 123–42.

Feldman, K. D., and E. Norton. 1995. 'Niqsaq and Napaaqtuq: Issues in Inupiaq Eskimo Life-form Classification and Ethnosciences', *Études Inuit Studies* 19(2): 77–100.

Fienup-Riordan, Ann. 1988. 'The Martyrdom of Brother Hooker: Conflict and Conversion on the Kuskokwim', *Alaska History* 3(1): 1–26.

———. 1990. *Eskimo Essays*. New Brunswick, NJ: Rutgers University Press.

———. 1994. *Boundaries and Passages: Rule and Ritual in Yup'ik Eskimo Oral Tradition*. Norman: University of Oklahoma Press.

————. 1999. 'Yaqulget Qaillun Pilartat (What the Birds Do): Yup'ik Eskimo Understanding of Geese and Those Who Study Them', *Arctic* 52: 1–22.

————. 2000. *Hunting Tradition in a Changing World*. New Brunswick, NJ: Rutgers University Press.

————. 2007. 'Compassion and Restraint: The Moral Foundations of Yup'ik Eskimo Hunting Tradition', in F. Laugrand and J. Oosten (eds), *La nature des esprits dans les cosmologies autochtones*. Quebec City: PUL, pp. 239–56.

Fienup-Riordan, A., with Marie Meade. 1994. 'The Boy Who Went to Live with the Seals', in Brian Swann (ed.), *Coming to Light: Contemporary Translations of the Native Literatures of North America*. New York: Random House, pp. 57–74.

Folger, Mosha. 2005. 'Bowhead Hunt among the Traditions That Strengthen Repulse Bay', *Inuktitut* (Fall): 25–30.

Foote, Lee, and George Wenzel. 2008. 'Conservation Hunting Concepts, Canada's Inuit and Polar Bear Hunting', in B. Lovelock (ed.), *Tourism and the Consumption of Wildlife*. London and New York: Routledge, pp. 115–28.

Forbes, G. J. 1986. 'The Birds of Igloolik Island, NWT', PhD dissertation. Toronto: York University.

Freeman, Milton R. 'Eskimo Thanking-acts in the Eastern Canadian Arctic', *Folk* 10: 25–28.

————. 2005. '"Just One More Time before I Die": Securing the Relationship between Inuit and Whales in the Arctic Region', *Senri Ethnological Studies* 67: 59–76.

Freeman, Milton R., Lyudmila Bogoslovskaya, Richard A. Caulfield, Ingmar Egede, Igor I. Krupnik and Marc G. Stevenson. 1998. *Inuit, Whaling and Sustainability*. Walnut Creek, CA: AltaMira Press.

Freeman, Milton R., and L. Foote (eds). 2009. *Inuit, Polar Bears, and Sustainable Use: Local National and International Perspectives*. Edmonton: Canadian Circumpolar Institute.

Freeman, Milton R., Eleanor E. Wein and Darren E. Keith. 1992. *Recovering Rights: Bowhead Whales and Inuvialuit Subsistence in the Western Arctic*. Edmonton: Canadian Circumpolar Institute and Fisheries Joint Management Committee.

Freeman, M., and G. Wenzel. 2006. 'The Nature and Significance of Polar Bear Conservation Hunting in the Canadian Arctic', *Arctic* 59(1): 21–30.

Freuchen, Peter. 1935a. *Arctic Adventure: My Life in the Frozen North*. New York: Farrar and Rhinehart.

Freuchen, Peter. 1935b. *Field Notes and Biological Observations*, vol. 2 (4–5) of *Report of the Fifth Thule Expedition 1921–24*. Copenhagen: Gyldendalske Boghandel, Nordisk Forlag.

Gagnon, Jeanne. 2011. 'Mosquito Country', *Northern News Services*, 2 August.

George, Jane. 1998. 'Pesky Bugs Pig Out on Kuujjuaq's Larches: An Insect Known as the Larch Sawfly Has an Insatiable Appetite for Kuujjuaq's Sub-Arctic Trees', *Nunatsiaq News*, 17 September.

————. 1999. 'When They Killed the Sled Dogs in Nunavik', *Nunatsiaq News*, 26 March.

————. 2007. 'Beluga Hunters Fight Quotas with Cameras', *Nunatsiaq News*, 21 December.

————. 2008b. 'New Bowhead Numbers Show Inuit Are Right: DFO Population Estimate Now 15 Times Greater', *Nunatsiaq News*, 14 March.

————. 2008c. 'Nunavut Wildlife Management Board Ponders Second Bowhead for Nunavut', *Nunatsiaq News*, 14 March.

————. 2009a. 'Community Leaders Say Inuit Values Hurt by Strict Limits: Nunavik Hunters Rejoice as Beluga Quota Upped', *Nunatsiaq News*, 28 May.

————. 2009c. '"If we push too far, we will lose": Biologist: Mining and Caribou
Herds Don't Mix', *Nunatsiaq News*, 16 April.

————. 2009d. 'NTI Demands Unrestricted Nunavut Bowhead Hunt', *Nunatsiaq News*, 13 February.

————. 2010. 'Nunavut Hunters Still Enraged Over Bear Quotas', *Nunatsiaq
News*, 4 April.

————. 2011a. 'NTI: Move to List Polar Bears under SARA "disappointing":
"That's What We Don't Need"', *Nunatsiaq News*, 15 July.

————. 2011b. 'Polar Bear to Be Added to SARA's "Special Concern" List', *Nunatsiaq News*, 5 November.

Gessain, Robert. 1978. 'L'Homme-Lune dans la mythologie des Ammassalim-
iut', in *Systèmes de signes: textes réunis en hommage à Germaine Dieterlen*.
Paris, Hermann.

Graburn, Nelson H. H. 1980. 'Man, Beast, and Transformation in Canadian
Inuit Art and Culture', in Marjorie M. Halpin and Michael M. Ames (eds),
*Manlike Monsters on Trial: Early Records and Modern Evidence*. Vancouver:
University of British Columbia Press, pp. 193–210.

Guemple, D. L. 1965. 'Saunik: Name Sharing as a Factor Governing Eskimo
Kinship Terms', *Ethnology* 4(3): 323–35.

Hall, Charles F. 1864. *Arctic Researches and Life with the Esquimaux*, vols 1 and
2. London: Sampson, Low, Son, and Marston.

————. (1867) 1970. *Life with the Esquimaux: The Narrative of Arctic Experience in Search of Survivors of Sir John Franklin's Expedition*. Rutland,
Vermont, and Tokyo: C. E. Turttle.

Hallowell, A. I. 1926. 'Bear Ceremonialism in the Northern Hemisphere', *American Anthropologist*, n.s., 28(1): 1–175.

Hamayon, Roberte. 1990. *La chasse à l'âme: Esquisse d'une théorie du chaman-
isme sibérien*. Nanterre, France: Société d'ethnologie.

————. 2012. *Jouer. Une étude anthropologique*. Paris: La Découverte.

Hawkes, Edward W. 1916. *The Labrador Eskimo*. Geological Survey Memoir
91. Anthropological Series 14. Ottawa: Department of Mines.

Hay, K., D. Aglukark, D. Igutsaq, J. Ikkidluak, and M. Mike. 2000. *Final Report
on the Inuit Bowhead Knowledge Study, Nunavut, Canada*. Iqaluit: Nunavut Management Board.

Henriksen, George. 2009. *I Dreamed the Animals: Kaniuekutat: The Life of an
Innu Hunter*. New York: Berghahn Books.

Holm, Gustav. 1887. 'Ethnological Sketch of the Angmagssalik Eskimo', ed. W.
Thalbitzer, *Meddelelser om Gronland* 39(2): 3–150.

Holtved, Erik. 1943. *The Eskimo Legend of Navaranaq*. Acta Artica Fascicule 1.
Copenhagen: Munksgaard.

————. 1962. 'Otto Fabricius' Ethnographical Works', trans. by W. E. Calvert,
introduction by W. Thalbitzer, *Meddelelser om Gronland* 140(2): 4–139.

Hugh-Jones, S. 1996. 'Bonnes raisons ou mauvaise conscience. De l'ambivalence de certains Amazoniens envers la consommation de la viande', *Terrain* 26(3): 123–48.

Idrobo, Carlos Julian. 2008. 'The Pangnirtung Inuit and the Greenland Shark', MA thesis. Winnipeg: University of Manitoba.

Ikeya, Kazenobu, 1997. 'Bear Ritual of the Matagi and the Ainu in Northeastern Japan', in T. Yamada and T. Irimoto (eds), *Circumpolar Religion and Ecology: An Anthropology of the North*. Tokyo: University of Tokyo Press, pp. 55–63.

Ingold, T. 1988. *What Is an Animal?* London: Unwin Hyman.

———. 1996. 'Hunting and Gathering as Ways of Peceiving the Environment', in R. Ellen and K. Fukui (eds), *Redefining Nature: Ecology, Culture and Domestication*. Oxford: Berg, pp. 117–55.

———. 2000. *The Perception of the Environment: Essays in Livelihood, Dwelling and Skill*. London: Routledge.

———. 2004. 'A Circumpolar Night's Dream', in J. Clammer, S. Poirier and E. Schwimmer (eds), *Figured Worlds: Ontological Obstacles in Intercultural Relations*. Toronto: University of Toronto Press, pp. 25–57.

Irving, L. 1953. 'The Naming of Birds by Nunamiut Eskimo', *Arctic* 6(1): 35–43.

———. 1958. 'On the Naming of Birds by Eskimos', *Anthropological Papers of the University of Alaska* 6(2): 61–77.

Issenman, Betty. 1997. *Sinews of Survival: The Living Legacy of Inuit Clothing*. Vancouver: University of British Columbia Press.

Issenman, Betty, and Catherine Rankin. 1988. *Ivalu: Traditions of Inuit Clothing*. Montreal: McCord Museum of Canadian History.

Jenness, Diamond. 1922. *The Life of the Copper Eskimos*, vol. 12 (A) of *Report of the Canadian Arctic Expedition, 1913–1918*. Ottawa: F. A. Acland.

Jensen, Bent. 1961. 'Folkways of Greenland Dogkeeping', *Folk* 3: 43–66.

Juel, Erik. 1945. 'Notes on Seal-Hunting Ceremonialism in the Arctic', *Ethnos* 10(2–3): 143–64.

Kalluak, Mark. 2010. *Unipkaaqtuat Arvianit: Traditional Stories from Arviat*. Iqaluit: Inhabit Media.

Kardosh, Robert. 2003. *The Art of Nick Sikkuark: Sculpture and Drawings*. Vancouver: Marion Scott Gallery.

Keith, Darren. 2005. *Inuit Qaujimajatuqangit Nanurmut: Inuit Knowledge of Polar Bears: A Project of the Gjoa Haven Hunters' and Trappers' Organization*. Edmonton: CCI Press.

Kilabuk, 1998. *A Study of Inuit Knowledge of the Southeast Baffin Beluga*. Iqaluit: Nunavut Wildlife Management Board.

Kimura, T. 1999. 'Bearing the "Bare Facts" of Ritual: A Critique of Jonathan Z. Smith's Study of the Bear Ceremony Based on a Study of the Ainu Iyomante', *Numen* 46(1): 88–114.

Kishigami, Nobuhiro. 1993. 'Dogs in the Spiritual World of Traditional Inuit Society of Canada: With Special Reference to Dogs in the Traditional Netsilik Inuit Society', *Proceedings of the 7th International Abashiri Symposium*, pp. 15–26.

———. 2005. 'Co-management of Beluga Whales in Nunavik (Arctic Quebec), Canada', in N. Kishigami and J. M. Savelle (eds), *Indigenous Use and Man-*

*agement of Marine Resources*, Senri Ethnological Studies 67. Osaka: The National Museum of Ethnology, pp. 121–44.

Kleivan, Inge. 1971. *Why Is the Raven Black? An Analysis of an Eskimo Myth.* Acta Arctica 17. Copenhagen: Munksgaard.

———. 1978. '"Lamb of God" = "Seal of God"? Some Semantic Problems in Translating the Animal Names of the New Testament into Greenlandic', *Papers from the 4th Scandinavian Conference of Linguistics, Hindsgavl, 7–8 January*, pp. 339–45.

Koester, David. 2002. 'When Fat Raven Sings: Mimesis and Environmental Alterity in Kamchatka's Environmentalist Age', in E. Kasten (ed.), *People and the Land: Pathway to Reform in Post Soviet Siberia.* Berlin: Deirtrich Reimez Verlag, pp. 45–62.

Kohn, Eduardo. 2007. 'How Dogs Dream: Amazonian Natures and the Politics of Transspecies Engagement', *American Ethnologist* 34(1): 3–24.

Kolb, Stéphane, and Samuel Law (eds). 2001. *Dreams and Dream Interpretation.* Inuit Perspectives on the 20th Century 4. Iqaluit: Nunavut Arctic College.

Koperqualuk, Lisa. 2011. 'Puvirniturmiut Religious and Political Dynamics', PhD dissertation. Quebec City: Université Laval.

Krech, Shepard. 1999. *The Ecological Indian: Myth and History.* New York: W. W. Norton.

Kretschmar, Freda. 1938. *Hundestammvater und Kerberos.* Stuttgart: Strecker und Schröder Verlag.

Kroeber, A. 1899. 'Tales of the Smith Sound Eskimo', *Journal of American Folk-Lore* 12(46): 166–82.

Krupnik, Igor I. 1981. *Arctic Adaptations: Native Whalers and Reindeer Herders of Northern Eurasia.* Hanover, NH: University Press of New England.

———. 1993. 'Prehistoric Eskimo Whaling in the Arctic: Slaughter of Calves or Fortuitous Ecology', *Arctic Anthropology* 30(1): 1–12.

Kublu, Alexina. 2004. *Edited Elders Glossary.* Iqaluit: Nunavut Arctic College.

Kulchyski, Peter, Don McCaskill and David Newhouse (eds). 2003. *In the Words of Elders.* Toronto: University of Toronto Press.

Kulchyski, Peter, and Frank James Tester. 2007. *Kiumajut (Talking Back): Game Management and Inuit Rights 1900–70.* Vancouver: University of British Columbia Press.

Kumlien, Ludvig. 1879. *Contributions to the Natural History of Arctic America.* Bulletin of the United States National Museum 15. Washington DC: United States Printing Office.

Kwon, H. 1999. 'Play the Bear: Myth and Ritual in East Siberia', *History of Religions* 38(4): 373–87.

Lantis, M. 1938. 'The Mythology of Kodiak Island, Alaska', *Journal of Folk-Lore* 51(200): 123–69.

———. 1946. 'The Social Culture of the Nunivak Eskimo', *Transactions of the American Philosophical Society*, n.s., 35(3), pp. 153–321.

———. 1947. *Alaskan Eskimo Ceremonialism.* American Ethnological Society Monograph 11. New York: J. J. Augustin.

Larsen, H. 1970. 'Some Examples of Bear Cult among the Eskimo and Other Northern People', *Folk* 11–12: 27–42.

Latour, Bruno. 1993. *We Have Never Been Modern*. Cambridge, MA: Harvard University Press.

———. 2009a. 'Perspectivism: "Type" or "Bomb"?', *Anthropology Today* 25(2): 1–2.

———. 2009b. 'Will Non-Humans Be Saved? An Argument in Ecotheology', *Journal of Royal Anthropological Institute* 15(3): 459–75.

Laugrand, Frédéric. 1997. 'Le Siqqitiq: Renouvellement religieux et premier rituel de conversion chez les Inuit du nord de la Terre de Baffin', *Études Inuit Studies* 21(1–2): 101–40.

———. 1999a. 'Mourir et renaître: La conversion au christianisme des Inuit de l'Arctique de l'Est', *L'Homme: Revue française d'anthropologie* 152: 115–42.

———. 1999b. 'Le mythe comme instrument de mémoire: Remémoration et interprétation d'un extrait de Genèse par un aîné inuit de l'île de Baffin', *Études Inuit Studies* 23(1–2): 91–115.

———. 2002. *Mourir et renaître: La réception du christianisme par les Inuit de l'Arctique de l'Est (1890–1940)*. Quebec City: Presses de l'Université Laval; Leiden: Centre of Non-Western Studies.

Laugrand, Frédéric, and Jarich Oosten. 2006. 'Connecting and Protecting: Lines and Belts in the Canadian Arctic', *Anthropological Papers of the University of Alaska* 4(1): 133–47.

———. 2008. *The Sea Woman: Sedna in Inuit Shamanism and Art in the Eastern Arctic*. Fairbanks: Alaska University Press.

——— (eds). 2009. *The Ethnographic Recordings of Inuit Oral Traditions by Father Guy Mary-Rousselière*. Iqaluit: Nunavut Arctic College.

———. 2010. *Transitions and Transformations: Shamanism and Christianity in the Canadian Arctic*. Montreal and Kingston: McGill-Queen's University Press.

———. 2012a. 'Elders, Oral Traditions and Shamanism', supplement, *Les Cahiers du CIÉRA* (October): 19–34.

———. 2012b. 'Maîtres de la vie et de la mort: La grandeur des "petites bêtes" du Grand Nord', *L'Homme* 202: 53–76.

Laugrand, Frédéric, Jarich Oosten, and Francois Trudel. 2001. *Representing Tuurngait*, vol. 1 of *Memory and History in Nunavut*. Iqaluit: Nunavut Arctic College/Nortext.

———. 2006. *Apostle to the Inuit: The Journals and Ethnographic Notes of Edmund James Peck: The Baffin Years: 1894–1905*. Toronto: University of Toronto Press.

Lee, David S., and G. Wenzel. 2004. 'Narwhal Hunting by Pond Inlet Inuit: An Analysis of Foraging Mode in the Floe-Edge Environment', *Études Inuit Studies* 28(2): 133–57.

Lévesque, Francis. 2008. 'Les Inuit, leurs chiens et l'administration nordique, de 1950 à 2007: Anthropologie d'une revendication inuit contemporaine', PhD dissertation. Quebec City: Université Laval.

———. 2010. 'Le contrôle des chiens dans trois communautés du Nunavik au milieu du 20e siècle', *Études Inuit Studies* 34(2): 149–66.

———. 2011. 'An Ordinance Respecting Dogs: Creating Insecurity by Imposing Security', in Michelle Daveluy, Francis Lévesque and Jeanne Ferguson (eds), *Security in the Arctic: Opportunities and Concern*. Edmonton: CCI Press, 73–90.

Lévi-Strauss, Claude. 1971. *L'homme nu.* Mythologiques 4. Paris: Plon.

Lewis, Arthur. 1904. *The Life and Work of The Reverend Edmund James Peck Among the Eskimos.* London: Hodder and Stoughton.

Lima, Tania S. 1999. 'The Two and its Many: Reflections on Perspectivism in Tupi Cosmology', *Ethnos* 64(1): 107–31.

Low, Albert L. 1906. *Cruise of the Neptune, 1903–1904: Report on the Dominion Government Expedition to Hudson Bay and the Arctic Islands on Board the D.G.S. Neptune.* Ottawa: Government Printing Bureau.

Lowenstein, Tom. 1993. *Ancient Land: Sacred Whale. The Inuit Hunt and Its Rituals.* New York: Farrar, Straus, and Giroux.

Lutz, Maija M. 1978. *The Effects of Acculturation on Eskimo Music of Cumberland Peninsula.* Ottawa: National Museum of Man, Mercure Collection, Canadian Ethnology Service.

Lynge, Fynn. 1992. *Arctic Wars, Animal Rights, Endangered Peoples.* Hanover, NH, and London: University Press of New England.

Lyon, George F. 1824. *The Private Journal of Captain G.F. Lyon of H.M.S. Hecla, During the Recent Voyage of Discovery under Captain Parry.* London: John Murray.

———. (1824) 1970. *The Private Journal of Captain G.F. Lyon of H.M.S. Hecla, During the Recent Voyage of Discovery under Captain Parry.* Barre, MA: Imprint Society.

Malaurie, Jean. 1976. *Les Derniers Rois de Thulé.* Paris: Plon.

Mannik, Hattie. 1998. *Inuit Nunamiut: Inland Inuit.* Altona, MB: Friesen Corporation.

Marquardt, Ole, and Rick Caufield. 1996. 'Development of West Greenlandic Markets for Country Foods since the 18th Century', *Arctic* 49(2): 107–19.

Marsh, Donald B. 1987. *Echoes from a Frozen Land.* Edmonton: Hurtig.

Mary-Rousselière, Guy. 1957. 'Une chasse à l'ours sur la péninsule de Simpson', *Eskimo* 45: 16–19.

———. 1969. *Les jeux de ficelle des Arviligjuarmiut.* Bulletin 233. Ottawa: Musée nationaux du Canada.

———. 1980. *Qitdlarssuaq. L'histoire d'une migration polaire.* Montreal: PUM.

Mathiassen, Therkel. 1928. *Material Culture of the Iglulik Eskimos,* vol. 6 of *Report of the Fifth Thule Expedition 1921–24.* Copenhagen: Gyldendalske Boghandel.

Mathieu, R. 1984a. 'Le corbeau dans la mythologie de l'ancienne Chine', *Revue d'histoire des religions* 201(3): 281–309.

———. 1984b. 'La patte de l'ours', *L'Homme* 24(1): 5–42.

Mauss, Marcel, in collaboration with Henri Beuchat. 1979. *Seasonal Variations of the Eskimo.* London: Routledge & Kegan Paul.

———. 1989. 'Essai sur le don. Forme et raison de l'échange dans les sociétés archaïques' (1923–24). In *Sociologie et Anthropologie,* Paris, PUF.

Mauzé, Marie. 1998. 'Northwest Coast Trees: From Metaphors in Culture to Symbols for Culture', in L. Rival (ed.), *The Social Life of Trees: Anthropological Perspectives on Tree Symbolism.* Oxford: Berg, pp. 223–51.

McCarney, A. P. 1995. *Hunting the Largest Mammals: Native Whaling in the Western Arctic and Subarctic.* Occasional Publication 36. Edmonton: Canadian Circumpolar Institute.

McComber, Louis (ed.). 2005. *We Call It Survival: Abraham Okpik*. Life Stories of Northern Leaders 1. Iqaluit: Nunavut Arctic College.

McDonald, John. 1998. *The Arctic Sky: Inuit Astronomy, Star Lore and Legend*. Toronto: Royal Ontario Museum/Nunavut Research Institute.

McDonald, M., L. Arragutainaq and Z. Novalinga. 1997. *Voices from the Bay: Traditional Ecological Knowledge of Inuit and Cree in the Hudson Bay Bioregion*. Sanikiluaq: Canadian Arctic Resources Committee and the Environmental Committee of Municipality of Sanikiluaq.

McMaster, G. 2011. *Inuit Modern: The Samuel and Esther Sarick Collection*. Toronto: Douglas and McIntyre.

McRury, Ian Kenneth. 1991. 'The Inuit Dog: Its Provenance, Environment and History', MA thesis. Cambridge: Scott Polar Research Institute.

Meletinsky, E. M. 1973. 'Typological Analysis of the Paleo-Asiatic Raven Myths', *Acta Ethnographica Academiae Scientiarum Hungaricae* 22(1–2): 107–55.

———. 1980. 'L'épique du corbeau chez les Paléoasiates', *Diogène* 110: 120–35.

Métayer, Maurice. 1973. *Unikpat*. Centre d'Études Nordiques. Quebec City: Université Laval.

Mitiarjuk Nappaaluk, Salumi. 1993. 'Encyclopédie inuit de Mitiarjuk', *Tumivut* 4: 16–24.

———. 1994. 'The Inuit Encyclopedia of Mitiarjuk', *Tumivut* 5: 73–80.

Müller-Wille, Ludger and Bernd Gieseking. 2011. *Inuit and Whalers on Baffin Island through German Eyes*. Montréal: Baraka Books.

Nadasdy, Paul. 2003. *Hunters and Bureaucrats: Power, Knowledge and Aboriginal State Relations in the Southwest Yukon*. Vancouver: University of British Columbia Press.

———. 2005. 'Transcending the Debate over The Ecological Noble Indian: Indigenous Peoples and Environmentalism', *Ethnohistory* 52(2): 291–329.

———. 2007. 'The Gift in the Animal: The Ontology of Hunting and Human-Animal Sociality', *American Ethnologist* 34(1): 25–43.

Nansen, Fridtjof. 1891. *Eskimoliv*. Kristiani: Giuseppe Castrovilli.

Nelson, Edward W. 1899. 'The Eskimo About Bering Strait', in *18th Annual Report of the Bureau of American Ethnology for the Years 1896–1897*. Washington DC: Government Printing Office, pp. 3–518.

Nelson, R. K. 1983. *Make Prayers to the Raven: A Koyukon View of the Northern Forest*. Chicago: University of Chicago Press.

Noble, Justin. 2008a. '"It's So Important That We Feel Small Trying to Encompass It": Music Festival Marks Revival of Bowhead Hunt', *Nunatsiaq News*, 7 August.

———. 2008b. 'Kangiqsujuaq Gets First Bowhead in a Century: "We're Back with Our Ancestors"', *Nunatsiaq News*, 15 August.

*Northern News Services*. 2008. 'Narwhal Cull Winds Down', 8 December.

*Nunatsiaq News*. 2009a. 'Cape Dorset Hunters Get Their Bowhead', 30 September.

*Nunatsiaq News*. 2009b. 'Whales Now Listed as of "Special Concern"', 7 May.

Nungak, Zebedee, and Eugene Arima. 1988. *Inuit Stories/Légendes inuit/Unikkatuat: Povungnituk*. Bulletin 235. Quebec City: Canadian Museum of Civilization.

Nuttall, Mark. 1992. *Arctic Homeland: Kinship, Community and Development in Northwest Greenland*. Toronto: University of Toronto Press.

————. 2000. 'Becoming a Hunter in Greenland', *Études Inuit Studies* 24(2): 33–45.

Oakes, Jill. 1988. 'Caribou and Copper Inuit Skin Clothing Production', PhD dissertation. Winnipeg: University of Winnipeg.

Oakes, Jill, and Rick Riewe. 1991. *Our Boots: An Inuit Women's Art*. London: Thames and Hudson.

Oosten, Jarich G. 1986. 'Male and Female in Inuit Shamanism', *Études Inuit Studies* 10(1–2): 115–37.

————. 1995. 'Inuit Cosmology and the Problem of the Third Sex', *Études mongoles et sibériennes* 26: 83–106.

————. 1997. 'Amulets, Shamanic Clothes and Paraphernalia in Inuit culture', in C. Buijs and J. Oosten (eds), *Braving the Cold: Continuity and Change in Arctic Clothing*. Leiden: Centre of Non-Western Studies, pp. 105–30.

————. 2005. 'Ideals and Values in the Participants' View of Their Culture: A View from the Inuit Field', *Social Anthropology* 13(2): 185–98.

Oosten, Jarich, and Frédéric Laugrand (eds). 1999a. *Introduction*. Interviewing Inuit Elders 1. Iqaluit: Nunavut Arctic College.

————. 1999b. *The Transition to Christianity*. Inuit Perspectives on the 20th Century 1. Iqaluit: Nunavut Arctic College.

————. 2001. *Travelling and Surviving on Our Land*. Inuit Perspectives on the 20th Century 2. Iqaluit: Nunavut Arctic College.

————. 2002. *Inuit Qaujimajatuqangit: Shamanism and Reintegrating Wrongdoers*. Inuit Perspectives on the 20th Century 4 Iqaluit: Nunavut Arctic College.

————. 2006. 'The Bringer of Light: The Raven in Inuit Traditions'. *Polar Record* 42(222): 187–204.

————. 2007. *Surviving in Different Worlds: Transferring Inuit Traditions from Elders to Youths*. Iqaluit: Nunatta-Campus/Arctic College.

————. 2010. *Hardships of the Past: Recollections of Arviat Elders*. Iqaluit: Nunavut Arctic College.

Oosten, Jarich, Frédéric Laugrand, and Willem Rasing (eds). 1999. *Perspectives on Traditional Law*. Interviewing Inuit Elders 2. Iqaluit: Nunavut Arctic College.

Ootova, Regilee. 2000. 'Inuit Midwifery: Inuit Irnisiksiijjusinginnik Miksaanut', *Inuktitut* (88): 11–23.

Ostermann, H. (ed.). 1938. 'Knud Rasmussen's Posthumous Notes on the Life and Doings of the East Greenlanders in Olden Times', *Meddelelser om Grønland* 109(1): [3]–212.

Ostermann, H., and E. Holtved (eds). 1952. *The Alaskan Eskimos as Described in the Posthumous Notes of Dr. Knud Rasmussen*, trans. W. E. Calvert, vol. 10 (pt. 3) of the *Report of the Fifth Thule Expedition, 1921–24*. Copenhagen: Gyldendalske Boghandel.

Paillet, Jean Pierre. 1973. 'Eskimo Language: Animal and Plants Taxonomies in Baker Lake'. Unpublished manuscript.

Panetta, Alex. 2009. 'Governor General Eats Seal to Show Support for Inuit', *Nunatsiaq News*, 29 May.

Paproth, H. J. 1976. *Studien über das Bärenzeremoniell. 1 Bärenjagdriten und Bärenfeste bei den tungusischte Volkern*. Uppsala: Toftens Trycheri AB.

Parry, William E. 1824. *Journal of a Second Voyage for the Discovery of a North-West Passage from the Atlantic to the Pacific: Performed in the Years 1821-22-23, in His Majesty's Ships Fury and Hecla*. London: John Murray.

Patridge, Shannon (ed.). 2009. *Niurrutiqarniq: Trading With the Hudson's Bay Company*. Iqaluit: Nunavut Arctic College.

Peary, Robert E. 1898. *Northward Over the 'Great Ice': A Narrative of Life and Work Along the Shores and Upon the Interior Ice-cap of Northern Greenland in the Years 1886 and 1891–97*, 2 vols. New York: Frederick A. Stockes.

Pedersen, M. A. 2001. 'Totemism, Animism and North Asian Indigenous Ontologies', *Journal of the Royal Anthropological Institute* 7(3): 411–27.

Pelly, David. 2001. *Sacred Hunt: A Portrait of the Relationship Between Seals and Inuit*. Vancouver: Greystone Books.

Pernet, Fabien. 2012. *Traditions relatives à l'éducation, la grossesse et l'accouchement au Nunavik*. Montreal and Inukjuak: Institut Culturel Avataq, Qaujimausivut.

———. 2013. 'Inuuiniq. La construction de la personne dans les rites de passage des Nunavimmiut', PhD dissertation. Quebec City: Université Laval.

Peter, Aaju, Myna Ishulutak, Julia Shaimaiyuk, Jeannie Shaimaiyuk, Nancy Kisa, Bernice Kootoo and Susan Enuaraq. 2002. 'The Seal: An Integral Part of Our Culture', *Études Inuit Studies* 26(1): 67–174.

Petit, Céline. 2011. 'Jouer pour être heureux: Pratiques ludiques et expressions du jeu chez les Inuit de la region d'Iglulik (Arctique oriental canadien), du XIXe siècle à nos jours', PhD dissertation. Quebec City: Université Laval.

Petitot, E. 1981. *Among the Chiglit Eskimos*, trans. E. Otto Höhn. Occasional Publication 10. Edmonton: Boreal Institute for Northern Studies.

Philippe, Jean. 1947. 'Psychologie esquimaude', *Eskimo* 9: 2–7.

———. 1951. 'Medecine and Taboos', *Eskimo* 23(3): 3–14.

Pitseolak, Peter, and Dorothy Harley Eber. (1978) 2003. *Pitseolak: Pictures out of My Life*. Montreal and Kingston: McGill-Queen's University Press.

———. 1993. *People from Our Side: A Life Story with Photographs and Oral Biography*. Montreal and Kingston: McGill-Queen's University Press.

Platenkamp, Jos.1996. 'The Healing Gift', in S. Howell (ed.), *For the Sake of Our Future: Sacrificing in Eastern Indonesia*. Leiden: CNWS, pp. 318–36.

Povungnituk. 1966. *The People of Povungnituk Independent through a Common Effort*. Quebec City: Povungituk Cooperative Society.

Preston, Richard. (1975) 2002. *Cree Narrative: Expressing the Personal Meaning of Events*. Montreal and Kingston: McGill-Queen's University Press.

Rainey, Froelich Gladstone. 1947. 'The Whale Hunters of Tigara', *Anthropological Papers of the American Museum of Natural History* 41(2): 231–32.

Randa, Vladimir. 1986. *L'ours polaire et les Inuit*. Paris: Selaf.

———. 1989. 'Esquisse du traitement lexical des categories zoologiques dans la langue d'Igloolik (Arctique canadien)', Revue d'ethnolinguistique, *Cahiers du LACITO* 4: 147–68.

———. 1994. 'Inuillu uumajuillu: Les animaux dans les savoirs, les représentations et la langue des Iglulingmiut (Arctique oriental canadien)', PhD dissertation. Paris: École des hautes études en sciences sociales.

———. 1996. 'Chasse au caribou en terre de Baffin: Un regard sur les pratiques cynégétiques des Iglulingmiut', *Anthropolozoologica* 23: 51–64.

———. 2002a. 'Perception des animaux et leurs noms dans la langue inuit (Canada, Groenland, Alaska)', in V. de Colombel and N. Tersis (eds), *Lexique et motivations: Perspectives ethnolinguistiques.* Paris: Peeters, pp. 79–114.

———. 2002b. '"Qui se ressemble s'assemble": Logique de constrution et d'organisation des zoonymes en langue Inuit', *Études Inuit Studies* 26(1): 71–108.

———. 2003. 'Ces "bestioles" qui nous hantent: Représentations et attitudes a l'égard des insectes chez les Inuit canadiens', in E. Motte-Florac and J. M. C. Thomas, *Les insectes dans la tradition orale.* Paris: Peeters, 449–63.

Rasing, Willem. 1994. *'Too Many People': Order and Non-conformity in Iglulingmiut Social Process.* Nijmegen, Netherlands: Katholieke Universiteit.

Rasmussen, Knud. 1908. *The People of the Polar North.* London: K. Paul, Trench, Trübner.

———. 1927. *Across Arctic America.* New York and London: G. P. Putnam's Sons.

———. 1929. *Intellectual Culture of the Iglulik Eskimos,* vol. 7 (pt. 1) of *Report of the Fifth Thule Expedition 1921–24.* Copenhagen: Gyldendalske Boghandel.

———. 1930. *Observations on the Intellectual Culture of the Caribou Eskimos: Iglulik and Caribou Eskimo Texts,* vol. 12 (pts 2–3) of *Report of the Fifth Thule Expedition 1921–24.* Copenhagen: Gyldendalske Boghandel.

———. 1931. *The Netsilik Eskimos: Social Life and Spiritual Culture,* vol. 8 (pts 1–2) of *Report of the Fifth Thule Expedition 1921–24.* Copenhagen: Gyldendalske Boghandel.

———. 1932. *Intellectual Culture of the Copper Eskimos,* vol. 9 of *Report of the Fifth Thule Expedition 1921–24.* Copenhagen: Gyldendalske Boghandel.

Rausch, R. 1951. 'Notes on the Nunamiut Eskimo and Mammals of the Anaktuvuk Pass Region, Brooks Range', *Arctic* 4: 147–95.

*Recollections of Inuit Elders.* 1986. Eskimo Point: Inuit Cultural Institute.

*Recollections of Helen Paungat.* 1988. Eskimo Point: Inuit Cultural Institute.

Rink, Henry. 1875. *Tales and Traditions of the Eskimo with a Sketch of Their Habits, Religion, Language and Other Peculiarities.* Edinburg: Wim Blackwood and Sons.

———. 1896. *Kahjakmaend: Fortaellinger af gronlandske saelhundefangere.* Odense, Denmark: Milo'ske Boghandel.

Rival, Laura. 2005. 'Soul, Body and Gender among the Huarorani of Amazonian Ecuador', *Ethnos* 70(3): 285–310.

Rogers, Sarah. 2009a. 'Nunavik Bowhead Landing No Easy Kill: Device Fails to Explode, Hunters Use Rifles', *Nunatsiaq News,* 27 August.

———. 2009b. 'Whale Hunt a Mix of Sadness, Joy for Lead Harpooner: Pregnant Female Died After 300 Rifle Rounds, One Lance Strike Through the Heart', *Nunatsiaq News,* 31 August.

———. 2011. 'Polar Bear Management Needs More Traditional Knowledge Input: NTI', *Nunatsiaq News,* 25 October.

Rombandeeva, E. I. 1993. 'Rituel de la fête de l'ours chez les Vogouls de la Sygma', *Etudes Finno-ougriennes* 25: 7–18.

Ross, W. Gillies. 1975. *Whaling and Eskimos: Hudson Bay 1860–1915.* Ottawa: National Museums of Canada.

————. 1977. 'Whaling and the Decline of Native Populations', *Arctic Anthropology* 14(2): 1–8.

————. 1984. *An Arctic Whaling Diary: The Journal of Captain George Comer in Hudson Bay 1903–1905*. Toronto: University of Toronto Press.

————. 1985. *Arctic Whalers, Icy Seas: Narratives of the Davis Strait Whale Fisheries*. Toronto: Irwin.

Roy, C. 1971. 'La chasse des mammifères marins chez les Ivujivimmiut', *Cahiers de Géographie du Québec* 15(36): 509–21.

Sabo, George, and Deborah Sabo. 1985. 'Belief System and the Ecology of Sea Mammal Hunting among the Baffin Island Eskimo', *Arctic Anthropology* 22(2): 77–86.

Sahlins, Marshall. 1972. *Stone Age Economics*. Hawthorne, NY: Aldine de Gruyter.

Sakakibara, Chie. 2009. '"No Whale No Music": Inupiaq Drumming and Global Warming', *Polar Record* 45(4): 289–303.

Saladin d'Anglure, Bernard. 1977. 'Iqallijuq, ou les reminiscences d'une âme-nom Inuit', *Études Inuit Studies* 1(1): 33–63.

————. 1978. *Vie et oeuvre de Davidialuk Alasuaq, artiste inuit du Québec arctique*. Quebec City: Gouvernement du Québec, Ministère des Affaires culturelles, Direction générale du patrimoine.

————. 1980a. 'Nanuq super-mâle: L'ours blanc dans l'espace imaginaire et le temps social des Inuit', *Études Mongoles et Sibériennes* 11: 63–94.

————. 1980b. 'Petit-ventre, l'enfant-géant du cosmos inuit (Ethnographie de l'enfant et enfance de l'ethnographie dans l'Arctique central inuit)', *L'Homme* 20(1): 7–46.

————. 1983. 'Ijjiqat: Voyage au pays de l'invisible inuit', *Études Inuit Studies* 7(1): 67–83.

————. 1984. 'Inuit of Quebec', in D. Damas (ed.), *Handbook of North American Indians*, vol. 5, *Arctic*. Washington DC: Smithonian Institution, pp. 476–507.

————. 1988a 'Kunut et les angakakkut' , *Études Inuit Studies* 12(1–2): 57–80.

————. 1988b. 'Penser le "féminin" chamanique, ou le "tiers-sexe" des chamanes inuit', *Recherches amérindiennes au Québec* 18(2–3): 19–50.

————. 1989. 'La part du chamane ou le communisme sexuel inuit revisité dans l'arctique central canadien', *Journal de la Société des Américanistes* 85: 133–71.

————. 1990a. 'Frère-lune (Taqqiq), soeur-soleil (Siqiniq) et l'intelligence du monde (Sila)', *Études Inuit Studies* 14(2): 75–140.

————. 1990b. 'Nanook, Super-Male: The Polar Bear in the Imaginary Space and Social Time of the Inuit of the Canadian Arctic', in R. G. Willis (ed.), *Signifying Animals: Human Meaning in the Natural World*. New York: Routledge, pp. 178–95.

————. 1992. 'Pygmées arctiques et géants lubriques ou les avatars de l'image de l'autre lors des premières rencontres entre Inuit et Blancs', *Recherches amérindiennes au Québec* 22(2–3): 73–88.

————. 1999. 'La chasse à la baleine chez les Inuit du Nord canadien', in S. Bobbé (ed.), *Baleines: Un enjeu écologique*. Paris: Autrement Éditions, pp. 88–126.

———. 2000. "'Pijariuniq": Performances et rituels inuit de la première fois', *Études Inuit Studies* 24(2): 89–113.

——— (ed.). 2001. *Cosmology and Shamanism*. Interviewing Inuit Elders 4. Iqaluit: Nunavut Arctic College.

———. 2006. *Être et renaître inuit: Homme, femme ou chamane*. Paris: Gallimard.

Saladin d'Anglure, Bernard, and Monique Vézinet. 1977. 'Chasses collectives au caribou dans le Québec arctique', *Études Inuit Studies* 1(2): 97–110.

Sales, Anne de. 1980. 'Deux conceptions de l'alliance à travers la fête de l'ours en Sibérie', *Études mongoles et sibériennes* 11: 147–213.

Sandell, B. 1996. 'Polar Bear Hunting and Hunters in Ittoqqortoormiit/Scoresbysund, NE Greenland', *Arctic Anthropology* 33(2): 77–93.

Santos-Granero, Fernando. 2009. *The Occult Life of Things: Native Amazonian Theories of Materiality and Personhood*. Tucson: University of Arizona Press.

Savard, Remi. 1966. *Mythologie esquimaude: Analyse de textes nord-groenlandais*. Travaux divers 14. Quebec City: CEN.

Schneider, Lucien. 1985. *Ulirnaisigutiit: An Inuktitut-English Dictionary of Northern Québec: Labrador and Eastern Arctic Dialects*. Quebec City: Presses de l'Université Laval.

Scott, Colin. 1996. 'Science for the West, Myth for the Rest?: The Case of James Bay Cree Knowledge Construction', in L. Nader (ed.), *Naked Science: Anthropological Inquiries into Boundaries, Power and Knowledge*. New York: Routledge Press, 69–86.

———. 2006. 'Spirit and Practical Knowledge in the Person of the Bear among Wemindji Bay Cree Knowledge', *Ethnos* 71(1): 51–66.

Seidelman, Harold, and James Turner. 1993. *The Inuit Imagination: Arctic Myth and Sculpture*. Seattle: University of Washington Press.

Sejersen, F. 2001. 'Hunting and Management of Beluga Whales (*Delphinapterus leucas*) in Greenland: Changing Strategies to Cope with New National and Local Interests', *Arctic* 54(4): 431–43.

Sharp, Henry. 2001. *Loon: Memory, Meaning and Reality in a Northern Dene Community*. Lincoln and London: University of Nebraska Press.

Smith, Eric Alden. 1991. *Inujjuarmiut Foraging Strategies: Evolutionary Ecology of an Arctic Hunting Economy*. New York: Walter de Gruyter.

Soby, Regitze Margarethe. 1970. 'The Eskimo Animal Cult', *Folk* 11–12: 43–78.

Sokolova, Z. P. 2002. 'The Bear Cult and the Bear Festivity in the Worldview and Culture of Siberian Peoples', *Ètnograficeskoe obozrenie* 1: 41–62.

Sonne, Birgitte. 1982. 'The Ideology and Practice of Blood Feuds in East and West Greenland', *Études Inuit Studies* 6(2): 21–50.

———. 1990. 'The Acculturative Role of the Sea Woman: early Contacts Relations between Inuit and Whites as Revealed in the Origin Myth of Sea Woman', *Man and Society* 13; 1–34.

Spalding, Alex. 1979. *Eight Inuit Myths*. Mercury Series, Canadian Ethnology Service 59. Ottawa: National Museum of Man.

———. 1998. *Inuktitut: A Multidialectical Outline*. Iqaluit: Nunavut Arctic College.

Spencer, Robert F. (1959) 1976. *The North Alaskan Eskimo: A Study in Ecology and Society*. New York: Dover Publications.

Stairs, A., and G. Wenzel. 1992. 'I Am I and the Environment: Inuit Hunting, Community, and Identity', *Journal of Indigenous Studies* 3: 1–12.

Stépanoff, Charles. 2009. 'Devenir-animal pour rester-humain: Logiques mythiques et pratiques de la métamorphose en Sibérie méridionale', *Images Re-vues* 6. Retrieved 22 December 2011 from http://imagesrevues.revues .org/388?lang=en.

Stevenson, Marc. 1997. *Inuit Whalers and Cultural Persistence: Structure in Cumberland Sound and Central Inuit Social Organization.* Oxford: Oxford University Press.

*Stories from Pangnirtung.* 1976. Edmonton: Hurtig Publishers.

Swanton, J. R. 1909. 'Contributions to the Ethnology of the Haida', *Memoirs of the American Museum of Natural History* 8(1): 1–300.

Tagoona, Armand. 1975. *Shadows.* Toronto: Oberon Press.

Tanner, Adrian. 1979. *Bringing Home Animals: Religious Ideology and Mode of Production of the Mistassini Cree Hunters.* London: C. Hurst.

Taylor, John G. 1985. 'The Arctic Whale Cult in Labrador', *Études Inuit Studies* 9(2): 121–32.

———. 1988. 'Labrador Inuit Whale Use during the Early Contact Period', *Arctic Anthropology* 25(1): 120–30.

———. 1993. 'Canicide in Labrador: Function and Meaning', *Études Inuit Studies* 17(1): 7–21.

Taylor, John G., and Helga Taylor. 1986. 'Labrador Inuit Summer Ceremonies', *Études Inuit Studies* 10(1–2): 233–44.

Tester, Frank. 2010. 'Mad Dogs and (Mostly) Englishmen: Colonial Relations, Commodities, and the Fate of Inuit Sled Dogs', *Études Inuit Studies* 34(2): 129–47.

Thalbitzer, William (ed.). 1914a. *The Ammasalik Eskimo,* pt. 1. Copenhagen: C. A. Reitzel.

Thalbitzer, William. 1914b. *Ethnographical Collections from East Greenland (Angmagsalik and Nualik).* Made by G. Holm, G. Amdrup and J. Petersen and Described by W. Thalbitzer in The Ammassalik Eskimo: Contributions to the Ethnology of the East Greenland Natives. Edited by William Thalbitzer; translated from the Danish by H. M. Kyle. In two parts. First part, *Meddelelser om Grønland* 39(7): 321–667.

——— (ed.). 1923. *The Ammasalik Eskimo,* pt. 2. Copenhagen: C. A. Reitzel.

———. 1925. 'Cultic Games and Festivals in Greenland', in *Congrès international des Américanistes, Compte-Rendu de la XIIe Session: Deuxième partie tenue à Göteborg en 1924,* 236–55.

———. 1930. 'Les magiciens esquimaux, leurs conceptions du monde, de l'âme et de la vie', *Journal de la Société des Américanistes* 22: 71–106.

Therrien, Michèle. 1987a. *Le Corps inuit (Québec arctique).* Paris: Selaf.

———. 1987b. 'La parole partagée: L'homme et l'animal arctiques', *Cahiers de Littérature Orale* 22: 105–30.

Therrien, Michèle, and Frédéric Laugrand (eds). 2001. *Perspectives on Traditional Health.* Interviewing Inuit Elders 5. Iqaluit: Nunavut Arctic College.

Thompson, John. 2007a. 'Davis Strait Polar Bear Flourishing, GN Says: "Scientific Knowledge Has Demonstrated That Inuit Knowledge Was Right"', *Nunatsiaq News,* 2 February.

————. 2007b. 'Nunavut Back-Tracks on Bear Numbers: GN Now Supports Science Over Observations of Hunters', *Nunatsiaq News*, 20 April.

Thorpe, Natasha L. 2000. *Contributions of Inuit Ecological Knowledge to Understanding the Impacts of Climate Change on the Bathurst Caribou Herd in the Kitikmeot Region, Nunavut.* Burnaby, British Columbia: Simon Fraser University.

————. 2001. 'Thunder on the Tundra: Inuit Qaujimajatuqangit of the Bathurst Caribou'. Tuktu and Nogak project. Ikaluktuuthak, NU.

————. 2004. 'Codifying Knowledge about Caribou: The History of Inuit Qaujimajatuqangit in the Kitikmeot Region of Nunavut, Canada', in D. Anderson and M. Nutall, *Cultivating Arctic Landscapes: Knowing and Managing Animals in the Circumpolar North.* Oxford: Berghahn Books, pp. 57–78.

Tookoome, Simon. 1999. *The Shaman's Nephew: A Life in the Far North.* Toronto: Stoddart Kids.

*Tumivut.* 2000. Special issue, 'Qimmiit-Eskimo Dogs', vol. 12.

Trott, Christopher G. 2006. 'The Gender of the Bear', *Études Inuit Studies* 30(1): 89–109.

Turner, Edith. 1990. 'The Whale Decides: Eskimos' and Ethnographer's Shared Consciousness on the Ice', *Études Inuit Studies* 14(1–2): 39–52.

Turner, Lucien. 1888. 'On the Indians and Eskimos of the Ungava District, Labrador', *Proceedings and Transactions of the Royal Society of Canada for the Year 1887* 5(2): 99–119.

————. (1894) 1979. *Indians and Eskimos in the Quebec-Labrador Pensinsula.* Quebec City: Coméditex.

Turner, Terence. 2009. 'The Crisis of Late Structuralism, Perspectivism and Animism: Rethinking Culture, Nature, Spirit, and Bodiliness', *Tipití* 7(1): 3–40.

Tyrrell, Marta. 2005. 'Inuit Perception, Knowledge and Use of the Sea in Arviat, Nunavut', PhD dissertation. Aberdeen: University of Aberdeen.

————. 2006. 'More Bears, Less Bears: Inuit and Scientific Perceptions of Polar Bear Populations on the West Coast of Hudson Bay', *Études Inuit Studies* 30(2): 191–208.

————. 2007. 'Sentient Beings and Wildlife Resources: Inuit, Beluga Whales and Management Regimes in the Canadian Arctic', *Human Ecology* 35(5): 575–86.

————. 2008. 'Nunavik Inuit Perspectives on Beluga Whale Management in the Canadian Arctic', *Human Organization* 6: 322–34.

Usher, Peter J. 2000. 'Traditional Ecological Knowledge in Environmental Assessment and Management', *Arctic* 53: 183–93.

Van de Velde, Franz. 1956. 'Les règles du partage des phoques pris par la chasse aux aglus', *Anthropologica* 3: 5–15.

————. 1957. 'Nanuk, le roi de la faune arctique', *Eskimo* 45: 4–15.

Vézinet, Monique. 1980. *Les Nunamiut: Inuit au coeur des terres.* Quebec City: Ministère des affaires culturelles.

Victor, Anne-Marie. 1987a. 'Éléments symboliques de la chasse à la baleine', *Études Inuit Studies* 11(2): 139–64.

————. 1987b. 'Les rituels de la chasse à la baleine: Les Eskimo de Sivugaq et de Tikigaq', PhD dissertation. Paris: Université de Paris-V (René Descartes).

Victor, Paul-Emile, and Joelle Robert-Lamblin. 1993. *La civilisation du phoque 2*. Bayonne, France: R. Chabaud éditions.

Vilaça, Aparecida, 2000. 'Relations between Funerary Cannibalism and Warfare Cannibalism: The Question of Predation', *Ethnos* 65(1): 83–106.

———. 2005. 'Chronically Unstable Bodies: Reflections on Amazonian Corporalities', *Journal of the Royal Anthropological Institute* 11: 445–64.

Vitebsky, P. 2005. *Reindeer People: Living with Animals and Spirits in Siberia*. London: Harper.

Viveiros de Castro, Eduardo B. 1998. 'Cosmological Deixis and Amerindian Perspectivism', *Journal of the Royal Anthropological Institute* 4: 469–88.

———. 2009. *Métaphysiques cannibales*. Paris: PUF.

Von Finckenstein, Maria (ed.). 2002. *Nuvisavik: 'Là où nous tissons.'* Ottawa: Canadian Museum of Civilization.

Wachowich, Nancy. 1999. *Sagiyuq: Stories from the Lives of Three Inuit Women*. Montreal and Kingston: McGill-Queen's University Press.

Waldmann, Samuel. 1909–10. 'Les Esquimaux du nord du Labrador', *Bulletin de la Société Neuchateloise de Géographie* 20: 430–44.

Watson, Paul. 2008. 'A Conversation with the Narwhal Butchers: Commentary by Captain Paul Watson', Sea Shepherd Conservation Society, 2 December. Retrieved 21 October 2009 from http://www.seashepherd.org/commen tary-and-editorials/2008/12/02/a-conversation-with-the-narwhal-butch ers-191.

Watt-Cloutier, Sheila. 2007. 'Nunavut Must Think Big, Not Small, on Polar Bears: "Allowing Ourselves to Remain Paralyzed by Anger against Certain Environmental Groups Only Keeps Us Stuck as Victims"', *Nunatsiaq News*, 17 January.

Weetaluktuk, Jobie, and Robyn Bryant. 2008. *Le monde de Tivi Etok: La vie et l'art d'un aîné inuit*. Quebec City: Multimondes, Institut Culturel Avataq.

Wenzel, George. 1983. 'Inuit and Polar Bears: Cultural Observations from a Hunt near Resolute Bay, N.W.T', *Arctic* 36(1): 90–94.

———. 1986. *The Ecology and Organization of Inuit Sealing Activities at Clyde River, NWT*. Royal Commission on Seals and the Sealing Industry in Canada 10. Ottawa: Government of Canada.

———. 1989. 'Sealing at Clyde River, NWT: A Discussion of Inuit Economy', *Études Inuit Studies* 13(1): 3–22.

———. 1991. *Animal Rights, Human Rights: Ecology, Economy and Ideology in the Canadian Arctic*. Toronto: University of Toronto Press.

———. 1995. 'Ningiqtuq: Resource Sharing and generalized Reciprocity in Clyde River, Nunavut', *Arctic Anthropology* 32(2): 43–60.

———. 1999. 'Traditional Ecological Knowledge and Inuit: Reflections on TEK Research and Ethics', *Arctic* 52: 113–24.

———. 2004. 'From TEK to IQ: Inuit Qaujimajatuqangit and Inuit Cultural Ecology', *Arctic Anthropology* 41: 238–50.

———. 2005. 'Nunavut Inuit and Polar Bear: The Cultural Politics of the Sport Hunt', *Senri Ethnological Studies* 67: 363–88.

———. 2008. *Sometimes Hunting Can Seem Like Business: Polar Bear Sport Hunting in Nunavut*. Edmonton: Canadian Circumpolar Institute Press.

Wenzel, George, and Martha Dowsley. 2008. '"The Time of the Most Polar Bears": A Co-management Conflict in Nunavut', *Arctic* 61(2): 177–89.

Weyer, Edward M. 1932. *The Eskimos, Their Environment and Folkways.* New Haven, CT: Yale University Press.

Whittaker, C. E. 1937. *Arctic Eskimo: A Record of 50 Years' Experience and Observation among the Eskimo.* London: Seeley.

Wight, Darlene Coward. 2001. *Art and Expression of the Netsilik.* Winnipeg: Winnipeg Art Gallery.

Willerslev, Rane. 2004. 'Not Animal, Not Not-Animal: Hunting Imitation and Empathetic Knowledge Among the Siberian Yukaghirs', *Journal of the Royal Anthropological Institute* 10: 629–52.

———. 2007. *Soul Hunters: Hunting, Animism and Personhood among the Siberian Yukaghirs.* Berkeley: University of California Press.

Willis, Roy. 1990. *Singnifying Animals: Human Meanings in the Natural World.* London: Unwin Hyman.

Windeyer, Chris. 2010a. 'Influx of Bears a Nuisance across Nunavut: Inuit Hunters Report Animals Are Healthy and Well Fed', *Nunatsiaq News,* 18 January.

———. 2010b. 'Nunavut Hotline Callers Claim Boom Times for Polar Bear', *Nunatsiaq News,* 11 January.

Wisniewski, Josh. 2007. 'Apprendre en perspective: Chasse, intentionalité et mimesis chez les chasseurs Inupiaq du nord-ouest alaskien', *Ethnographiques .org* (13). Retrieved 23 April 2014 from http://www.ethnographiques.org/2007/Wisniewski.

Zarate, Gabriel. 2008. 'Government Slams Activist Leader', *Northern News Services,* 15 December.

———. 2010. 'Nunavut Plans Big Survey of Baffin Caribou Herds: Researchers Hope to Solve the Riddle of Caribou Scarcity', *Nunatsiaq News,* 10 February.

# Index